On Fc
Through E

A TRAIL GUIDE TO
THE BRITISH ISLES

INCLUDES:*England, Ireland, Northern Ireland, Scotland and Wales*

Here's What Europe's Walking Organizations Say About this Book

"The most complete reference for the hiker in Germany." —LUDWIG LENZ, 3rd Direktor, Deutscher Alpenverein (German Alpine Club), Munich.

"Extraordinarily comprehensive." —JOHN NEWNHAM, assistant secretary, The Ramblers' Association, London.

"Excellent. Many more or less experienced alpinists could learn quite a lot on how to prepare a tour and on what to do in cases of emergency."— LUCETTE DUVOISIN, general secretary, Schweizerische Arbeitsgemeinschaft für Wanderwege (Swiss Footpath Protection Association), Basel.

"A very comprehensive and most valuable book." —DR. SONJA JORDAN, Österreichische Fremdenverkehrswerbung (Austrian National Tourist Office), Vienna.

"I was very impressed. This book will be of great value to all hikers who want to go to other countries." —FINN HAGEN, Den Norske Turistforening (Norwegian Mountain Touring Association), Oslo.

"You've done a helluva good job assembling and organizing a truly awesome amount of data. You seem to have thought of every contingency—and then some—so the prospective walker will be able to plan his vacation well in advance of departure. . . . This guide should become something of a classic in its field—a backpacker's Baedeker." —STEPHEN R. WHITNEY, former managing editor, Sierra Club Books, and author of *A Sierra Club Naturalist's Guide: The Sierra Nevada*.

"Your work is very complete and accurate (something we find seldom, even in our own country)." —FREDDY TUERLINCKX, general secretary, Grote Routepaden (Long-Distance Footpath Association), Antwerp.

"I am really impressed with the enormous work that you have been able to do in a short time—and by the amount of knowledge and experience that you show!" —INGEMUND HÄGG, Svenska turistföreningen (Swedish Touring Club), Stockholm.

On Foot Through Europe

A TRAIL GUIDE TO THE BRITISH ISLES

INCLUDES: *England, Ireland, Northern Ireland, Scotland and Wales*

by Craig Evans

Walking, Backpacking, Ski Touring,
Climbing—Everything You Can Do On Foot

QUILL

New York 1982

Library of Congress Catalog Card Number: 82-604

ISBN: 0-688-01164-0 (pbk)

Printed in the United States of America

First Quill Edition

1 2 3 4 5 6 7 8 9 10

Behind the Scenes

M ANY PEOPLE HAVE contributed to this book—people in tourist offices, weather bureaus, forestry services, sport shops, guidebook and map outlets and holiday associations. In addition, the members of the mountaineering councils and federations, sports councils and walking associations in the British Isles have been especially helpful. Without the assistance of these people—and the time and effort they devoted to answering questions, researching information and reviewing the final manuscript—this book would not have been possible.

To all who helped prepare the manuscript—typists, proofreaders, friends—I also owe my sincere gratitude.

And to those who helped the most, a special thanks:

For reviewing the entire manuscript, helping offset my American bias and providing otherwise hard-to-get information:

Arthur Howcroft, president of the European Ramblers' Association's Walking Committee and a tour leader for England's Country-Wide Holidays Association.

Ingemund Hägg, secretary of the European Ramblers' Association's Walking Committee, consultant to the Svenska turistföreningen (Swedish Touring Club) and author of *Walking in Europe,* a 40-page booklet on where to get information to go walking in 25 countries, published in England by the Swedish Touring Club, 1978 (a handy booklet, incidentally, that is well worth owning).

For providing information on walking in their areas and for reviewing the accuracy of the chapters on their countries:

ENGLAND

P.H.E. Carter of the South West Way Association, Newton Abbot, Devon.
Eric Gurney, National Organizing Secretary of the Backpackers' Club, Reading, Berkshire.
John Newnham and *John Trevelyan* of the Ramblers' Assocation, London.
Bernie Sluman, head of public relations for the Countryside Commission, Cheltenham, Gloucestershire.

Celia Smith, information projects officer of the British Tourist Authority, London.

And the following voluntary officials of the Ramblers' Association:

John Bainbridge, Moorland Group, Teignmouth, South Devon.

Major Brett Collier, Lincolnshire and South Humberside Area, North Carlton.

H. Comber, East Sussex Area, Eastbourne.

L. Hensman, Sussex Area, Horsham.

E.W. Hibberd, Lake District Area, Lancaster.

S. Hodgson, Somerset Area, Bridgwater (cq).

Joan Kelland, Gloucestershire Area, Cheltenham.

Rowland Y. Pomfret, Oxfordshire Area, Oxford.

Walter Richards, Cornwall Area, St. Eval.

C.G. Smith, Nottinghamshire Area, Nottingham.

W.G. Stothard, Northern Area, Newcastle-upon-Tyne.

A. Toomer, Wiltshire Area, Swindon.

Joe Turner, Devon Area, Exeter.

A. Richards, West Riding Area, Leeds.

L.M. Wickens, Isle of Wight Area, Shanklin.

IRELAND

J.C. (Joe) Gallagher, Bord Fáilte (Irish Tourist Board), Dublin.

Joss Lynam, Federation of Mountaineering Clubs of Ireland, Dublin.

J.B. Malone, author, inveterate walker, *Evening Herald* columnist and member of An Taisce, Dublin.

Dan Tracy, An Óige (Irish Youth Hostel Association), Dublin.

NORTHERN IRELAND

Wilfrid Capper, Sports Council for Northern Ireland, Belfast.

Ian J. Hill, manager, public relations, Northern Ireland Tourist Board, Belfast.

R.F. MacKenzie, Forest Service, Belfast.

J. McClatchey, Forest Service, Belfast.

Ernest Sandford, publicity officer, Northern Ireland Tourist Board, Belfast.

SCOTLAND

Alex G. (Sandy) Cousins and William S. Myles, The Mountaineering Council of Scotland, Glasgow.

Roney Dugal, Scottish Landowners' Federation, Edinburgh.

John A. Hutchinson, publications editor, Scottish Tourist Board, Edinburgh.

Eric Langmain, Mountain Rescue Committee of Scotland, Edinburgh.

D.H. McPherson, Scottish Rights of Way Society, Edinburgh.

Denis Mollinson, Mountain Bothies Association, Edinburgh.

Hazel Pottinger, senior information officer, Forestry Commission, Edinburgh.

WALES

Roy Mason, publicity manager, Bwrdd Croeso Cymru (Wales Tourist Board), Cardiff.
A.D. Parsons, Comisiwn Coedwigaeth (Forestry Commission), Cardiff.
Gordon Probert, county planning officer, Cwmbran, Gwent.
Arthur Roberts, chairman, The Ramblers' Association, Welsh Council.

There was also the enormous dedication of the people who made the trail guide series come to physical reality. The basic team was: Ed Meehan who drew the maps, Brian Sheridan who did the illustrations, Vincent Torre who designed the cover and Elisabeth Kofler Shuman, my research and editorial assistant.

There was also Stephen R. Whitney, my editor, whose involvement in this book escalated beyond that of simply an editor, and whose commitment to its completion became much more than he—or his wife—ever bargained for. As deadlines approached and the size of each chapter swelled, he evolved from copy editor and devil's advocate to co-author, writing first short sections of unfinished chapters from my notes, then whole chapters. And I, in turn, became his rewriter and editor. Together, we were able to complete seven books, ensure their accuracy and oversee every detail of their production, a job I could never have accomplished alone and still have met the final deadline.

In this book, he co-authored the chapter on Northern Ireland.

Finally, there was William Kemsley, Jr., president of Foot Trails Publications, Inc., whose own passion for detail sustained his unfaltering belief in this trail guide series through all of its growing pains, despite the advice of his accountants. Few publishers would have put up with so much when lesser books could have been produced much more economically. Yet he rarely asked that compromises be made. He only asked that it be done. And done well.

Thank you, each of you. You've been great friends.

Craig Evans
Washington, D.C., 1981

How to Use this Book

THIS BOOK IS PACKED with information. It describes every aspect of walking, backpacking and climbing in England, Ireland, Northern Ireland, Scotland and Wales: all the places you can go, the maps and guidebooks you need, where you can get information on trail lodgings and camping, the weather conditions you can expect and the telephone numbers to call for weather forecasts. There's even a list of special train and bus fares that can save you money in each country. And more: the clothing and equipment you will need, walking tours and mountaineering courses you might like to take advantage of, what you should know about property rights and footpath laws, even some tidbits of history and folklore.

There are also hundreds of addresses: places you can write for maps and guidebooks, obtain train and bus schedule information and get specific answers on walking, climbing and traveling in particular areas. And you get a lot more than just an address. Everything is spelled out: the information and services available and, if useful publications are available, what their titles are and what information they contain.

The result is a complete sourcebook to all the information on walking, backpacking, ski touring and climbing in the British Isles.

This book has been designed to make finding the specific information you need as easy as possible. The table of contents lists the major divisions in each chapter, plus some minor divisions, so you can turn right to the page where, say, the services provided by the walking organizations or the emergency telephone numbers for search and rescue are given. The name of each organization has been set off from the rest of the text by means of a darker type face and additional spacing so it can be found easily—again and again. And all the addresses and telephone numbers are listed in an alphabetical *Address Directory* at the back of each chapter so you only have one place to look when you need to use one. There is even a section entitled *A Quick Reference* at the end of the chapters on each country, which gives you the page numbers where the most important information is located on walking in that country.

Another help: this book was bound so you can remove pages—and thus save lugging the entire book along—when you just want one chapter on the trail for easy reference. To remove pages: 1) open the book to the first page you wish to remove; 2) bend the book open as far as it will go; 3) turn to the end of the section you wish to remove; 4) again, bend the book open as far as it will go; 5) with one hand, hold down the pages on either side of the section you wish to remove; 6) with the thumb and index finger of the other hand, grasp the top part of the section at the point where it attaches to the spine, and 7) slowly pull the section away from the spine. The pages should come out in a complete section, with all the pages attached to one another.

When you wish to return a chapter you have removed to the book, simply slip it back into the space where it belongs. Then put a rubber band around the book so the loose sections don't fall out.

Finally, one last note: every attempt has been made to ensure the information in this book is both complete and accurate. Nonetheless, those who worked on the book—myself, the reviewers in each country, copy editors and typesetters—are not perfect. An occasional mistake might have slipped past. Two numerals in a telephone number might have been transposed and never caught. A name may have been misspelled or a valuable guidebook overlooked. If so, it was not intentional.

There are the inevitable changes to consider, too. All addresses, telephone numbers and prices were verified prior to publication. But people and organizations move, telephone numbers change and prices go up. Hence, I cannot accept responsibility or liability for any inaccuracies or omissions.

Prices, of course, change constantly. *Those quoted are meant only as guides.* For each year after 1981, expect a yearly increase of *at least 15 percent.* Maybe more.

This book describes the opportunities in the different regions of the British Isles. Six other books cover the rest of Europe:

- *On Foot Through Europe: A Trail Guide to Austria, Switzerland & Liechtenstein*
- *On Foot Through Europe: A Trail Guide to West Germany*
- *On Foot Through Europe: A Trail Guide to Scandinavia*
- *On Foot Through Europe: A Trail Guide to Spain & Portugal*
- *On Foot Through Europe: A Trail Guide to France & the Benelux Nations*

Use this or any of the area guides in conjunction with *On Foot Through Europe: A Trail Guide to Europe's Long-Distance Footpaths,* which gives you an overview of walking in Europe and tips on how to plan your hikes. All the background information available—and the places where you can get it—is here. It includes how to get information by mail, how to get to and stay along the trails, how to follow the paths safely, what to do in an emergency, and what equipment to bring, and many other facts to get you started hiking through Europe.

I welcome your comments. If you find an address or telephone number has changed, or you think some additional information should have been included in the book and was not, please let me know. Write to me at: Foot Trails Publications, Inc., Bedford Road, Greenwich, Connecticut 06830, U.S.A.

Contents

xii   **CONTENTS**

Difficulty:
What the Footpath Gradings Mean

The footpaths described in this book have been graded according to their difficulty. These gradings are based upon the *Schwierigkeitsgrade*—or difficulty gradings—developed for walkers in Austria. They are:

Easy (Schwierigkeitsgrad A & B). A path across either level or gently undulating terrain. Differences in altitude are small—less than 250 meters. The path requires minimal effort. It can be walked in any weather. Suitable for families with young children.

Easy to Moderately Difficult (Schwierigkeitsgrad C). A path across hilly terrain or mountains of medium height (up to 1,800 meters in altitude). The path presents few complications: climbs and descents are rarely steep, altitude differences are less than 600 meters and route finding is generally not difficult. Except in extremely bad weather, the path can be walked without great effort.

Moderately Difficult (Schwierigkeitsgrad D). A path with regular climbs and descents. Sections of the path may cross steep, rocky or marshy terrain. Some sections may also be above treeline or partially obstructed with undergrowth. The path generally can be walked without difficulty in good weather—providing you are physically fit, have the proper equipment and know how to use a map and compass. In bad weather use caution. Check with local authorities before you set out to be sure you are aware of any peculiarities in the local weather and path conditions.

Difficult (Schwierigkeitsgrad E). A strenuous route across rough terrain. Climbs and descents are steep and difficult. Precipices, swiftly flowing streams, thick undergrowth or snowfields may be encountered. In some places use of a map and compass may be essential to follow the route. On particularly exposed or dangerous sections safety devices—such as fixed cables and ladders—may be installed along the path. No climbing skills nor climbing equipment are required. Sections of some routes, however, will require that you are sure footed and are not subject to acrophobia. Novices and families with young children should not attempt such a route. In bad weather, *all* walkers should avoid it.

For Experienced Mountain Walkers Only (Schwierigkeitsgrad F). An extremely difficult route—across glaciers, on routes with exposed or dangerous sections (and no fixed cables or other safety devices), or cross-country through rough terrain where accurate route-finding with a map and compass is essential. Climbs and descents are steep and treacherous and may require rock climbing (up to Class II). Stream crossings are tricky and may require use of a rope. Severe, quick-changing weather conditions also may be encountered. To follow this route mountaineering experience is imperative, as is specialized equipment—crampons, ice axe or rope—and knowledge of its use.

Where & How to Go Hiking in the British Isles

ENGLAND

SCOTLAND

North Sea

NORTHUMBRIA

• Carlisle
Newcastle
upon Tyne

CUMBRIA

ISLE OF MAN

Kendal

YORKSHIRE AND
HUMBERSIDE

Scarborough

Lancaster

• York

NORTH WEST
ENGLAND

Leeds

Liverpool

Manchester

Irish Sea

Lincoln

Nottingham

EAST
MIDLANDS

Norwich

HEART
OF ENGLAND

Cambridge

WALES

Stratford-
upon-Avon

EAST
ANGLIA

Gloucester

THAMES AND
CHILTERNS

Oxford

London

Canterbury

• Bristol

Dover

SOUTHERN
ENGLAND

Eastbourne

WEST COUNTRY

Southampton

SOUTH EAST
ENGLAND

Exeter

Plymouth

ISLE OF WIGHT

Falmouth

English Channel

ISLES OF
SCILLY

KILOMETERS

0   100

England

ENGLAND IS A LAND of diversity and contrast, a land where each region
brings surprises: moated castles nestled in shady dales; rugged
highlands surrounded by fertile farmlands; and undulating valleys with
centuries-old towns of gray, squared-stone walls and overflowing rose
gardens.

Each region is distinctive, with its own characteristic geology, varied
wildlife and dramatic contrasts in scenery.

Much of this diversity springs from the land's complex geological
structure. Within its small area—130,447 square kilometers (50,365
square miles)—England contains rocks of virtually every major geological
epoch. Moreover, the many settlers and invaders who influenced Britain's
history and whose descendants still retain—and, in many cases, even
nurture—a distinct individuality, also contribute to the country's diversity.

For the walker, these differences are one of Britain's great attractions.
The countryside is easily accessible and includes nearly every kind of rural
beauty: gracious old cities dominated by Gothic cathedrals; country
estates with magnificent grounds; quiet footpaths linking hamlets,
churches and farmhouses of flint and brick.

You can walk the length of Offa's Dyke, the great earthwork constructed
about 800 A.D. to mark the frontier between Mercia and Wales, or
Hadrian's Wall, built by the Romans to defend England against marauding
tribesmen from the north. There is the "Wessex" of Thomas Hardy's
novels to explore and the mountainous Lake District, made famous by
William Wordsworth and the other Lake poets.

There is also the gracious British hospitality—polite, reserved and
helpful—an aspect of the country that the walker, in particular, seems to
receive in large measure.

In total, there are 165,700 kilometers (103,000 miles) of public
footpaths and bridleways in England and Wales. Of these, 2,413 kilometers (1,499 miles) are long-distance routes.

Although England's long-distance footpaths are popular and heavily
used, most of the country's walking is on the myriad of interconnecting
local paths, which grew up through the centuries as part of the communications system of the countryside.

The vast majority of these footpaths are rights-of-way protected by law.
Since the days of William the Conqueror, every Briton has had the right to

5

own property, but every other Briton has had the right to use existing paths to cross it. Because of this, you have the right to walk through private land from one point to the next on these established paths.

But you also have a responsibility to respect England's *Country Code*. This means you must:

- Enjoy the countryside and respect its life and work.
- Guard against all risks of fire.
- Fasten all gates, even if you find them open. (The sole exception to this is if an open gate is secured. If the gate won't open, climb it only at the hinge end.)
- Keep yours dogs under close control.
- Keep to public paths across farmland.
- Use gates and stiles to cross fences, hedges and walls. (Dry stone walls are particularly vulnerable. Never climb them or remove any stones from them. Building and repairing these walls is a highly skilled—and expensive—craft.)
- Leave livestock, crops and machinery alone.
- Take your litter home.
- Help to keep all water clean.
- Protect wildlife, plants and trees.
- Take special care on country roads. Always walk in single file and face oncoming traffic.
- Make no unnecessary noise.

Stopping to picnic outside of designated areas, leaving a gate open where livestock can stray, or persistently walking back and forth on a public path all constitute a trespass, for which you—technically—can be prosecuted.

The right-of-way issue also has another twist: the waymarking of footpaths in England is, at best, sporadic. The locations of paths are required to be signposted where they intersect with paved roads. But, while some paths are signposted (usually with wooden finger posts or green and white "Public Footpath" signs), many are not. Also, few paths are waymarked throughout their full length. Some even aren't well trod and may only exist as dotted lines on a map. As a result, it is sometimes difficult to know if you are keeping to the legal right-of-way. In fact, you might find that some paths have been plowed up and have had crops planted across them. This is illegal, so you are entitled to walk through the crop, providing you stay as close as practicable to the line of the path. If a path has been obstructed by barbed wire or overgrowth you are entitled to remove as much as necessary to enable you to get by, unless there is an obvious short way around.

Sometimes a path might take you through a farmyard or, occasionally, even through a private garden. In these cases, you need to know where the path goes. Because a path's route may not always be obvious, it is important to carry the Ordnance Survey maps on which rights-of-way are marked. Then, if you still are in doubt about where the right-of-way is, ask.

In addition to England's extensive network of footpaths, there are large areas of uncultivated countryside over which you may usually roam at will. This countryside is of three types:

Access land. This is land to which formal agreements allowing the public to walk over it have been made. Such land is relatively rare, although there are 181 square kilometers (70 square miles) in the Peak National Park to which these agreements apply. Access land is clearly indicated on site, usually at its points of access.

Common land. This land originally was the property of local landowners to which villagers had pasture and grazing rights. Commons may consist of a few acres of rough grazing ground to extensive tracts of open land. There is no *right* of access to it (unless the common land is in a former urban district or borough), but in practice the public may walk freely over it. In total, there are approximately 607,000 hectares (1.5 million acres) of common land. Most of Dartmoor, for instance, and large stretches of the Lake District mountains and the Pennines are common land. This land usually is not indicated on site. Also, although the word "common" may be part of a place name on a map, this is no guarantee that the area is still a common.

Mountain and moorland. In much of England you will have no trouble in walking over high grazing country, even though it is private property. But if there are notices warning you off, you are well advised to obey them.

England has seven national parks and numerous Areas of Outstanding Natural Beauty in which you can walk. In addition, there is an extensive network of nature trails, which are signposted to point out local flora and fauna. Numerous walking-holiday arrangements are also available to take you to some of the most beautiful parts of the country.

Those interested in antiquities such as Roman roads and Norman castles will find many marked on the Ordnance Survey maps. In some areas, such as the Pennines, there are many traces of past industry—old mine workings, disused canals and old red-brick foundries—to explore.

Another enjoyable aspect of walking in England is visiting its country pubs. These are scattered throughout the country and offer a hospitable haven where a tired walker can have a pint of bitter, play a game of darts and absorb some local color. Some pubs prefer not to have walkers because they are trying to attract a different clientele. It is their privilege to discriminate; they are not obliged to serve anyone they do not wish to. Other pubs welcome walkers. But, because you are likely to arrive travel-stained with muddy boots and possibly soaking wet, it is advisable to use

the public bar and, unless the pub caters especially to walkers, to leave
your boots and pack outside the door.

England's Rights-of-Way Laws

Although the right of passage has been a part of British common law since
Norman times, the legal niceties were not sharply defined until Britain's
Public Rights of Way Act of 1932. Further provisions were laid down by
the National Parks and Access Act of 1949, the Highways Acts of 1959,
1971, and 1980 and the Countryside Acts of 1968 and 1981.

These acts have not always been popular with property owners. The
result has been occasional friction between landowners and walkers.
When the Chiltern Society began mapping footpaths in the early 1960s to
record them as rights-of-way, for instance, many farmers tried to dis-
courage the walkers from crossing their land—and the discouragement
was far from mild. Some farmers even took guns to frighten ramblers away,
but the ramblers—as walkers are known in Britain—fought back with
cameras, tape recorders and newspaper headlines. The guns have since
been put away, and peaceful cooperation has steadily been growing
among ramblers and most landowners.

Nevertheless, occasional path blockages, *Trespassers will be prosecuted*
signs and, in a few instances, outright intimidation still occur. One
careless walker who forgets to close a gate or knocks off a stone while
climbing over a wall can cause a landowner to turn against all walkers. It
is therefore essential to insure you are not that careless hiker.

When walking in England, it is important to understand the major
highlights of its rights-of-way laws. Essentially, they provide the following:

Classification

> *Footpath*—a highway over which the public has a right-of-way on
> foot only.
>
> *Bridleway*—a highway over which the public has a right-of-way on
> foot, on horseback and on bicycle.
>
> *Roads used as a public path*—RUPPs, as they are commonly known,
> are usually green lanes or unsurfaced tracks that were originally used
> by carts and pack horses. They are legal rights-of-way which, under
> the Countryside Act of 1968, are soon to be reclassified as either
> byways, bridleways or footpaths.
>
> *Byway*—a minor road, open to all traffic, including motor vehicles.

Protection. Legally, a public footpath is part of the Queen's highway and
subject to the same protection as a trunk road. It is just as much of an
offense to obstruct a road with barbed wire as it is to erect a fence across a

public path without giving proper access—and the penalty for doing so is exactly the same. The same is true of signposts and waymarkings; it is a punishable offense to destroy or damage one.

The creation of public paths. In theory, most paths become rights-of-way because the owner dedicates them to public use. In fact very few paths have been formally dedicated, but the law assumes that if the public uses a path without interference for upwards of 20 years, then the owner intends dedication. Most public paths came about in this way. Paths can also be established by mutual agreement between local authorities and owners, or by compulsory creation order. Creation orders, however, are rare and difficult to obtain.

The closure of public paths. A path cannot cease to be a public right-of-way if it is not used. This was decided as long ago as 1315 (R vs. Inhabitants of St. James, Taunton, Selwyn's Nisi Prius Reports). Disuse, however, can be the basis for an application by a landowner for an order to close the path. A path can be closed or diverted, but only by an order carried out by local authorities—county and district councils—or the central government. Also, the order can be enacted only after proper public notice has been given, time has been allowed for objections and the objections have been considered at a public enquiry or in writing.

The right of passage. A person's right is limited to passing and repassing along a public path on *bonafide* journeys. A person may also pause or sit down to rest along a path. A reporter walking back and forth along a right-of-way taking notes, for instance, has exceeded his right of passage and is considered a trespasser. Pitching a tent without permission is also a trespass.

Rights-of-way maps. A clearly defined path may not always exist along a public right-of-way. Also, not all paths in England are rights-of-way. The safest way to determine if a path is a right-of-way is to check the *Definitive Map* of paths, which all county councils have been required to prepare. If a footpath or bridleway appears on the definitive map, that is conclusive evidence in law of its existence as a right-of-way. This holds true even if the path is overgrown, obstructed by barbed wire, has houses built across it or is plowed up. There is still a legal right to use it—unless an extinguishment or diversion order has been granted by due legal process. The local authority can use its statutory powers to have the path opened for public use. If a path has been legally closed or diverted, this won't be shown on the Definitive Map until after the next review. The county council, however, will have a copy of the order, which you may inspect on request.

   The definitive maps can be seen at county council and district council offices, usually in the surveyors' department. Some counties sell copies of their definitive map, and some place copies in libraries.

Rights-of-way are also shown on the 1:63,360, 1:50,000 and 1:25,000 Second Series Ordnance Survey maps. Further information on the Ordnance Survey maps will be found in the section on *Maps* later in this chapter.

Footpath maintenance. The responsibility for the maintenance of footpaths falls upon the county councils, although other local authorities can assume this responsibility. In practice, private groups of volunteers in each region often help maintain path surfaces, keep markers in repair and free the way of overgrowth.

Gates and stiles. The maintenance of the gates and stiles on a path is the responsibility of the property owner, although the county council must contribute one-quarter of the cost if asked. If the landowner fails to keep his gates and stiles in proper repair, the authority can, after 14 days' notice, do the job and send the bill to the landowner.

Obstructions. Obstructions on a path—barbed wire, an overgrown hedge or a pile of manure—should be reported to the county councils. Or you may report them to the Ramblers' Association. County councils have the power to require owners to remove obstructions and to prosecute those who fail to do so.

Waymarking. County councils have the power to waymark paths, or may delegate the work to individuals, societies or other local authorities. But the law provides few specifics as to where or to what extent footpaths are to be waymarked. Instead, section 27 of the Countryside Act of 1968 simply imposes a general duty on county councils to waymark paths to the extent they think necessary. The result is that waymarking—where it exists—varies considerably in England. There are acorn-shaped markings, wooden arrows, stenciled paint arrows and cairns—sometimes all on the same path. The Countryside Commission has recommended a standardized system of painted arrows—yellow for footpaths and blue for bridleways. This recommendation has been endorsed by the Ramblers' Association. But not all local authorities have adopted this system. Also, although the Countryside Commission has suggested that paths be signposted and waymarked "to the extent that any visitors who are unfamiliar with the area will not lose their way," there are still many paths in England which are neither signposted nor waymarked.

As Richard Wilson noted in a recent issue of a British walkers' magazine, *The Great Outdoors:* "The relationship of rambles to brambles may be unclear to those who have never attempted to walk along the course of one of those red dotted lines which are liberally and, as will become apparent, optimistically scattered far and wide over the Ordnance Survey's 1:50,000 maps; it will require no explanation to anybody who has . . . fought his way through a bramble hedge, six foot high and six foot wide, has been playfully released by that hedge with just enough momentum to carry him headlong into a ditch whose bottom consists of a six-inch layer of evil-smelling slime, and has emerged therefrom to find himself nose-to-nose with an exceptionally fearsome specimen of Hereford bull . . . .

"It is for this reason that I have learnt that I cannot rely solely on the 1:50,000 map for navigations purposes: though it is ideal for following paths of whose existence there is some evidence on the ground, such as stiles or a well-worn trail, I have found that it requires supplementation by the 1:25,000 map, with its much greater amount of information, in order to follow accurately the course of a path across fields between one non-existent stile and the next."

Some footpaths in England, of course, offer you a clear, trouble-free route. But the exceptions are notable—and many.

Dangerous animals. Most, but not all, county councils have adopted bylaws prohibiting mature bulls in fields crossed by public paths. In some counties, bulls may be kept in fields crossed by public paths providing they are accompanied by cows or heifers. Other than bulls, it is not an offense to have dangerous animals in a field crossed by a public path. But the owner of the animal is liable for any damage or injury it may cause.

Plowing. Farmers have a right to plow up a path providing they restore the path to a reasonably usable condition within three weeks of starting to plow. Failure to restore a path is illegal and offenders may be prosecuted. Also, the right to plow does not extend to paths along the edges of fields nor to green lanes (RUPPs). Nonetheless, many farmers ignore their obligation to restore a path—and plow where they darn well please, law or no law.

How to cross a plowed field. Although it may seem more sensible to walk around the edge of a field if a path has been plowed up and crops are planted over it, you can be warned off for walking in a place where you have no right to be. Instead, stick to the right-of-way, try to stay as close to the line of the path as you can, and hope you brought the 1:25,000 Second Series Ordnance Survey maps on which rights-of-way—and field boundaries—are marked.

Trespassing. Property owners have the right to insist that trespassers leave their land and return to the right-of-way. And they may use any reasonable and necessary force to compel you to do so. Property owners may also prosecute a person for any unauthorized entry on their property. But, in this case, they must prove injury to their property. If a landowner sues for trespass and is unable to prove injury, he may only recover nominal damages—although you might have to meet his legal costs. For this reason, a sign saying *Trespassers will be prosecuted* aimed, for instance, at keeping you off a private drive might be meaningless. Prosecution is likely to occur only if you trespass and damage property. If you are ever accused of trespass, a polite apology and a willingness to follow the (usually irate) accuser's directions often closes the incident—even amicably.

Misleading notices. You may occasionally see posted notices that are calculated to deter you from using a public footpath—a sign saying *Private* where a footpath enters a field, for instance. Such notices are illegal. They should be reported to the county council. Before proceeding, however, you should check your map to ensure the path is a legal right-of-way. If it isn't, you may have to do some quick explaining to an irate property owner.

Further information on England's rights-of-way laws is available from the Ramblers' Association (for its address and telephone number, see the *Address Directory* at the back of this chapter). Among the publications the RA sells on the laws are:

- *Right of Way.* A short pamphlet that summarizes the laws in 24 questions and answers.
- *A Practical Guide to the Law of Footpaths and Bridleways* by Ian Campbell of the Commons Society. Describes the right-of-way laws in detail. Cites examples of court cases that have been heard on various aspects of the laws.
- *The Creation, Diversion and Closure of Public Paths.* By the Ramblers' Association. Explains the procedures governing the changes that can be made and cites the appropriate legislative sections.
- *A Guide to Definitive Maps of Public Paths* by Mary McArevey for the Commons Society. Tells you everything you need to know about definitive maps, including where they can be inspected.

A complete list of publications, plus their prices, is available on request from the Ramblers' Association.

The English Landscape

England can be divided roughly into two main regions—lowland England and highland (or upland) England.

The lowlands—located in the south and east—are a region of broad river valleys, low undulating hills and a succession of asymmetrical chalk scarplands that rise gently on one side, and on the other drop sharply into clay vales. The farmland is fertile and the fields, often enclosed with hedgerows, alternate with areas of woodland, heath and a close succession of quaint villages and towns, each with its old churches and bits of literary or historical antiquity.

The highlands—lying in the north and west—consist of mountainous outcroppings of very old rocks, interspersed with valleys and plains. This area contains all the mountainous parts of England—the granite mass of Dartmoor in Devon, the igneous mountains of the Lake District and the gritstone and limestone of the Pennines, which stretch from the Peak District to the Scottish border, forming what is often called the "backbone of England." On the fringes of the Pennines, where the Coal Measures occur, heavy industry and mining support dense populations. But, on the whole, the highlands constitute a sparsely populated region of grasslands and rough pasture, where sheep farms, dairies and small livestock operations predominate.

Throughout England, you encounter regional variations. The central part of the Lake District, for instance, is rugged and precipitous, formed by volcanic rocks. But as the lake-filled valleys radiate out from the central dome of mountains, the volcanics give way to slate, which dominates the smoother and softer scenery north of Derwentwater and around Coniston and Windermere.

Less than 50 kilometers to the east are the Yorkshire Dales, an area of carboniferous limestone, remarkable for its cliffs, caves, potholes and underground streams.

In the lowlands, billowing rounded hills of chalk abut sandy heaths and rich clay basins. And in the midlands, isolated inliers of ancient rocks project through the layers of clay and rich red sandstone.

Even along the coast, the land is varied. There are bold headlands formed by the ancient rocks of the highlands: the granite cliffs of Land's End and the red sandstone of St. Bees Head. Around lowland England, soft-white limestone—the chalk—forms white cliffs as at Dover and in the Needles off the Isle of Wight. Yet, the eastern coast between the Humber and Thames estuary is low-lying and some stretches have for centuries been protected from the sea by embankments.

Flora & Fauna

England also has a diverse pattern of vegetation. On heavy soils, the natural cover is oak forest, with alder along river banks and marsh or fen in areas of persistent flooding. On chalk and limestone, ash and beech grow, and on sandy soils, Scots pine, birch and heathland flora.

Through the ages, England's natural forest has gradually disappeared, a victim of the plow, cattle and sheep raising and the demand for wood, charcoal and coal. Today, woodland covers only about 4.5 percent of the country. Most of this woodland occurs along the Welsh border and in parts of the southeast. Yet much of England appears to be well wooded because of the numerous hedgerows and isolated trees.

In the highlands there are large stretches of moorland and, at higher altitudes, a tundralike vegetation of lichens, mosses and bilberry. In these areas cultivated land is limited primarily to the valleys and plains, where the typically thin, poor highland soils are deeper and richer.

In contrast, most of lowland Britain has been cultivated, the exceptions being urban areas and a few patches of heath and forest. More than a third of the farmland is arable. The rest is pasture and meadow with indigenous grasses and flowering plants.

Because of Britain's cool temperate climate and evenly distributed rainfall, streams rarely dry up, grasslands are green throughout the year, and a succession of wildflowers bloom from spring to autumn. In fact, there is scarcely a month in which some flowers may not be found in hedgerows and sheltered woodland glades (hence, the saying: "Kissing's out of season when the gorse is not in bloom.").

Animal life in England has suffered even more than plants from human activities. Many of the native large animals, such as the wolf, the bear, the boar and the reindeer, have become extinct. But red deer, often protected for sporting reasons, still flourish in the west of England on Exmoor, while other deer are increasing in the plantations of the Forestry Commission. There are foxes in most rural areas, and otters occasionally are found near fast-flowing rivers and streams. The stoat, weasel, hedgehog, hare and rabbit occur practically everywhere, as do squirrels (although the imported gray squirrel has almost driven out the native red squirrel). On the Atlantic coast, gray seals and common seals are frequently seen and, on the Farne Islands off the coast of Northumberland, there is a large colony of gray seals.

Birds are numerous. Some 460 species have been recorded, of which nearly 200 species breed in England. The rest are migrants or winter visitors.

On the other hand, reptiles and amphibians are few. Only three snakes occur, of which only the viper, or adder, is venomous. The viper is found chiefly on pine and heath lands. Its bite is usually not fatal—just painful. If you are bitten, however, you should seek medical assistance immediately.

Climate

The chief characteristic of the English climate, even in summer, is its changeability. On the highlands, low-lying mists are common, and can quickly obliterate the sun. Or it can rain. In fact, throughout England it can rain just about anytime—and usually does.

You have to be prepared.

Temperatures generally decrease from west to east in winter and from south to north in summer. But rarely are temperatures either very hot or very cold.

During a normal summer, the temperature in southern England occasionally rises to about 27°C. (81°F.), but temperatures of 32°C. (90°F.) and above are infrequent. On the other hand, you may need a wool sweater even in the middle of July, especially if you are walking in the highlands.

Extreme minimum temperatures depend largely on local conditions. In some areas, *minus* 7°C. (20°F.) may occur on a still, clear winter's night, but in most of England, *minus* 12°C. (10°F.) is rare, and *minus* 18°C. (0°F.) has been recorded only during exceptionally cold periods.

On the whole, England has an average annual rainfall of 854 mm (34 inches). The amount of rainfall in local areas, however, is greatly influenced by its topography and exposure to the Atlantic. In the center of the Lake District, as much as 4,394 mm (173 inches) of precipitation may fall during an average year, whereas some places in southeast England record less than 508 mm (20 inches). Throughout England, rain is fairly well distributed throughout the year, although the driest months generally are from March to June and the wettest are from October to January. Nonetheless, a period of three weeks without rain is unusual.

In the highlands, the damp climate and high winds often combine to create extremely severe conditions, and the weather can rapidly change from sun to storm. Where the possibility of severe weather conditions exists—on the fells (hills) of the Lake District, for instance—warnings to walkers are sometimes posted, along with advice on the clothing and equipment required to cope with the conditions. These warnings should be heeded religiously.

Weather Forecasts

Local weather forecasts for many parts of England can be obtained by telephone. Details of the services available in each area and their telephone numbers are listed under *Weather Forecasts* in the *Telephone Information Services* section at the front of area directories.

The recordings generally provide an overall forecast for one of England's 14 forecast districts. These are large areas, however, so vagaries in local topography may cause weather conditions to vary from the forecasts—sometimes drastically.

For this reason, it is sometimes best to call the district Meteorological Office, especially if you plan to walk along the coast or in the highlands. You can then request a 24-hour forecast for the specific locality in which you intend to walk.

If you do this, you should ask for the officer-in-charge and tell him:

1. The locality for which you wish a forecast.
2. The purpose for which the forecast is required.
3. The weather features that are of special interest to you—wind, rain and temperature, for instance.
4. The time at which the information is desired.
5. The telephone number to which the information is to be sent.

The Meteorological Office will then prepare a forecast for you and call back with the information. There is a nominal charge for this service, but it's worth it. You won't be able to get a more accurate forecast.

Even so, remember that weather conditions can still change, so pack your rucksack accordingly.

The telephone number of the Meteorological Office will be listed in the area directories along with the other weather forecast numbers, usually under the heading, "For more detailed enquiries call the Meteorological Office."

In London, this number is:

London Weather Centre: Tel. (01) 836 4311.

Where to Get Walking Information

There are three organizations that can provide information on walking in England.

For general information:

Ramblers' Association (see *Address Directory*).

The Ramblers' Association—or, as it is known by its common acronym, the RA—is the best single source of information on walking in Britain. Its staff can answer just about any question you have—or at least refer you to whoever can answer it. And, barring an overload of work, replies are prompt.

The RA also publishes a series of useful *Fact Sheets*, which summarize the essential information a person should know when planning a walk in England. They include:

- *Fact Sheet 1—Equipment for Ramblers.* Four pages of sensible suggestions.
- *Fact Sheet 2—Long-Distance Paths.* Gives a brief description of the long-distance paths over 50 miles in length. Also lists the sheet numbers of maps required to walk the paths, nearest railway stations to the route ends and the publications available to each path, their prices and the addresses of their publishers.
- *Fact Sheet 3—Maps for Walkers.* Gives a brief description of the various Ordnance Survey maps on which footpaths are indicated, gives their prices and tells you how to order them.
- *County Sheets—Path Guides.* A must for planning your trip, this series of Fact Sheets lists by county all the path guides and local footpath maps known to the RA. Prices for the guides and maps are given, as are the charges for postage (within Britain) and the addresses of their publishers. The County Sheets also include the

names and addresses of the area secretaries of the RA, the names of RA groups in each county, and information on guided walks and excursions. The series covers each of England's 45 counties plus Scotland and Wales. When ordering please specify the name of the county in which you plan to walk.

- *Fact Sheet 5—Walking in Britain.* Provides an overview of walking in Britain. Gives a brief description of the footpath network, long-distance paths, mountaineering, maps, trail lodgings, the national parks, Areas of Outstanding Beauty and what you need to bring with you to walk in Britain. Also includes a sales list with overseas postage prices. Designed for foreign walkers who are coming to Britain for the first time.

The Fact Sheets are available for a nominal charge. In addition, the RA asks that you send enough stamps or international postal reply coupons to cover the mailing costs.

A list of other publications available from the RA is free on request. All the publications are available only in English.

For information on England's long-distance footpaths:

Countryside Commission (see *Address Directory*).

A statutory body set up under the Countryside Act of 1968, the Commission is responsible for drawing up proposals for the establishment of long-distance footpaths. The Commission also assists local authorities in negotiations of rights-of-way agreements for the long-distance paths. The Commission, which took over the work of the National Parks Commission in running the national parks, also designates Areas of Outstanding Natural Beauty, provides grants for public access to open country, helps create country parks and provides recreational facilities in the countryside. A series of free pamphlets to the long-distance footpaths can be obtained on request.

For information on backpacking in Britain:

Backpacker's Club (see *Address Directory*). A club organized specifically to meet the needs of the lightweight walker-camper. Will answer questions about where and how you can go backpacking in Britain. Also will provide details of the routes and paths where you can backpack and camp along the trails.

Walking Clubs in England

There are more than 600 walking clubs and societies in England. Of these, the most important national organizations are:

See *Address Directory:*

The Ramblers' Association. A politically active organization, the RA is devoted to protecting the interests of ramblers and to improving access on foot to the countryside. Formed in 1935, it has 37,000 individual members and 450 affiliated organizations. Its branches—known as Areas—cover Britain. Within most Areas there also are organized Groups of the RA that center on particular towns and districts. At Area and Group level, rambles are organized for members. But most of the time and funds of the association go toward protecting the countryside and the right of all people to walk across it.

Since its founding, the RA has campaigned for public access to uncultivated land, the creation of definitive maps to establish conclusively the status of public paths as rights-of-way, and the signposting of paths at their junctions with paved roads. It successfully fought a threat by the government in 1973 to curtail the 1:25,000 Ordnance Survey maps, and recently has even been successful in having the rate of publication of these maps speeded up. RA members also carried out much of the survey work and campaigned hard for the necessary legislation to create the nationally designated long-distance paths such as the Pennine Way, the South Downs Way and the Offa's Dyke Path.

RA inspectors and wardens—all voluntary—maintain a vigilant watch over attempts to close and divert public paths. Illegal interference—barbed wire, padlocked gates, high fences and missing bridges—are taken up with local authorities and through the courts. RA representatives also appear at scores of public enquiries into path closures and diversions every year. As a result of RA opposition, many path extinguishment orders are withdrawn or turned down.

In addition, RA members waymark paths, clear them of overgrowth and, in the National Parks, act as voluntary wardens to protect the countryside and inform visitors.

Wherever you walk in England, you are indebted to the efforts of the RA. The paths you walk, the maps you use, the waymarks and signposts along your route—each has been influenced by the RA.

Members receive the RA's journal, *Rucksack*. This is published three times a year and includes news on the country's footpaths, RA activities, new legislation and book reviews. In addition, they receive a copy of the RA's annual *Bed and Breakfast Guide*. Members are also free to join in the Area and Group activities of the association.

Although the RA has more than 400 clubs and societies affiliated to it in

Britain—including the Country-wide Holidays Association, Holiday Fellowship and Youth Hostels Association—no reciprocal membership agreements exist. Instead, many ramblers also belong to one or more of these other organizations.

Membership applications will be sent on request from the head office. Foreign members are welcomed.

Backpackers' Club. Known as the "club for the un-clubbables," the Backpackers' Club is a specialized organization for the lightweight walker-camper—the person who carries shelter, sleeping bag, clothing and food on the trail so he or she can be totally self-sufficient. The club functions successfully without controlling committees. Instead, it has numerous County Co-Ordinators scattered across the country, each of whom is a volunteer. And its charter is simply the *Country Code.*

The purpose of the club is to represent and safeguard the rights of backpackers; to ensure their continual rights of access to meadow, mountain, moorland and beach; to fight moves to legislate camping; to encourage the full use of the established long-distance footpaths, national parks and open areas; and to encourage and aid in the development of lightweight walking and camping equipment.

Members of the club receive:

1. Discounts on the purchase of equipment from various camping equipment and clothing retailers in the U.K.

2. A comprehensive advisory and information service on backpacking. This includes advice on choosing equipment as well as advice on routes, camp sites, food and clothing.

3. A confidential *Farm Pitch Directory,* which lists places where members may pitch their tents. Most of the pitches are on farms and well off the beaten track.

4. Camping equipment and personal-effects insurance which, for a nominal charge, covers loss or damage to equipment.

5. Invitations to attend monthly Backpacking Weekends, held in various parts of the country.

6. Use of the club's exclusive camping sites in forest areas.

7. *Backchat,* the club's quarterly newsletter.

Membership applications will be sent on request. Foreign members are welcomed.

British Mountaineering Council. The British Mountaineering Council (BMC) is not a walkers' organization. Its concern is mountaineering. Founded in 1944, it promotes the interests of British mountaineers and mountaineering in the United Kingdom and overseas. Jointly with the Mountaineering Council of Scotland it is the representative body of British mountaineers. Full membership is open to mountaineering clubs and organizations whose principal objectives are mountaineering, who have headquarters in the United Kingdom and who are owned and controlled by their members. Associate membership is open to bodies who do not qualify for full membership and to individuals.

The BMC assists member clubs—of which there are more than 200 in the U.K.—and, with their cooperation, works to improve guidebooks and huts and to arrange reciprocal rights in club huts. It also ensures adequate training for novice, intermediate and advanced mountaineers; resists encroachments on the mountain environment; negotiates access rights to mountain areas, outcrops and sea cliffs; and helps expeditions overseas in cooperation with the Mount Everest Foundation and the Alpine Club. In addition, it tests the safety of mountain equipment and, in cooperation with the Mountaineering Council of Scotland, provides a British Mountain Guide qualification for experienced mountaineers who wish to perform as mountain guides in Britain.

BMC publications include guidebooks, safety handbooks, pamphlets, posters and equipment test reports. Sets of safety filmstrips and slides covering summer and winter mountaineering are also available. Lists of the publications and films are free on request from the BMC.

Members of the BMC receive its official magazine, *Climber & Rambler*, published 12 times per year. In addition, they may take part in the BMC's insurance plan, which provides coverage for personal accidents in the British Isles; mountain rescue in the Alps; and public liability for member clubs, associated bodies and individual members. The BMC also offers to clubs and organizations a Hut Insurance Scheme that provides coverage for burglary, theft and breaking and entry. It also issues insurance to instructors and guides for their personal climbing, whether professional or private. Premiums for BMC insurance vary, depending upon the coverage desired. Complete information is available from the BMC's Insurance Department.

Membership applications are available on request. Although foreigners may join the BMC, they do not qualify for insurance coverage.

An address list of affiliated clubs is available on request.

Camping Club of Great Britain and Ireland, Ltd. The Camping Club looks after camping interests. It has 45 camping sites of its own and publishes a directory of 2,500 British and Irish sites. In addition, it has groups devoted to lightweight camping and mountaineering. Members receive its journal, *Camping and Caravanning*. Information on membership may be obtained by writing the club.

The Commons, Open Spaces and Footpaths Preservation Society. This society, founded in 1865, promotes knowledge of England's rights-of-way laws so that paths and commons may be preserved for the public benefit. It publishes a journal (free to members) that contains articles and a summary of important legal cases.

Country-Wide Holidays Association. The CHA runs a wide range of walking holidays in Britain and abroad. It is also one of England's major walking clubs—devoted, simply, to encouraging people to walk. Founded in the 1890s, the CHA owns 24 guesthouses in Great Britain, most of which are country mansions adapted to meet CHA purposes. Each guest house accommodates between 50 and 85 people.

There are more than 100 CHA member clubs in Britain. These offer weekly social programs, rambles, weekends at guesthouses, special-interest visits, film and slide shows, dances, and a variety of other activities.

Guests who spend a week or more at any CHA center during a year and who sign the Official Form of Membership automatically become members of the CHA. Membership continues from the date of the holiday until September 30 of the following year.

Members receive the biannual *CHA Magazine* as well as its summer and winter brochures, which list the CHA holidays.

Further information on the CHA holidays, its guesthouses and its club activities is available from the head office.

The Holiday Fellowship, Ltd. The Holiday Fellowship has more than 100 rambling and social clubs in various parts of the country. In addition, it organizes a wide variety of walking holidays in Britain and abroad. Members receive the club magazine, *Over the Hills,* as well as current brochures describing its numerous holiday programs.

Long-Distance Walkers Association. This association exists to further the interests of those who enjoy long-distance walking. It organizes and supports long-distance walking events and marathons. It also provides members with information on long-distance paths. No emphasis is placed on any form of racing or road walking. Members receive a thrice-yearly magazine, which gives details of forthcoming events.

Mountain Bothies Association. The MBA is a voluntary organization formed to maintain simple unlocked shelters in remote country for the use of walkers, climbers and other outdoor enthusiasts. Members receive an up-to-date list of the bothies and their locations.

Youth Hostels Association. Yes, a walking club. And a large one, too. In addition to operating more than 250 hostels in England and Wales, the YHA offers to its members rock-climbing and mountaineering courses, walking tours (among others) and a variety of travel services. The YHA also has a regional system of area associations. Many of these have groups that organize walking activities throughout the year. (Details on these activities are often posted in nearby hostels or YHA shops.) Membership in any youth hostel association is honored. Or, if you are not already a member of the youth hostel association in your country, you may join the YHA. It is also possible to become a life member.

Maps

The Ordnance Survey (OS), a government department, publishes five map series that are suitable for walkers:

1:25,000—First Series. Because of their great detail, these maps are particularly valuable for walking across difficult terrain and in cultivated areas. Each map covers an area of 10 kilometers by 10 kilometers and has contours drawn in at vertical intervals of 25 feet (7.62 meters). They show tracks as surveyed on the ground. In addition, they show field boundaries, perhaps the most important feature for walkers in lowland areas. This enables you to follow more easily the true line of a path and to recognize immediately which field you are in. No distinction is made on the maps between public and private paths, nor between footpaths and bridleways, so before the maps can be used with certainty they should be compared with the smaller scale OS maps or, better yet, with the definitive maps prepared by the county councils. Only 13 sheets in the series— SD-92, SH-52, SH-53, SH-61, SH-62, SH-64, SH-71, SH-72, SH-74, SH-83, SH-93, SO-49 and SO-59—have been overprinted with rights-of-way information at the request of the county council concerned. The series covers England, Wales and most of Scotland, except where superceded by the Second Series.

1:25,000—Second Series. Each of these excellent maps covers an area of 20 kilometers east to west by 10 kilometers north to south— the same as two First Series maps side by side. Details are basically the same as on the First Series except that the Second Series maps have been redrawn to make the presentation of details clearer. In addition, rights-of-way are shown in green where the information was available from the definitive maps at the time of preparation. This makes them even more useful than the First Series maps. The series eventually will cover the whole of England, Scotland and Wales, and will replace the First Series maps. To date, more than 450 maps have been produced out of a total of 1499. The rate of production, however, has recently been speeded up; if this is maintained the series should be complete by 1990.

Outdoor Leisure Maps, 1:25,000. A recent development, these maps cover popular walking areas. Nearly all sheets cover an area of 26 kilometers by 21 kilometers. Based on the 1:25,000 maps, they show rights of way, youth hostels, camping and caravanning sites, mountain rescue posts, boundaries of access land and access paths. Information on the map is also given in three languages—English, French and German. For the areas they cover, they are the best walkers' maps available from the OS. To date, the following maps have been published:

- *Outdoor Leisure Maps based on the First Series, 1:25,000.* These maps have a brown cover. They are available for Dark Peak (Northern Peak District), Three Peaks, Malham and Upper Wharefedale (both Yorkshire Dales), English Lakes (four sheets— NE, NW, SE, SW), Wye Valley and Forest of Dean, South Pennines, and in Wales: Brecon Beacons (three sheets—East, Central and West) and Snowdonia National Park (six sheets—Snowdon, Conwy Valley, Bala, Harlech, Cader Idris and Dovey Forest).
- *Outdoor Leisure Maps based on the Second Series, 1:25,000.* These have a yellow cover. They are available for Cuillin and Torridon Hills (two maps back to back), High Tops of the Cairngorms (Scotland), Brighton and Sussex Vale, South Devon, Purbeck (Dorset), New Forest, and White Peak (Southern Peak District).

1:50,000 Maps. The 204 maps in this series are the successors to the old one-inch-to-the-mile maps. They cover the whole of England, Scotland and Wales. Rights-of-way information recorded on county council definitive maps is reproduced on the 1:50,000 maps in red (except for Scotland, where no rights-of-way information is given). Paths whose status is not known are marked in black, and the OS keys emphasize that this depiction is no guarantee of a right of way. Fifty-two sheets have been redrawn to Second Series specifications. These maps show additional tourist information, which is being added to First Series maps as they are reprinted. Legends on the maps are also translated into French and German. These maps are primarily suited for walking in uncultivated areas. Because they do not show field boundaries, even the most skilled map reader will have difficulty using them to follow the exact line of a path in intensively farmed areas. Nonetheless, they are invaluable in planning walks, especially in areas where you must use the First Series 1:25,000 maps, which do not provide rights-of-way information.

Tourist Maps, one-inch (1:63,360). These are the last relics of the one-inch-maps system. They give both rights-of-way and tourist information similar to that contained on some of the 1:50,000 maps: ancient monuments, viewpoints, archeological sites, ecclesiastical buildings, museums and stately homes open to the public. Maps for hilly areas also show contour relief by means of shading. Like the 1:50,000 maps they are primarily suited for use in high, uncultivated areas, and in lowland areas should be used only for route planning. Maps available: Exmoor, Dartmoor, New Forest, Peak District, Lake District, North York Moors, and in Scotland: Loch Lomond and the Trossachs, and Ben Nevis and Glen Coe.

Where to Buy OS maps

Most major booksellers, stationers and outdoor-leisure-equipment specialists in larger towns stock the OS maps, as does the Ramblers' Association.

A list of retailers, a catalog with a map index and a price list are available from:

Ordnance Survey (see *Address Directory*).

The Ordnance Survey does not sell maps directly to the public. Orders by mail should instead be sent to the OS's main agent in London:

Cook, Hammond & Kell, Ltd. (see *Address Directory*).

When ordering maps by mail, you should list the map title, scale, publisher and, if possible, the sheet number of the maps desired. If the sheet number is not known, briefly describe the area covered by the map. Also, specify whether you want a flat or folded map—the prices are different.

Payment should be by Bankers Draft made out in sterling and should include enough to cover packing and postage charges.

You may write in English, French or German.

Because few local booksellers and stationers stock the complete set of OS maps, it is advisable to either order your maps by mail before you arrive in England or to buy them in London at the beginning of your trip.

Other Maps

Local Footpath Maps. These maps, produced for the most part by local path enthusiasts, are listed in the RA's *County Sheets* (see the section on *Where to Get Walking Information*). Most of these maps are based on the OS maps and include additional information of interest to walkers. Some of the maps, such as those produced by the Chiltern Society, are extremely well done. In most cases, these maps are only available locally and, by mail, only from the club or society responsible for the maps.

Finally, another series of maps worth mention are those produced by:

John Bartholomew & Son Ltd. (see *Address Directory*).

These maps cover all of Britain and are stocked by most booksellers. An index and price list may be obtained from the publisher on request.

Guidebooks

Numerous guidebooks are available. Many new publications for walkers also appear annually—so many that it is difficult for even the Ramblers' Association to keep up with them.

Most of the walk guides—including many of the best—are amateur in origin. They are written, produced and published by a local footpath or amenity society. Style, format and content vary, as does their reliability. Few, if any, are available in any language besides English. Also, many of the guides are only on sale locally and may be unknown to booksellers in other areas.

The best way to find out which guidebooks exist for the area in which you intend to walk, how much they cost and where you can purchase them is to write to the Ramblers' Association for the *County Sheet* covering that area (see *Where to Get Walking Information*). The County Sheets are the most complete listing of path guides available.

Another source of information on path guides are the reviews published in *Rucksack*, the RA's journal; *Climber & Rambler*, the BMC's official magazine, and *The Great Outdoors* (for more information on magazines for walkers, see the section on *Walkers' Magazines*).

Browsing the bookshelves at camping-equipment shops and local booksellers is also beneficial. Occasionally you may find a path guide that is now out of print or a new publication that has not yet been included on the RA Fact Sheet. In London, the best browsing is at:

See *Address Directory:*

YHA Services Ltd. and

Edward Stanford Ltd. Very well-stocked—for *all* European areas.

The YHA shops in Manchester and Birmingham also have a good supply of guidebooks.

Finally, a list of publications of interest to walkers—including books on the English geology, flora and fauna, weather and national parks—may be obtained from their publishers. The publishers can also tell you of forthcoming publications and the dates when they will be available. The major guidebook publishers are listed below. For their addresses, see the *Address Directory.*

Constable & Company Ltd. One of England's leading general-interest publishers, with more than 600 titles in print. Among the books it publishes for walkers are John Hillaby's *Journey through Britain* and *Journey through Europe,* W.A. Poucher's Peak guides *(The Lakeland Peaks, The Peak and Pennines, The Scottish Peaks* and *The Welsh Peaks),* Hamish MacInnes's *International Mountain Rescue Handbook* and a series of guides to the long-distance footpaths. You may write in English, French or German.

Cordee. A publisher, distributor and importer of books on mountaineering, rock climbing, skiing and backpacking. Titles cover Britain, Ireland, the Alps, North America, Nepal and Peru and include textbooks on technique and safety, mountaineering narratives and autobiographies of famous climbers.

Dalesman Publishing Co. Publishes nearly 20 path guides, most to walks in northern England.

Footpath Publications. Publishes a series of very well done guides to some of southern England's long-distance footpaths by H.D. Westacott.

Forestry Commission. Publishes a series of free leaflets with maps. These give details of recreational facilities provided in Britain's forest areas. The leaflets, entitled *See Your Forests,* come in four editions— Scotland, North England, South England and Wales. They describe forest walks, trails, campsites and picnic places, as well as facilities such as wayfaring courses.

Warne Gerrard Ltd. Publishers of the *Walks for Motorists* series. The series, which includes nearly 20 guides, outlines more than 500 circular walks in the English countryside.

Her Majesty's Stationery Office (HMSO). Publishes the *Long Distance Footpath Guides* and *National Park Guides* for the Countryside Commission, and the *Forestry Commission Guides,* as well as books on British regional geology, plants, animals, birds, insects, trees, historic buildings, monuments and castles. You may write in English, French, German, Italian or Spanish.

National Trust. *Publishes National Trust—Nature Walks,* a booklet describing more than 80 marked trails on England's national-trust lands.

Ramblers' Association. In addition to its free *Fact Sheets,* the RA publishes and sells path guides and accommodation lists to several long-distance footpaths, rights-of-way publications, footpath-policy statements and a series of periodicals of interest to those concerned with public paths.

Shire Publications Ltd. Publishers of the *Discovering Walks in . . .* series and the Chiltern Society Footpath Maps.

Spurbrooks Ltd. Publishes nearly 20 path guides in addition to the *Spur Venture Guide* series that includes sensible, down-to-earth advice and tips on backpacking, maps and compass, survival and rescue, weather lore, rock climbing and outdoor first aid.

Thornhill Press Ltd. Publishes guides to several long-distance walking routes.

West Col Productions. England's leading publisher of climbing guides. Also publishes numerous district guides with general information for touring and walking. Its titles include 35 walking, climbing and skiing guides to the Alps. Of its British titles, most concentrate on Scotland and Wales. West Col also sells maps for ramblers and mountaineering expeditions to the major mountain ranges of the world.

Western National Omnibus Company. Publishes several leaflets to footpaths in England's West Country.

Westmorland Gazette. Publishers of Alfred W. Wainwright's *Pictorial Guides.* The 19 books in this series—of which 13 are walking guides and 6 are sketchbooks—are some of the most attractive books done by anyone anywhere. The text is handwritten by the author and contains entertaining, but erudite commentaries on what is to be seen along the way. The maps are superb and numerous. Each is drawn on a scale of 1:25,000 and gives details not found on Ordnance Survey maps, such as gates, stiles, cairns and individual trees along each path. In addition, each book is liberally graced with delightful line drawings. The result is an exquisite book that is entertaining and a delight to look through. The only drawback is that people to whom English is a second (or third) language may have difficulty reading the text, despite Wainwright's neat printing. Nonetheless, it is worthwhile to buy one of the books, just to own one. The series includes seven guides to the Lakeland Fells, plus *Fellwanderer, Pennine Way Companion, Walks in Limestone Country, Walks on the Howgill Fells* and *A Coast to Coast Walk.*

Numerous path guides, as well as other publications for walkers, are available from each of England's national parks. Lists of these publications may be obtained by writing the individual parks (see *Address Directory):*

Dartmoor National Park Department.
Exmoor National Park Authority.
Lake District National Park Information Service.
Northumberland National Park.
North York Moors National Park.
Peak District National Park.
Yorkshire Dales National Park.

For a general guide on walking in Britain, one of the best is:

• *The Walker's Handbook* by H.D. Westacott, Penguin Books Ltd., Harmondsworth, Middlesex, 2nd ed., 1980. Includes sensible advice on clothing and equipment, use of a map and compass, walking techniques, weather and behavior in the countryside. Also provides in-depth information on the rights-of-way laws in England and Wales and on footpath law in Scotland. Describes each of Britain's national parks, Areas of Outstanding Beauty and long-distance footpaths, and lists the maps, guidebooks and locations and telephone numbers of rescue posts for each. A well-done book.

Walkers' Magazines

Several British magazines contain articles on walking, climbing and ski touring, equipment test reports, book reviews and numerous other features of interest to walkers. A few also include suggested walking itineraries, both in Britain and abroad. They include:

- *Camping*, Link House Publications Ltd. Monthly. Covers all aspects of camping. Has a regular feature on backpacking.
- *Climber & Rambler*, Holmes McDougall Ltd. Monthly. A beautifully done magazine. Articles tend to concentrate on climbing and fell walking. But the magazine also has features of interest to lowland walkers. Test reports on new equipment are good, and book reviews are incisive. It has an independent editorial policy, even though it is the official journal of the British Mountaineering Council.
- *Footpath Worker*, The Ramblers' Association. A mimeographed newsletter that is published occasionally. Includes articles of interest to those concerned with preserving rights-of-way. Gives detailed information about court cases involving paths.
- *The Great Outdoors*, The Walking, Camping & Backpacking Monthly, Holmes McDougall Ltd. This is Britain's leading magazine for walkers. Regular features include equipment reports, tips on outdoor photography, reviews of books and path guides, and footpath profiles. Articles cover all subjects of interest to walkers and backpackers.
- *Practical Camper*, Haymarket Publishing Ltd. Monthly. Provides comprehensive coverage of news of interest to campers. Has a regular feature on backpacking.
- *Rucksack*, The Ramblers' Association. Three issues a year. The official journal of the Ramblers' Association. A good magazine for walkers, with a comprehensive news section covering all matters related to paths and the countryside. Has good book reviews and notices of new footpath guides.

The addresses of the publishers are given in the *Address Directory*.

Trailside Lodgings

There are many types of accommodation in England for one-center walking holidays—everything from campsites to five-star hotels.

But before you set off on a walk from one point to another, you should be sure you know where lodgings are located—and how you can get to them from the trail.

Most towns and villages have bed-and-breakfast accommodation. These may be in pubs, guesthouses or private homes. But not all bed-and-breakfast establishments advertise. Instead, you often find that if one is full you are sent on to the next until someone somewhere finally puts you up.

There also are youth hostels, hotels and, occasionally, an old inn in which you can stay. In fact the hostel network—from a walker's standpoint—is one of the best in Europe. But, again, you have to know how to get to them. In sparsely populated areas of the highlands, lodgings are often far apart and a considerable distance from the trail. Even in the lowlands, you must sometimes take a bus into a town to find accommodation. And the road you come out on may only have twice-a-day bus service, if that.

In popular holiday centers—the Lake District and the coastal areas of Cornwall and Devon on the southwest peninsula, for instance—lodgings for the summer are often booked as much as a year in advance. If you plan to walk in one of these areas at this time of year, advance reservations are essential.

Even elsewhere you should try to book in advance. This way you are assured you won't have to spend the night in a local barn—or worse if you can't find a barn in which the farmer will let you stay. Normally, a phone call each morning is sufficient to book ahead. If you are unable to walk as far as you had planned, be sure to let the person you booked with know.

Calling in advance also has another advantage: the person you talk with can usually tell you how to reach the lodgings from the trail and, if you have to catch a bus, when and where it stops.

How to Find Lodgings

Many guidebooks tell you where lodgings are located and how you can get to them. But there are exceptions. Some path guides do not include lodging information. In others, the lodging and bus-schedule information may be obsolete.

For this reason, it is advisable to supplement the path guides with an up-to-date accommodation list. Those that are recommended for walkers are listed below. For the addresses of the outlets from which they can be obtained, see the *Address Directory*.

- *Bed and Breakfast Guide.* Published annually by the Ramblers' Association. This lists more than 1,500 recommended lodgings in the U.K. where ramblers are welcome and the price is reasonable. A coding system is used to indicate which of the lodgings are near the long-distance footpaths. The guide is free to members. Non-members may purchase it from the RA for a nominal charge.

- *Forestry Commission Cabins and Holiday Houses.* This includes a brief description of the cabins and holiday houses in 12 forest areas in Great Britain. Booking addresses and telephone numbers, overnight charges and the facilities provided are given for each, along with its grid-reference number on OS maps. The booklet is free from the Forestry Commission.

- *Long-Distance Footpath Accommodation Lists.* These are published for the Pennine Way, Offa's Dyke Path, Cotswold Way, South West Way, Dale's Way, Hadrians Wall and the Viking Way. Several also include transportation information. All but the latter two can be obtained from the Ramblers' Association head office, which can, however, give you the addresses of associations from which they can be obtained. Charges for the lists vary.

- *Mountain Huts Available for Groups.* Lists 15 mountain huts in the Lake District in which private groups (including small groups of two or three people) may stay. Gives information on the number of sleeping spaces and available facilities. Also gives the names and addresses of the people to contact for bookings. Free from the Lake District National Park Information Service. Similar lodging lists also are available from several of the other national parks.

- *Mountain Huts Available to Members.* This lists the huts maintained by mountaineering and climbing clubs affiliated with the British Mountaineering Club and the Mountaineering Club of Scotland. The huts are open only to members—and then only if there is room. The huts—of which there are between 75 and 80—vary widely in size and amenities. Some sleep only 10 or 12 people and have no blankets, cutlery or fuel for cooking. Members who use the huts should bring their own food and a sheet sleeping bag or, for huts without blankets, a down sleeping bag. They also must book in advance—sometimes as much as 12 weeks ahead. The list gives a brief description of each hut—including its facilities, location and grid reference number—and tells to whom bookings should be directed. It is published each year and is available to members only from the BMC.

- *YHA Handbook.* The Youth Hostels Association which, despite its name, caters to outdoor people of any age, has more than 250 hostels scattered throughout England and Wales. Many, especially those in the more popular areas, are within a day's walk of each other. A few hostels also have special units in which families can stay for two weeks or so instead of the normal maximum of three nights. Most hostels provide inexpensive meals and cooking facilities for members. Those who stay in the hostels have to do a few household duties before leaving in the morning, which keeps prices low. The YHA Handbook gives full details on the hostels and includes sketch maps to help you find them. The YHA also publishes a map of England and Wales that shows the locations of its hostels. The handbook and map are both available from the YHA for a nominal charge.

Other Accommodation Lists

While not specifically geared to the needs of walkers, there are several other accommodation lists of use to walkers traveling in England. These include:

- *Britain: Hotels and Restaurants.* Published annually by the British Tourist Authority. This large, thorough publication lists all classes of hotels, including some guesthouses. Available for a nominal charge from many booksellers, as well as from all BTA offices. (For the locations of BTA offices, see the section on *Useful Addresses & Telephone Numbers* later in this chapter.)

- *Britain: Meet the British.* This booklet from the BTA tells you how you can arrange to spend time with a British family as a paying guest. It has a foreword translated into French, German, Dutch, Italian and Spanish and is divided into three sections: 1) the names, addresses and telephone numbers of organizations that can arrange or give advice on paying-guest accommodation, exchange visits and *au pair* situations, 2) organizations that welcome foreign visitors at their meetings and social events, and 3) the names, addresses and telephone numbers of private individuals who offer accommodation in their homes. Prices are also included. The booklet is free from BTA offices abroad.

- *Britain: Stay at an Inn.* Another BTA publication. This lists old inns of Britain in which you can stay. Some have been in existence for more than 600 years. Full details are given on each. The publication is available for a nominal charge from all BTA offices.

- *Britain: Stay on a Farm.* Describes farmhouse lodgings and farm holidays in Britain. Some of these are located in prime walking areas. Available from all BTA offices.

- *Britain: Youth Accommodation.* This gives suggestions on a variety of reasonably priced lodgings available to students and young people. It includes youth hostels, country guesthouses and holiday centers. Available from all BTA offices.

- *Where to Stay.* A series of 12 regional accommodation guides published by the English Tourist Board. Each guide covers all types of accommodation in: the Lake District, Northumbria, North West England, Yorkshire & Humberside, Heart of England, East Midlands, Thames & Chilterns, East Anglia, London, West Country, South of England and South East England. Full details on the lodgings are given. The guides are available for a nominal charge from many booksellers as well as from the English Tourist Board (see *Address Directory*).

- *Where to Stay: Hotels in England.* A comprehensive one-volume guide to England's hotels, motels, guesthouses, hostels, bed and breakfast homes, inns and farmhouse accommodation. Large and expensive. Available from many booksellers as well as from the English Tourist Board.
- *Where to Stay: Self Catering Accommodation in England.* This guide includes details on a wide variety of accommodation from holiday houses and flats to camping and caravan sites. Available from booksellers and the English Tourist Board.

Camping

In many parts of England you can camp along the trails. In fact, on some trails you might *have* to camp. The last stretch of the Pennine Way, for instance, is a grueling 43.5-kilometer (27-mile) walk across the Cheviots, which rise up to 760 meters (2,500 feet). The only chance for accommodation is 4½ kilometers (3 miles) off the path at a shepherd's croft. There is also a mountain hut 11 kilometers (7 miles) from Kirk Yetholm at the end of the path. But there is no other shelter of any kind.

Lodgings on other highland paths can also be few and far between.

Throughout England you may camp on private land—providing you ask the landowner and he or she gives consent. Many farmers are good about letting you camp, but some are not. The only way to be sure is to ask—and be prepared for a negative reply.

Some country inns will allow you to camp nearby, as will many filling stations, but, again, this varies from one to another.

In mountain areas and on open moorland, few people will object if you camp on uncultivated countryside above the valley field walls and away from roads. In fact, the best policy here is to make yourself as inconspicuous as possible so nobody has the chance to object. But if someone does, move on.

In the national parks it is wise to ask what its policies are on open camping. You cannot always camp anywhere you please—even on open uncultivated land. Camping is also restricted in many forest parks.

Campers should be sure to leave their campsites in such a condition that no one can ever tell they were there. (For suggestions on how to minimize your impact, see the chapter on *What You Should Know About Camping in Europe* in *On Foot Through Europe: A Trail Guide to Europe's Long-Distance Footpaths.*) Otherwise, the next walker who shows up with a tent may not be welcome. And the next walker could be you.

Guides to official campsites are available for a nominal charge from the Camping Club of Great Britain and Ireland and the British Tourist Authority. And a free guide to campsites in Britain's forest parks is available from the Forestry Commission. (The addresses to write will be found in the *Address Directory.*)

For further information on lightweight walking and camping—away from the beaten track—contact the Backpackers' Club. The club willingly gives advice on where and how to camp in Britain, providing you specify where you want to go. And if you join the club, you can obtain a copy of its confidential *Farm Pitch Directory*.

Water

The overall quality of water in England is extremely good. Highland brooks and streams generally can be trusted—unless you are directly below a sheep pasture. Even in the lowlands, brook water is generally okay, as long as it is fast flowing and looks clear. There are, of course, exceptions. And just because a stream looks clear is no guarantee it is.

The English are very conscious of their water purity—and have taken great pains to protect it. But something can always happen upstream which you are unaware of—a chance you take when you drink from natural water sources. Hence, caution is always advisable.

Tap water on the other hand can always be trusted. If not, it will be posted with a sign that says *not for drinking*.

Water can usually be obtained from guesthouses. Pubs are also good sources of water (to name just one beverage). But don't just go into a pub and ask for water; the reception may not be overly friendly.

Some mountain huts, however, do not have water—a point you should check if you intend to stay in one.

Equipment Notes

The two most important pieces of equipment for walking in England are good raingear and a windproof anorak. You can get by with stout walking shoes on some lowland paths, but if you have to cross a muddy field that has just been plowed you will want a pair of boots. A wool sweater is also advisable at all times of year.

In the highlands conditions can sometimes be arctic-like even in summer, and in winter walkers may need an ice axe and crampons. You should always check weather reports, and carry spare woolens—including a cap and mittens—as well as a spare ration of high-energy food.

Crowded Trails

The most crowded trail in England is the southern section of the Pennine Way in the Peak District National Park. The impact on the trail has been so bad, in fact, that airline pilots report they can see the path as they fly over Britain. Several measures have been taken in an attempt to reduce the erosion of the path, including putting plastic mats down in particularly muddy sections. But so far few of the measures have been effective.

Path erosion and overuse have also become a problem in the Lake District. And the rocks on some trails have become so polished with vibram soles that even the slightest trace of wetness makes footing treacherous.

Crowding is, of course, at its worst during the summer months. But the effects last all year. If you must walk in the Lake District or the Pennine Way—and you probably will want to—you should do it at some time of year other than midsummer. During May and early June, the weather is generally good, lodgings are easier to find and the trails, while not deserted, are much less crowded. September is also a good month.

In the summer, the best advice is to walk somewhere else.

Walking & Climbing Tours

Numerous walks are organized locally and on a national scale. Many of these are one-week holidays based in a single center. But numerous day and weekend rambles in local areas are also available.

Often, such rambles are advertised in the local press. Foreign walkers are always welcome.

Many Ramblers' Association Areas and Groups conduct city-based rail- and coach-excursion rambles into the countryside, as do other rambling clubs and footpath societies. These guided walks are open to the general public, often at no charge beyond the price of the excursion ticket.

Advance bookings are usually unnecessary for these rambles. You simply buy a ticket and show up at the appointed time and place. As you ride out to your hiking destination, details of the walks are passed out. On arrival, parties of moderate size are then formed, each with an experienced leader.

Details on these rambles are contained in the RA's County Sheets (see the section on *Where to Get Walking Information*).

The County Sheets also give details on the guided walks organized by most National Parks. These day-long walks are usually conducted between April and September. For these, a small charge may be payable to the leader at the start of the ramble.

On a national scale, the major organizers of walking holidays are:

See *Address Directory:*

Country-Wide Holidays Association. This is one of the oldest and best established organizers of walking holidays in Britain. It has week-long walking holidays based at its guesthouses in the Lake District, Snowdonia, Somerset, Cornwall, Isle of Wight, Devon, Hampshire, the Cotswolds, Scotland, Isle of Man, the Yorkshire and Norfolk coasts, Derbyshire and Northumberland, as well as holidays abroad.

There are also youth weeks, senior-citizen weeks, mountain weeks, caving and climbing tours, coastal walks, special-interest holidays for yoga, bird watching, photography and field studies, plus a variety of walking tours to many of Europe's most notable walking areas. And this is just the beginning. Day and weekend rambles are also organized by local groups of the CHA throughout England. All excursions and walks are led by experienced leaders, and it is possible to go on one at practically any time of year. Full details are given in the CHA's free brochures, *Summer Holidays at Home and Abroad* and *Winter Holidays.*

Holiday Fellowship. Another old, well-established organizer of walking holidays. It offers week-long holidays at centers throughout England, Scotland and Wales, as well as abroad. There are one-, two- and three-week walking tours on several of England's long-distance footpaths, holidays for young people and special holiday weeks for pony trekking, archeology, exploring canals, photography and orienteering. Day and weekend rambles are also organized by its local groups throughout England. Full details are given in its free brochures: *Holidays that are Different; Autumn, Winter and Spring Holidays; Holidays for Young People and School Parties; Great Britain, Great Holidays,* as well as a series of leaflets to its walking tours on the long-distance footpaths.

Ramblers Holidays Ltd. Offers numerous mountain walking and trekking holidays, ski touring holidays and special holidays for photography, birdwatching and studying alpine flowers, abroad and in Britain from a permanent center in the Lake District. Full details are given in its free brochure, *Ramblers Holidays.*

YHA Adventure Holidays. These holidays—open to people of all ages—are operated by the Youth Hostel Association. The walking holidays last for a week and are based in centers throughout most of England, Scotland and Wales. There are also holidays for climbing and mountaineering, underwater swimming, pony trekking, cycling, sailing, fishing and fossil hunting. Full details are given in its free brochure, *YHA Adventure Holidays.*

Another source of information on walking tours is the British Tourist Authority. It publishes two booklets on holiday arrangements that are available throughout Britain:

- *Britain: Activity Holidays.* A manual held at BTA offices, this lists the names, addresses and telephone numbers of multi-activity centers, as well as of the centers and organizations that offer holidays for caving and potholing, climbing and mountaineering, skiing and walking. Details are given on the holiday programs available, accommodation and the charges for each. The list includes more than 50 organizations that offer walking tours in

England alone. Copies of individual pages from these sections of the manual will be sent on request.

- *Young Visitors to Britain.* Gives information on activity centers and organizations that cater to children, teenagers and students in varying age groups. The booklet is free from all BTA offices.

The English Tourist Board also publishes two booklets that list walking holidays:

- *Outdoor Activity and Sport Holidays.*
- *Special Interest and Hobby Holidays.*

Both are available for a nominal charge from the English Tourist Board.

Mountain Guides

Mountain guides may be hired for rock climbs and winter tours in the Lake District, the Peak District and Cornwall, as well as in the Scottish Highlands and North Wales. On rock climbs, the guides will take a maximum of three people. Ropes are provided by the guide, as is any necessary hardware, but the client must bring the rest of his equipment, including an anorak, vibram sole boots and, where necessary, a climbing belt, helmet, ice axe and crampons.

Also, if you expect to climb with a guide on Britain's sea cliffs and highland peaks, you must be in good physical condition.

Arrangements are made directly with the guide. Also, you must book in advance. Fees are reasonable, but the number of guides is limited, so the earlier you book the better.

A list of mountain guides, with their addresses and a list of recommended minimum fees, can be obtained by sending a stamped, self-addressed envelope to:

Colin G. Firth (see *Address Directory*).

Mountaineering Courses

Courses in basic and advanced rock climbing, mountaineering, caving, hillwalking and mountain rescue are offered by nearly 25 organizations in England.

A list of these organizations, entitled *Mountaineering Courses in Britain and Abroad,* is available from the British Mountaineering Council.

The list gives the address of each organization, a brief description of the courses available, their duration and the age groups accepted. The list is designed to help you choose the right course, not to answer all your questions. For full details, you must write the individual organizations.

In addition to these organizations, mountaineering courses are offered by:

See *Address Directory:*

Lake District National Park. Offers courses in climbing, mountain navigation and mountain safety for people between the ages of 14 and 18, as well as courses in mountain walking and field-party leadership. Full details are available from Lake District National Park Centre.

Youth Hostels Association. Arranges basic, intermediate and advanced courses led by qualified guides in mountaineering, high-altitude climbing and mountain leadership. Also has weekend courses. Details are given in its brochure *YHA Adventure Holidays.*

The Sports Council. Operates the Plas y Benin National Centre for Mountain Activities in Snowdonia National Park, North Wales. A wide range of courses are offered—basic, advanced and instructors' courses in rock climbing; rock, snow and ice courses; a one-month mountaineering course; training in mountain leading and mountain rescue; family courses; mountain photography and mountain weather. A booklet describing the center and its courses is available on request. The booklet also lists the regional offices of the Sports Council, many of v/hich run day courses on weekends.

Cross-Country Skiing

There is very little organized ski touring in England, primarily due to the lack of predictable snow. When it does snow, people go out into the countryside on their own. The rest of the year, skiing is limited to grass slopes.

Nonetheless, there are several active ski clubs in England. Information can be obtained from:

The National Ski Federation of Great Britain (see *Address Directory).*

Special Train & Bus Fares

Unlike many other countries, Britain offers few really great bargain tickets for extensive rail and bus travel once you arrive in the country. The way to save money is to buy a Britrail Pass *before* you arrive. Here's a rundown of the special fares:

Britrail Pass. This allows unlimited rail travel throughout England, Scotland and Wales, including continental boat trains, BR Lake Windermere steamers and Sealink Isle of Wight ferry services. First- and second-class tickets are available for a duration of 8, 15, 22 days or one month (monthly pass on sale outside Europe only). The only ticket that saves you more money is a Youth Pass, which is available only to people under 23 years of age. Even so, the cost of an eight-day pass is less than the normal second-class return fare between London and Aberdeen. Britrail passes *cannot* be purchased in Britain. You must obtain them in advance from British Rail General Agents in Europe or from a principal travel agent in your country. If you have difficulty locating an agent who sells the ticket, the British Tourist Authority office in your country can tell you where the Britrail passes are sold.

Britrail Youth Pass. Available for people between the ages of 14 and 22 (children under 14 ride for half fare). Only second-class tickets are available, again for a duration of 8, 15, 22 days or one month. This offers a discount of an additional 25 percent over the Britrail Pass.

If you arrive without a Britrail Pass and still want to save money, all is not lost. There are several special fares you can take advantage of and, while they will not save you as much as a Britrail Pass, they are much cheaper than paying full fare for single and return tickets. These special fares include:

Railrovers. There are nine railrover tickets available. These offer either 7 or 15 days of unlimited travel in first or second class. There are also special reduced prices for families. The nine railrover tickets include: 1) Freedom of Wales, 2) Southern, 3) Western, 4) West of England, 5) Freedom of Scotland, 6) East Anglia, 7) Eastern, 8) London Midland and 9) the All-line Railover. These may be purchased between March 1 and October 31 from any British Rail ticket office.

Awayday Return. This saves you up to 45 percent on the standard return fare and entitles you to travel to and from a destination on any day of the week. You can also travel on most trains, except for some rush-hour services on Mondays to Fridays. You should check details when you buy the ticket.

Weekend Return. This saves you up to 35 percent on the regular fare if you travel more than 121 kilometers (75 miles), leave on a Friday, Saturday or Sunday and return the same weekend on a Saturday, Sunday or Monday. Again, you should check specific details when you buy the ticket.

Monthly Return. This saves you up to 12½ percent on the regular fare on rail travel in excess of 121 kilometers. It entitles you to travel to a destination and return within one calendar month of the date shown on the ticket. You can travel on most trains any day of the week. The only catch is that if you make your outward journey any day Monday to Friday, you cannot return before Saturday.

Further information on rail travel can be obtained from the ticket sellers in the stations.

Bus & Coach Travel

Long-distance coach services operate all over Britain. These are normally the most economic form of public transport. Information about coach services starting from London, on which it is advisable to book in advance, is available from:

Victoria Coach Station (see *Address Directory*).

Elsewhere, information should be obtained at the local bus and coach stations. No advance bookings are necessary on these services.

If you expect to travel extensively by coach and bus, it is wise to obtain a copy of the *National Express Service Guide*. Issued twice a year— summer and winter—the guide gives detailed timetable information for the majority of coach services throughout Britain.

National Travel (NBC) Ltd. (see *Address Directory*).

To save money on coach and bus travel, you can buy the:

Coachmaster Pass. Issued by National Travel (NBC) Ltd., this provides unlimited travel on most of Britain's express coach network and discounts on day and half-day coach tours. The passes are available for a duration of 8, 15, 22 and 29 days. There are also reductions for children.

Public Transport in the National Parks

Most of the national parks operate special transport services to fill the gaps left by regularly scheduled services. These are designed primarily for visitors who have no other means of getting about and strive to ease the congestion caused by too many cars.

A free leaflet, entitled *Public Transport in the National Parks*, describes the services and tells you where you can obtain current timetables. The leaflet is available from:

The Countryside Commission (see *Address Directory*).

Minibus Services

A variety of minibus services have evolved to supplement regular services and cater to special needs. Often, they provide the only link to places lacking other forms of public transport. For walkers, they are sometimes the only way in which some paths—and overnight lodgings—can be reached on public transport. A reference sheet, entitled *Minibus Services*, provides details. It is free on request from the British Tourist Authority.

Useful Addresses
& Telephone Numbers

General Tourist Information

In England:

British Tourist Authority (see *Address Directory*). Between Easter and September, the office is open weekdays from 9 a.m. to 6 p.m. and Saturdays from 9 a.m. to 2:30 p.m. Between October and Easter, it is open weekdays from 9:15 a.m. to 5:30 p.m. and Saturdays from 9:15 a.m. to 1 p.m. Closed Sundays. Publishes a useful list of tourist information centers throughout Britain:

• *Britain Tourist Information Centres.* Gives you the addresses and telephone numbers of the national, regional, local and specialized tourist information centers throughout Britain. Also includes addresses and telephone numbers of the travel enquiry and booking offices for British Rail. Advice on how to use the booklet is translated into French, German, Dutch, Italian and Spanish. Very complete.

English Tourist Board (see *Address Directory*). Open from 9:15 a.m. to 5:30 p.m. weekdays.

Abroad:

Branch offices of the British Tourist Authority are located in EUROPE: Brussels, Copenhagen, Paris, Frankfurt, Amsterdam, Rome, Oslo, Madrid, Stockholm and Zurich; AUSTRALIA: Sydney; NEW ZEALAND: Wellington; SOUTH AFRICA: Johannesburg; JAPAN: Tokyo; CANADA: Toronto, and in the U.S.A.: Los Angeles, Chicago, Dallas and New York.

New York: British Tourist Authority, 680 Fifth Avenue, New York, New York 10019. Tel. (212) 581-4700.

Sport Shops

There are numerous shops scattered throughout England that cater to backpackers, climbers and walkers. An *Equipment Directory* giving their addresses, telephone numbers and a brief description of the equipment each carries is published at the back of each issue of *The Great Outdoors* and *Climber & Rambler* (see the section on *Walkers' Magazines).*

In London, one shop you can visit is:

YHA Adventure Centre (see *Address Directory*).

Search & Rescue

In an emergency: Go to the nearest rescue post or telephone—whichever is quickest. At the telephone, **dial 999.** Ask for the **police.**

In Britain the police forces are the main coordinators of the search-and-rescue effort. Unless it is quicker to get to a manned Mountain Rescue Post, all calls for help must go to the police. They will then call out the volunteer rescue teams and public services needed.

There is no charge for search and rescue. When needed, helicopters are provided gratis, and rescuers are volunteers who exist on donations (you will see donation boxes for the mountain rescue squads in many sport shops). Medical care is also free—even for foreigners—thanks to Britain's social medicine.

Before you go walking in Britain, you should obtain a copy of:

- *Mountain and Cave Rescue,* The Handbook of the Mountain Rescue Committee, Herald Press, Arbroath, Angus. This lists the official rescue teams and posts throughout Britain, gives their locations, grid reference numbers and the names, addresses and telephone numbers of their supervisors. The booklet also has sections on mountain safety, how to deal with a mountain accident, first aid, distress signals and a description of Britain's rescue service.

This booklet is the most complete, up-to-date listing of rescue posts available. Nonetheless, the position of a post is sometimes changed and should be verified locally. If there is a change, write it directly in the booklet, then carry it in your pack—opened to the page on which the rescue posts are listed for the area in which you are walking. This way, the booklet will be ready for quick reference—just in case.

The booklet is available only in English. Even so, it can be used by walkers who do not speak English. It can be obtained for a nominal charge from:

Mountain Rescue Committee (see *Address Directory*).

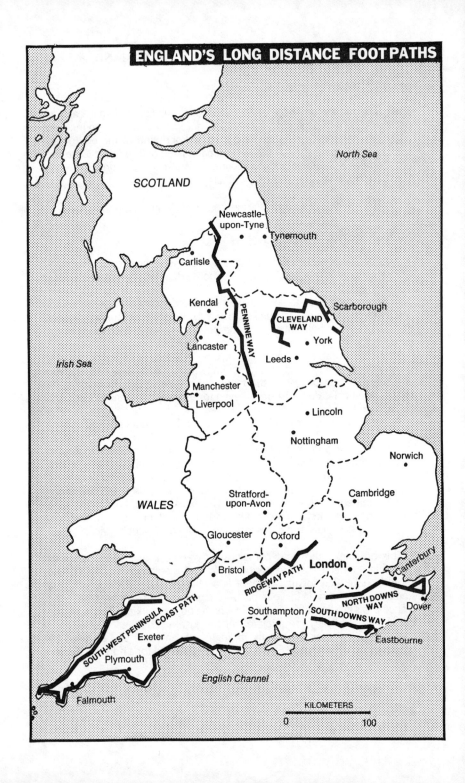

ENGLAND'S LONG DISTANCE FOOT PATHS

SCOTLAND

North Sea

Newcastle-upon-Tyne

Tynemouth

Carlisle

Kendal

Scarborough

CLEVELAND WAY

PENNINE WAY

Lancaster

York

Irish Sea

Leeds

Manchester

Liverpool

Lincoln

Nottingham

Norwich

WALES

Stratford-upon-Avon

Cambridge

Gloucester

Oxford

London

Canterbury

Bristol

RIDGEWAY PATH

NORTH DOWNS WAY

Dover

Southampton

SOUTH DOWNS WAY

SOUTH-WEST PENINSULA COAST PATH

Eastbourne

Exeter

Plymouth

English Channel

KILOMETERS

Falmouth

0   100

England's Long-Distance Footpaths

There are nine official long-distance footpaths in Britain—one in Scotland, two in Wales and six in England. These have a combined length of 2,413 kilometers (1,499 miles).

In addition, there are more than 120 (and increasing every week) unofficial long-distance footpaths, which were created by local path enthusiasts because progress on the official paths had proceeded so slowly. Although the legislation providing for the creation of long-distance paths was passed as part of the National Parks and Access to the Countryside Act in 1949, the first long-distance path—the Pennine Way—was not opened until 1965.

Nonetheless, in the end, walkers have benefited. In total, there are now more than 6,100 kilometers (3,800 miles) of long-distance paths which you can walk in England.

Each of the official long-distance paths traverses an Area of Outstanding Natural Beauty or national park, and is highlighted by numerous scenic, historic and prehistoric features. Also, all are waymarked with the symbol of an acorn, except in Scotland, where long-distance footpaths are marked with the symbol of a thistle.

The agency responsible for these paths is the Countryside Commission (see *Address Directory*), which proposes new routes, helps secure rights-of-way agreements and pays the cost of maintaining the paths. The actual responsibility for establishing and maintaining the paths, however, falls upon the county councils in the areas concerned.

The unofficial routes—which lack official backing by the Countryside Commission—are overseen by local footpath groups. On these, the standards of maintenance vary. And a few are not waymarked. But then, they are often less crowded than the official routes.

Nearly all the paths lend themselves to walking in sections—except for some of the shorter unofficial routes. And most can be walked at any time of year. Only the Pennine Way—the most difficult of the paths—should not be attempted between November and April except by the hardiest and most experienced walkers.

Finding accommodation on some of the paths can be a problem, particularly during the busy season when demand often outpaces supply. Camping is not always practical because of a lack of convenient sites and potable water. Therefore, you should be sure to obtain the accommodation guide to the path you intend to walk—or the RA's *Bed and Breakfast Guide* (see the section on *Trail Lodgings* earlier in this chapter)—and book your lodgings well in advance.

Where possible, the 1:25,000 Ordnance Survey maps should be used to walk the paths. Generally, however, the 1:50,000 maps will suffice if supplemented with one of the path guides. For the addresses of guidebook publishers and other organizations listed in the footpath descriptions, see the *Address Directory*.

The Official Long-Distance Footpaths

The Cleveland Way

From Helmsley—on the edge of North York Moors National Park—to Filey on the Yorkshire coast. Stretches around three sides of the park through wooded valleys, across open moorlands and, for nearly a third of the way, along coastal cliffs. **Length:** 150 kilometers (93 miles). **Walking Time:** 6 to 8 days. **Path Markings:** Marked throughout with an acorn symbol.

Lodgings: Plentiful along the coast, but limited inland—especially for the 35 kilometers (22 miles) between Helmsley and Osmotherley and for the 40 kilometers (25 miles) between Osmotherley and Guisborough. It is, however, possible to camp—both on the open moors and in organized sites along the coast. *The Cleveland Way Bed and Breakfast List* is free on request from the North York Moors National Park Department.

Special Notes: Weather can be bleak and cold. Changes are sudden, with fogs along the coast and sharp drops in temperature. Warm clothing and a compass are essential. The moorland path should not be attempted alone.

Maps:
- Ordnance Survey 1:50,000, sheets 93, 94, 99, 100 and 101.
- Ordnance Survey 1:25,000, sheets NZ-40, NZ-50, NZ-51, NZ-60, NZ-61, NZ-62, NZ-71, NZ-81, NZ-90, SE-48, SE-49, SE-58, SE-68, SE-99 and TA-08.

Guidebooks:
- *The Cleveland Way* by Alan Falconer, HMSO, 1972. (Recommended)
- *A Guide to the Cleveland Way* by Malcolm Boyes, Constable & Company.
- *The Cleveland Way* by William Cowley, Dalesman Publishing Company.

The North Downs Way

From Farnham to Dover through the Surrey Hills and Kent Downs, a rolling, pastoral countryside. At Boughton Alup near the eastern end of the path, an alternate route loops up to Canterbury, then goes over the Barham Downs and down to Dover, passing through pleasant orchard country. **Length:** With the loop to Canterbury, 227 kilometers (141 miles). **Walking Time:** 10 to 12 days. **Path Markings:** Marked throughout with an acorn symbol and, except in Surrey, yellow arrows.

Lodgings: Tend to be sparse, although it is possible to find bed-and-breakfast accommodation and inns in towns near the route. Several youth hostels are also located near the route. No accommodation guide to the path has yet been published, although the addresses of several lodgings are listed in the RA's *Bed and Breakfast Guide*. Camping is impractical as there are few suitable sites and no potable water on the downs.

Special Notes: The walking is easy. No special equipment is required.

Maps:
- Ordnance Survey 1:50,000, sheets 178, 179, 186, 187, 188 and 189.
- Ordnance Survey 1:25,000, sheets SU-84, SU-94, TQ-04, TQ-14, TQ-15, TQ-25, TQ-35, TQ-45, TQ-65, TQ-66, TQ-75, TQ-76, TQ-85, TQ-95, TQ-94, TR-04, TR-05, TR-13, TR-14, TR-15, TR-23, TR-24, TR-25 and TR-34.
- *North Downs Way Map Book,* Publication No. CCP 113, Countryside Commission. Also sold by the Ramblers' Association.

Guidebook:
- *The North Downs Way* by John Trevelyan and Tom Doggett, Ramblers' Association, 1978. Revised and expanded 1980.

Offa's Dyke Path

See the section on *Long-Distance Footpaths in Wales* in the chapter on Wales.

Pembrokeshire Coast Path

See the chapter on Wales.

The Pennine Way

From Edale in Derbyshire to Kirk Yetholm just over the border in Scotland. The path winds through the Peak District, Yorkshire Dales and Northumberland national parks and crosses the High Pennines and the Cheviots. It follows old footpaths and bridleways, pack horse and drove roads, shepherd's tracks, Roman roads and, in Northumberland National Park, a portion of Hadrian's Wall. There are waterfalls, huge limestone cliffs and, for the naturalist, subalpine flora. In all, it offers some of the wildest—and most rugged—walking in England. **Length:** 402 kilometers (250 miles). **Walking Time:** 16 to 21 days. **Path Markings:** Some of the route is well-marked and trod, but in many places it crosses expanses of wild moorland, devoid of prominent landmarks, consisting largely of peat, heather, bog and tussocks of grass. The route in these areas is marked, in part, by stakes and cairns. But they are never numerous enough to obviate the need of a map and compass.

Lodgings: Availability varies. Several youth hostels are accessible from the route and bed-and-breakfast accommodation can be found near parts of the path. But there are also long stretches with no towns or villages—the longest of which is a 43-kilometer section at the northern end that must be walked in one day. The best solution is to camp. There is rarely a shortage of drinking water, and there are many suitable sites on the fells. Nonetheless, an accommodation list is a must. *The Pennine Way Accommodation List,* published by the Pennine Way Council, is available for a nominal charge from the Ramblers' Association.

Special Notes: The path is a strenuous, high-level path through predominantly wild country. It should not be attempted by anyone who cannot steer by a map and compass or cannot walk 20 to 25 kilometers (12 to 15 miles) a day over rough ground and through bogs. The weather is notorious even in summer for heavy rainfall, high winds and mists. Wind and rain protection are essential, as are stout boots, warm clothing, a wool hat and mittens, flannel or woolen trousers (or pair of climbing breeches of closely woven material) and an emergency ration of high-energy food.

Maps:
- Ordnance Survey 1:50,000, sheets 74, 80, 86, 91, 92, 98, 103, 109 and 110.
- Ordnance Survey 1:25,000, sheets NT-70, NT-71, NT-81, NT-82, NT-91, NT-92, NY-62, NY-63, NY-64, NY-65, NY-66, NY-72, NY-73, NY-74, NY-76, NY-77, NY-79, NY-80, NY-82, NY-83, NY-87, NY-88, NY-89, NY-90, NY-91, NY-92, SD-86, SD-87, SD-88, SD-89, SD-91, SD-92, SD-93, SD-94, SD-95, SD-96, SD-99, SE-00, SE-01, SK-08, SK-09 and SK-18.
- Parts of the route are also covered by four of the Ordnance Survey 1:25,000 Outdoor Leisure Maps: *Dark Peak, Three Peaks, Malham and Upper Wharfedale* and *South Pennines.*

Guidebooks:
- *Pennine Way Companion: A Pictorial Guide* by Alfred W. Wainwright, Westmorland Gazette, 1968. (Highly recommended)
- *The Pennine Way* by Tom Stephenson, HMSO, 1981. (Also recommended)
- *Walking the Pennine Way* by Alan Penrose Binns, Gerrard Publications, 1972.
- *The Pennine Way: Britain's Longest Continuous Footpath* by Kenneth Oldham, Dalesman Publishing Company, 1972.
- *A Guide to the Pennine Way,* Christopher J. Wright, Constable & Company, 1975.
- *Read About Walks on the Pennine Way,* by and from Photo Precision (color booklet).

Further Information: Contact the Pennine Way Council (see *Address Directory).*

The Ridgeway Path

From Ivinghoe in Buckinghamshire to Overton Hill near Avebury in Wiltshire. Passes through the North Wessex Downs and Chilterns Areas of

Outstanding Natural Beauty. Follows, for the most part, the ancient Wessex Ridgeway and Icknield Way. The region has many religious monuments, fortifications, burial places and agricultural systems dating from the Bronze and early Iron Ages. **Length:** 137 kilometers (85 miles). **Walking Time:** 6 to 7 days. **Path Markings:** Marked throughout with an acorn symbol and, in places, with yellow or white arrows.
Lodgings: Limited, although small inns can be found in some towns. It is necessary to plan your route carefully and book in advance. Camping is not recommended as there is little water. No accommodation guide is published specifically for the path. You must, instead, rely upon local tourist authorities and the RA's *Bed and Breakfast Guide*.
Special Notes: This is one of the easiest of the long-distance paths to walk. No special equipment is required, outside of stout shoes.
Maps:
• Ordnance Survey 1:50,000, sheets 165, 173, 174 and 175.
• Ordnance Survey 1:25,000, sheets SU-16, SU-17, SU-27, SU-28, SU-38, SU-48, SU-58, SU-68, SU-69, SU-79, SP-70, SP-80, SP-90 and SP-91.
Guidebooks:
• *A Practical Guide to Walking the Ridgeway Path* by H.D. Westacott, Footpath Publications, 1978. (Recommended)
• *The Ridgeway Path* by Sean Jennett, HMSO, 1977.
• *Walks along the Ridgeway* by Elizabeth Cull, Spurbooks, 1976.
• *Discovering the Ridgeway* by Vera Burden, Shire Publications, revised, 1981.
• *The Oldest Road, an Exploration of the Ridgeway* by J.R.L. Anderson and Fay Godwin, Wildwood House.

The South Downs Way

From the outskirts of Eastbourne in East Sussex to Buriton in Hampshire. This is the only long-distance bridleway yet created in Britain and, hence, can be used by riders and cyclists as well as walkers. One small section is an alternate route for walkers only. This follows coastal cliffs known as the Seven Sisters. The entire route lies within the Sussex Downs Area of Outstanding Natural Beauty—an open, rolling countryside with clumps of woodland. **Length:** 129 kilometers (80 miles). **Walking Time:** 5 to 7 days.
Path Markings: Vary. In East Sussex, there are short concrete plinths with an acorn symbol that are variously labeled "South Downs Way," "Public Bridleway" and "Public Footpath," and in West Sussex there are oak fingerboards marked "South Downs Way." It is also possible to extend the walk into Hampshire, but this is not part of the "official" route and there are no signposts, only an occasional acorn symbol painted on gateposts, stiles and walls.
Lodgings: Many possibilities for accommodation are available, both on and near the path, some with stabling and grazing for horses. Camping is

not recommended because of a lack of water. A list of lodgings is included in the path guide, *Along the South Downs Way* (see below).

Special Notes: Although there are some steep climbs, the walking is generally easy. No special equipment is required.

Maps:
- Ordnance Survey 1:50,000, sheets 197, 198 and 199.
- Ordnance Survey 1:25,000, sheets, SU-71, SU-81, SU-91, TQ-01, TQ-10, TQ-11, TQ-20, TQ-21, TQ-30, TQ-31, TQ-40, TQ-50 and TV-59.
- The Ordnance Survey 1:25,000 Outdoor Leisure Map, *Brighton and the Sussex Vale*, also covers part of the route.

Guidebooks:
- *Along the South Downs Way* by the Eastbourne Rambling Club. (Recommended) Available from the Ramblers' Association.
- *South Downs Way Public Transport Guide,* a free leaflet available from the West Sussex County Council. (Recommended)
- *The South Downs Way* by Sean Jennett, HMSO.
- *The South Downs Way* by the Ramblers' Association, available from the RA head office.

The South West Peninsula Coast Path

Recently completed, this path stretches from Minehead in Somerset to Studland on Poole Harbour in Dorset. It is the longest continuous footpath in Britain, following the coast for 829 kilometers (515 miles). It is based on an old path used by coastguard men and is seldom out of sight of the sea. The path is divided into five sections, each of which can be walked in their entirety or in segments. The specifics pertaining to these sections are described below. Some comments, however, can be made on the path in its entirety: **Walking Time:** For the full route, a minimum of five weeks. **Path Markings:** Marked throughout with an acorn symbol.

Lodgings: There are many possibilities for accommodation on the route, including numerous youth hostels and campsites. But advance bookings are necessary during summer. An accommodation list is included in *The South West Coastal Path Guide.* It is available for a nominal charge from The South West Way Association as well as from the Ramblers' Association.

Special Notes: On some parts of the path the going is rough and there is no way off once you commit yourself. Advance planning is essential. The weather is often warm and sunny. Combined with salt spray and reflection from the ocean, this makes the risk of sunburn high. A wide-brimmed hat and sun cream are advisable. Shorts, however, should be avoided; much of the path is bordered with thorny plants. Heavy winds and fog can also occur, so you should carry good wind and raingear, as well as a warm sweater.

Maps:
• Listed by section below.
Guidebooks:
• *The South West Coastal Path Guide,* available from the South West Way Association. This lists lodgings, transportation connections, path guides, maps and useful addresses, plus gives brief descriptions of each part of the route. Published annually. (Recommended)
• *The South West Peninsula Coast Path:* 1) *Minehead to St. Ives,* 2) *St. Ives to Plymouth,* and 3) *Plymouth to Poole.* All published by Letts & Company. Despite some errors and a gap, this is the best series of path guides covering the entire path. (Recommended)
Further Information: Write the South West Way Association (see *Address Directory).*

1) *The Somerset and North Devon Coast Path.* From Minehead to Marsland Mouth near Bude. Across the heights of Exmoor. **Length:** 132 kilometers (82 miles). **Walking Time:** 6 to 7 days.
Maps:
• Ordnance Survey 1:50,000, sheets 180, 181 and 190.
• Ordnance Survey 1:25,000, sheets SS-21, SS-22, SS-32, SS-42, SS-43, SS-44, SS-54, SS-64, SS-74, SS-84 and SS-94.
Guidebooks:
• *A Practical Guide to Walking the Devon North Coast Path* by H.D. Westacott, Footpath Publications. (In preparation.) Should be supplemented with:
• *The South West Peninsula Coast Path:* 1) *Minehead to St. Ives,* Letts & Company. Covers the full route. (Recommended)
• *Somerset and North Devon Coast Path—Exmoor Section.* Available from Exmoor National Park Authority.
• *Somerset and North Devon Coast Path* by Clive Gunnell, HMSO.
• A complete list of other guides to the path is included in *The South West Coastal Path Guide.*

2) *The North Cornwall Coast Path.* From Marsland Mouth to Penzance. Past towering cliffs and headlands, sandy beaches, sheltered harbors and fishing villages. **Length:** 217 kilometers (135 miles). **Walking Time:** 9 to 11 days.
Maps:
• Ordnance Survey 1:50,000, sheets 190, 200, 203 and 204.
• Ordnance Survey 1:25,000, sheets SS-20, SS-21, SW-32, SW-33, SW-42, SW-43, SW-53, SW-54, SW-64, SW-75, SW-86, SW-87, SW-97, SX-08 and SX-19.
Guidebooks:
• *The South West Peninsula Coast Path:* 1) *Minehead to St. Ives* and 2) *St. Ives to Plymouth,* Letts & Company.
• *Walking the North Cornwall Coastal Footpath* by Mark Richards, Thornhill Press. Available from the South West Way Association. (Highly recommended)

- A complete list of other guides to the path is included in *The South West Way Coastal Path Guide.*

3) *The South Cornwall Coast Path.* From Penzance to Cremyll on the Tamar estuary. Along a coastline broken by inlets with many small seaports and places of historic interest. **Length:** 214 kilometers (133 miles). **Walking Time:** 9 to 11 days.
Maps:
- Ordnance Survey 1:50,000, sheets 200, 201, 203 and 204.
- Ordnance Survey 1:25,000, sheets SW-43, SW-52, SW-53, SW-61, SW-62, SW-71, SW-72, SW-73, SW-83, SW-94, SX-04, SX-05, SX-15, SX-25, SX-35 and SX-45.
Guidebooks:
- *The South West Peninsula Coast Path: 2) St. Ives to Plymouth,* Letts & Company. (Recommended)
- *A Practical Guide to Walking the Cornwall South Coast Path* by H.D. Westacott, Footpath Publications. (In preparation)
- A complete list of other guides to the path is included in *The South West Way Coastal Path Guide.*

4) *The South Devon Coast Path.* From Cremyll to Lyme Regis along a geologically complex coastline of estuaries, sandy flats and impressive promontories of chalk and red sandstone. **Length:** 149 kilometers (93 miles). **Walking Time:** 6 to 8 days.
Maps:
- Ordnance Survey 1:50,000, sheets 192, 193, 201 and 202.
- Ordnance Survey 1:25,000, sheets SX-45, SX-54, SX-64, SX-73, SX-84, SX-85/95, SX-86/96, SX-97, SX-08/18, SY-29 and SY-39.
Guidebooks:
- *A Practical Guide to Walking the Devon South Coast Path* by H.D. Westacott, Footpath Publications. (Recommended)
- *The South West Peninsula Coast Path: Plymouth to Poole* by Ken Ward and John Mason, Letts & Company. (Also recommended)
- *South Devon Coast Path Guide* by Brian Le Messurier, HMSO.
- A complete list of other guides to the path is included in *The South West Coastal Way Path Guide.*

5) *Dorset Coast Path.* From Lyme Regis to Studland, along limestone cliffs, past an extraordinary pebble formation at Chesil Beach and across grassy downlands and sand dunes. **Length:** 116 kilometers (72 miles). **Walking Time:** 5 to 6 days.
Maps:
- Ordnance Survey 1:50,000, sheets 193, 194 and 195.
- Ordnance Survey 1:25,000, sheets SY-39, SY-49, SY-58, SY-68, SY-67/77, SY-78, SY-88, SY-87/97, SZ-07 and SZ-08.
Guidebooks:
- *A Practical Guide to Walking the Dorset Coast Path* by H.D. Westacott, Footpath Publications. (Recommended)

- *Dorset Coast Path* by Brian Jackman, HMSO.
- *The South West Peninsula Coast Path: Plymouth to Poole* by Ken Ward and John Mason, Letts & Company. (Also recommended)
- A complete list of other guides to the path is included in *The South West Way Coastal Path Guide.*

Other Long-Distance Footpaths

The Calderdale Way

A circular route around the Borough of Calderdale in West Yorkshire, beginning in Halifax. The walk can be done in short stages and the many points of access make it ideal for families. It is the first major Recreation Footpath of the Countryside Commission. **Length:** 89.5 kilometers (50 miles). **Walking Time:** 3 days. **Path Markings:** Waymarked throughout. **Lodgings:** Available in towns near the route.
Maps:
- Ordnance Survey 1:50,000, sheets 103, 104 and 110.
Also:
- Ordnance Survey 1:25,000 Outdoor Leisure Map, *South Pennines.*
Guidebook:
- *The Calderdale Way.* Available from H.C. Morris, Calderdale Way Association.

The Coast to Coast Walk

From St. Bees Head on the Irish Sea to Robin Hood's Bay on the North Sea. Passes through the Lake District, Yorkshire Dales and North York Moors national parks. A recommended walk. **Length:** 306 kilometers (190 miles). **Walking Time:** 14 days. **Path Markings:** Intermittent. There are cairns along some of the paths the route follows. The route itself, however, is not marked.
Lodgings: Limited except for youth hostels and accommodation for small parties.
Special Notes: The weather is changeable and can be severe. Wind and rain protection are essential, as are a compass, stout boots, warm clothing, a wool cap and mittens and an emergency ration of food.
Maps:
- Ordnance Survey 1:50,000, sheets 89, 90, 91, 92, 93, 94, 98 and 99. These are sufficient when used in conjunction with the path guide.
Guidebook:
- *A Coast to Coast Walk: A Pictorial Guide* by Alfred W. Wainwright, Westmorland Gazette.

The Cotswold Way

From Chipping Camden to Bath along the Cotswold escarpment in Gloucestershire. The route lies within the Cotswold Area of Outstanding Natural Beauty. Hilly farming country with extensive views over Severn Vale to the Welsh mountains. **Length:** 161 kilometers (100 miles). **Walking Time:** 8 days. **Path Markings:** Marked with a white spot. Signposted and marked throughout.
Lodgings: Many available near—although not always on—the route. Accommodation and transportation information is listed in the *Cotswold Way Handbook*, available for a nominal charge from the Ramblers' Association.
Maps:
• Ordnance Survey 1:50,000, sheets 150, 151, 162, 163 and 172.
Guidebooks:
• *Cotswold Way: A Walker's Guide* by Mark Richards, Thornhill Press.
• *Cotswold Way Handbook* by the Gloucestershire Area Ramblers' Association. Available from the RA head office.

The Crosses Walk

A circular route across the North York Moors, starting at Goathland. A challenge walk is organized over this route each year by the Scarborough Search and Rescue Team. **Length:** 85 kilometers (53 miles). **Walking Time:** 4 days. **Path Markings:** None.
Lodgings: Scarce. It is best to camp.
Special Notes: Weather can be bleak and cold. Changes are sudden with sharp drops in temperature. Warm clothing and a compass are essential. The route should not be attempted alone.
Maps:
• Ordnance Survey Tourist Map, 1:63,360, *North York Moors*.
Guidebook:
• *The Crosses Walk* by Malcolm Boyes, Dalesman Publishing Company.

The Cumbria Way

From Ulverston to Carlisle. Traverses the length of the Lake District from south to north. Follows field paths, lake shore, valleys and crosses heather moorland through the mountain area. **Length:** 113 kilometers (70 miles). **Walking Time:** 5 to 6 days. **Path Markings:** None. The route, however, is generally signposted.
Lodgings: Many lodgings in towns along the route. But you should book in advance—way in advance. Lodging information can be obtained from the Cumbria Tourist Board, as well as from the RA's *Bed and Breakfast Guide*.

Special Notes: The weather is changeable and can be severe. You should carry warm clothing and a compass.
Maps:
• Ordnance Survey 1:50,000, sheets 85, 90 and 97.
• Ordnance Survey 1:25,000, sheets SD 17/27, SD 28, SD 29, SD 39, NY 20, NY 21, NY 22, NY 23, NY 25/35, NY 30, NY 33 and NY 34.
• Ordnance Survey 1:25,000 Outdoor Leisure Maps, three sheets: *Lake District SE, SW* and *NW.*
Guidebook:
• *The Cumbria Way* by John Trevelyan, Dalesman Publishing Company.

The Dales Way

A riverside walk from Ilkley in West Yorkshire to Bowness on Windermere in Cumbria. **Length:** 130 kilometers (81 miles). **Walking Time:** 6 days.
Path Markings: Waymarked only in part.
Lodgings: Reasonably available. Refer to the RA's *Bed and Breakfast Guide* and *Dale's Way Handbook.*
Maps:
• Ordnance Survey 1:50,000, sheets 97, 98, 99 and 104.
Guidebooks:
• *The Dales Way* by Colin Speakman, Dalesman Publishing Company.
• *The Dales Way Handbook,* available from the Ramblers' Association.

The Derwent Way

From Barmby to Lilla Howe on the North York Moors. Roughly follows the River Derwent through Stamford Bridge, Malton and the Vale of Pickering to its source on the North York Moors. Links up with the Cleveland Way at Lilla Howe. **Length:** 129 kilometers (80 miles). **Walking Time:** 5 days.
Path Markings: Waymarked throughout.
Lodgings: Available in towns along the route.
Maps:
• Ordnance Survey 1:50,000, sheets 94, 100, 101 and 106.
Guidebook:
• *The Derwent Way* by R.C. Kenchington, Dalesman Publishing Company.

The Ebor Way

From Helmsley, North Yorkshire, to Ilkley, West Yorkshire, linking the Cleveland Way with the Dales Way. **Length:** 113 kilometers (70 miles).
Walking Time: 3 days. **Path Markings:** Waymarked throughout.

Lodgings: Refer to the RA's *Bed and Breakfast Guide*.
Maps:
• Ordnance Survey 1:50,000, sheets 100, 104 and 105.
Guidebook:
• *The Ebor Way* by J.K.E. Piggin, Dalesman Publishing Company.

The Eden Way

Follows the Eden for most of its length; a long and beautiful stretch of river in Cumbria with woods, shingle beds and bridges. **Length:** 89 kilometers (55 miles). **Walking Time:** 3 days. **Path Markings:** Partially waymarked. **Lodgings:** Refer to the RA's *Bed and Breakfast Guide*.
Maps:
• Ordnance Survey 1:50,000, sheets 85, 86, 90, 91 and 98.
Guidebook:
• *Across Northern Hills* by Geoffrey Berry, Westmorland Gazette.

Essex Way

From Epping to Dedham in Essex. Mainly on field paths and country lanes. **Length:** 81 kilometers (50 miles). **Walking Time:** 4 days. **Path Markings:** Signposted.
Lodgings: Available in towns near the route.
Maps:
• Ordnance Survey 1:50,000, sheets 167 and 168.
Guidebooks:
• *Essex Way* by the East Anglia Tourist Board.
• *Alternative Route Sections*, a supplement to *Essex Way*, by the West Essex Ramblers' Association.

Hadrian's Wall

From Wallsend near Newcastle to Bowness on the Solway Firth. The wall, built by the Romans, once stretched from coast to coast. Now its continuity is disrupted by paved roads and, in areas, only scattered fragments of the wall remain. The finest open, unspoiled section is in a central 24-kilometer (15-mile) stretch from Sewingshields Crag, six miles west of Chollerford, to Walltown Crags, one mile northeast of Green Head. In some other areas you must walk along paved roads. **Length:** 118 kilometers (73 miles). See the special note below. **Walking Time:** 6 days. **Path Markings:** None. And there is an absence of rights-of-way in places. **Lodgings:** The youth hostel at Once Brewed is located at the midway point of the route. Other lodgings are available in towns along—and a short distance from—the route. The towns, however, are sometimes as much as a 32-kilometer (20-mile) walk apart. Camping generally is not practical. An accommodation list is included in the path guide, *Rambling along the Roman Wall.*

Special Notes: Brian Jackson, in a recent article in the *London Times,* observes: "As the Roman crow flew, it is about 80 miles—a Roman mile being a thousand paces. Several times when we were very weary, hungry and wet, we tried counting a thousand paces from one milecastle to the next. We always fell short. Maybe Romans had longer legs than Yorkshiremen, or maybe Hadrian's surveyors fiddled the distances (the Emperor was hardly likely to return on his small black pony and check). But for us it meant a tramp—given detours, descents into the valley to an overnight pub, the reluctant climb back after breakfast, and simply getting lost—of nearly 120 blistery modern miles." The most enjoyable part of the wall to walk is between Sewingshields Crag and Walltown Crags. And that can easily be done in two days.

Maps:
• Ordnance Survey 1:50,000, sheets 85, 86, 87 and 88.
• Archaeological Map of Hadrians's Wall, 2 inches to 1 mile. Does not show rights-of-way.

Guidebooks:
• *A Guide to Hadrian's Wall* by A.R. Birley, HMSO. (Recommended)
• *Rambling along the Roman Wall* by the Northern Area Ramblers' Association. (Recommended for its accommodation list)
• *Roman Wall Summer Bus Service.* Free from the Northumberland National Park. A self-addressed, stamped envelope should accompany orders. (Useful)
• *A Walk along the Wall* by Hunter Davies, Weidenfeld and Nicolson.
• *Along Hadrian's Wall* by David Harrison, Cassell Publishers.

Isle of Wight Coastal Path

A circular walk around the island. Can be started at any point. **Length:** 113 kilometers (70 miles). **Walking Time:** 5 days. **Path Markings:** Signposted, but not fully waymarked.

Lodgings: Best to book in advance. An accommodation list is available from the Isle of Wight Tourist Board.

Maps:
• Ordnance Survey 1:50,000, sheet 196.
• Ordnance Survey 1:25,000, sheets SZ-28, SZ-38, SZ-47, SZ-48, SZ-49, SZ-57, SZ-58, SZ-59 and SZ-68.

Guidebooks:
• *Isle of Wight Coastal Path,* a series of leaflets available from the County Surveyor and Planning Officer, Isle of Wight.

London Countryway

An orbital route around London, based on existing footpaths. **Length:** 330 kilometers (205 miles). **Walking Time:** 15 days. Also can be done in sections from London. **Path Markings:** Signposted.
Lodgings: Many possibilities. Listed in the path guide (below).
Maps:
• Ordnance Survey 1:50,000, sheets 165, 166, 167, 175, 177, 186, 187 and 188.
Guidebook:
• *Guide to the London Countryway* by Keith Chesterton, Constable & Company.

Lyke Wake Walk

From Osmotherly to Ravenscar across the North York Moors. Supposedly follows an old coffin track (hence, the word "wake"). **Length:** 71 kilometers (44 miles). **Walking Time:** 3 days (24 hours to qualify for the Lyke Wake Club). **Path Markings:** None. The route, however, is signposted.
Lodgings: Limited. Camping is possible. Lodging information is available from the North York Moors National Park Department.
Special Notes: Weather can be bleak and cold with sudden changes and sharp drops in temperature. Warm clothing and a compass are essential.
Maps:
• Ordnance Survey Tourist Map, 1:63,360, *North York Moors*.
• Ordnance Survey 1:50,000, sheets 94, 100 and 101.
Guidebook:
• *Lyke Wake Walk* by Bill Cowley, Dalesman Publishing Company.

North Buckinghamshire Way

From the Chiltern Ridgeway at Chequers Knapp to Wolverton through the Vale of Aylesbury. The route can also be extended to Green Norton by using the Grafton Way and to Badby on the Knightley Way. Many fine viewpoints. **Length:** 48 kilometers (30 miles) or, with the extensions, 87 kilometers (54 miles). **Walking Time:** 2 to 4 days. **Path Markings:** Yellow arrows.
Lodgings: Listed in the path guide, *North Buckinghamshire Way*. Transportation information is also included.
Maps:
• Ordnance Survey 1:50,000, sheets 152 and 165.
Guidebooks:
• *North Buckinghamshire Way* by the Southern Area Ramblers' Association.
• *The Grafton Way* by the Northamptonshire County Council Leisure and

Amenities Department. Available for a nominal charge. Also, please send a self-addressed, stamped envelope.
• *The Knightley Way*, also by the Northamptonshire County Council.

The Oxfordshire Way

From Bourton-on-the-Water to Henley-on-Thames. **Length:** 97 kilometers (60 miles). **Walking Time:** 4 days. **Path Markings:** Signposted throughout. Waymarking is currently in progress.
Lodgings: Available in towns near the route.
Maps:
   ordnance Survey 1:50,000, sheets 163, 164 and 175.
• A set of three maps in the scale of 1:25,000 is published to the path by CPRE Oxfordshire Branch.
Guidebook:
• *The Oxfordshire Way* by the CPRE.

Peakland Way

A circular walk around the Peak District National Park on existing rights-of-way. **Length:** 155 kilometers (96 miles). **Walking Time:** 7 to 8 days. **Path Markings:** Some sections signposted; others have no markings.
Lodgings: Refer to the RA's *Bed and Breakfast Guide*. Information is also available from the Peak District National Park.
Maps:
• Ordnance Survey Tourist Map, 1:63,360, *The Peak District*.
• Ordnance Survey 1:50,000, sheets 110 and 119.
Guidebook:
• *The Peakland Way* by John Merrill, Dalesman Publishing Company.

The Peddars Way

From Cromer to near Thetford in Norfolk. Begins on the Norfolk coast, then heads inland along an ancient Roman road. **Length:** 122 kilometers (76 miles). **Walking Time:** 4 days. **Path Markings:** Partially waymarked.
Lodgings: Available in towns near the route. Listed in *Walking the Peddar's Way* (see below).
Maps:
• Ordnance Survey 1:50,000, sheets 132 and 144.
Guidebook:
• *The Peddars Way* by Bruce Robinson, Weathercock Press.
• *Walking the Peddars Way and Norfolk Coast Path* by and from Peddars Way Association.

Pennine Link

Joins the Pennine Way, near Horton-in-Ribblesdale in North Yorkshire, with the Lake District at Keswick. **Length:** 113 kilometers (70 miles). **Walking Time:** 4 days. **Path Markings:** Partially waymarked.
Lodgings: Refer to the RA's *Bed and Breakfast Guide*.
Maps:
• Ordnance Survey 1:50,000, sheets 89, 90, 91 and 98.
Guidebook:
• *Across Northern Hills* by Geoffrey Berry, Westmorland Gazette.

The Roman Way

Joins the Roman forts of Brougham, Ambleside, Hardknott and Ravenglass in the Lake District National Park. Fine fell-walking over the Roman road of High Street. **Length:** 77 kilometers (48 miles). **Walking Time:** 3 days. **Path Markings:** None.
Lodgings: Many available, but book in advance. A list is available from the Cumbria Tourist Board and the Lake District National Park Information Service.
Maps:
• Ordnance Survey Tourist Map 1:63,360, *Lake District*. Or:
• Ordnance Survey 1:50,000, sheets 85, 89, 90 and 97. Or:
• Ordnance Survey 1:25,000 Outdoor Leisure Map, four sheets: *English Lakes* NE, NW, SE and SW. (Recommended)
Guidebook:
• *Across Northern Hills* by Geoffrey Berry, Westmorland Gazette.

The Sandstone Trail

From Delamere Forest to the Shropshire border in Cheshire. **Length:** 40 kilometers (25 miles). **Walking Time:** 2 days. **Path Markings:** Fully signed and waymarked.
Lodgings: Refer to the RA's *Bed and Breakfast Guide*.
Maps:
• Ordnance Survey 1:50,000, sheet 117.
Guidebook:
• *Sandstone Trail* by the Cheshire County Council.

The Staffordshire Way

From Mow Cop to Kinver Edge. Canal towpath and hilltop walking. **Length:** 145 kilometers (90 miles). **Walking Time:** 6 to 7 days. **Path**

Markings: To date, only 97 kilometers (60 miles) from Mow Cop to Cannock Chase have been signposted and waymarked.
Lodgings: Refer to the RA's *Bed and Breakfast Guide.*
Maps:
• Ordnance Survey 1:50,000, sheets 118 and 128.
Guidebook:
• *The Staffordshire Way* by the Staffordshire County Council Planning Department.

St. Peter's Way

From Chipping Ongar to St. Peter's Chapel near Bradwell in Essex. Devised by Fred Matthews and Harry Bitten. Takes you across farmlands and over the Bagshot Hills. Finishes with a fine walk along the Essex coast. **Length:** 72.5 kilometers (45 miles). **Walking Time:** 3 days. **Path Markings:** none.
Lodgings: Available in towns near the route.
Maps:
• Ordnance Survey 1:50,000, sheets 167, 168, 177 and 178.
Guidebook:
• *St. Peter's Way* by Fred Matthews and Harry Bitten, West Essex Area Ramblers' Association.

Sussex Border Path

From Emsworth to Rye around the border of West Sussex. Beautiful rolling countryside. **Length:** 196 kilometers (150 miles). **Walking Time:** 6 to 7 days. **Path Markings:** None at present. May be waymarked in the near future by the West Sussex County Council.
Lodgings: Available in towns near the route.
Maps:
• Ordnance Survey 1:50,000, sheets 186, 187, 188, 189, 197, 198, and 199.
Guidebook:
• *Sussex Border Path: West Sussex* by Aeneas Mackintosh and Ben Perkins. Available from Dr. B. Perkins, East Sussex.

The Thamesdown Trail

A circular route around Swindon. Passes through the Thames Valley, the Vale of White Horse and the Marlborough Downs. **Length:** 87 kilometers (54 miles). **Walking Time:** 3 days. **Path Markings:** Partly waymarked.

Lodgings: Available in towns near the route.
Maps:
• Ordnance Survey 1:50,000, sheets 163, 165, 173 and 174.
Guidebook:
• *The Thamesdown Trail* (available in English and French) by Laurence Main.

Three Forests Way

A circular route linking the three forests of Epping, Hatfield, and Hainault in Essex. **Length:** 97 kilometers (60 miles). **Walking Time:** 4 days. **Path Markings:** None.
Lodgings: Available in towns near the route.
Maps:
• Ordnance Survey 1:50,000, sheets 166, 167 and 177.
Guidebook:
• *The Three Forests Way* by Fred Matthews and Harry Bitten, West Essex Group Ramblers' Association.

Two Moors Way

From Ivybridge in South Devon to Lynton on the North Devon coast. Passes through Dartmoor and Exmoor national parks. Follows green lanes and field paths across open moor and through wooded valleys. **Length:** 166 kilometers (103 miles). **Walking Time:** 7 to 8 days. **Path Markings:** Waymarked in mid-Devon only. Use of a compass is essential across the two moors.
Lodgings: An accommodation list is included in the path guide, *Two Moors Way.*
Special Notes: Much of the route is hilly and the field paths are often muddy. The open moor also is liable to be wet. Waterproofed boots and gaiters are essential.
Maps:
• Ordnance Survey 1:50,000, sheets 180, 181, 191 and 202.
• Ordnance Survey 1:25,000, sheets SS-70, SS-73, SS-74, SS-81, SS-82, SS-83, SX-65/75, SX-66, SX-68/78, SX-76, SX-77, and SX-79.
Guidebook:
• *Two Moors Way* by Helen Rowett, Devon Area Ramblers' Association. Available from J.R. Turner.

The Viking Way

From the Humber Bridge, near Barton-on-Humber in South Humberside, to Oakham in Rutland, Leicestershire. Passes through the Lincolnshire

Wolds, an Area of Outstanding Natural Beauty. An easy walk along lowland footpaths and bridleways through a rolling landscape with wide views, peaceful villages and country inns. **Length:** 258 kilometers (160 miles). **Walking Time:** 10 to 12 days. **Path Markings:** A yellow square with a stylized symbol of a viking helmet. The route has not yet been fully marked.
Lodgings: An accommodation list is included in the path guide, *The Viking Way.*
Maps:
• Ordnance Survey 1:50,000, sheets 112, 113, 121, 122, 130 and 141.
Guidebooks:
• *The Viking Way* by the Lincolnshire and South Humberside Area Ramblers' Association. (Recommended)
• *Viking Way Accommodation and Transport Sheet,* also available from the Lincolnshire and South Humberside Area Ramblers' Association. (Recommended)
• *Viking Way Leaflets:* 1) *Bigby to Walesby,* 2) *Walesby to Donnington,* and 3) *Donnington to Horncastle.* Several other leaflets covering the rest of the path are also available. All by the Lincolnshire County Council.

The Wealdway

From Gravesend in Kent to Eastbourne in East Sussex. Links the North and South Downs. Passes through the Kent and Sussex Weald, a wooded, fertile region. **Length:** 134 kilometers (83 miles). **Walking Time:** 6 days, although strong walkers can do it in three. **Path Markings:** Intermittent. Also, the markings are not consistent throughout.
Lodgings: The walker is never far from villages where accommodation can be found. For details, refer to the RA *Bed and Breakfast Guide.*
Maps:
• Ordnance Survey 1:50,000, sheets 177, 178, 188 and 199.
Guidebooks:
Three separate guides in sections:
• *Gravesend to Tonbridge.* Available from Moopham Publications.
• *Tonbridge to Uckfield* and, in preparation, *Uckfield to Eastbourne.* Both available from the Sussex Area Ramblers' Association.
• *Wealdway Guide.* Available from Sussex RA.

The Wear Valley Way

Traverses the length of the Wear Valley in Durham, running from the Killhope Wheel picnic site to the Willington (Jubilee Bridge) picnic site, both of which have parking facilities and are near bus service. Follows a unused railway along the Wear and Derwent watershed for much of the way. Crosses open moors and pastures, passes through forests and climbs several hills. Laid out by the Association of Fell Ramblers and Wayfarers.

Length: About 64 kilometers (40 miles). **Walking Time:** As a challenge walk, 24 hours (upon the completion of which you are awarded a patch and certificate), or at a more leisurely pace, 3 days. **Path Markings:** None. **Lodgings:** None. You must plan on camping.
Maps:
• Ordnance Survey 1:50,000, sheet 92.
Guidebook:
• Not yet available. Information on walking the path can be obtained from Alan Earnshaw, general secretary, Association of Fell Ramblers & Wayfarers. There is also a useful regional path guide:
• *Walking in Weardale* by T. R. Spedding, Dalesman Publishing Company.

Heart of England Way

From Chipping Campden to Cannock Chase, linking the Cotswold Way with the Staffordshire Way. May eventually form part of a through route all the way from Bath to Scotland. **Length:** 106 kilometers (80 miles). **Walking Time:** 4 days. **Path Markings:** None.
Lodgings: Refer to the RA's *Bed and Breakfast Guide*.
Maps:
• Ordnance Survey 1:50,000, sheets 127, 128, 139, 150 and 151.
Guidebook:
• *The Heart of England Way*. MRT Westwood, in the croft, Meridon, West Midlands. A useful regional path guide is:
• *West Warwickshire Walks* by and available from Wootten Wamen Footpaths Group.

Wey-South Path

From Guildford to Amberley along the towpath of the former Wey and Arun Canal in the South Downs. **Length:** 58 kilometers (36 miles). **Walking Time:** 2 days. **Path Markings:** None, but the towpath is clearly defined.
Lodgings: Refer to the RA's *Bed and Breakfast Guide*.
Maps:
• Ordnance Survey 1:50,000, sheets 186 and 197.
Guidebooks:
• *Wey-South Path* by A. Mackintosh. Available from the Wey and Arun Canal Trust.

White Rose Walk

From Kilburn White Horse to Roseberry Topping in the North York Moors National Park. Follows a portion of the Cleveland Way. **Length:** 64 kilometers (40 miles). **Walking Time:** 3 days. **Path Markings:** Signposted where it follows the Cleveland Way. No other path markings.
Lodgings: Limited. Accommodation information is available from the North York Moors National Park Department.
Maps:
• Ordnance Survey Tourist Map, 1:63,360, *North York Moors.* Or:
• Ordnance Survey 1:50,000, sheets 93, 94, 99 and 100.
Guidebook:
• *White Rose Walk* by Geoffrey White, Dalesman Publishing Company.

Wolds Way

From Filey (at one end of the Cleveland Way) to Ferriby in Humberside (over the Humber Bridge from the Viking Way). Passes through the chalk hills of the Yorkshire Wolds. Has been designated as an official long-distance footpath, but remains to be officially opened. **Length:** 113 kilometers (70 miles). **Walking Time:** 5 days. **Path Markings:** Signposted.
Lodgings: An accommodation list is included in the RA Area path guide, *The Wolds Way.*
Maps:
• Ordnance Survey 1:50,000, sheets 100, 101 and 106.
Guidebooks:
• *The Wolds Way* by the East Yorkshire and Derwent Area Ramblers' Association. Principally an accommodation and transport guide. (Recommended)
• *The Wolds Way* by David Rubinstein, Dalesman Publishing Company.

Yorkshire Dales Centurion Walk

A circular route through the Yorkshire Dales National Park. **Length:** 161 kilometers (100 miles). Not recommended due to problems with public access in unmarked areas.

Land's End to John O'Groats

There is no single long-distance path connecting the furthest extremities of Britain, although judging by the number of enquiries the Ramblers' Association receives from people who want to follow the route outlined in John Hillaby's *Journey Through Britain* (Constable & Company), a well-beaten path could by now exist. Suggestion: To those who wish to attempt this marathon walk, the Ramblers' Association suggests that maximum use be made of the existing long-distance footpaths—South West Peninsula Coast Path, Two Moors Way, Offa's Dyke and the Pennine Way—and that suitable routes through Scotland be taken from D.G. Moir's books, *Scottish Hill Tracks* (see the section on *Guidebooks* in the chapter on Scotland). The Ordnance Survey maps covering the gaps can then be used to help you plot routes on existing rights-of-way to link up these paths.

Canal Towpaths and Riverside Paths

Some canal towpaths and riverside paths are public rights-of-way; others are privately owned. The only way to determine the status of a towpath is to examine the appropriate 1:50,000 Ordnance Survey map.

Even if a canal towpath is not a public right-of-way, there are often few obstacles in rural areas to prevent you from walking along one—except, perhaps, the complete absence of a towpath. Nonetheless, you may be warned off if the path is not a right-of-way.

Further Reading:

- *The Thames Walk,* a guide to paths along the Thames from Putney to Thames Head. Available from the Ramblers' Association.
- *Lost Canals of England and Wales* by Ronald Russell, David and Charles.
- *Towpath Guide Series:* 1) *Staffs and Worcs Canal* and 2) *Brecknock & Abergavenney and Menmouthshire Canals.* Available from Waterway Productions Ltd.
- *Nicholson's Guides to the Water-Ways:* 1) *South East,* 2) *North West,* 3) *South West,* 4) *North East,* and 5) *Midlands.* Also available from Waterway Productions Ltd.
- *Nicholson's Guide to the Thames,* from Waterway Productions Ltd.
- *Towpath Trek* by George Birtill, Guardian Press. Describes a section of the Leeds and Liverpool canal in southwest Lancashire.
- *The Navigation Way* by Peter Grotes, Tetradon Publications Ltd. Describes a 100-mile towpath walk around Birmingham and the west Midlands.

England's National Parks

In Britain, national parks are not owned by the state as in many other countries. Most of the areas included in the parks are in private ownership. People live and work in the parks just as they do in other parts of the country. Also, access for walkers is no greater than in other parts of the country, except in cases where local arrangements have been negotiated.

The parks, however, are protected by legislation to prevent intrusive and damaging developments. And most include relatively wild countryside—mountains, moors, heaths, downs and, in some cases, towering seacliffs.

When walking in the parks, you must stick to public paths, to land designated for public access and to common land. If in doubt, ask local people. Because much of the terrain is rugged, novices should not venture out alone. Many of the parks organize walks with experienced leaders. And, for those who do not wish to venture into the moors and mountains, there are often numerous walks in the valleys of the national parks.

Many of the parks publish leaflets for walkers—including transportation schedules, accommodation lists, information on guided walks and mountaineering courses, and path guides. A list of these publications and their prices can be obtained on request from the parks. Their addresses are given in the *Address Directory* at the back of this chapter.

Most national parks also maintain rescue teams and have manned rescue posts scattered throughout the park. The locations of these rescue posts are listed in *Mountain and Cave Rescue,* the handbook of the Mountain Rescue Committee. You should obtain a copy of this booklet (see description under "Search & Rescue" in the section on *Useful Address & Telephone Numbers).* Because the location of a post is sometimes changed, you should verify the locations locally. You can do this at one of the park information offices.

The Parks

Dartmoor

This park is located in Devon on the South West Peninsula. It encompasses the largest piece of really wild country left in southern England. At the heart of Dartmoor is an expanse of heather-clad moorland that rises to an altitude of 621 meters (2,038 feet) at Willhays, the highest point in southern England. This part of the park is noted for its many outcrops of granite—or *tors,* as they are known locally—that have been weathered

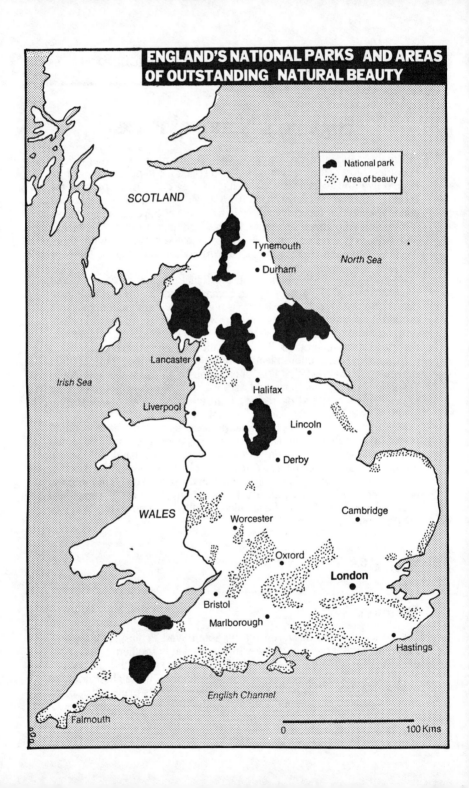

ENGLAND'S NATIONAL PARKS AND AREAS
OF OUTSTANDING NATURAL BEAUTY

SCOTLAND

North Sea

Tynemouth
Durham

Lancaster

Irish Sea

Halifax

Liverpool

Lincoln

Derby

WALES

Worcester

Cambridge

Oxford

London

Bristol

Marlborough

Hastings

English Channel

Falmouth

■ National park
∴ Area of beauty

0   100 Kms

into strange shapes. Scattered over the moor are the ruins of Bronze Age huts, enclosures, burial chambers and ritualistic stone rows—more than are found anywhere else in England.

On the fringes of the park are steep-sided valleys and streams, thick woods and moorstone villages. There are also many medieval churches, bridges and castles throughout the park.

Area: 946 square kilometers (365 square miles).

Towns with Park Information Centers: See *Address Directory.*

Special Notes: Advance planning and good equipment are necessary for walks on the moors. Heavy rain, mists and hill fogs can set in quickly. These conditions pose a special hazard, since many tracks over the moors are poorly defined and there are large areas of deep, treacherous bog.

In the northern part of the park, the army uses a large area for training exercises and artillery practice. This area is marked on Ordnance Survey maps. Red flags are flown when firing is taking place. Information on the dates and times of firing can be obtained from the park information center and local post offices.

Lodgings: All types of accommodation are available. Accommodation lists are available from the Dartmoor National Park Department. Campsites are located on the perimeter of the park. It is also possible to camp on common land within the park. Elsewhere, you must ask the landowner's permission.

Maps:
- Ordnance Survey Tourist Map, 1:63,360, *Dartmoor.*
- Ordnance Survey 1:50,000, sheets 191, 201 and 202.
- Ordnance Survey 1:25,000, sheets SX-46, SX-47, SX-48/58, SX-55, SX-56, SX-57, SX-59, SX-65/75, SX-66/76, SX-67, SX-68/78, SX-69/79, SX-77, SX-87, SX-88/98 and SX-89/99.

Guidebooks:
- *Dartmoor National Park* by W.G. Hoskins, HMSO. A general guide to the park. Does not include path descriptions.
- *Visitors Guides:* 1) *Southern Dartmoor,* 2) *Eastern Dartmoor,* 3) *Northern Dartmoor,* 4) *South Hams,* 5) *Torbay,* 6) *Exeter,* and 7) *Plymouth.* All by Arthur L. Clamp, Westway Publications. Each contains 11 walks.
- *Walks and Rides on Dartmoor* by H.D. Westacott, Footpath Publications. (Recommended)
- *Walks in the Dartmoor National Park,* No. 1, from Moretonhampstead, Manaton and Lustleigh. By Elizabeth Prince. Available from Dartmoor National Park Department. (Recommended)
- *Read about Walks on Dartmoor and Exmoor,* Photo Precision.

Exmoor

Most of this park lies in Somerset, although a part of it spills over into Devon. It is a moorland plateau seamed by deep wooded valleys, known as *combes*. The highest point is Dunkery Beacon (532 meters; 1,708 feet), a massive dome that catches all the clouds from the Atlantic, has an annual rainfall of 1,524 mm (60 inches) and forms the gathering ground for numerous rivers and streams. Because of the steep ground, those that flow north are fast and treacherous with water slides and deep pools.

On the fringes of the moor, to the south and west, is steep broken country, with small farms and large areas of rough land. In the north the coastal scenery is dominated by dramatic hogback cliffs and wild sea approaches. Like Dartmoor National Park to the south, there are also many prehistoric remains.

Area: 663 square kilometers (256 square miles).

Towns with Park Information Centers (open April through September): See *Address Directory*.

Special Notes: Exmoor offers some of the easiest walking in any of the national parks. Still, weather changes on the moors can be sudden and should be taken into account.

Lodgings: Plentiful. See the RA's *Bed and Breakfast Guide*.

Maps:
- Ordnance Survey Tourist Map, 1:63,360, *Exmoor*.
- Ordnance Survey 1:50,000, sheets 180 and 181.
- Ordnance Survey 1:25,000, sheets SS-44/54, SS-63, SS-64, SS-72, SS-73, SS-74, SS-82/92, SS-83, SS-84, SS-93, SS-94, ST-03 and ST-04.

Guidebooks:
- *Exmoor National Park* by John Coleman-Cooke, editor, HMSO. A general guide to the park. Does not include path descriptions.
- *Rambles in West Somerset and on Exmoor*, available from Western National Omnibus Company.
- Read about *Walks on Dartmoor and Exmoor*, Photo Precision.
- *Exmoor National Park: Waymarked Walks 1, Waymarked Walks 2* and *Waymarked Walks 3*, available from Exmoor National Park Authority. (Recommended)
- *Suggested Walks & Bridleways:* 1) *Combe Martin*, 2) *Woody Bay*, 3) *Lynton & Lynmouth*, 4) *Malmsmead* and 5) *Brendon Common*. Also available from the park authority.
- *Exmoor Walks, Exmoor Coastal Walks* and *Exmoor Riverside Walks*. All by Tim Abbot, Books of Wessex Ltd.
- A list of other path guides and leaflets is available from the park authority.

The Lake District

This is the largest of Britain's national parks—and the most popular. Located in Cumbria, it includes England's largest lakes and its highest mountains—Scafell Pike (978 meters; 3,210 feet), Helvellyn (950 meters; 3,117 feet) and Skiddaw (931 meters; 3,054 feet). The central part of the park is rugged and precipitous. Steep-sided mountains rise dramatically from the low ground near the sea, 16 kilometers away, a contrast that makes them appear higher than they actually are. Radiating out from the mountains are a series of valleys dotted with long, narrow lakes and small villages with stone buildings. During the summer and on weekends, the valley towns teem with tourists. But, providing the popular walks are avoided, you can get away from the crowds by taking to the *fells,* as the lakeland mountains are known. And while you still might not be entirely alone, you will be able to enjoy much more the ever-repeating succession of mountain, dale and lake.

Area: 2,244 square kilometers (866 square miles).

Towns with Park Information Centers (open daily from Easter until late September): See *Address Directory:*

Special Notes: Weather can change quickly, and that on the fells often contrasts sharply to that in the valleys. On the heights, you should be prepared for high winds, rain and heavy mists. For local weather forecasts and fell conditions, Tel. Windermere (09662) 5151.

Lodgings: Many available, but book in advance. Lists are available from the Cumbria Tourist Board and the Lake District National Park Information Service.

Maps:
• Ordnance Survey Tourist Map, 1:63,360, *Lake District.* (Recommended)
• Bartholomew, 1:63,360, *Lake District.* (Recommended)
• Ordnance Survey 1:50,000, sheets 85, 89, 90, 96 and 97.
• Ordnance Survey 1:25,000 Outdoor Leisure Map, four sheets: *English Lakes* NE, NW, SE and SW. (Recommended)

Guidebooks:
• *The Lake District National Park* by W.H. Pearsall, HMSO. A general guide to the park. Does not include footpath descriptions.
• *A Pictorial Guide to the Lakeland Fells* by Alfred W. Wainwright, Westmorland Gazette: Vol. 1 *The Eastern Fells,* Vol. 2 *The Far Eastern Fells,* Vol. 3 *The Central Fells,* Vol. 4 *The Southern Fells,* Vol. 5 *The Northern Fells,* Vol. 6 *The North Western Fells* and Vol. 7 *The Western Fells.* (All highly recommended)
• *Lake District Walks for Motorists:* 1) *Central Area,* 2) *Northern Area* and 3) *Western Area.* All by John Parker, Warne Gerrard Ltd.
• *The Lakeland Peaks* by W.A. Poucher, Constable and Company. A guide for both walkers and climbers. (Recommended)
• A list of other publications—including a series of free leaflets to short walks throughout the district, guides to nature trails and information on guided walks—is available from the Lake District National Park Information Service as well as from the Brockhole National Park Centre. The RA's *County Sheet—Cumbria* also lists numerous path guides (see the section on *Where to Get Walking Information* earlier in this chapter).

North York Moors

This park encompasses the largest heather moor in England. It is located in North Yorkshire and Cleveland. Deep, narrow valleys cut through the moorland on its southern and eastern sides, and along its rock-bound coast, fishing villages perch on the cliffs. Inland, there are numerous prehistoric burial places, medieval crosses and an occasional small market town. In August, the heather on the moors is in bloom, a sight that is more than worth the trip.

Area: 1,433 square kilometers (553 square miles).

Towns with Park Information Centers (open from April to October): See *Address Directory.*

Special Notes: Weather can be bleak and cold. Changes are sudden, with fogs along the coast and sharp drops in temperature. Warm clothing and a compass are essential. The moorland paths should not be attempted alone.

Lodgings: Plentiful along the coast, but limited inland. Even so, with advance planning you should have no difficulties. There are 10 youth hostels located in or on the boundaries of the park. An accommodation list is available from the North York Moors National Park Department. It is also possible to camp on some areas of the moors.

Maps:
- Ordnance Survey Tourist Map, 1:63,360, *North York Moors.*
- Ordnance Survey 1:50,000, sheets 93, 94, 99, 100 and 101.
- Ordnance Survey 1:25,000, sheets NZ-40, NZ-50, NZ-51, NZ-60, NZ-61, NZ-70, NZ-71, NZ-80, NZ-81, NZ-90, NZ-91, SE-48, SE-49, SE-57, SE-58, SE-59, SE-67, SE-68, SE-69, SE-78, SE-79, SE-88, SE-89, SE-98, SE-99, TA-08 and TA-09.

Guidebooks:
- *The North York Moors National Park,* Arthur Raistrick, editor, HMSO. A general guide to the park. Does not include footpath descriptions.
- *Waymarked Walks:* 1) *to Roseberry,* 2) *to Cook Monument* and 3) *to Lonsdale.* Also, *Lealholm Bank Walk* and *Lealholm to Glaisdale Walk.* All available from the North York Moors National Park Department.
- *Walking on the North York Moors* by the North Yorkshire and South Durham Area Ramblers' Association, Dalesman Publishing Company. (Recommended)
- *Green Tracks and Heather Tracks, Vols. 1 and 2* by Wade Balmain, F. Graham. (Recommended)
- *North York Moors Walks for Motorists:* 1) *North and East* and 2) *West and South.* Both by Geoffrey White, Warne Gerrard Ltd. (Recommended)

Northumberland

Embracing a region of hills and moorland, this park stretches from Hadrian's Roman Wall in the south to the Cheviot Hills on the Scottish border. It encompasses the best-preserved section of Hadrian's Wall, plus several Roman forts, all in a setting little changed since the time of the Romans.

Area: 1,031 square kilometers (398 square miles).

Towns with Park Information Centers: See *Address Directory.*

Special Notes: Much of the park is common land. Walkers have traditionally been permitted access—providing livestock and game are not disturbed—but there is no *right* of access. Hence, you are obliged to leave if you are asked to do so.

Lodgings: Scarce in some areas. An accommodation list is available from Northumberland National Park. It is also possible to camp, providing you keep a low profile and do not disturb livestock or game.

Maps:
- Ordnance Survey 1:50,000, sheets 74, 75, 80, 81, 86 and 87.
- Ordnance Survey 1:25,000, sheets NU-00, NU-01, NU-02, NT-60, NT-70, NT-71, NT-80, NT-81, NT-82, NT-83, NT-90, NT-91, NT-92, NT-93, NY-66, NY-67, NY-68, NY-69, NY-76, NY-77, NY-78, NY-79, NY-86, NY-88, NY-89, NY-99 and NZ-09.

Guidebooks:
- *Northumberland National Park,* John Philipson, editor, HMSO. A general guide to the park. Does not include footpath descriptions.
- *Ramblers through Northumberland* by the Northern Area Ramblers' Association. Available from Bab Hiley. (Recommended)
- *Ramblers' Cheviot* and *Ramblers' Tyneside,* both by the Northern Area Ramblers' Association Harold Hill & Son. (Recommended)
- *North Ramble Land* by Sidney Fisher. Available from the author.
- *Green Tracks and Heather Tracks,* Vols. 1 and 2 by Wade Balmain, F. Graham.

Peak District

This was England's first national park. It is also one of the most heavily used, especially on weekends. The Peak District lies primarily in Derbyshire, although parts of the park extend into Staffordshire, Cheshire, Yorkshire and Greater Manchester. In the north, the Dark Peak region, a high, bleak moorland plateau ringed by gritstone crags, is covered by somber, forbidding banks of black peat, known as *hags,* and deep drainage channels, or *groughs.* To the south and east, a limestone plateau, known as the White Peak, features a softer, greener landscape, crisscrossed by drystone walls and divided by wooded dales with swift, clear rivers and gray, stone-wall villages. Much of this area is honeycombed with old lead workings and natural caves and caverns, some of which are open to the public, primarily around Castleton.

Area: 1,404 square kilometers (542 square miles).

Towns with Park Information Centers: See *Address Directory.*

Special Notes: Walkers in the Dark Peak area must be well-equipped and prepared for any change in the unpredictable weather. The Kinder

Plateau, at 636 meters (2,088 feet) the highest point in the park, can be bleak and cold and, even in the best conditions, is a rugged test for walkers. Between August 12 and December, parts of the park's access land is closed for grouse shooting. Specific closed areas are posted on information boards and in the local press. The information centers also can give you information on the closures.

Lodgings: Many possibilities in the White Peak area; less so in the Dark Peak area. An accommodation list is available from the Peak District National Park. Details on lodgings are also given in the RA's *Bed and Breakfast Guide*.

Maps:
- Ordnance Survey Tourist Map, 1:63,360, *Peak District*.
- Ordnance Survey 1:50,000, sheets 109, 110, 118 and 119.
- Ordnance Survey 1:25,000 Outdoor Leisure Map, *Dark Peak* (covers most of the northern part of the park).
- Ordnance Survey 1:25,000, sheets SE-00, SE-01, SE-10, SE-20, SJ-96, SJ-97, SK-04, SK-05, SK-06, SK-07, SK-14, SK-15, SK-16, SK-17, SK-25, SK-26, SK-27, SK-36 and SK-37 (covers the rest of the park).

Guidebooks:
- *Peak District National Park*, Patrick Monkhouse, editor, HMSO. A general guide to the park. Does not include footpath descriptions.
- *Peak District Walks:* 1) *Short Walks* and 2) *Long Walks*. Both by John Merrill, Dalesman Publishing Company.
- *The Peak and Pennines* by W.A. Poucher, Constable & Company.
- *Peak District Walks for Motorists* by Clifford Thompson, Warne Gerrard Ltd.
- *Peak District*, Photo Precision.
- Numerous pamphlets and path guides are available from the Peak District National Park. A free publication list can be obtained from the park authority on request. The RA's *County Sheets* covering Derbyshire, Staffordshire, Cheshire, Yorkshire and Greater Manchester also list many path guides for the Peak District and the surrounding area (see the section on *Where to Get Walking Information* earlier in this chapter).

Yorkshire Dales

The Yorkshire Dales is an area of upland moor cut by long, narrow valleys with limestone cliffs, caves, potholes and underground streams. The park includes some of the finest limestone scenery in Britain, as well as the Three Peaks (Ingleborough, Whernside and Pen-y-Ghent) and many relics of the past, including the ruins of old stone smelting mills, Roman fortifications and ancient abbeys. The Pennines run through the center of the park, forming part of England's watershed. On the mountainsides, streams descend through rocky gorges, tumbling toward the steep-sided dales in a succession of waterfalls.

In total, there are 600 buildings of Historical or Architectural Importance and more than 100 designated Ancient Monuments in the park. In addition, there are more than 1,610 kilometers (1,000 miles) of footpaths and bridleways.

Area:
1,762 square kilometers (680 square miles).

Towns with Park Information Centers: See *Address Directory.*

Special Notes: Weather conditions can be as severe as in the Peak and Lake districts. The Yorkshire Dales is generally drier, but also colder and particularly severe in winter. Its potholes are well worth visiting, but you must use caution when walking to avoid falling into one.

Lodgings: There are several youth hostels. Most towns in the dales also have bed-and-breakfast accommodation. Information is available from the Yorkshire Dales Tourist Association.

Maps:
- Ordnance Survey 1:50,000, sheets 91, 92, 97, 98, 99, 103 and 104.
- Ordnance Survey 1:25,000 Outdoor Leisure Map, two sheets, *The Three Peaks* and *Malham and Upper Wharfedale.*

Guidebooks:
- *Yorkshire Dales National Park* by I.G. Simmons, HMSO. A general guide to the park. Does not include footpath descriptions.
- *Walks in Limestone Country* and *Walks on the Howgill Fells.* Both by Alfred W. Wainwright, Westmorland Gazette.
- *The Peak and the Pennines* by W.A. Poucher, Constable & Company.
- *Rambles in the Dales, Yorkshire Dales Walks for Motorists* and *Further Dales Walks for Motorists.* All by the West Riding Ramblers' Association, Warne Gerrard Ltd.
- *Walking in the Northern Dales* by North Yorkshire and South Durham Area Ramblers' Association, Dalesman Publishing Company.
- *Walks in Swaledale* and *Walks in Wensleydale,* both by Geoffrey White, Dalesman Publishing Company.
- *Walking in the Craven Dales* by Colin Speakman, Dalesman Publishing Company.

All of these guides, with the exception of the HMSO's *Yorkshire Dales National Park,* may be obtained by mail from the West Riding Area Ramblers' Association, via Harry Saynor. A price list is available on request when you send a self-addressed, stamped envelope. The guides also may be obtained from their publishers.

Further Guidebooks:
- *The Yorkshire Dales National Park* publishes a series of nominally priced leaflets to walks in the park. These include: 1) *Walks in Wensleydale,* four leaflets, 2) *Walks in Wharfedale,* five leaflets, 3) *Walks in Swaledale,* three leaflets, and 4) *Walks in Ribblesdale,* two leaflets. These may be obtained at the Park Information Centers or by mail from Yorkshire Dales National Park.

Areas of Outstanding Natural Beauty

In addition to the national parks, there are currently 32 designated Areas of Outstanding Natural Beauty in Britain. These also have special legislative protection, although it is less strict than for the national parks.

The Areas of Outstanding Natural Beauty generally offer much easier walking than the more rugged parts of the national parks. And the regional tourist boards responsible for the areas sometimes have leaflets that give details of walks within them. Not all paths, however, are well marked—or well trod—and only a few Areas of Outstanding Natural Beauty have special facilities for walkers, but with the proper Ordnance Survey maps you will be able to find many places to walk.

Further details on the Areas of Outstanding Natural Beauty are given under the following regional descriptions:

Cumbria & the Lake District
East Anglia
East Midlands
Heart of England
Northumbria
North West England
South East England
Thames & Chilterns

Country Parks

England and Wales have more than 130 country parks. Many of these have forest walks and nature trails. A booklet gives details:

- *Country Parks.* This lists the locations of all the country parks in England and Wales by county, provides their grid reference numbers and briefly describes their terrain and notable features. Includes a map. It is available only in English. Free from the Countryside Commission (see *Address Directory*).

Forests and Forest Parks

There are also many footpaths in England's forests. Two leaflets give details:

- *See Your Forests: Northern England* and *See Your Forests: Southern England.* These list all of the Forestry Commission forests and forest parks by county. They include a brief description of forest walks and trails, give the grid reference number of the starting points and tell where leaflets to the walks may be obtained. Grid reference numbers of information centers, campsites and wayfaring courses are also given. Includes maps. The leaflets are available only in English. Free from the Forestry Commission.

Cumbria & the Lake District

For years, Cumbria was a no-man's-land: in the 11th century it was described as the land lying *between* England and Scotland. It was a wild, thinly populated region frequently devastated by the Danes and the Scots, belonging first to one side, then the other. Ruins of former castle strongholds remain in several villages and many stone towers, built for protection during border frays, are strewn across the countryside. From Carlisle (originally Scottish), fragments of Hadrian's Wall are easily reached. The town also has a 12th century cathedral and castle to explore.

Cumbria's tumbling valleys, moors and spruce forests are as imposing as ever, but today peace reigns.

For walkers, the most noted region in Cumbria is the mountainous Lake District (for details, see the section on *England's National Parks*), but there are also many footpaths along the coast. The small town of Millom in the south makes a good base for fell walking around Black Combe Mountain (from the top of which you can sometimes see the Isle of Man). And in the north there is the Solway Coast Area of Outstanding Natural Beauty. Both are good places where you can escape from the Lake District's summer crowds.

Useful Addresses

See *Address Directory:*

Brockhole National Park Centre.

Cumbria Tourist Board. Provides general tourist information, accommodation lists and leaflets on walks in the Solway Coast Area of Outstanding Natural Beauty. Also can provide the addresses and telephone numbers of local tourist information centers. Written enquiries only.

Lake District Area Ramblers' Association. Written enquiries only. Please enclose a self-addressed envelope and sufficient international postal reply coupons to cover postage. Information available includes:

1. A list of the RA's guided walks.
2. A list of the footpath guides that can be purchased from the RA, plus their prices. Includes more than 26 titles.

For more detailed enquiries, write to the head office of the Ramblers' Association.

Guidebooks

Listed in the RA's *County Sheet—Cumbria.* The Fact Sheet includes prices, the cost of postage (within Britain) and the addresses of publishers for each guidebook, plus information on guided walks and excursions. The Fact Sheet is available only from the head office of the Ramblers' Association. It cannot be obtained from the Lake District RA.

Areas of Outstanding Natural Beauty

Arnside and Silverdale
A region of limestone hills with views to the south across Morecambe Bay and, to the north, to the mountains of the Lake District. Located on the southern tip of the Lake District National Park. Covers 75 square kilometers (29 square miles).
Maps:
• Ordnance Survey 1:50,000, sheet 97.
• Ordnance Survey 1:25,000, sheets SD-46, SD-47 and SD-48.
Guidebooks:
• None.
Further Information: Contact the Cumbria Tourist Board.

Solway Coast
This is a relatively flat area with sandy beaches and wide views across

Solway Firth to the hills in Scotland. It lies between Maryport and the Scottish border. Covers 106 square kilometers (41 square miles).

Maps:
- Ordnance Survey 1:50,000, sheet 85.
- Ordnance Survey 1:25,000, sheets NY-16 and NY-26.

Guidebooks:
- *Allerdale Ramble.* Available from Allerdale District Council, Cockermouth, Cumbria.
- *Read About Walks on the Solway Coast.* Available from Photo Precision Ltd.

Further Information: Contact the Cumbria Tourist Board.

Suggested Walks

The Cumbria Way, through the Lake District (described under "Other Long-Distance Footpaths" in the section on *England's Long-Distance Footpaths*). Both Ulverston and Carlisle, the beginning and end points for the walk, can be reached by train. The Coast to Coast Walk (also described in the section on *England's Long-Distance Footpaths)* is another fine walk. There are also many rewarding day hikes in the Central Fells. Scafell Pike (978 meters), the highest mountain in England, is strenuous. Particularly recommended as areas for day hikes are: 1) Coniston Old Man, 2) Langdale Pikes, 3) Helvellyn, and 4) Great Gable.

East Anglia

A pastoral region with a low-lying, softly undulating countryside and many rivers and estuaries, East Anglia encompasses the counties of Norfolk, Suffolk, Essex and Cambridgeshire. The area abounds with nature reserves, small villages and market towns with a wealth of churches, ivy-covered houses and Tudor buildings, and prosperous farmlands that stretch toward the horizon beneath a great dome of sky. It is the driest part of England.

Useful Addresses

See *Address Directory:*

> **East Anglia Tourist Board.** Provides general tourist information and accommodation lists. Can provide the addresses and telephone numbers of local tourist information centers. Also publishes a path guide to the *Essex Way* (see *England's Long-Distance Footpaths*).
>
> **Cambridgeshire Area Ramblers' Association.** See note below.
>
> **Southern Area Ramblers' Association** (for Essex). See note below.
>
> **Norfolk Area Ramblers' Association.** See note below.
>
> **Suffolk Area Ramblers' Association.** See note below.

The secretaries of the RA Areas are volunteers who must answer correspondence during spare time in the evenings. Please respect this. Only make written enquiries and be sure to enclose a self-addressed envelope and sufficient international postal reply coupons to cover postage. The information you can obtain from the area secretaries includes:

1. Lists of the Area's guided walks and excursions.
2. Path guides published by the RA Area.
3. Addresses of affiliated clubs.

For more detailed enquiries, write to the head office of the Ramblers' Association.

Guidebooks

For the addresses of the following publishers and mail-order outlets, see the *Address Directory*.

Cambridgeshire

- *Country Walks around Cambridge* by the Cambridge RA Group.
- *Country Walks in Huntingdonshire* by the Huntingdon RA Group.
- *Country Walks* by the Peterborough RA Group.

Essex

- *London Countryside Walks for Motorists: North East* by William A. Bagley, Warne Gerrard Ltd.
- *Short Walks in West Essex* by Fred Matthews. Available from the author.
- *Short Walks in London's Epping Forest* by Fred Matthews. Available from the Southern Area Ramblers' Association.
- *Essex Way* by the East Anglia Tourist Board.

Norfolk

- *Six Walks in Ludham* by the Ludham Parish Council, Yarmouth.
- *Twenty North Norfolk Walks* by the North Norfolk District Council.
- *More Rambles in Norfolk* by "Rambler." Available from the Norfolk Area RA.

Suffolk

- *Walking around Hadleigh* by Alec O'Reilley. Available from Keith Avis.

Additional details on guidebooks to East Anglia, including their current prices, are contained in RA's *County Sheets—Cambridgeshire, Essex, Norfolk* and *Suffolk*, are available from the head office of the Ramblers' Association.

Areas of Outstanding Natural Beauty

Dedham Vale
A pastoral region full of charming villages. Covers 57 square kilometers (22 square miles) of the Constable Country in Essex and Suffolk.
Maps:
• Ordnance Survey 1:50,000, sheets 155, 168 and 169.
• Ordnance Survey 1:25,000, sheets TL-93, TM-03 and TM-13.
Guidebooks:
• None.
Further Information: Contact the East Anglia Tourist Board.

Norfolk Coast
A region of beaches, salt marsh and mud flats between Kings Lynn and Mundesley in northern Norfolk. Covers 451 square kilometers (174 square miles).
Maps:
• Ordnance Survey 1:50,000, sheets 131, 132, 133 and 134.
• Ordnance Survey 1:25,000, sheets TF-52, TF-62, TF-63, TF-64, TF-73, TF-74, TF-83, TF-84, TF-93, TF-94, TG-03, TG-04, TG-13, TG-14, TG-23/33, TG-24 and TG-42.
Guidebook:
• *Twenty North Norfolk Walks* by the North Norfolk District Council.
Further Information: Contact the East Anglia Tourist Board.

Suffolk Coast and Heaths
An area of wooded estuaries laced with creeks. Covers 391 square kilometers (151 square miles) of coast between Ipswich and Lowestoft.
Maps:
• Ordnance Survey 1:50,000, sheets 156 and 169.
• Ordnance Survey 1:25,000, sheets TM-13, TM-14, TM-23, TM-24, TM-25, TM-33, TM-34, TM-35, TM-44, TM-45, TM-46, TM-47, TM-48, TM-57 and TM-58.
Guidebooks:
• None.
Further Information: Contact the East Anglia Tourist Board.

Suggested Walks

The Essex Way. For details, see the section on *England's Long-Distance Footpaths*.

East Midlands

The East Midlands district is comprised of five counties: Derbyshire, Leicestershire, Lincolnshire, Northamptonshire and Nottinghamshire. It is a pleasant region with rolling hills and wooded valleys in the west and agricultural lands in the east. Scattered throughout the countryside are historic houses and castles, market towns and villages built of local stone. The opportunities for walking are numerous. Here is a brief breakdown:

Derbyshire: Many hill and valley footpaths and walks along quiet rivers. In the north is the Peak District National Park—indisputably the East Midlands' top walking area. The park contains the largest area of open land in Britain with access agreements as well as the Peakland Way and a sizable section of the Pennine Way. Around Castleton, there are numerous underground caverns, some of which are open to the public.

Leicestershire: In the east, footpaths wind through a rolling landscape with rural villages and thatched cottages of local stone. One of the best walking areas is the Charnwood Forest in the northwest, a woodland with rocky outcrops.

Lincolnshire: As a whole, this county has one of the lowest densities of footpaths in England. To the south and southeast are low-lying *fens,* wetlands that have been drained to yield fertile farmlands. These have few footpaths. But in the north and northeast, the farmland gives way to the chalk hills of the Lincolnshire Wolds, an Area of Outstanding Natural Beauty with many grassland paths, including the Viking Way.

Northamptonshire: The county's agricultural lands are laced with canals and waterways, many of which are bordered by stone-wall villages and steepled churches. Many canal towpaths can be walked, including the one along the Grand Union Canal. There is also good walking on footpaths in the Northampton uplands, south of Peterborough, as well as in the Nene Valley and its wooded tributaries.

Nottinghamshire: Home of D.H. Lawrence, Lord Byron and the legendary Robin Hood. Includes Sherwood Forest with its majestic oak trees, Clumber Park and Rufford Abbey—all good walking country.

Useful Addresses

See *Address Directory:*

> **East Midlands Tourist Board.** Provides general tourist information, accommodation lists and free information sheets on walking in the English Shires. Also can provide the addresses and telephone numbers of local tourist information centers.
>
> **Derbyshire Area Ramblers' Association.** See note below.
>
> **South Yorkshire and North East Derbyshire Area Ramblers' Association.** See note below.
>
> **East Midlands Area Ramblers' Association.** (Covers Leicestershire and Northamptonshire). See note below.
>
> **Lincolnshire and South Humberside Area Ramblers' Association.** See note below.
>
> **Nottinghamshire Area Ramblers' Association.** See note below.

The secretaries of the RA Areas are volunteers who must answer correspondence during spare time in the evenings. Please respect this. Only make written enquiries and be sure to enclose a self-addressed envelope and sufficient international postal reply coupons to cover postage. The information you can obtain from the area secretaries includes:

1. Lists of the Area's guided walks and excursions.
2. Path guides published by the RA Area.
3. Addresses of affiliated clubs.

For more detailed enquiries, write to the head office of the Ramblers' Association.

Guidebooks

For the addresses of the following publishers and mail-order outlets, see the *Address Directory.*

Derbyshire

- *Walking in Derbyshire, Walks in the Derbyshire Dales* and *Dovedale Guide.* All published by Derbyshire Countryside Ltd.
- *Derbyshire Trails* by John Merrill, Dalesman Publishing Company. (Recommended)
- *Walking in South Derbyshire* by John Merrill, Dalesman Publishing Company.

Leicestershire

- *More Walks in Leicestershire* by the Leicestershire Footpaths Association. Describes 22 circular walks. Available from the Leicester City Information Bureau.

Lincolnshire

- *Rambling in Lincolnshire* by Brian Dixon. Available from the Lincolnshire Area RA.
- *Walks around Grantham* and *Walks around Lincoln.* Both describe local walks up to 9.5 kilometers (6 miles) in length. Also available from the Lincolnshire Area RA.

Northamptonshire

- *The Grafton Way* and *The Knightley Way.* Both by the Northamptonshire County Council Leisure and Amenities Department. The guides describe two 19-kilometer (12-mile) waymarked footpaths that link up with the North Buckinghamshire Way (see *England's Long-Distance Footpaths.*
- *Waterside Walks in Northamptonshire* by Dave Goodwin. Available from J. Anderson.

Nottinghamshire

- *Walks in Nottinghamshire: Series 1* (14 walks) and *Series 2* (16 walks). Both published by the Nottinghamshire County Council.
- *Walks in Nottinghamshire:* 1) *Laxton, Moorhouse Hamlet, Laxton Circular,* 2) *Kneeton to East Bridgford over the Trent Hills,* 3) *Thurgaton and Halloughton,* 4) *The Dunham, Church Laneham, Laneham, Dunham Circular,* 5) *Maplebeck to Eakring, Circular over Mansey Common,* 6) *Lowdham, Woodborough, Epperstone,* and 7) *Ossington to Moorhouse.* Available from the Nottinghamshire County Council.
- *Walks around Ruddington, Nottinghamshire* by the Ruddington Footpaths Preservation Group.

- Many Parish Councils and local footpath societies publish guides. If you are visiting a small town or village, enquire at the local bookshops. The books normally cost only a few pence.

Additional details on guidebooks to the footpaths in the East Midlands are contained in the RA's *County Sheets—Derbyshire, Leicestershire, Lincolnshire, Northamptonshire* and *Nottinghamshire*, available from the head office of the RA.

Areas of Outstanding Natural Beauty

Lincolnshire Wolds
A region of valleys and undulating chalk hills. Covers 560 square kilometers (216 square miles) in northern and western Lincolnshire.
Maps:
- Ordnance Survey 1:50,000, sheets 113, 121 and 122.
- Ordnance Survey 1:25,000, sheets TA-10, TA-20, TF-09, TF-18, TF-27, TF-28, TF-29, TF-36, TF-37, TF-38, TF-39, TF-46 and TF-47.

Guidebooks:
- *The Viking Way* by the Lincolnshire and South Humberside Area RA.

Further Information: Contact the East Midlands Tourist Board.

Suggested Walks

The possibilities are numerous. And they all are pleasant. The best thing to do is to purchase a few of the guidebooks or—where guidebooks do not exist for the areas suggested at the beginning of this section—to look at the maps and make your own decision.

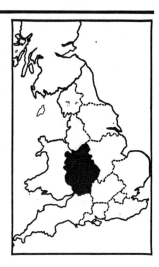

Heart of England

This region offers a wide scope of pleasant country walking. There is the Shakespeare country around Stratford-upon-Avon in Warwickshire with its half-timbered villages and thatched cottages, a rich farming region scattered with forests. In western Hereford and Worcester, the rolling red-earth countryside rises to the Black Mountains along the Welsh border, crossed in great loops by the deep-wooded banks of the Wye River. Here, you find fields of hops, fruit orchards and dairy farms, as well as the black-and-white buildings characteristic of the area. There is also the Forest of Dean, not far from the ruins of Tintern Abbey. And throughout Shropshire (Salop) there are many castles, reminders of border struggles.

Some of the choicest walking is in the designated Areas of Outstanding Natural Beauty—the Cotswolds, the Malvern Hills, Cannock Chase, the Wye Valley and the Shropshire Hills.

It is a lovely region. And well deserving of its name.

Useful Addresses

See *Address Directory:*

> **Heart of England Tourist Board.** Provides general tourist information and accommodation lists, plus a booklet on *Nature Trails and Wildlife Centres* and a fact sheet on *Town Trails.* Also can provide the addresses and telephone numbers of local tourist information centers.
>
> **Gloucestershire Ramblers' Association.** See note below.

Midland Area Ramblers' Association. (Covers the counties of Hereford and Worcester, Shropshire, Warwickshire, West Midlands and the southern half of Staffordshire.) See note below.

North Staffordshire Area Ramblers' Association. See note below.

The information you can obtain from the area secretaries includes:

1. Details on the Area's guided walks and excursions.
2. Path guides published by the RA Area.
3. Addresses of affiliated clubs.

Be sure to enclose a self-addressed envelope and sufficient international postal reply coupons to cover postage. For more detailed enquiries, write to the head office of the Ramblers' Association.

Guidebooks

Numerous guidebooks are available. Full details are given in the RA's *County Sheets—Gloucestershire, Herefordshire and Worcestershire, Shropshire, Staffordshire, Warwickshire* and *West Midlands,* available from the head office of the Ramblers' Association.

Areas of Outstanding Natural Beauty

Cannock Chase
A region of heathland and woods crossed by valleys. Some of the wilder parts are reserved solely for walkers and riders. Located near Stafford. Covers 67 square kilometers (26 square miles).
Maps:
• Ordnance Survey 1:50,000, sheet 127.
• Ordnance Survey 1:25,000, sheets SJ-81/91, SJ-92, SK-01 and SK-02.
Guidebooks:
• Contact the Staffordshire County Council Department in Stafford for details (see *Address Directory*).
Further Information: Contact the Heart of England Tourist Board.

The Cotswolds
A region of broad-backed hills cut in the south by deep wooded valleys. To the north and west, a steep scarp drops to the fertile, fruit-growing lands along the Severn and Avon rivers. Towns and villages are built with the warm honey-colored stone of the hills and capped with moss-covered roofs of Stonesfield slate. On the fringes of the Cotswolds are the cathedral cities of Gloucester and Oxford, the spas of Bath and Cheltenham and English country towns like Banbury, Evesham and Tewkesbury. Excellent walking country. Covers 1,508 square kilometers (582 square miles).

Maps:
- Ordnance Survey 1:50,000, sheets 150, 151, 163, 164, 172 and 173.
- Ordnance Survey 1:25,000, sheets SO-70, SO-80, SO-81, SO-90, SO-91, SO-92, SO-93, SO-94, SP-00, SP-01, SP-02, SP-03, SP-04/14, SP-10, SP-11, SP-12, SP-13, SP-20, SP-21, SP-22, SP-23, ST-66/76, ST-77, ST-78, ST-79, ST-87, ST-88, ST-98 and ST-99.
- *Ramblers Maps of the Cotswolds* (1:25,000): *No. 2 Cleeve Hill* and *No. 3 Birdlip*, available from Gloucestershire RA Services through Miss M.A. Brooks.

Guidebooks:
- *Cotswold Rambles* by P. Drinkwater and H. Hargreaves, Thornhill Press.
- *Discovering Walks on the Cotswolds* by R. Kershaw and B. Robson, Shire Publications.
- *Read about Walks on the Cotswolds.* Photo Precision Ltd.
- *Cotswold Walks for Motorists:* 1) *Northern Area* and 2) *Southern Area.* Both by Peter A. Price, Warne Gerrard Ltd.

Further Information: Contact the Heart of England Tourist Board.

Malvern Hills
A region of grass-covered hills between Great Malvern and Ledbury, with sweeping views over the surrounding countryside (you can often see the Welsh hills). Several summits exceed 300 meters (984 feet) in height. Covers 104 square kilometers (40 square miles). Recommended for a very pleasant day of walking.

Maps:
- Ordnance Survey 1:50,000, sheets 149 and 150.
- Ordnance Survey 1:25,000, sheets SO-73, SO-74 and SO-75.

Guidebook:
- *Country Walks: East Malvern Area* by the Malvern Hills District Footpath Society.

Further Information: Contact the Heart of England Tourist Board or the Malvern Hills District Footpath Society.

Shropshire Hills
Another hilly region, the Shropshire Hills rise to a height of nearly 550 meters (1,800 feet) along the Welsh border. Located south of Shrewsbury, a historic town with timbered houses and narrow lanes in a bend of the Severn River. Covers 777 square kilometers (300 square miles). The Stiperstones area is particularly recommended for walking.

Maps:
- Ordnance Survey 1:50,000, sheets 126 and 137.
- Ordnance Survey 1:25,000, sheets SO-38, SO-39, SO-48 and SO-49

Guidebook:
- *Church Stretton and South Shropshire Rambles* by Robert Smart. Available from the author.

Further Information: Contact the Heart of England Tourist Board.

The Wye Valley
A meandering river valley with deeply wooded banks, gorges and high limestone cliffs. Flows past the Forest of Dean, Tintern Abbey and small, historic riverbank towns with half-timbered buildings. Part of the river's course is followed by the Wye Valley Walk (details below). Covers 324 square kilometers (125 square miles).
Maps:
• Ordnance Survey 1:50,000, sheets 149, 161, 162, 171 and 172.
• Ordnance Survey 1:25,000 Outdoor Leisure Map, *Wye Valley and Forest of Dean.*
• *Wye Valley Footpath Maps* (1:25,000): *No. 1 Beachley to St. Briavels* (includes Tintern Abbey, Severn Bridge and Wye Valley Walk) and *No. 2 St. Briavels to Monmouth* (includes Wye Valley and Forest of Dean). Available from Gloucestershire RA Services through R.A. Long.
Guidebooks:
• *Dean Forest and Wye Valley,* Forestry Commission Guide, HMSO. Includes maps and footpath descriptions.
• *Inter-hostel routes:* 1) *Mitcheldean-Welsh Bicknor* and 2) *Welsh Bicknor-Mitcheldean.* Duplicated route descriptions with sketch maps. Available from Gloucestershire RA Services through Mr. R.A. Long.
• *Exploring the Wye Valley and Forest of Dean* by Roger Jones. Available from the author.
Further Information: Contact the Heart of England Tourist Board.

Suggested Walks

For starters, there is the Cotswold Way, the Staffordshire Way and the Sandstone Trail (see the section on *England's Long-Distance Footpaths*). In addition, there is:

In Shropshire: Stiperstones, the Long Mynd, the Wrekin and the Clee Hills.

In Staffordshire: Cannock Chase. Also the southern fringe of the Peak District (near Leek). Here, the Roaches (a rock-climbing edge) is particularly recommended.

The Wye Valley Walk: From Chepstow to Symond's Yat. Passes through Tintern and Monmouth (site of the only remaining fortified bridge in England). On the Wyndcliff, it climbs to a lookout known as Eagle's Nest, 213 meters (700 feet) above the river. **Length:** 35 kilometers (21.5 miles). **Walking Time:** 2 days. **Path Markings:** White arrows with orange dots. **Lodgings:** Available in Chepstow, Tintern and Monmouth.
Maps:
• Ordnance Survey 1:25,000 Outdoor Leisure Map, *Wye Valley and Forest of Dean.*

Guidebook:
• *Wye Valley Walk* (map cards) by the Gwent County Council. Available from the Gwent County Public Relations Officer.

Northumbria

Memories of the past haunt Northumbria. Castles abound, as do the ruins of ancient towers and hill forts, gaunt reminders of the centuries of battle and feud in this border region. There are Roman ruins—survey barracks, granaries, bath houses—and long, snaking sections of Hadrian's Wall. There are also prehistoric rock carvings, many of which are found in the remote uplands of the Cheviot Hills.

To the west are the rolling moorland fells of the Pennines, sparsely populated, swathed in heather and bracken, their vast vistas broken only by an isolated gray stone farmstead or flock of sheep. The region also includes the Border Forest Park; the Northumberland Coast, an Area of Outstanding Natural Beauty; and Northumberland National Park.

Some parts of the county of Durham are disfigured by coal mining, and there is extensive industrialization in the county of Tyne and Wear, but much of the north county is wild and lonely, crossed only by remote mountain tracks, an occasional stone village—and the reminders of the past.

Useful Addresses

See *Address Directory:*

Northumbria Tourist Board. Provides general tourist information and accommodation lists. Also can provide the addresses and telephone numbers of local tourist information centers.

Northern Area Ramblers' Association. Can provide information on guided walks and excursions. Also sells several footpath guides. For more detailed enquiries, please contact the head office of the Ramblers' Association.

Guidebooks

For the addresses of the following publishers and mail-order outlets, see the *Address Directory*.

Cleveland

• None.

Durham

• *Walking in Weardale* by T.R. Spedding, Dalesman Publishing Company.
• *Green Tracks and Heather Tracks* by Wade Balmain, F. Graham. Covers Cheviot, Cross Fell and North Yorks Moors in two volumes.

Northumberland

• *Ramblers' Cheviot, Ramblers' Tyneside, Ramblers' through Northumberland, Rambling along the Roman Wall* and *The Pennine Way in Northumberland*. All by the Northern Area Ramblers' Association. Available from the RA Area Secretary.
• *Let's Go for a Walk in Stocksfield* by M. Burke. Available from the author.
• *North Ramble Land* by Sidney Fisher. Available from the author.

Additional details on guidebooks, including their prices and the cost of postage, are included in the RA's *County Sheets,* available from the head office of the Ramblers' Association.

Areas of Outstanding Natural Beauty

The Northumberland Coast
Ruined priories, mist-laden castles and weed-strewn rocky outcrops swept by the sea line this coast. Includes several picturesque fishing villages, Holy Island and the Farne Islands. Covers 130 square kilometers (50 square miles).
Maps:
• Ordnance Survey 1:50,000, sheets 75 and 81.

- Ordnance Survey 1:25,000, sheets NU-04, NU-05, NU-13, NU-14, NU-20, NU-21, NU-22 and NU-23.
Guidebooks:
- None.
Further Information: Contact the Northumbria Tourist Board.

Suggested Walks

For starters:

Hadrian's Wall: From Sewingshields Farm to Gilsland. **Walking Time:** 2 days. **Path Markings:** Yellow arrows.
Lodging: Twice Brewed Hotel on the Military Road. Also, the Once Brewed youth hostel (next door to Twice Brewed).
Maps:
- Ordnance Survey 1:50,000, sheets 86 and 87.
Guidebook:
- *Rambling along the Roman Wall* by the Northern Area RA.
Further Information: See full description in the section on *England's Long-Distance Footpaths.*

Also, Northumberland National Park (see *England's National Parks*) and the Coast to Coast Walk (see *England's Long-Distance Footpaths*).

North West England

This region includes the counties of Lancashire, Greater Manchester, Merseyside and Cheshire, as well as the port city of Liverpool and the city of Manchester, one of the centers where the Industrial Revolution began. The North West is rich with industrial history, as well as with some of the scars it left behind. It is still an industrial center, but outside the cities, footpaths can be found in farmlands, a corner of the Peak District National Park and the Forest of Bowland. There is also good walking country in the Pennines and on the edges of many of the smaller industrial towns. Walking clubs in the area are numerous and active (many are listed in the *RA's County Sheets*), and they will make you welcome.

Useful Addresses

See *Address Directory:*

> **North West Tourist Board.** Provides general tourist information and accommodation lists. Also can provide the addresses and telephone numbers of local tourist information centers. Written and telephone enquiries only.
>
> **Lancashire North-East Area Ramblers' Association.** See note below.
>
> **Manchester Area Ramblers' Association.** See note below.
>
> **Merseyside Area Ramblers' Association.** See note below.
>
> **Lake District Area Ramblers' Association.** Covers part of Lancashire as well as Cumbria.

The secretaries of the RA Areas can provide you with:

1. Lists of the Area's guided walks and excursions.
2. Path guides published by the RA Area.
3. Addresses of affiliated clubs.

Enquiries should be accompanied by a self-addressed envelope and sufficient international postal reply coupons to cover postage. For more detailed enquiries, write to the head office of the Ramblers' Association.

Guidebooks

For the addresses of the following publishers and mail-order outlets, see the *Address Directory*.

Cheshire

- *Walking in Cheshire* by Jack Baker and Jack Hanmer, Dalesman Publishing Company.
- *Cheshire Walks for Motorists* by Peter A. Price, Warne Gerrard Ltd.
- *Twenty Walks in Mid-Cheshire* by "Rambler" of the Liverpool Echo. Available from Philip, Son & Nephew Ltd.
- *Gritstone Trail* by the Cheshire County Council.

Greater Manchester

- *Walks around the Wigan Metro* by and available from K.A. Johnson.
- *Over the Five Barred Gate* (Clayton, Whittle and Brindle area) by G.A. Birtill, Chorley Guardian.

Lancashire

- *Walking in Central Lancashire* by Cyril Spiby, Dalesman Publishing Company. Available from the Lake District Area Ramblers' Association.
- *The Round Preston Walk* by Ian Brodie, also available from the Lake District Area Ramblers' Association.
- *Walking around Preston* by Ian Brodie and Peter Davy, Dalesman Publishing Company.
- *Green Pastures* (Leyland area), *Hikers' Book of Rivington*, *Enchanted Hills* (Rivington area), *Follow Any Stream* (Euxton, Eccleston and Mawdesley areas), *Let's Take a Walk* (Chorley, Euxton and Whittle areas), *Heather in My Hat* (Rivington area) and *Towpath Trek* (from Cherry Tree, Blackburn to Tarleton by Leeds and Liverpool Canal). All by G.A. Birtill, Chorley Guardian.

Merseyside

- *Ten Walks for Motorists in the Wirral* by "Greenways," Belvidere Press.

Additional details on guidebooks to the North West, including their prices and the cost of postage, are contained in the RA's *County Sheets,* available from the head office of the Rambler's Association.

Areas of Outstanding Natural Beauty

Forest and Trough of Bowland
A region of open moorland between Carnforth, Settle and Clitheroe. Covers 803 square kilometers (310 square miles).
Maps:
- Ordnance Survey 1:50,000, sheets 97, 98 and 103.
- Ordnance Survey 1:25,000, sheets SD-53, SD-54, SD-55, SD-56, SD-57, SD-63, SD-64, SD-65, SD-66, SD-74, SD-75, SD-83, SD-84, SD-85 and SD-86.
Guidebook:
- *Access Areas in the Forest of Bowland* (leaflet) by the Lancashire County Council.
Further Information: Contact the North West Tourist Board.

South East England

The South East is ringed by gentle, humpbacked hills, scattered woodland and a white-cliffed seascape. Between its two ranges of chalk hills—the North and South Downs—is the Kent and Sussex Weald, a rich farming country with small Georgian towns and Tudor villages. Along the coast, there are elegant seaside resorts and small, half-timbered villages with a history of smuggling.

Footpaths are numerous, winding through the wooded hills and gorse-covered heaths of Surrey, past the cathedral city of Canterbury and to the white cliffs of Dover. Three of the South East's four Areas of Outstanding Natural Beauty are traversed by long-distance footpaths. There are also numerous nature reserves and more than 4,452 hectares (11,000 acres) of National Trust Lands—including areas such as Box Hill, Frensham, Hindhead, Headly Heath and Leith Hill—in which you can walk.

Useful Addresses

See *Address Directory:*

South East England Tourist Board. Provides general tourist information and accommodation lists. Also can provide the addresses and telephone numbers of local tourist information centers. Written and telephone enquiries only.

Southern Area Ramblers' Association. (Covers Kent and Surrey.)

Sussex Area Ramblers' Association. Can provide lists of the Area's guided walks and excursions, addresses of affiliated clubs and path guides published by the RA Area. Written enquiries only.

Guidebooks

More than 80 are available. Full details are contained in the RA's *County Sheets—Kent, Surrey* and *Sussex,* available from the head office of the Ramblers' Association. Another comprehensive list is:

• *Keys to the Kent & Sussex Countryside: A Map and Book List for Walkers and Riders* by the Kent Rights of Way Council. Available from Kent County Council, County Secretary's Department. Gives details on more than 50 guidebooks. Also lists the names and sheet numbers of maps covering Kent and Sussex. Gives the addresses of outlets where the books and maps can be obtained, as well as the names and addresses of more than 20 walking groups in the two counties. (Recommended)

Areas of Outstanding Natural Beauty

Chichester Harbour
A large semi-enclosed area of harbour and estuary, in parts still relatively wild. Covers 75 square kilometers (29 square miles).
Maps:
• Ordnance Survey 1:50,000, sheet 197.
• Ordnance Survey 1:25,000, sheets SU-30, SU-40, SU-70, SU-80,

SZ-29, SZ-39, SZ-49, SZ-79 and SZ-89.

Guidebooks:
- *A Ramblers' Atlas of West Sussex: Vol. 2 Chichester Area* by J.C. Rammell and L.H.H. Rush. Available from the Sussex Area Ramblers' Association.

Further Information: Contact the South East England Tourist Board.

Kent Downs

A wide curve of chalk hills stretching from the Surrey Hills near Westerham to the white cliffs of Dover and Folkestone. Traversed by the North Downs Way and Pilgrims' Way (see the section on *England's Long-Distance Footpaths*). Provides fine views over the Kent and Sussex Weald. Covers 845 square kilometers (326 square miles).

Maps:
- Ordnance Survey 1:50,000, sheets 178, 179, 187, 188 and 199.
- Ordnance Survey 1:25,000, sheets TQ-44, TQ-45/55, TQ-46/56, TQ-54, TQ-64/74, TQ-65/75, TQ-66/76, TQ-67/66, TQ-85/95, TQ-86/96, TR-03, TR-04, TR-05, TR-13, TR-14, TR-15, TR-23, TR-24 and TR-25.

Guidebooks:
- *London Countryside Walks for Motorists: South East* by William A. Bagley, Warne Gerrard Ltd.
- *Walks in the Hills of Kent* by Janet Spayne and Audrey Krynski, Spurbooks Ltd.
- *Country Walks around Sevenoaks* and *More Country Walks around Sevenoaks*. Both by R.H. Oakely. Available from the Sevenoaks Bookshop.
- *Walks on the North Downs:* 1) *Hollingbourne to the Medway* by Cyril Davis and 2) *Doddington and Lenham* by Alan Smith, editor. Both available from the Swale Footpaths Group.

Further Information: Contact the South East England Tourist Board.

Surrey Hills

A popular area for Londoners, the Surrey Hills sweep across Surrey from Titsey Hill on the Kent border to Haslemere. At Leith Hill, they reach the highest point in the South East—294 meters (965 feet). Much of the land is owned by the National Trust, hence there is good access to popular areas such as Ranmore Common, the Devil's Punch Bowl, Newlands Corner and Box Hill. Covers 415 square kilometers (160 square miles).

Maps:
- Ordnance Survey 1:50,000, sheets 186 and 187.
- Ordnance Survey 1:25,000, sheets SU-83, SU-84, SU-93, SU-94, TQ-03, TQ-04, TQ-05, TQ-14, TQ-15, TQ-25, TQ-35 and TQ-45/55.

Guidebooks:
- *London Countryside Walks for Motorists: South West* by William A. Bagley, Warne Gerrard Ltd.
- *Walks in the Surrey Hills* by Janet Spayne and Audrey Krynski, Spurbooks Ltd.

- *Walks in Surrey* by Geoffrey Hollis, Surrey Daily Advertiser. Also available from the Southern Area Ramblers' Association.

Further Information: Contact the South East England Tourist Board.

Sussex Downs

A range of whale-backed hills, cut by several small rivers. The downs are covered with short springy turf in the east, and wooded in the west. They stretch from Petersfield to the 152-meter (500-foot) high cliffs at Beachy Head, near Eastbourne, and are traversed by the South Downs Way. The region covers 982 square kilometers (379 square miles).

Maps:
- Ordnance Survey 1:50,000, sheets 197, 198 and 199.
- Ordnance Survey 1:25,000, sheets SU-70, SU-71, SU-72, SU-81, SU-82, SU-83, SU-90, SU-91, SU-92, SU-93, TQ-00, TQ-01, TQ-02, TQ-10, TQ-11, TQ-20/30, TQ-21/31, TQ-40, TQ-41, TQ-50 and TV-59.

Guidebooks:
- *Along the South Downs Way* and *On Foot in East Sussex*. Both by the Eastbourne Rambling Club.
- *South Sussex Walks* by Lord Teviot and M.B. Quinion, BBC Publications.
- *A Rambler' Atlas of West Sussex: Vol. 1 Midhurst Area* and *Vol. 3 Pulborough Area*. Both by J.C. Rammell and L.H.H. Rush. Available from the Sussex Area Ramblers' Association.
- *Adur to Arun* by H.L. Reeves, Optimus Books.
- *Discovering Walks in West Sussex* by T.W. Hendrick, Shire Publications. Also available from the Sussex Area Ramblers' Association.

Suggested Walks

The possibilities are numerous. For starters, however, you might try the North Downs Way, the South Downs Way, the Weald Way and the Wey-South Path (see the section on *England's Long-Distance Footpaths*).

Southern England

This region encompasses the counties of Hampshire and Dorset as well as the Isle of Wight, first colonized by the Romans in A.D. 43. Legend, true or almost true, has played a large role in shaping the area's historical backdrop. Literary associations are also strong. Jane Austen wrote novels in her cottage at Chawton in Hampshire. Dickens was born in Portsmouth. Keats settled for the mild climate of Shanklin on the Isle of Wight. And Thomas Hardy wrote about such places as Knowlsea (Swanage) and Budmouth (Weymouth), to name a few.

Hampshire is a county of woodland, babbling brooks, slow meandering rivers and green open countryside scattered with thatched cottages of flint and chalk. At its center is the country town of Winchester, the first capital of England, where Alfred the Great had his court. Nearby is the New Forest, with its majestic stands of Douglas fir and oak trees, expanses of heath and Bronze Age earthworks.

Along the Dorset coast are bustling seaside resorts, shingle banks and sandy coves ringed by cliffs. Inland, the countryside is rolling and strewn with medieval abbeys, Georgian mansions, cathedrals and Neolithic burial mounds.

Long-distance footpaths include the Isle of Wight Coastal Path and the Dorset Coast Path (see the section on *England's Long-Distance Footpaths*). There are also many country walks described in leaflets available from local tourist information centers.

Useful Addresses

See *Address Directory*:

Southern Tourist Board. Provides general tourist information and accommodation lists. Also can provide the addresses and telephone numbers of local tourist information centers.

Dorset Area Ramblers' Association. See note below.

Hampshire Area Ramblers' Association. See note below.

Isle of Wight Area Ramblers' Association. See note below.

The Area secretaries of the Ramblers' Association can provide:

1. Lists of the Area's guided walks and excursions.
2. Path guides published by the RA Area.
3. Addresses of affiliated clubs.

Enquiries should be accompanied by a self-addressed envelope and sufficient international postal reply coupons to cover postage. For more detailed enquiries, write to the head office of the Ramblers' Association.

Guidebooks

Dorset

- *Rambles in Dorset* by Western National Omnibus Company.
- *Purbeck Paths, Vols. 1 and 2,* by M. Bibby. Available from Mr. F. Baxter.
- Also, see the guidebooks listed for the Dorset Coast Path in the section on *England's Long-Distance Footpaths.*

Hampshire

- *Walks in East Hampshire* by Brenda M. Parker, Paul Cave Publications.
- *Explore the New Forest,* Forestry Commission Guide, HMSO.
- *Read about Walks in the New Forest,* Photo Precision Ltd.
- *Discovering Walks in the New Forest* by Derrick Knowlton, Shire Publications Ltd.
- *Walks in the New Forest* by W. Wenban-Smith, Spurbooks Ltd.
- *New Forest Walks* by Anne-Marie Edwards, BBC Publications.
- *Ten Walks in and around Winchester* by the Winchester RA Group.

Isle of Wight

- Walk Guides: *Bembridge Trail, Hamstead Trail, Nunwell Trail, Shepherds Trail, Stenbury Trail, Tennyson Trail, Worsely Trail* and *Isle of Wight Coastal Path* (leaflets). All available from the County Surveyor and Planning Officer, Isle of Wight.

- *Russel's Walks and Rambles in the Isle of Wight,* available from W.J. Nigh & Sons, Publishers.

Additional details on guidebooks to Southern England, including their current prices, are contained in the RA's *County Sheets,* available from the head office of the Ramblers' Association.

Areas of Outstanding Natural Beauty

Dorset
A region of coastal cliffs and downland with extensive prehistoric remains. Covers more than one-third of Dorset and most of its coast—1,036 square kilometers (400 square miles). In some areas there are occasional military maneuvers. You should check on this before you set out.
Maps:
- Ordnance Survey 1:50,000, sheets 193, 194 and 195.
- Ordnance Survey 1:25,000, sheets SY-29/39, SY-49, SY-58/68, SY-59, SY-67, SY-68/78, SY-69, SY-79, SY-88/98, SY-97, SZ-07 and SZ-08.
Guidebook:
- *Rambles in Dorset* by Western Omnibus Company.
Further Information: Contact the Southern Tourist Board.

East Hampshire
A region of hills and rolling farmland between Winchester and Petersfield on the Hampshire and Sussex border. Covers 391 square kilometers (151 square miles).
Maps:
- Ordnance Survey 1:50,000, sheets 185, 186, 196 and 197.
- Ordnance Survey 1:25,000, sheets SU-41/51, SU-42/52, SU-53, SU-61, SU-62, SU-63, SU-71, SU-72, SU-73 and SU-83.
Guidebook:
- *Walks in East Hampshire* by Brenda M. Parker, Paul Cave Publications.
Further Information: Contact the Southern Tourist Board.

Isle of Wight
A region of rolling downland, beach, cliff and valley. Many footpaths with views to the sea. Covers nearly two-thirds of the island—189 square kilometers (73 square miles).
Maps:
- Ordnance Survey 1:50,000, sheet 196.
- Ordnance Survey 1:25,000, sheets SZ-28, SZ-38, SZ-48, SZ-49, SZ-57, SZ-58, SZ-59 and SZ-68.
Guidebooks:
- See list for *Isle of Wight,* above.
Further Information: Contact the Southern Tourist Board.

South Hampshire Coast
A coastal region and sailing center. Abuts the southern edge of the New Forest. Covers 78 square kilometers (30 square miles).
Maps:
• Ordnance Survey 1:50,000, sheets 195 and 196.
• Ordnance Survey 1:25,000, sheets SU-20/30, SU-40/50, SZ-29 and SZ-39.
Guidebooks:
• None.
Further Information: Contact the Southern Tourist Board.

Suggested Walks

Dorset Coast Path and Isle of Wight Coastal Path (see the section on *England's Long-Distance Footpaths*).

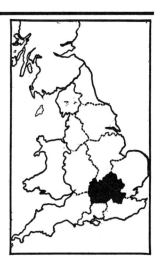

Thames & Chilterns

This region includes the city of London and the countryside to the north and west—the counties of Bedfordshire, Berkshire, Buckinghamshire, Hertfordshire and Oxfordshire. It is an area of vales and valleys and sweeping downlands rich in history and literary associations.

Footpaths are practically everywhere, crossing gentle hills, leading past ponds and greens, and into the shade of peaceful dells. They take you down a lane to the cottage where Milton wrote the last part of *Paradise Lost*, through the Chequers estate (the official country home of prime ministers) and over the ground Disraeli strode.

To the west of London, the beech-covered Chiltern Hills rise gently from the London Basin, then drop sharply to the rich farmland of the Vale of Aylesbury. Farther west are the Cotswolds, with their honey-stone villages, moss-covered roofs and village greens. To the north is the remote moorland of Otmoor, the Vale of Aylesbury and the watermills and windmills of Bedfordshire. There is also the Thames Valley, home of royalty, and St. Albans which, like Verulamium, was one of the Roman Empire's leading cities.

There are towpaths that can be walked along the Kennet and Avon Canal, Oxford Canal, Grand Union Canal and Lee and Stort Navigation. And everywhere: castles and abbeys, Roman ruins, prehistoric remains and small, centuries-old thatched cottages.

Useful Addresses

See *Address Directory:*

> **Thames and Chilterns Tourist Board.** Provides general tourist information and accommodation lists. Also can provide the addresses and telephone numbers of local tourist information centers.
>
> **The Chiltern Society.** An extremely active footpath society—and very helpful to foreign walkers. Oversees footpaths in the Chilterns Area of Outstanding Natural Beauty. New members welcome.
>
> **Southern Area Ramblers' Association.** (Covers Bedfordshire, Berkshire, Buckinghamshire and Hertfordshire). See note below.
>
> **Oxfordshire Area Ramblers' Association.** See note below.

The Area secretaries of the Ramblers' Association can provide:

1. Lists of the Area's guided walks and excursions.
2. Path guides published by the RA Area.
3. Addresses of affiliated clubs.

Enquiries should be accompanied by a self-addressed envelope and sufficient international postal reply coupons to cover postage. For more detailed enquiries, write to the head office of the Ramblers' Association.

Guidebooks

Numerous guidebooks and local footpath maps are available. Full details are given in the RA's *County Sheets.*

A few selected guides of use include:

Berkshire

- *Walks in Berkshire* by Vera Burden, Spurbooks Ltd.
- *Walks around the Downs* by Roy Chapman, Countryside Books.

Buckinghamshire

- *Discovering Walks in Buckinghamshire* by Ronald Pigram, Shire Publications.
- *On Foot in the Vale of Aylesbury* by Peter and Diana Gulland, available from the Southern Area Ramblers' Association.

Hertfordshire

- *Footpath Walks in Mid-Hertfordshire for Motorists* by the Mid-Herts Footpath Society.
- *Footpath Walks around St. Albans* by the St. Albans and District Footpath Society.

Oxfordshire

- *Walks in Oxfordshire* by Nigel Hammond, Spurbooks Ltd.
- *Walking around Oxford* by the Oxford Fieldpaths Society, Oxford Illustrated Press.

Around London—General

- *Country Walks* by London Transport. Can be bought at Underground stations, news agents and bookshops in London.
- *Short Walks in London's Epping Forest* by F. Matthews and H. Bitten. Available from F. Matthews.
- *London Countryside Walks for Motorists: 1) North East, 2) North West, 3) South East* and *4) South West*. All by William A. Bagley, Warne Gerrard Ltd.

Areas of Outstanding Natural Beauty

The Chilterns
A region of chalk hills with stately beech woods, picturesque villages and wide views over the farmland to the north. Easily accessible from London. Excellent walking country. Many paths can be muddy, so a pair of good boots and gaiters are necessary. Covers 801 square kilometers (309 square miles).
Maps:
- Ordnance Survey 1:50,000, sheets 165, 166 and 175.

- Chiltern Society Footpath Maps 1:25,000, *Marlow, Henley NW, Wendover, Henley SW, Sarratt and Chipperfield, The Penn Country, Wycombe NW, Chartridge, The Hampden Country,* and *Hambledon Valley.* All available from Shire Publications.

Guidebooks:
- *Discovering Walks in the Chilterns* by Ronald Pigam, Shire Publications.
- *Walks along the Ridgeway* by Elizabeth Cull, Spurbooks Ltd.

Further Information: Contact The Chiltern Society.

North Wessex Downs
A large, unspoiled tract of chalk downland south of Oxford. Includes some of the most important prehistoric sites in England. Good walking country. Covers 1,751 square kilometers (676 square miles).

Maps:
- Ordnance Survey 1:50,000, sheets 173, 174, 184 and 185.
- Ordnance Survey 1:25,000, sheets ST-96, SU-05, SU-06, SU-07, SU-15, SU-16, SU-17, SU-18, SU-25, SU-26, SU-27, SU-28, SU-34, SU-35, SU-36, SU-37, SU-38, SU-44, SU-45, SU-46, SU-48/58, SU-54, SU-55, SU-56, SU-57, SU-59, SU-66 and SU-77.

Guidebooks:
- *Walks around the Downs* by Roy Chapman, Countryside Books.
- *Walks along the Ridgeway* by Elizabeth Cull, Spurbooks Ltd.

Further Information: Contact the Thames and Chilterns Tourist Board.

Suggested Walks

The possibilities are numerous. Long-distance paths in the area include the North Buckinghamshire Way, the Oxfordshire Way, the Ridgeway Path and the London Countryway (see the section on *England's Long-Distance Footpaths*). Beyond that, refer to the guidebooks above.

The West Country

The West Country has the longest coastline of any region in England. From the Severn Estuary, it stretches for nearly 1,050 kilometers (650 miles) around Land's End to Poole Harbour, presenting the walker with an ever-changing panorama of rugged headlands, sandy coves, pebble ridges and lowland marshes. The region also includes two of England's national parks—Dartmoor and Exmoor—six Areas of Outstanding Natural Beauty and all or part of four long-distance footpaths. In addition, there are numerous country parks, nature reserves and National Trust lands with footpaths.

The West Country encompasses five counties—Avon, Cornwall, Devon, Somerset, Wiltshire—and a part of a sixth, Dorset. The county of Avon stretches north and south from the River Avon—from the Severn Estuary eastwards to the Cotswolds and from the Mendip Hills north to the vale of Berkeley. Within these boundaries are two ancient cities—Bristol and Bath—and portions of two Areas of Outstanding Natural Beauty—the Cotswolds and the Mendip Hills.

Cornwall is an ancient Celtic land with a coastline of soaring cliffs and clifftop castles to the north, and a coastline of wooded estuaries, sheltered coves, small fishing ports and popular resorts to the south.

Devon also has two contrasting coastlines, plus quiet villages of cob and thatch, the historic city of Exeter and a host of bustling country towns, as well as the wild open spaces of the two national parks.

Somerset includes a portion of the heather-covered heights of Exmoor, the sea-level marshes of Sedgemoor and a peaceful countryside of thatched cottages, stately homes and romantic legends. The south of the county is a land of rolling countryside, legendary site of Arthur's Camelot and of Glastonbury, the mythical island of *Avalon*, burial place of Arthur.

To the east are the woods and bracken covered slopes of the Quantocks and, in the north, the limestone heights of the Mendip Hills.

Wiltshire is a rural, inland county. From the Thames-side meadows in the north, hill and vale stretch south. Here, crystalline chalk streams flow through verdant valleys and, on the Salisbury Plain, cloud shadows drift over expanses of rolling corn fields. At every turn you see the works of prehistoric man—Yarnbury Castle, Bratton Castle and, the greatest of all, the Bronze Age Circle of standing stones at Stonehenge.

It is an ideal spot for a walking holiday. But if you go in summer, be sure to book your accommodation well in advance. Also, in Wiltshire you should check on current military maneuvers—which are often intense, especially on the Salisbury Plain—and choose your walking areas accordingly.

Useful Addresses

See *Address Directory:*

> **West Country Tourist Board.** Provides general tourist information and accommodation lists. Also can provide the addresses and telephone numbers of local tourist information centers.
>
> **The South West Way Association.** See note below.
>
> **Avon Area Ramblers' Association.** See note below.
>
> **Cornwall Area Ramblers' Association.** See note below.
>
> **Devon Area Ramblers' Association.** See note below.
>
> **Somerset Area Ramblers' Association.** See note below.
>
> **Wiltshire Area Ramblers' Association.** See note below.

The association secretaries can provide:

1. Lists of guided walks and excursions.
2. Path guides published by the association.
3. Addresses of affiliated clubs.

Enquiries should be accompanied by a self-addressed envelope and sufficient international postal reply coupons to cover postage. For more detailed enquiries, write to the head office of the Ramblers' Association.

Guidebooks

There are nearly 80 guidebooks to the footpaths in the West Country. Full details are given in the RA's *County Sheets,* available from the head office of the Ramblers' Association.

Areas of Outstanding Natural Beauty

Cornwall

Encompasses a large portion of the Cornwall coast. Includes the Cornwall Coast Path (see the section on *England's Long-Distance Footpaths*). Covers 933 square kilometers (360 square miles).

Maps:
- Ordnance Survey 1:50,000, sheets 190, 200, 201, 203 and 204.
- Ordnance Survey 1:25,000, sheets SS-20/30, SS-21/31, SW-32/42, SW-33, SW-43, SW-52, SW-53, SW-54, SW-61, SW-62, SW-64, SW-71, SW-72, SW-73, SW-74, SW-75, SW-83, SW-84, SW-86, SW-87, SW-93, SW-94, SW-97, SX-04, SX-05, SX-07, SX-08, SX-15, SX-16, SX-17, SX-18, SX-19, SX-25, SX-26, SX-27, SX-28/38, SX-29/39, SX-35 and SX-45.

Guidebooks:
- *Rambles in West Cornwall* and *Rambles in South Devon and East Cornwall*. Both by Western National Omnibus Company.
- *Walks in West Cornwall: Penzance and St. Ives* by Winifred M. White, West Cornwall Footpaths Preservation Society.
- *Cornish Walks:* 1) *Around Tregony,* 2) *Harrowbeer and Metherell,* and 3) *St. Michaels Mount.* All by Cornwall Federation of Womens' Institutes.
- Route Descriptions: 1) *St. Gluvias Church and Mylor Bridge,* 2) *Burdock Church,* 3) *Mabe Village,* 4) *Mabe Church,* 5) *Looe* and 6) *Boscawen Park,* Truro. All by Miss W. Weston. Available from the author.
- Also, see the guidebooks for the North and South Cornwall Coast Paths in the section on *England's Long-Distance Footpaths*.

Further Information: Contact the West Country Tourist Board.

East Devon

A region of coastline with red sandstone cliffs and rolling farmland with many charming villages. Covers 267 square kilometers (103 square miles).

Maps:
- Ordnance Survey 1:50,000, sheets 192 and 193.
- Ordnance Survey 1:25,000, sheets ST-00/10, ST-01/11, SY-08/18, SY-09/19, SY-28 and SY-29/39.

Guidebooks:
- *Walks in Devon* by Christina Green, Spurbooks Ltd.

Further Information: Contact the West Country Tourist Board.

Mendip Hills

A region of limestone hills, some more than 300 meters (984 feet) in height, with extensive views over Bristol Channel. Includes Wookey Hole and Cheddar Gorge, part of a large cave system for which the area is noted. Located between Weston-super-Mare and Wells in the counties of Avon and Somerset. Covers 202 square kilometers (78 square miles).

Maps:
- Ordnance Survey 1:50,000, sheet 182.
- Ordnance Survey 1:25,000, sheets ST-35, ST-44/54, ST-45, ST-55 and ST-56.

Guidebooks:
- None.

Further Information: Contact the West Country Tourist Board.

North Devon

A region of rugged coastline with high cliffs. Includes all of the north Devon coast. Covers 171 square kilometers (66 square miles).

Maps:
- Ordnance Survey 1:50,000, sheets 180 and 190.
- Ordnance Survey 1:25,000, sheets SS-21/31, SS-22/32, SS-42/52, SS-43/53, SS-44/54 and SS-64.

Guidebooks:
- *Rambles in North Devon* by Western National Omnibus Company.
- *Walks around Lynton and Lynmouth* by Lyn Publicity Association.
- *Coastal Rambles* by North Devon Printing Works.
- Also, see the guidebooks for the North Devon Coast Path in the section on *England's Long-Distance Footpaths*.

Further Information: Contact the West Country Tourist Board.

Quantock Hills

A region of wooded valleys and grass-covered hills between the port of Watchet (from which Coleridge's Ancient Mariner sailed) and the Vale of Taunton Deane. Covers 98 square kilometers (38 square miles).

Maps:
- Ordnance Survey 1:50,000, sheet 181, 182 and 193.
- Ordnance Survey 1:25,000, sheets ST-04, ST-12, ST-13, ST-14, ST-22 and ST-23.

Guidebooks:
- *Rambles in West Somerset and on Exmoor* by Western National Omnibus Company.

Further Information: Contact the West Country Tourist Board.

South Devon

A region of coastal cliffs, beaches, estuaries and deep inlets located between Plymouth and Torbay. A popular summer resort area. Covers 332 square kilometers (128 square miles).

Maps:
- Ordnance Survey 1:50,000, sheets 201 and 202.
- Ordnance Survey 1:25,000, sheets SX-45, SX-54, SX-55, SX-63/73, SX-64, SX-65/75, SX-74, SX-83, SX-84/94 and SX-85/95.

Guidebooks:
- *Read about Walks in South Devon,* Photo Precision.
- *Rambles in South Devon and East Cornwall* and *Rambles in Torbay and District.* Both by Western National Omnibus Company.

- *Torbay Coast Path* by A.S. Kingdon, Torbay Leisure Services Ltd.
- Also, see the guidebooks for the South Devon Coast Path in the section on *England's Long-Distance Footpaths.*

Suggested Walks

Many walks are possible along the various sections of the South West Peninsula Coast Path—either for a continuous walking holiday or for a day's ramble. Another long-distance path in the area is the Two Moors Way. Portions of the Cotswold Way and Ridgeway Path also extend into the West Country. All are highly recommended. For details, see the section on *England's Long-Distance Footpaths.*

Many paths can be muddy, so a pair of good boots and gaiters are necessary. It is also best to avoid summer when the weather is lovely, but crowds can overwhelm the area. The best times for walking are in the spring and autumn.

Yorkshire & Humberside

North Yorkshire is England's largest county—8,288 square kilometers (3,200 square miles). Together with the counties of West Yorkshire, South Yorkshire and Humberside, it encompasses a region of stunning contrast. Along the coast are precipitous chalk cliffs, deeply indented bays and bluff promontories that rise more than 180 meters (590 feet) above the sea. Inland, there are old country boroughs, small villages and hamlets, as well as rolling pastureland, craggy limestone dales and wild, windswept moors. There is the medieval city of York, with its timber-framed brick buildings, and Sheffield, an important steel-making center.

On the North York Moors, ancient stone crosses stand like solitary sentinels above peat bog and heather, and sheep roam wild and free. Farmsteads are few and walls rare. You are completely exposed—surrounded by total desolation—an eerie feeling when the sudden mists, for which the area is noted, descend. Suitable clothing, maps and a compass are essential.

The Yorkshire Dales appear more tame, with sheep grazing on grassy hills, but weather conditions can be just as severe, especially in winter. Here, as in the Lake District, hill, valley and waterfall become fell, dale and force—the *fjell, dal* and *foss* of the Scandinavian settlers who came to this region centuries ago. This is limestone country—an area of dramatic white pinnacles, potholes, gorges and waterfalls. In West Yorkshire, there are steep, wooded valleys, ruined abbeys and crooked streets of stone-built houses. And south of Sheffield, a corner of the Peak District National Park spills into South Yorkshire.

Long-distance footpaths are numerous. There are eight—the Cleveland Way, Coast to Coast Walk, Crosses Walk, Dales Way, Lyke Wake Walk, White Rose Walk and Wolds Way, plus a portion of the Pennine Way. In addition, there are many short, interconnecting local paths, many of which are located in Yorkshire's two national parks.

Useful Addresses

See *Address Directory:*

Yorkshire and Humberside Tourist Board. Provides general tourist information and accommodation lists. Also can provide the addresses and telephone numbers of local tourist information centers. Written and telephone enquiries only.

East Yorkshire and Derwent Area Ramblers' Association. (Covers the northern portion of Humberside and part of North Yorkshire.) See note below.

North Yorkshire and South Durham Area Ramblers' Association. See note below.

West Riding Area Ramblers' Association. See note below.

South Yorkshire and North East Derbyshire Area Ramblers' Association. See note below.

The Area secretaries of the Ramblers' Association can provide:

1. Lists of the Area's guided walks and excursions.
2. Path guides published by the RA Area.
3. Addresses of affiliated clubs.

Enquiries should be accompanied by a self-addressed envelope and sufficient international postal reply coupons to cover postage. For more detailed enquiries, write to the head office of the Ramblers' Association.

Guidebooks

A few of the guides available include:

North Yorkshire

- *Rambles in the Dales, Yorkshire Dales Walks for Motorists* and *Further Dales Walks for Motorists.* All by the West Riding Area Ramblers' Association, Warne Gerrard Ltd.
- *Walking in the Northern Dales* by the North Yorkshire and South Durham Area Ramblers' Association, Warne Gerrard Ltd.
- *Walks in Swaledale* and *Walks in Wensleydale.* Both by Geoffrey White, Dalesman Publishing Company.
- *Walking in the Craven Dales* by Colin Speakman, Dalesman Publishing Company.
- *Walks around Harrogate* by Harrogate RA Group, West Riding Ramblers' Association.
- *Walks in Limestone Country* and *Walks on the Howgill Fells.* Both by Alfred W. Wainwright, Westmorland Gazette. (Highly recommended)

West Yorkshire

- *Kiddiwalks: A Book of Family Rambles* and *Footpaths of Leeds.* Both by the West Riding Ramblers' Association.
- *Walking in Brontë Country* by the West Riding Ramblers' Association, Dalesman Publishing Company.
- *Pennine Walks around Hebden Bridge* by Calder Civic Trust, West Riding Ramblers' Association.
- *Wetherby and Tadcaster Walks* by the Wetherby RA Group and Ainsty Footpaths Society, West Riding Ramblers' Association.
- *Leeds to the Sea* by the West Riding Area Ramblers' Association.

All of the above guides are available from:

Elizabeth Green, West Riding Area (see *Address Directory*)

A list of other guides sold by the West Riding RA—and their prices—may also be obtained on request.

Other Recommended Guides

- *Walking in South Yorkshire* by J.F. Ferns, Dalesman Publishing Company.
- *Yorkshire's Three Peaks,* Dalesman Publishing Company.
- *Walks in the Vale of York* by the York RA Group.
- *Walks in the Yorkshire Dales* by H.O. Wade, Spurbooks Ltd.
- *Ten Walks in Meltham and District* by the Meltham and District Civic Society.
- *Pendleside and Brontë Country Walks for Motorists* by George Banks, Warne Gerrard Ltd.
- Also, see the guidebooks listed for the North York Moors National Park and Yorkshire Dales National Park (see the section on *England's National Parks),* as well as the Cleveland Way, the Coast to Coast Walk, the Crosses Walk, the Dales Way, the Lyke Wake Walk, the White Rose Walk and the Wolds Way (see the section on *England's Long-Distance Footpaths).*

A complete list of guidebooks and local footpath maps to Yorkshire and Humberside is included in the RA's *County Sheets,* available from the head office of the Ramblers' Association.

Suggested Walks

The possibilities are practically unlimited. Any of the guidebooks listed above will get you started. There also are eight long-distance paths from which to choose. And the two national parks—the North York Moors and Yorkshire Dales—have numerous footpaths. The choice is yours. Still, don't ignore the rest of England.

Address Directory

A

- *Ambleside Park Information Center,* At the Old Courthouse, Church Street, Ambleside. Tel. Ambleside 3084. Accommodation Bureau: Tel. Ambleside 2582.
- *Anderson, L.,* 29 The Fairway, Blaby, Leicestershire.
- *Association of Fell Ramblers & Wayfarers,* Alan Earnshaw, General Secretary, 45 Moorland Close, Sunnybrow, Crook, Durham DL15 0BX.

- *Avis, Keith,* 68 High Street, Hadleigh, Suffolk.
- *Avon Area Ramblers' Association,* Miss E. M. Branton, Secretary, 7 Nedge Hill, Chewton Mendip, Bath, Avon BA3 4LP.
- *Aysgarth Falls Park Information Center.* At the car park, Leyburn. Tel. Aysgarth (09693) 424.

B

- *BBC Publications,* Distribution Department, 144 Bermondsey Street, London SE1.
- *BMC,* see *British Mountaineering Council.*
- *BTA,* see *British Tourist Authority.*
- *Bab Hiley,* see *Hiley, Bab.*
- *Backpacker's Club,* Eric R. Gurney, Honorary National Organizing Secretary, 20 St. Michaels Road, Tilehurst, Reading, Berkshire RG3 4RP. Tel. (home) Reading (0734) 28754 or (business) Checkendon (0491) 680541 ext. 250.
- *Bakewell Park Information Center.* At Market Hall, Bridge Street. Tel. 3227.
- *Baxter, Mr. F.,* 3 Rempstone Cottage, Corfe Castle, Wareham, Dorset BH20 5JH.
- *Bitten, Harry,* see *Matthews, Fred.*
- *Belvidere Press,* 221 Rake Lane, Wallasey, Merseyside.
- *Books of Wessex Ltd.,* Priory Bridge Road, Taunton, Somerset.
- *Bowness-on-Windermere Park Information Center.* At Bowness Bay, Glebe Road, Bowness-on-Windermere. Tel. Windermere 2895. Accommodation Bureau: Tel. Windermere 2244.
- *British Mountaineering Council,* Crawford House, Precinct Centre, Booth Street East, Manchester M13 9RZ. Tel. (061) 273 5835.
- *British Tourist Authority, London,* 64 St. James's Street, London SW1A 1NF. Tel. (01) 499 9325. Tube: Green Park (Picadilly and Victoria lines).
- *British Tourist Authority, New York,* 680 Fifth Avenue, New York, New York 10019, U.S.A. Tel. (212) 581-4700.
- *Brockhole Park Information Center,* National Park Centre, Windermere. Tel. Windermere 2231.
- *Brooks, Miss M.A.,* 85 Broadoak Way, Hatherley, Cheltenham GL51 5LL.
- *Burke, M.,* High Garth, Apperly Road, Stocksfield, Prudhoe, Northumberland.
- *Buxton Park Information Center.* At St. Ann's Well, The Crescent. Tel. 5106.

- *Byrness Park Information Center.* At 9 Otterburn Green, Byrness. Tel. Otterburn 622.

C

- *CHA,* see *Country-Wide Holidays Association.*
- *CPRE Oxfordshire Branch,* Sandford Mount, Charlbury, Oxford OX7 3TL.
- *Calderdale Way Association,* 7 Trinity Place, Halifax HX1 1BD.
- *Cambridgeshire Area Ramblers' Association,* Mr. G. Smith, Secretary, 5 Garlic Row, Cambridge CB5 8HW. .
- *Camping Club of Great Britain and Ireland, Ltd.,* 11 Lower Grosvenor Place, London SW1W 0EY. Tel. (01) 828 9232.
- *Cassell Publishers,* 35 Red Lion Square, London WC1.
- *Castleton Park Information Center.* On Castle Street. Tel. Hope Valley 20679.
- *Cheshire County Council,* Countryside Division, County Hall, Chester CH1 1SF.
- *Chiltern Society,* Cherry Cottage, Stokenchurch, High Wycombe, Buckinghamshire.
- *Chorley Guardian,* 32A Market Street, Chorley PR7 2RY.
- *Clapham Park Information Center* (via Lancaster). In The Reading Room. Tel. Clapham (04685) 419.
- *Colin Firth,* see *Firth, Colin.*
- *Combe Martin Park Information Center,* Combe Martin, North Devon. Located in a caravan at the beach car park. Tel. Combe Martin 3319.
- *Commons, Open Spaces and Footpaths Preservation Society,* 25a Bell Street, Henley-on-Thames (Oxon). Tel. Henley 3535.
- *Constable & Company Ltd.,* 10 Orange Street, London WC2H 7EG.
- *Cook, Hammond & Kell, Ltd.,* London Map Centre, 22-24 Caxton Street, London, SW1H 0QU. Tel. (01) 222 2466. Tube: St. James's Park (Circle and District Lines).
- *Cordee,* 249 Knighton Church Road, Leicester LE2 3JQ.
- *Cornwall Area Ramblers' Association,* A. Palmer, Secretary, 1 Whitley Barn, Tresarrett, Bodmin, Cornwall PL30 4QH.
- *Cornwall Federation of Women's Institutes,* 10 Strangeways Terrace, Truro, Cornwall.
- *County Surveyor and Planning Officer,* County Hall, Newport, Isle of Wight.
- *Countryside Books,* 4 Turners Drive, Thatcham, Berkshire.

- *Countryside Commission,* Public Relations Department, John Dower House, Crescent Place, Cheltenham, Gloucestershire GL50 3RA. Tel. Cheltenham (0242) 21381.
- *Country-Wide Holidays Association,* Birch Heys, Cromwell Range, Manchester M14 6HU. Tel. (061) 224 2887.
- *County Surveyor and Planning Officer,* County Hall, Newport, Isle of Wight.
- *Cumbria Tourist Board,* Ellerthwaite, Windermere, Cumbria LA23 2AQ.

D

- *Dalesman Publishing Co.,* Clapham, via Lancaster, North Yorkshire, LA 2 8 EB0.
- *Danby Park Information Center.* At Danby Lodge National Park Centre, near Whitby. Tel. Castletor 654. Day visitors only.
- *Dartmoor National Park Department,* Courtenay House, Fore Street, Bovey Tracey, Devon.
- *Dartmoor National Park Information Centre:*
  —*Dovey Tracey.* Located at the Lower Car Park. Tel. 832047. Open mid-April to early October. Several caravan information centers are also located on the moor during the summer months.
- *David and Charles,* Brunel House, Newton Abbot, Devon TQ12 2 DW.
- *Derbyshire Area Ramblers' Association,* Mrs. M. R. Treece, Secretary, Dene Cottage, Alport, Bakewell, Derbyshire.
- *Derbyshire Countryside Ltd.,* Lodge Lane, Derby DE1 3HE.
- *Devon Area Ramblers' Association,* Mr. E. R. Vinnicomb Beechcroft, Secretary, Combe Crosse, Bovey Tracey, Newton Abbot, Devon TQ13 9AU.
- *Dorset Area Ramblers' Association,* Mr. F. Baxter, Secretary, 3 Rempstone Cottages, Corfe Castle, Wareham, Dorset.
- *Dovestones Park Information Center.* On Dovestones Reservoir, near Greenfield.

E

- *East Anglia Tourist Board,* 14 Museum Street, Ipswich, Suffolk IP1 1HU. Tel. Ipswich 214211.
- *East Midlands Area Ramblers' Association.* (Covers Leicestershire and Northamptonshire), Miss F. Fewings, Secretary, 17 Haddon Close, Rushden, Northamptonshire.

- *East Midlands Tourist Board,* Bailgate, Lincoln LN1 3AR. Tel. Lincoln 31521.
- *East Yorkshire and Derwent Area Ramblers' Association,* Dr. G. R. Eastwood, Secretary, Bridgend, 60 Front Street, Lockington, Driffield, North Humberside.
- *Eastbourne Rambling Club,* 28 Kinfauns Avenue, Eastbourne, East Sussex BN22 8SS.
- *Edward Stanford Ltd.,* The International Map Centre, 12-14 Long Acre, London WC2E 9LP. Tel. (01) 836 1321. Tube: Covent Garden (Picadilly line) or Leicester Square (Northern and Picadilly lines).
- *Elizabeth Green,* see *Green, Elizabeth.*
- *Emergency,* dial 999. Ask for the police.
- *English Tourist Board,* Department A.H., 4 Grosvenor Gardens, London SW1W 0DU. Tel. (01) 730 3451. A two-block walk from Victoria Station.
- *Exmoor National Park Authority,* Exmoor House, Dulverton, Somerset TA22 9HL.
- *Exmoor National Park Information Centres* (open April through September):
  —*Combe Martin,* North Devon. Located in a caravan at the beach car park. Tel. Combe Martin 3319.
  —*Lynmouth,* North Devon. At the Parish Hall, Watersmeet Road. Tel. Lynton 2509.
  —*Minehead,* Somerset TA24 5NB. At the Market House, The Parade. Tel. Minehead 2984.

F

- *Firth, Colin G.,* Secretary, Association of British Mountain Guides, 64 Barco Avenue, Penrith, Cumbria,
- *Fisher, Sidney,* 37 Lesbury Road, Alnwick, Northumberland.
- *Footpath Publications,* Adstock Cottage, Adstock, Buckingham MK18 2HZ.
- *Forestry Commission,* 231 Corstorphine Road, Edinburgh EH12 7AT, Scotland.
- *Fred Matthews,* see *Matthews, Fred.*

G

- *Glenridding Park Information Center.* Located in a caravan at the Glenridding car park. Tel. Glenridding 414.
- *Gloucestershire RA Services,* R. A. Long, 27 Lambert Avenue, Shurdington, Cheltenham.

- *Gloucestershire Ramblers' Association,* Miss Joan Kelland, Secretary, 55 Eldon Road, Cheltenham, GL52 6TX.
- *Graham, F.,* 6 Queen's Terrace, Newcastle-on-Tyne NE 2 Ph.
- *Green, Elizaebth,* 5 Huby Banks, Huby, Leeds S17 OAH.
- *Guardian Press,* 32A Market Street, Chorley, Lancashire.
- *Gwent County Public Relations Officer,* County Hall, Cwmbran, Gwent NP4 2XF.

H

- *Hampshire Area Ramblers' Association,* Miss B. Frost, Secretary, 103 Mill Road, Fareham, Hampshire PO16 0UA.
- *Harold Hill & Son,* Killingworth Place, Gallowgate, Newcastle-on-Tyne NE1 4SL.
- *Harry Bitten,* see *Matthews, Fred.*
- *Hawes Park Information Center.* Located in a caravan at the Station Yard. Tel. Hawes (09696) 450.
- *Hawkshead Park Information Center.* Located in a caravan at the Hawkshead car park. Tel. Hawkshead 525.
- *Haymarket Publishing Ltd.,* Gillow House, 5 Winsley Street, London W1A 2HG.
- *Heart of England Tourist Board,* P. O. Box 15, Worçester WR1 2JT. Tel. Worcester 29511.
- *Her Majesty's Stationery Office (HMSO),* Atlantic House, Holborn Viaduct, London EC1P 1BN. (Bookshop: 49 High Holborn, London WC1V 6HB.)
- *Hiley, Bab,* 44 Montague Avenue, Newcastle-on-Tyne NE3 4JN.
- *Holiday Fellowship, Ltd.,* 142-144 Great North Way, London NW4 1EG. Tel. (01) 203 3381.
- *Holmes McDougall Ltd.,* 12 York Street, Glasgow G2 8LG, Scotland.
- *Huntingdon RA Group,* 125 Mill Road, Buckden, Cambridgeshire.

I

- *Ingram Park Information Center.* At the Old School House, Ingram. Tel. Powburn 248.
- *Isle of Wight Area Ramblers' Association,* Mr. L. M. Wickens, Secretary, 8 Spring Gardens, Shankin, Isle of Wight PO37 7AQ.
- *Isle of Wight Tourist Board,* 21 High Street, Newport, Isle of Wight PO30 1JS. Tel. Newport 4343.

J

- *John Bartholomew & Son Ltd.,* Duncan Street, Edinburgh EH9 1TA, Scotland. Tel. (031) 667 9341.
- *Johnson, K.A.,* 45 Glenside, Wrightington, Wigan.
- *Jones, Roger,* 45 Greyhound Lane, Stourbridge, West Midlands DY8 3AD.

K

- *Keith Avis,* see *Avis, Keith.*
- *Kent County Council,* County Secretary's Department, County Hall, Maidstone, Kent.
- *Keswick Park Information Center.* At Moot Hall, Market Square, Keswick. Tel. Keswick 72803. Accommodation Bureau: Tel. Keswick 72645.

L

- *Lake District Area Ramblers' Association,* E. W. Hibberd, Secretary, "Rowan," 4 Lentworth Drive, Scotforth, Lancaster LA1 4RJ.
- *Lake District National Park Centre,* Youth and Schools Liaison Officer, Brockhole, Windermere, Cumbria LA 23 1LP. Tel. Windermere 2231.
- *Lake District National Park Information Service,* Bank House, High Street, Windermere, Cumbria LA 23 1AF.
- *Lake District National Park Information Centres* (open daily from Easter until late September):
—*Ambleside.* At the Old Courthouse, Church Street. Tel. Ambleside 3084. Accommodation Bureau: Tel. Ambleside 2582.
—*Bowness-on-Windermere.* At Bowness Bay, Glebe Road. Tel. Windermere 2895. Accommodation Bureau: Tel. Windermere 2244.
—*Brockhole.* National Park Centre, Windermere. Tel. Windermere 2231. Day visitor center only. This is one of the best National Park interpretive centers in Britain—if not the best. It is also by far the best information center in the Lake District. Highly recommended, especially for overseas visitors.
—*Glenridding.* Located in a caravan at the Glenridding car park. Tel. Glenridding 414.
—*Hawkshead.* Located in a caravan at the Hawkshead car park. Tel. Hawkshead 525.
—*Keswick.* At Moot Hall, Market Square. Tel. Keswick 72803. Accommodation Bureau: Tel. Keswick 72645.
—*Windermere.* At Bank House, High Street. Tel. Windermere

2498. No personal callers. Information Officer and Head Warden Offices only.

- *Lancashire County Council,* Estates Office, Winkleigh House, Winkleigh Square, Preston.
- *Lancashire North-East Area Ramblers' Association,* Mr. J. Lees, Secretary, 23 Pendle Road, Great Harwood, Blackburn BB6 7TN.
- *Leicester City Information Bureau,* 12 Bishop Street, Leicestershire.
- *Letts & Company,* Borough Road, London SE1 1DW.
- *Lincolnshire and South Humberside Area Ramblers' Association,* Major Brett Collier, Secretary, "Lukenya," Hillfoot, North Carlton, Lincoln LN1 2RR.
- *Lincolnshire County Council,* County Offices, Lincoln LN1 1YL.
- *Link House Publications Ltd.,* Dingwell Avenue, Croydon CR9 2TA.
- *London Transport,* 55 Broadway, Westminster, London SW1.
- *Long-Distance Walkers Association,* John Feist, Membership Secretary, Lowry Drive, Marple Bridge, Stockport, Cheshire SK6 5BR.
- *Ludham Parish Council,* 29 Willow Way, Ludham, Yarmouth, Norfolk NR29 5QS.
- *Lyn Publicity Association,* Lynton, Devon.
- *Lynton Park Information Center.* At the Parish Hall, Watersmeet Road, Lynmouth, North Devon. Tel. Lynton 2509.

M

- *Mackintosh, A.,* 253 Hawthorne Road, Bongnor Regis, West Sussex.
- *Main, Laurence,* 25 Kimmeridge Close, Nythe, Swindon, Wiltshire SN3 3PZ.
- *Malham Park Information Center.* Located in a caravan in the Malham car park. Tel. Airton (0723) 363.
- *Malvern Hills District Footpath Society,* Barnards, Green House, Great Malvern, Worcestershire.
- *Manchester Area Ramblers' Association,* Miss R. Irlam, Secretary, 4 Sunningdale Road, Urmston, Manchester M31 1DG.
- *Matthews, Fred,* and *Harry Bitten,* Glen View, London Road, Abridge, Essex.
- *Merseyside Area Ramblers' Association,* Miss A. Thayer, Secretary, 53 Bramwell Avenue, Prenton, Birkenhead, Merseyside.
- *Mid-Herts Footpath Society,* 1 Templewood, Welwyn Garden City, Hertfordshire.
- *Midland Area Ramblers' Association,* Mr. M. Bird, Secretary, 58

Minehead, Somerset TA24 5NB. At the Market House, The Parade. Tel. Minehead 2984.

* *Moopham Publications,* Wrenbury, Wrotham, Kent.
* *Mountain Bothies Association,* Richard Butrym, 15 Merton Road , Histon, Cambridge.
* *Mountain Rescue Committee,* The Secretary, 9 Milldale Avenue, Temple Meads, Buxton, Derbyshire SK17 9BE.

N

* *National Ski Federation of Great Britain,* 118 Eaton Square, London SW1 9AF. Tel. (01) 235 8227.
* *National Travel (NBC) Ltd.,* Victoria Coach Station, London SW1W 9TP.
* *National Trust* (Country Walks), 42 Queen Anne's Gate, London SW1H 9AS.
* *Nigh & Sons, W.J.,* Publishers, 62 Landguard Road, Shanklin, Isle of Wight.
* *Norfolk Area Ramblers' Association,* Mrs. Jeanne le Surf, Secretary, 6 Atthill Road, Norwich NR2 4HW.
* *North Devon Printing Works,* 5 Oxford Grove, Ilfracombe, Devon EX34 9HG.
* *North Norfolk District Council,* Holt Road, Cromer, Norfolk.
* *North Staffordshire Area Ramblers' Association,* Mr. R. W. Gregg, Secretary, Kent House, Leek, Staffordshire ST13 7SY.
* *North West Tourist Board,* The Last Drop Village, Bromley Cross, Bolton BL7 9PZ. Tel. Bolton 591511.
* *North York Moors National Park,* Bondgate, Helmsley, North Yorkshire YO6 5BP.
* *North York Moors National Park Information Centres* (open from April to October):
  —*Danby.* At Danby Lodge National Park Centre, near Whitby. Tel. Castleton 654. Day visitors only.
  —*Sutton Bank.* At the top of Sutton Bank alongside the A170 road. Personal callers only.
* *North Yorkshire and South Durham Area Ramblers' Association,* Mr. R. M. Bettinson, Secretary, 6 Lynmouth Road, Norton, Stockton, Teesside TS20 1QA.
* *Northamptonshire County Council Leisure and Amenities Department,* Northampton House, Northampton NN1 2JP.
* *Northern Area Ramblers' Association,* W.G. Stothard, Secretary, 14 Mill Hill Road, East Denton, Newcastle-upon-Tyne NE5 2AR.

- *Northumberland National Park,* Bede House, All Saints Centre, Newcastle-upon-Tyne NE1 2DH.
- *Northumberland National Park Information Centres:*
  —*Byrness.* At 9 Otterburn Green. Tel. Otterburn 622.
  —*Ingram.* At the Old School House. Tel. Powburn 248.
  —*Once Brewed.* On the Military Road, Hexham. Tel. Bardon Mill 396.
  —*Rothbury.* In Church House, Church Street.
- *Northumbria Tourist Board,* Prudential Building, 140-150 Pilgrim Street, Newcastle-upon-Tyne NE1 6TQ. Tel. Newcastle 28795.
- *Nottinghamshire Area Ramblers' Association,* Mr. C. G. Smith, Secretary, 361 Nottingham Road East, Eastwood, Nottingham NG16 2AP.
- *Nottinghamshire County Council,* Footpaths Office, Trent Bridge House, Fox Road, West Bridgford, Nottingham NG2 6B1.

O

- *Once Brewed Park Information Center.* On the Military Road, Hexham. Tel. Bardon Mill 396.
- *Optimus Books,* 13 Montague Place, Worthing, West Sussex BN11 3BG.
- *Ordnance Survey,* Romsey Road, Maybush, Southampton SO9 4DH. Tel. Southampton 775555 ext. 706.
- *Oxford Illustrated Press,* Shelley Close, Headington, Oxford OX3 8HB.
- *Oxfordshire Area Ramblers' Association,* Mr. D. Smith, Secretary, Brackenmount, Chacombe, Banbury, Oxfordshire.

P

- *Paul Cave Publications,* 13 Portland Street, Southampton, Hampshire.
- *Peak District National Park,* Aldern House, Baslow Road, Bakewell, Derbyshire DE4 1AE.
- *Peak District National Park Information Centres:*
  —*Bakewell.* At Market Hall, Bridge Street. Tel. 3227.
  —*Buxton.* At St. Ann's Well, The Crescent. Tel. 5106.
  —*Castleton.* On Castle Street. Tel. Hope Valley 20679.
  —*Dovestones.* On Dovestones Reservoir, near Greenfield. Open on Sundays only.
- *Peddars Way Association,* 6 Atthill Road, Norwhich NR2 4HO.
- *Penguin Books Ltd.,* Harmondsworth, Middlesex.

- *Pennine Way Council,* 14 St. Barnabas Drive, Littleborough, Lancashire OL15 8EJ.
- *Perkins, Dr. B.,* 11 Old London Road, Patcham, Brighton, East Sussex BN1 8XR.
- *Peterborough RA Group,* 32 Fitzwilliam Street, Peterborough PR1 2RX.
- *Philip, Son & Nephew Ltd.,* 7 Whitechapel, Liverpool L69 1AN.
- *Photo Precision Ltd.,* Caxton Road, St. Ives, Huntingdon, Cambridgeshire.

R

- *Ramblers' Association,* 1/5 Wandsworth Road, London SW8 2LJ. Tel. (01) 582 6878. Located outside Vauxhall Station (Victoria Line Underground and British Rail) above Barclay's Bank. Take Bondway (east side) exit from Underground.
- *Ramblers Holidays Ltd.,* 13 Longcroft House, Fretherne Road, Welwyn Garden City, Hertfordshire AL8 6PG. Tel. Welwyn Garden 31133.
- *Robert Smart,* see *Smart, Robert.*
- *Roger Jones,* see *Jones, Roger.*
- *Rothbury Park Information Center.* In Church House, Church Street.
- *Ruddington Footpaths Preservation Group,* Willowbrook, 8 Devon Drive, Ruddington, Nottinghamshire.

S

- *St. Albans and District Footpath Society,* 48 Stanley Avenue, St. Albans, Hertfordshire.
- *Sedbergh Park Information Center,* 72 Main Street. Tel. Sedbergh (0587) 20125.
- *Sevenoaks Bookshop,* 147 High Street, Sevenoaks, Kent.
- *Shire Publications Ltd.,* Cromwell House, Church Street, Princes Buckinghamshire HP17 9AJ.
- *Sidney Fisher,* see *Fisher, Sidney.*
- *Smart, Robert,* Brackendale, Longhills Road, Church Stretton, Salop.
- *Somerset Area Ramblers' Association,* Mr. S. Hodgson, Secretary, 33 Broadlands Avenue, North Petherton, Bridgewater, Somerset TA6 6QR.
- *South East England Tourist Board,* Cheviot House, 4-6 Monson Road, Tunbridge Wells, Kent TN1 1NH. Tel. Tunbridge Wells 33066.

- *South West Way Association,* Mrs. D. Y. Lancey, Assistant Secretary, Kynance, 15 Old Newton Road, Kingskerswell, Newton Abbot, Devon TQ12 5LB.

- *South Yorkshire and North East Derbyshire Area Ramblers' Association,* Mr. R. Bullen, Secretary, 18 Furniss Avenue, Sheffield S17 3QL.

- *Southern Area Ramblers' Association* (for Essex), Mr. T. Dogget, Secretary, 1/5 Wandsworth Road, London SW8 2LJ.

- *Southern Tourist Board,* Canute Road, Southampton, Hampshire SO1 1FH. Tel. Southampton 20438.

- *Sports Council,* Department B, 70 Brompton Road, London SW3 1EX. Tel. (01) 581 1212.

- *Spurbrooks Ltd.,* 6 Parade Court, Bourne End, Buckinghamshire.

- *Staffordshire County Council Planning Department,* County Building, Martin Street, Stafford, ST16 2LE.

- *Suffolk Area Ramblers' Association,* Mr. A. Pratt, Secretary, Sidegate Avenue, Ipswich, Suffolk.

- *Surrey Daily Advertiser,* Martyr Road, Guildford, Surrey.

- *Sussex Area Ramblers' Association,* 31 Forestfield, Horsham, West Sussex RH13 6DY.

- *Sussex Area Ramblers' Association,* Mr. Gray, Secretary, 21 Solent Road, East Wiltering, Chichester, West Sussex PO20 8DJ.

- *Sutton Bank Park Information Center.* At the top of Sutton Bank alongside the A170 road.

- *Swale Footpaths Group,* "Scillonia," Lewson Street, Teynham, Sittingbourne, Kent.

T

- *Tetradon Publications, Ltd.,* Bridge House, Shalford, Guildford, Surrey.

- *Thames and Chilterns Tourist Board,* P. O. Box 20, 8 The Market Place, Abingdon, Oxfordshire OX14 3HG. Tel. Abingdon 22711.

- *Thornhill Press,* 24 Moorend Road, Cheltenham, Gloucestershire.

- *Torbay Leisure Services Ltd.,* Lymington Road, Torquay TQ1 3EY.

- *Turner, J.R.,* Coppins, The Poplar, Path Lane, Pinhoe, Exeter, Devon EX4 8JX.

V

- *Victoria Coach Station,* Buckingham Palace Road, London SW1W 9TP. Tel. (01) 730 0202. A 10-minute walk from British Rail's Victoria Station.

W

- *Warne Gerrard Ltd.*, Warne House, Vincent Lane, Dorking, Surrey RH4 3FW.
- *Waterway Productions Ltd.*, Kottingham House, Dale Street, Burton-on-Trent DE14 3TD.
- *Weather Centre*, London. Tel. (01) 836 4311.
- *Weather Forecasts: Windermere* Tel. (09662) 5151.
- *Weathercock Press*, Gunton Mall, Lowestoft, Suffolk.
- *Weidenfeld and Nicolson*, 11 St. John's Hill, London SW11.
- *West Col Productions*, 1 Meadow Close, Goring-on-Thames, Reading, Berkshire RG8 9AA.
- *West Cornwall Footpaths Preservation Society*, Spindrift House, Marazion, Cornwall.
- *West Country Tourist Board*, Trinity Court, 37 Southernhay East, Exeter, Devon EX1 1SQ. Tel. Exeter 76351.
- *West Essex Ramblers' Association*, Glen View, London Road, Abridge, Essex.
- *West Riding Area Ramblers' Association*, Mrs. A. Richards, Secretary, Old School House Lane, Dave Banks, Harrogate, North Yorkshire HG3 4ER.
- *West Sussex County Council*, County Hall, Chichester, West Sussex.
- *Western National Omnibus Company*, National House, Queen Street, Exeter, Devon EX4 3TF.
- *Westmorland Gazette*, 22 Stricklandgate, Kendal, Cumbria.
- *Weston, Miss W.*, 2 Lanaton Road, Penryn, Cornwall.
- *Westway Publications*, 203 Elburton Road, Plymouth, Devon 9L9 8HX.
- *Wey and Arun Canal Trust*, 24 Griffiths Avenue, Lancing, West Sussex.
- *Wildwood House*, 1 Prince of Wales Passage, 117 Hampstead Road, London NW1 3EE.
- *Wiltshire Area Ramblers' Association*, Mr. A. Toomer, Secretary, 24 Carisbrook Terrace, Chiseldown, Swindon, Wiltshire.
- *Winchester RA Group*, 29a Old Kennels Lane, Winchester, Hampshire.
- *Windermere Park Information Center.* At Bank House, High Street, Windermere. Tel. Windermere 2498. No personal callers. Information Officer and Head Warden Offices only.
- *Wootten Wamen Footpaths Group*, Sunnybrook, Wooten Wamen, via Solihull, Birmingham.

Y

- *YHA,* see *Youth Hostels Association.*
- *YHA Adventure Centre,* 14 Southampton Street, London WCZE 7HY. Tel. (01) 836 8541. Tube: Covent Garden (Picadilly line), Leicester Square (Northern line) or Embankment (Circle, District and Bakerloo lines).
- *YHA Adventure Holidays,* Department HB, Trevelyan House, St. Albans, Hertfordshire AL1 2DY. Tel. St. Albans 55215.
- *YHA Services Ltd.,* 14 Southampton Street, London WC2E 7HY. Tel. (01) 836 8541. Tube: Covent Garden (Piccadilly line), Leicester Square (Northern line) or Embankment (Circle District and Bakerloo lines).
- *York RA Group,* 26 Fir Tree Close, York YO2 4EU.
- *Yorkshire Dales National Park,* Colvend, Hebden Road, Grassington, North Yorkshire BD23 5LB.
- *Yorkshire Dales National Park Information Centres:*
  —*Aysgarth Falls.* At the car park, Leyburn. Tel. Aysgarth (09693) 424.
  —*Clapham* (via Lancaster). In The Reading Room. Tel. Clapham (04685) 419.
  —*Grassington.* At "Colvend," Hebden Road. Tel. Grassington (0756) 752748.
  -*Hawes.* Located in a caravan at the Station Yard. Open Tuesdays and weekends only. Tel. Hawes (09696) 450.
  —*Malham.* Located in a caravan in the Malham car park. Tel. Airton (0723) 363.
  —*Sedbergh.* 72 Main Street. Tel. Sedbergh (0587) 20125.
- *Yorkshire Dales Tourist Association,* Burnsall, Nr. Skipton, North Yorkshire.
- *Yorkshire and Humberside Tourist Board,* 312 Tadcaster Road, York YO2 2HF. Tel. York 67961.
- *Youth Hostels Association,* Trevelyan House, 8 St. Stephen's Hill, St. Albans, Hertfordshire AL1 2DY. Tel. St. Albans 55215.

A Quick Reference

In a hurry? Turn to the pages listed below. They will give you the most important information on walking in England.

Search & Rescue, page 41.

Weather Forecasts, page 15.

Associations to Contact for Information:
On Walking, page 16.
On Climbing, page 34.
On Skiing, page 37.
Tourist Offices, National, page 40.

Maps, page 22.

Guidebooks, page 24.

Equipment, page 33.

Address Directory, page 112.

Also, see the special notes on equipment—and the listings of maps and guidebooks—for:

Long-Distance Footpaths, pages 43–64.

National Parks, pages 65–75.

Ireland, Republic of

IRELAND—A GREEN CARPETED ISLE, the land of shamrocks and leprechauns, where the wind's rustle carries the bleating of sheep and the haunting melody of an Irish ballad. Aye, and so it is.

But that is only one of its many surfaces—and but a small one at that.

To know this land, with its unhurried, simple ways, and its people, with their open, unassuming friendliness and soft speech—the famous "gift o'th'gab"—is something that is hard to rush. You may try, but Ireland has a strange way with time, a way of turning a week-long overland excursion into two, of softly changing itineraries and time schedules to lure you up backroads where green lanes lead into the hills, hills of solitude and seeming isolation.

In the countryside life is a quiet drama of simple things: the surprise of donkeys and sheep competing with an occasional bicycle or car on the twisting backroads; farmers with a horse and cart delivering fresh milk to the cooperative creamery; the early morning mist lifting off stone-walled fields. Above a gleaming white cottage, smoke curls from a chimney, the rich, earthy smoke of burning turf. In an isolated field a farmer pitches hay, his dog a companion. Time seems to be measured not by clocks or any sense of immediacy, but by the sun and moon and the ebb and flow of the tide. Ask a shopkeeper what time the day's delivery of milk will arrive and he is likely to reply, "When it gets here," adding: "Take a spot o' mine if you need it for your tea."

The simple things, the small kindnesses, the easy-going manner of people ever ready to talk with a stranger . . . they're qualities you find again and again.

Ireland is a small country—only 84,260 square kilometers (32,524 square miles). Yet its scenery is varied, including more than 800 lakes and rivers and a deeply indented coastline so winding that no place in the country is more than 112 kilometers (70 miles) from the sea. In the center of the country is an undulating limestone plain with peat bogs and glacial deposits of sand and clay. Toward the sea, the land rises to low mountains: the granite domes of Wicklow, the sandstone ridges of Cork and Kerry, the jagged quartzite peaks of Connemara, the cliff-lined limestone plateaus of Sligo and Leitrim. Like the rim of a saucer, they encircle the central plain.

The highest peak—Carrauntoohill, located near Killarney in County

IRELAND, REPUBLIC OF

Kerry—is only 1,041 meters (3,414 feet) high. But what the mountains lack in height, they make up for in diversity. There are deep, lake-filled glens; caves, narrow gorges and underground streams; and gentle, bog-covered highlands. Along the west coast, in the counties of Donegal, Mayo, Galway and Kerry, the mountains tower dramatically above narrow fjords. Here one finds most of Ireland's Gaeltacht areas—the bastions of Ireland's social and cultural traditions—where Irish Gaelic is the spoken language and English, while understood, is rarely used in everyday speech.

Many traditions from the simpler, older way of life still survive in the Irish countryside. You can see Saint Brigid's cross hanging over a combine-harvester in country barns and hear a farm wife murmur the old prayer, "the light o' heaven to the souls o' the dead," as she turns an electric switch. Prehistoric and medieval remains abound—dolmens, cairns, stone circles, pillar stones and earthen forts dating from the Iron Age (of which there are nearly 40,000 in Ireland). Yet practically everywhere you go, the countryside is uncrowded and, because of minimal industrialization, relatively unspoiled.

Although there is no "Public Rights of Way Act" or "Access Act," as in neighboring England and Wales, to guarantee a walker's freedom, access to the mountains and hills is virtually unrestricted. In fact you may roam practically anywhere you wish. An occasional farmer may refuse to let you cross his property, but this is rare. Generally, the only place where you may be denied access is near Dublin, where the abuses of weekend vandals and motorcyclists have—sadly—strained the welcome of the local hill-farmers. Beyond the Dublin area, however, the overwhelming majority of landowners are tolerant of those who cross their property. In fact, many even offer a friendly wave and a wish of "God speed"—or engage you in a moment of animated conversation—as you pass.

Also, because relatively few walkers venture into the Irish hills, you can travel for an entire week in some areas, such as the Sligo Mountains, without seeing another walker.

One reason for this is Ireland's lack of marked footpaths. Several nature paths have been waymarked in the State Forests, and a few youth hostels in County Kerry are connected by marked tracks, but these account for barely 100 kilometers of paths. Elsewhere, there are old green lanes, fire breaks, sheep tracks and mountain tracks that often can be followed into the hills and, in some cases, back out again. But once you are in the highlands, you must rely primarily on your own wits—and a map and compass—to navigate across the terrain.

There are also many old canals along which you can walk—the best known of which are the Royal and Grand canals, which link Dublin with Shannon, and the Barrow Navigation, which links the Grand Canal and Dublin with the southeast corner of Ireland. But again, the tow paths along the canals are unmarked, and you must be willing to hop an odd fence and go through some knee-high grass to walk their banks.

Few if any of the tow paths and green lanes are shown on Irish maps.

The number of guidebooks is also limited, but those that exist can help you work out routes across the hills. The handbook published by An Óige—the Irish Youth Hostel Association—also includes information on suggested walks that start and end near Ireland's youth hostels.

Many of the youth hostels, in fact, are ideally suited for walkers. Most are located within a day's walk of each other and usually have at least two days of enjoyable rambles that can be undertaken from the hostel. Thus you can stay in a hostel, spend two days walking in the local area, then walk on to the next hostel and repeat the sequence.

Another valuable source of information is the local people. They can suggest routes and tell you about the history and folklore of their areas. On occasion, they may even invite you around the corner to the local pub to bend your ear in the friendly Irish way over a pint of Guinness.

The local tourist information offices operated by *Borde Fáilte*—the Irish Tourist Board—are also extremely helpful and can alert you to local events, such as the Midsummer fire blazes in County Galway or the dances and traditional music at a *ceili,* that you might otherwise miss.

You should remember, however, that the freedom to roam where you wish in Ireland also carries a large responsibility. Because no legal rights of way exist, the *privilege* to cross a person's property can be revoked at any time. And the loss of that privilege can be caused by just one careless walker. As one Irishman points out, "You can despoil a man's wife and, if you are caught, only get bruised up. But despoil a man's property and you're likely to get shot."

It is imperative that each walker take care not to litter and not to camp without first asking permission. In addition, all gates along the way should be closed and latched properly. If you respect property rights, you will be welcomed. If not, you—and all future walkers—will be greeted by the ire of the Irish.

Flora & Fauna

Ireland has a wealth of wetlands. Bogs alone, with their dwarf shrubs, sedges and sphagnum mosses, cover nearly one-seventh of the land area. In addition, there are fens, freshwater marshes, callows (flat areas adjoining rivers that are subject to flooding in winter) and turloughs, or semi-dry lakes covered with a closely cropped, grassy sward, which are subject to dramatic fluctuations in their water levels, changing from lake to pond to swamp to dry depression and back again, according to the cycle of rainfall.

Clumps of trees follow fence lines. There are also pockets of mountain oak, hazel, beech and primeval oak in valleys and along rivers. Forestry plantations—made up primarily of Norway spruce, Sitka spruce and Scots pine—cover 303,750 hectares (750,000 acres) and are scattered throughout the country's 359 state forests. For the most part, however, the countryside is open and the rocky, grass-covered flanks of the hills stick out against the skyline, giving much of the country a wild, rugged appearance.

Ireland was once completely forested, except on the tops of mountains. Mixed hardwoods covered the lowlands, and pines grew on the uplands and in parts of the west. But human interference, beginning with the earliest Stone Age settlers around 5000 B.C., greatly altered the Irish landscape. Much of the existing farmland was created by draining bogs. Cutting vegetation—reeds for thatch, and willows and rushes for baskets—is still locally practiced and has been a major factor influencing vegetation type. Turf cutting for fuel, another traditional activity, has also molded the landscape and, where the demands for fuel are great or where bogs are not common, cutting has removed the bog, or at least its upper layers, completely.

The fact that Ireland became an island before Britain has also had an important effect on the distribution of its animals and plants. Highland plants found in Britain are generally lacking in Ireland. On the other hand, a group of plants called Cantabrian, which are most fully developed in Spain, are indigenous to Ireland. These include the arbutus of southwest Ireland, the large flowered butterwort, the St. Palmicks cabbage and certain heaths.

The mole and weasel, common animals in England, are not found in Ireland. There are only two kinds of mice (as opposed to four in Britain) and no snakes of any kind. Several species of woodlice are found in Ireland (the next colony is on the Pyrenees), and in many Irish lakes there is a small freshwater sponge that is unknown elsewhere in Europe, but is abundant in North America.

Other animals include the red deer, the imported Sitka deer, badgers, grey and red squirrels and hedgehogs. There are also numerous waders and seabirds and many of the songbirds common to England.

A series of booklets on Ireland's wetlands, forests and bird life are available for a nominal charge from the Forest and Wildlife Service (for its address and telephone number, see the *Address Directory* at the back of this chapter). These include:

- *Wetlands Discovered* (in English). Gives a description of all the various types of wetlands in Ireland. Describes their evolution and plant life. Illustrated with numerous colored line drawings.
- *Some Irish Bird Haunts* (in English). Lists the names and locations of places in Ireland which are notable for their bird life. Includes a physical description of each area, the species of birds which can be seen and a sketch map showing their locations.
- *A List of Commoner Irish Birds* (in English). Lists Ireland's common birds and describes the habitats in which each is most likely to be seen.

Bord Fáilte (see *Address Directory*) also publishes a free Information Sheet entitled *Notes for Birdwatchers*.

Climate

Mild southwesterly winds and the Gulf Stream give Ireland a fairly equable climate. Average temperatures in January and February range between 4° C. (39°F.) and 7°C. (45°F.), while average temperatures in July and August range between 14°C. (57°F.) and 16°C. (61°F.). During the summer, daytime temperatures occasionally reach 24°C. (75°F.), but rarely go much higher.

The driest area in the country is along the coast near Dublin, where the average annual rainfall is less than 750 mm (30 inches). In contrast, most of the low-lying areas in the northwest, west and southwest record between 1,125 mm (45 inches) and 1,500 mm (60 inches) of precipitation per year.

Many of Ireland's mountains abut the sea and, as a consequence, their weather can be erratic—fog one hour, sunshine the next, rain and wind anytime. As a result, walkers must always be prepared for cold, wet weather, and those who venture onto the unmarked tracks in the Irish hills must be capable of navigation with a map and compass in adverse weather. If you aren't, it is best to stick to the marked trails in the state forests and to paths near the youth hostels.

April is generally the driest month, receiving about 54 mm (2.2 inches) of rain, except in Kerry, where June is the driest. In Meath and parts of Kildare September is the wettest month, whereas December or January is usually the wettest month in the rest of Ireland. Snow is rare, although the mountains occasionally receive a powdering—sometimes even during the summer.

One thing can safely be assumed about the Irish weather, however: it will change, and can do so extremely rapidly.

Weather Forecasts

The weather forecasts given in newspapers and on radio and television broadcasts are usually too general to be of much use to walkers. Instead, you should telephone the meteorological service directly:

Meteorological Service: Dublin, Tel. (01) 74 33 20 or Cork Airport, Tel. (021) 2 67 86.

Be sure to tell the person to whom you speak the exact area where you are going to walk; variations in weather can occur even over short distances.

You should also specify the dates you intend to be in an area and the weather features that are of interest to you, such as wind speed and direction, temperature and anticipated rainfall. In addition, be sure to ask for the anticipated cloud level. Clouds often hang below 600 meters (2,000 feet) and can envelop the mountain tops in swirling mists.

Where to Get Walking Information

Bord Fáilte publishes a useful Information Sheet which provides a good overview on hill walking in Ireland:

- *Ireland. Information Sheet No. 11: Hill Walking and Rock Climbing* (in English). This includes: 1) the addresses and telephone numbers of Ireland's mountain rescue teams; 2) the locations, telephone numbers and grid reference numbers of mountain rescue posts; 3) the address where Ordnance Survey maps can be purchased; 4) the titles of guidebooks to walking and climbing in Ireland; 5) the locations of mountaineering club huts; 6) the addresses of organizations that offer climbing courses and walking holidays; and 7) a brief description of each of Ireland's principal mountain areas with the sheet numbers of the appropriate Ordnance Survey maps and the names and altitudes of the principal peaks in each area.

Every walker should obtain a copy of this Information Sheet, if only to have the current information on Ireland's mountain rescue facilities. The one-page Information Sheet is free upon request from Bord Fáilte as well as from most of its branch offices abroad. It also can be obtained from:

Federation of Mountaineering Clubs of Ireland (F.M.C.I.). See *Address Directory.*

The F.M.C.I. is an invaluable source of information on hill walking and climbing in Ireland. It is the coordinating body for mountaineering in Ireland, to which practically all of Ireland's mountaineering clubs belong. The F.M.C.I. also publishes guidebooks, runs mountaineering courses, and is responsible for setting the standards for the training of instructors, guides and tour leaders through Bord Oiliunt Sleibhe—the Irish Mountain Leadership Board.

By most European standards the F.M.C.I. is relatively small. Correspondence goes to the home of its honorary secretary, who answers it in her spare time. Consequently, requests for information should be specific (see the chapter on *Trail Information—and Where to Get It* in *On Foot Through Europe: A Trail Guide to Europe's Long-Distance Footpaths*) and in writing. Nonetheless, the F.M.C.I. can answer just about any question you might have on walking in Ireland.

Once you have decided where you want to walk in Ireland, you can also contact the local mountaineering clubs (see the section on *Irish Mountaineering Clubs* later in this chapter). Members of the local clubs will be glad to meet with you and can provide detailed information on their areas which, as yet, is not to be found in any published sources.

An Óige

Another valuable source of information on walking is An Óige—the Irish Youth Hostel Association. An Óige organizes outings for walking, rock climbing and orienteering; has marked several trails (with a red T painted on rocks) that lead from one hostel to another in County Kerry; and publishes several leaflets describing the walking opportunities around its hostels. The leaflets, entitled *An Óige: A Walking Guide for Hostellers,* include:

- *No. 1—Aughavannagh and Ballinclea;*
- *No. 2—Glenbride and Ballinclea;*
- *No. 3—Glencree and Knockree;* and
- *No. 4—Aughavannagh, Glenmalure, Glendalough and Tiglin.*

The leaflets include route descriptions and a sketch map. They are available for a nominal charge from the local youth hostel wardens, or by mail from:

An Óige (see *Address Directory*).

Most youth hostel wardens can give you a wealth of information on the areas in the immediate vicinity of the hostels and, if you have the appropriate Ordnance Survey maps, they often will mark out suggested walks on them.

The *An Óige Handbook* is also packed with useful information for the walker, climber, cyclist and spelunker. In fact, of all the youth hostel association handbooks in Europe, it is one of the best available for this purpose. The descriptions of each hostel take up a full page in the handbook and—in addition to the usual information on their addresses, opening and closing dates and facilities—include: 1) the scale and sheet numbers of the Ordnance Survey maps that cover the area around each hostel, with the grid reference number of the hostel; 2) the names and distances to the nearest youth hostels; 3) the names and altitudes of nearby mountains; 4) a notation of points of interest; and 5) a one- or two-paragraph description of the surrounding terrain and the opportunities it offers for walking, climbing, cycling, fishing and spelunking. In a few cases, brief route descriptions are also given for suggested walks near the hostels.

The handbook has a section entitled "Adventure Sports and Other Activities," which gives useful information on speleology, orienteering, rock climbing, sport training courses and pony trekking in Ireland, along with the addresses where additional information on each activity can be obtained. A summary of the recreation activities near each hostel is even included to help you decide which hostels you would like to visit.

In addition, the handbook lists the addresses and telephone numbers of Ireland's mountain rescue facilities, includes a series of sketch maps to help you locate the hostels and gives the addresses of the other youth hostel associations throughout the world. The handbook is updated each year.

Nature Trails

Nature Trails have been laid out and marked in nearly 20 of Ireland's State Forests. Each of the trails—which range from 2 to 5 kilometers in length—is described in a series of leaflets published by the Forest and Wildlife Service. The leaflets can be obtained from dispenser boxes at the entrances to the State Forests, in which case payment is made to a nearby "honesty box." They can also be purchased individually or in complete sets from:

Forest and Wildlife Service (see *Address Directory*).

The leaflets include:

- *1—Bellevue Woods Nature Trail* (County Wicklow);
- *2—Tibradden Forest Trail* (County Dublin);
- *3—Cruagh Forest Trail* (County Dublin);
- *4—Glendalough Woods Nature Trail* (County Wicklow);
- *5—Gougane Barra Nature Trail* (County Cork);
- *6—Ravensdale Wood Nature Trail* (County Louth);
- *7—Glenbower Wood Nature Trail* (County Cork);
- *8—Devil's Glen Wood Nature Trail* (County Wicklow);
- *9—Dooney Wood Nature Trail* (County Sligo);
- *10—Glengarriff Woods Nature Trail* (County Cork);
- *11—Currabinny Wood Nature Trail* (County Cork);
- *12—Glengarra Wood Nature Trail* (County Tipperary);
- *13—Monicknew Woods Nature Trail* (County Laois);
- *14—Portumna Woods Nature Trail* (County Galway);
- *15—Coole Woods Nature Trail* (County Galway);
- *16—Townley Hall Wood Nature Trail* (County Louth); and

• *17—Lorg Dúlra Coill Thuar Mhic Éadaigh/Tourmakeady Wood Nature Trail* (County Mayo).

The Forest and Wildlife Service also publishes a series of attractively illustrated booklets to Ireland's State Forest Parks—Killykeen, Lough Key, Dún a Ri, Avondale, Guagán Barra, Kennedy Park, and Ards and Rossmore—which, among other information, include descriptions of several walks in each park. All the leaflets and booklets are written in Gaelic and English, and include sketch maps of the trails.

Another useful booklet available from the Forest and Wildlife Service is:

• *The Open Forest: A Guide to Areas Open to the Public* (in English). This lists each of Ireland's State Forests and Forest Parks by county, gives directions on how they can be reached by road, and briefly describes their recreation facilities, trails and scenic and historic sites. At the back is a list of all the Forest and Wildlife Service publications and their prices. Free upon request.

National Library of Ireland

If you like libraries and have some spare time while you are in Dublin, you might want to spend an afternoon or two in the reading room of the National Library of Ireland. The library has a wealth of old manuscripts and rare, out-of-print books which can give you information on areas to ramble and help you plan walks. Three resources that are particularly useful to walkers are:

• *Hayes List of Sources, Volume 9, Places—Dates.* This lists all the information which has been published on each town, village, locality and mountain in Ireland since the 19th century. It is current up until 1970. Place names are listed alphabetically by county. Thus, to find the list of published information on Carrauntoohill, Ireland's highest mountain, you would first look under "County Kerry," then under "Carrauntoohill."

• *Hayes List of Sources, Volume 8, Ireland—Roads.* This lists all the information which has been published on Ireland's roadways and tracks, including its green lanes and mountain tracks (which are not shown on the one-inch Ordnance Survey maps). By digging up the histories of Ireland's roadways out of the book stacks, you can probably find several old, unused country tracks which no one has walked for years. (That is, if you don't mind a little detective work.) Again, entries are alphabetized by county.

• *Geological Survey of Ireland: Memoirs Sheets.* This book includes exquisite line drawings of Ireland's mountains by George Du Noyer. In addition, there are extremely accurate mountain panoramas on which each peak is named, cross-sections of selected mountains, and detailed descriptions of the terrain. Each plate in the book corresponds to a single one-inch Ordnance Survey sheet so you can match up the mountain views to your own maps (which you should bring into the library with you). At the front of each volume is an index of Ordnance Survey maps, with the area covered by the volume outlined in red. Ordnance Survey sheets 160 to 205, for instance, are covered in the volume on County Kerry (call number IR 5540941-G13).

The library is noted for going to great lengths to provide information. You can also request photocopies of specific pages in any of the resource books. (Or, in the case of the Du Noyer drawings, you can specify the names of the mountains you intend to visit.) It takes from 7 to 10 days before the photocopies can be picked up, however, so you must order them in advance if you are in a hurry. Written enquiries should be addressed to:

National Library of Ireland, Librarian (see *Address Directory*).

Irish Mountaineering Clubs

The F.M.C.I. is currently composed of 22 member clubs with 2,100 members. Most of the clubs take a keen interest in foreign walkers who are visiting Ireland and often go out of their way to provide assistance.

Members of foreign mountaineering clubs—and indeed all foreign walkers—are generally welcome as visitors in the club huts (providing you book in advance). Foreign walkers can often take part in club activities as well.

F.M.C.I. Member Clubs

See *Address Directory:*

Comeragh Mountaineering Club.
Cork Mountaineering Club.
Dalriada Mountaineering Club.
Danum Mountaineering Club.
Dublin University Mountaineering Club
Eastern Command Mountaineering Club.
Glenfoffany Climbing Club.
Irish Mountaineering Club, Belfast Section.

Irish Mountaineering Club, Dublin Section.
Irish Ramblers Club.
Laune Mountaineering Club.
New University of Ulster Mountaineering Club.
Northwest Mountaineering Club.
Queens University Mountaineering Club.
Peaks Climbing Club.
Slieveadore Club.
Sligo Mountaineering Club.
Tralee Mountaineering Club.
Ulster Polytechnic Mountaineering Club.
University College Dublin Mountaineering Club.
University College Galway Mountaineering Club.
Wayfarers Association.

Other Walking & Climbing Associations

See *Address Directory:*

Association for Adventure Sports.
C.H.A. Walking Club.
Holiday Fellowship.
Irish Orienteering Association.
Slieve Bloom Association.

It is advisable to check the club addresses with the F.M.C.I.; they change often. A list of the clubs' current officers and addresses is available upon request from the F.M.C.I. Please enclose a self-addressed envelope and sufficient international postal reply coupons to cover postage.

Maps

When it comes to hill walking, the Irish topographical maps leave something to be desired. The half-inch (1:126,720) maps contain several inaccuracies. And some of the one-inch (1:63,360) maps have not been updated since 1900, when they were originally drawn—in black and white—to record who had how much land for the purposes of taxation. Because no one lived in the mountain regions, these areas were considered unimportant. As a result, the contours on one-inch maps change from 100-foot to 250-foot intervals at an elevation of 1,000 feet. At the very least this can be confusing. At worst, it is dangerous. A 250-foot contour interval can hide a large cliff. And, indeed, the cliffs around Lugnaquillia in the Wicklow Mountains are not shown on the Ordnance Survey one-inch maps.

A series of newly surveyed 1:50,000 maps is planned. But, because of limited funds, the Ordnance Survey may not be able to complete this series for another 20 years.

In the meantime, the F.M.C.I. is cooperating with the Ordnance Survey by asking its members to review each of Ireland's existing half-inch and one-inch sheets to pinpoint inaccuracies that should be corrected in future editions.

Until these corrections are made, however, you should be aware of the maps' shortcomings and be prepared to allow for them. In a letter to the Ordnance Survey, reprinted in the Winter, 1978 *F.M.C.I. Newsletter*, Joss Lynam writes:

> There are, I think, in the ½" map of nearly every mountain area in Ireland that I have climbed in, errors which are serious for hill-walkers, even if they do not seriously affect the general public.
>
> We do not in general complain constructively because we recognise that the ½" map is not really suitable for hill-walking by reason of its small scale, and we have become resigned to a long wait until the finance for a 1:50,000 is available.
>
> The errors are of two kinds. In the Nephins we were testing Mountain Leader candidates in accurate navigation, and for this to be done properly demands a map that is at least as accurate as the navigator. Unfortunately we did not find this degree of accuracy in the lakes and streams in the boggy area west of the range—very possibly they have changed since they were surveyed. We find the same situation in Wicklow (on both ½" and 1"). The Tiglin Centre does a lot of training on the hills, and finds that junctions and bends in streams may or may not be as marked. These are errors which are annoying and frustrating, but not dangerous.
>
> Some errors are serious—I take one example which is well-documented. On sheet 10, in the Maum Turks, the magnetic bearing taken from the map from Pt. 2076 (MR 900 514) to ring contour MR 883 525 is 346°; on the ground it is 331°, a difference of 15°. Generally if I find myself off route I blame my navigation, not the map. But after a large number of people (including myself) had gone off route on this section of the Maum Turks Walk in 1975 and 1976, and what is more, had all erred in the same direction, east into the Failmore valley, I checked the bearing on a fine day, and found the error I mention above. Members of the U.C.G. Mountaineering Club have confirmed my bearing within ± 2° . . . .

The lack of marked footpaths in Ireland makes a walker heavily dependent upon the Ordnance Survey maps for navigation. Even with their occasional shortcomings, however, the maps are reliable enough to allow you to explore the mountain areas. Route finding may be more exacting and demand more skill than in other areas where footpaths are marked and the maps can be trusted without question, but it is also more challenging.

As an alternative, you can choose one place as a base and take short walks on trails in the surrounding area, or stick to the nature trails in the State Forests and the tow paths along Ireland's canals. But even here, you should always carry the appropriate half-inch sheets or, in the few areas where they exist, the one-inch District Maps. And, wherever possible, you should supplement the maps with the available guidebooks and large doses of advice from the locals.

The maps available for walkers are:

Half-Inch Series (1:126,720). The 25 sheets in this series cover all of Ireland. The maps show the locations of youth hostels. Many unclassified roads are shown, but few of the mountain tracks, green lanes and forest fire breaks which may be of use to the walker. Relief is depicted by layer tints and contours. Contours are drawn in at 100-foot intervals. Other features, such as water and roads, are shown in color. The National Grid is printed in black at 10-kilometer intervals with marginal ticks at 1 kilometer.

One-Inch District Maps (1:63,360). The four sheets in this series cover the areas surrounding Dublin, Cork, Killarney and Wicklow. All features represented on the half-inch maps are shown in color on this series, with additional place names and prominent features. Many mountain tracks and green lanes, however, are not shown. Contours change from 100- to 150-foot intervals at an elevation of 1,000 feet. The National Grid is shown at one-kilometer intervals. For the areas they cover, these are the best maps available for the walker.

One-Inch Black Outline (1:63,360). The 205 sheets in this series cover all of the Republic of Ireland, except for some areas along the border with Northern Ireland. None of the sheets have been updated since 1900. All features on the series—roads, railways, rivers, contours and heights—are shown in black. At 1,000 feet, contours change from 100- to 250-foot intervals. These sheets provide details on many byroads, paths and cart tracks which have fallen into disuse and can be used as walking routes. While useful, these maps should be supplemented with the appropriate half-inch sheets.

Six-Inch Series (1:10,560). The 1,770 sheets in this series cover all of Ireland, including the islands off its coast. They provide the best record of Ireland's green lanes and mountain tracks. All fields, houses and townland and barony boundaries are also shown. All features are in black. The sheets covering most mountain areas have not been revised since 1912. Hence, details of State Forests and forest roads are lacking. Also many sheets have *no* contours at all, and none have them above 1,000 feet. While useful for their record of mountain tracks, they are six times the cost of the one-inch and half-inch maps. And to be of any use, they must be supplemented with the appropriate half-inch or one-inch maps.

The Ordnance Survey maps can be purchased in Dublin from:

Government Publications Sales Office (see *Address Directory*).

The maps, plus a free index and price list, can also be obtained from:

Ordnance Survey Office (see *Address Directory*).

The index to the Six-Inch Series must be specifically requested. There is a nominal charge for this index.

In towns other than Dublin, the maps often can be purchased from tourist offices and booksellers. A list of designated map agents in Cork, Galway, Kilkenny, Ballina, Limerick, Waterford, Sligo, Wexford, Tralee, Dubdalk, Athlone and Ennis can be obtained upon request from the Ordnance Survey.

Aerial Photographs

For walkers with plenty of time for advance planning there is an alternative to the Ordnance Survey maps. A series of aerial photographs taken between 1973 and 1978 cover the entire Republic of Ireland. The vertical-format photographs have a scale of 1:26,000 and show mountain tracks, cliffs, forests and all other features of interest to walkers. They are more reliable than any published Ordnance Survey map. But there is a hitch: the negatives are held in Paris by the French aerial survey contractors who took the shots, and it takes up to three months to obtain prints.

Further information on the aerial photographs, including how you can obtain prints to specific regions and their prices, can be obtained from:

Geological Survey (see *Address Directory*). A full set of aerial photographs is on file at the survey office.

Guidebooks

Ireland has long had a dearth of guidebooks for hill walkers. The situation is steadily improving, although there are still places in Ireland where your best—and, indeed, only—resources are an Ordnance Survey map and advice from the locals.

The F.M.C.I. began to focus attention on Ireland's lack of guidebooks in the mid-1970s. Since then, nine new guides for hill walkers have appeared, including six regional hill walking guides covering all of Ireland. Several new climbing guides have also been published, with promises of more on the way.

Many possible routes, of course, remain unmentioned (perhaps even on purpose so they do not become crowded). But the guidebooks provide descriptions of more routes than a person can ever hope to complete in a decade of walking holidays in Ireland—a vast improvement over the situation a mere five years ago.

These guidebooks include:

General Guides

- *Climbing in the British Isles: Ireland* by H.C. Hart, Longmans, Green & Co., London and New York, 1895, reprinted by Joss Lynam, Dublin. This reprint of the original 1895 book is still useful to the hill walker, and thoroughly enjoyable to anyone with an interest in the history of mountaineering in Ireland.

- *Mountaineering in Ireland* by Claud W. Wall (revised), Federation of Mountaineering Clubs of Ireland, Dublin, 1976. This is an updated version of the original book, which appeared in 1939. It covers all mountain areas of Ireland, with details on the best walks; includes a list of the 257 mountains in Ireland with an altitude of 610 meters (2,000 feet) or more; and gives information on hut and hostel accommodation. Recommended.

- *The Irish Peaks,* Joss Lynam, general editor, Constable & Company, London. Due to be released in 1982. This hill walkers' guide will have detailed descriptions, maps and photographs of more than 50 hill walks in Ireland. Compiled in cooperation with the member clubs of the F.M.C.I. Recommended.

- *Rock Climbs in Ireland,* edited by Calvin Torrans, Constable & Company, London. Due to be released in 1982. Will include pitch-by-pitch descriptions and photographs of nearly 200 selected rock climbs in Ireland.

- *The Mountains of Ireland* by Dr. D. Pochin, B.T. Batsford, London, 1955, new edition 1977. Fine illustrations, but stresses historical background, rather than route details.

Regional Hill Walking Guides

- *Dublin and Wicklow Mountains: Access Routes for the Hill Walker,* edited and published by members of the Irish Ramblers Club, 1976. This book was an immediate sellout (1,000 copies in two weeks) and is now in its sixth printing. It gives detailed descriptions on how to get into the hills around Dublin—Ireland's most popular hill walking area. Sketch maps, on which grid reference numbers are indicated, are included along with information on accommodation, mountain rescue and dangerous areas not explicitly marked on OS maps.

- *The Twelve Bens,* edited by Joss Lynam, Federation of Mountaineering Clubs of Ireland, 1971. This is a hill walkers' and rock climbers' guide to the most interesting mountain area in Connemara. Includes suggestions for cross-country hikes and a pitch-by-pitch description of selected climbs.

- *The Mountains of Killarney* by J.C. Coleman, Dundalgan Press, Dundalk, 1948. An excellent hill walkers' guide to the Reeks and other mountains around Killarney. Includes sketch maps and photographs. Route descriptions generally are still accurate, despite some changes in the past 30-odd years.

- *Journeys into Muskerry: Wanderings and Excursions in the Country West of Cork City and the Kerry Borderland of Southern Ireland* by J. C. Coleman, Dundalgan Press (W. Tempest) Ltd., Dundalk. A beautifully written book with wood block prints by the author. The route descriptions are more literary than are typically found in walking guides, woven within the author's commentaries on place, history and experiences. While the commentaries are delightful, they may pose a problem for walkers who want to follow Coleman's routes and to whom English is a second language.

- *Irish Walk Guides,* Joss Lynam, general editor, Gill & Macmillan (see *Address Directory*). This series of six regional hill walking guides covers all of Ireland. Each guide gives detailed descriptions of up to 40 of the best hill walks of varying lengths in the region covered, includes a map of each walk and contains notes on the climate, history, geology, flora and fauna of the region. The six guides in the series are:

—*Irish Walk Guides/1: South West* by Sean O'Suilleabhain of the Laune Mountaineering Club, 1978. Covers Kerry and West Cork.
—*Irish Walk Guides/2: West* by Tony Whilde of the University College Galway Mountaineering Club, 1978. Covers Clare, Galway and Mayo.
—*Irish Walk Guides/3: North West* by Gerry Foley of the Sligo Mountaineering Club and Patrick Simms of the North West Mountaineering Club, 1979. Covers Sligo and Donegal.
—*Irish Walk Guides/4: North East* by Richard Rogers, 1980. Covers Northern Ireland.
—*Irish Walk Guides/5: East* by David Herman, Jean Boydell, Michael Casey and Eithne Kennedy of the Irish Ramblers Club, 1979. Covers Dublin, Wicklow and Wexford.

—*Irish Walk Guides/6: South East* by Frank Martindale of Tipperary Adventure Sports Club, 1979. Covers Waterford, Kilkenny and South Tiperary.

Rock-Climbing Guides

• *Wicklow* by Ken Higgs, F.M.C.I., 1981.
• *Dalkey* by Stephen Young, F.M.C.I., 1979.
• *Antrim Coast* by Calvin Torrans and Clare Sheridan, F.M.C.I., 1981.
• *Mournes* by John Forsythe, F.M.C.I., 1980.
• *Donegal* by the Irish Mountaineering Club, 1962, reprinted 1978.
• *Coum Gowlaun* by Joss Lynam, F.M.C.I., 1979.
• *Twelve Bens* (see description under *Regional Hill Walking Guides*).
• *Clare* by Tom Ryan, F.M.C.I., 1978.
• *Malinberg* by Jim Leonard, F.M.C.I., 1979.
• *Bray Head and Minor Crags around Dublin,* Joss Lynam, and Liam Convery, F.M.C.I., 1978.
• *F.M.C.I. New Climbs Bulletin.* Issued annually. Lists all the new climbs made in Ireland each year. Also gives full details on climbs in areas which are not yet described in separate guidebooks. The bulletins are available for every year since 1973.

Where to Buy Guidebooks

The Gill & Macmillan *Irish Walk Guides* are widely distributed and can be purchased from most booksellers in Ireland. The other hill walking and climbing guides are usually—but not always—available from booksellers near the areas covered by the guides. It is best to order these guides by mail from the F.M.C.I. to ensure you obtain the ones you want. A list of the guides sold by the F.M.C.I. and their prices is available upon request.

Tow Path Guides

Information on Ireland's canals can be obtained from Bord Fáilte and from the reference sources in the National Library of Ireland (see the section on *Where to Get Walking Information*). One of the best-documented walks is on the tow path along the River Barrow from Athy to St. Mullins village, southeast of Dublin, a distance of 69 kilometers (43 miles). Tow paths along the Grand and Union canals can also be walked. Two useful publications to the River Barrow are:

• *Guide to the River Barrow* compiled by T.F. O'Sullivan, Emerald Star Line Ltd., Graiguenamanagh. A mimeographed description of the castles, abbeys, bridges, locks and towns along the River Barrow. Includes historical notes. Although written for those who plan to navigate the river, it is also useful to walkers. The description of the areas along the tow path begins with Athy (mile 20) and takes you to St. Mullins (mile 63).

- *Emerald Star Line Limited: The Barrow Navigation.* A ring binder with mimeographed reproductions of the river charts. Notations on the charts include historical notes, as well as useful addresses and telephone numbers in the towns through which the river passes. The tow path is not shown on the charts, although their large scale is useful for those who wish to walk along the river, since all bridges are shown.

Both publications can be obtained for a nominal charge from:

Emerald Star Line Ltd. (see *Address Directory*).

Other Books

Numerous other books are available which can provide useful background on the areas in which you might like to walk in Ireland. Bord Fáilte (see *Address Directory*) publishes an information sheet with a list of selected books on Ireland's archeology, architecture, art, folklore, genealogy and history. The list also includes the titles of regional travel guides and the addresses of booksellers in Irish towns. The sheet is entitled:

- *Ireland. Information Sheet No. 18: Books of Irish Interest.* Free upon request.

Several books of historic, architectural, archeological and conservation interest are published by:

An Taisce (see *Address Directory*). A list of titles and prices is available upon request.

An Taisce also publishes a bi-monthly journal, *An Taisce: Ireland's Conservation Journal,* and can provide information on the National Trust lands it manages, most of which are open to walkers.

A few books now out of print are worth perusing in the National Library of Ireland. These include:

- *The Festival of Lugnasa* by Maire McNeill, Oxford University Press, 1965. This gives details of almost every mountain pilgrimage and high-level gathering in Ireland. Many such functions come down from prehistoric times, and the folklore details in this book make it highly recommended reading.
- *The Way I Went* by R. L. Praeger. A very personal description of

Ireland by a leading naturalist. Praeger had a bias toward mountains; he was the first president of the Irish Mountaineering Club.

- *The Open Road* by J.B. Malone, Independent Newspapers Ltd., Dublin, 1950. Gives details for walks around Dublin. Includes historical notes.
- *Walking in Wicklow* by J.B. Malone, Helícon Ltd., Dublin, 1964. Gives details on walks using green lanes, mountain tracks and old abandoned roadways in the Wicklow Mountains. Written by a man who probably knows the Wicklows better than any other Irishman.

J.B. Malone also wrote weekly articles for Dublin's *Evening Herald* from 1938 through 1976. These cover the Wicklows in detail and include maps. Most of the papers are now on microfilm, but with advance notice, the National Library of Ireland can provide photocopies of the articles that interest you.

Trailside Lodgings

There is a wide variety of lodgings in which walkers can stay near the Irish mountains—family hotels and guesthouses, country homes, youth hostels, even castles and thatched-roof cottages. There are also four mountaineering club huts in Kerry and Wicklow. Walks can be planned between the available lodgings in many areas, but you should be sure to consult a map and accommodation list beforehand to ensure the lodgings can be easily reached from your planned route. Most of the lodgings are located either in valleys or in towns and villages near the mountains, and sizeable detours are sometimes required to reach them. Advance reservations are also highly advisable, especially in July and August.

One welcome feature of the family hotels and guesthouses is the ever-present Irish breakfast—hot or cold cereal, juice, eggs, sausage or bacon, slabs of fresh soda bread heaped with butter and marmalade, and pots of strong tea—which is included in the room price. Evening meals are also available for a nominal charge, but you sometimes have to give advance notice (usually about four hours) if you want them.

Several accommodation lists are available on request from Bord Fáilte. These include:

- *Ireland Tourism: Hotels and Guesthouses* (in English, French and German). Gives full details on Ireland's hotels, guesthouses, holiday hostels and holiday camps. Includes prices (not guaranteed). The towns and villages in which the lodgings are located are listed alphabetically by county.
- *Ireland Tourism: Irish Homes Accommodation* (in English, French and German). Gives full details on the town and country homes and Irish farmhouses in which you can stay. A great way to meet the Irish.

Bord Fáilte also can provide lists of the restored castles and thatched-roof cottages in which you can stay.

Youth Hostels

Many of Ireland's 50-odd youth hostels are located in prime hill walking areas and are excellent bases for hikes into the surrounding areas, especially where lodgings are scattered and seldom within a day's walk of each other.

The hostels, which may be converted castles, cottages, shooting lodges or coast guard stations, have separate dormitories for men and women. Beds and blankets are provided, but you must bring your own sheet sleeping bag. None of the hostels provide meals, although there are usually places where you can buy food nearby and all the hostels have a kitchen in which you can cook. Cooking utensils and dishes are provided in the kitchens, but you must bring your own cutlery. A cup and tin plate are also useful to have along for one of the spontaneous "drum ups" (outdoor meals).

Most of the hostels remain open all year. During July and August the hostels are heavily used and reservations made at least a month in advance are essential to ensure a bed. Advance bookings are also advisable if you intend to stay in the hostels during weekends in May and June or in September and October. Booking should be made directly to the hostels in which you intend to stay, except for those in Wicklow, Louth and Meath, which should be booked through the An Óige office in Dublin (see *Address Directory*).

The hostels have a policy of never turning away anyone who is walking or bicycling and, when they reach their capacity, they will give you a spare mattress for the floor. But the hostels sometimes run out of mattresses and, because of bitter experience, camping near the hostels is now forbidden.

Full details on the hostels, including their booking addresses, are included in the *An Óige Handbook* (described under *"An Óige"* in the section on *Where to Get Walking Information*).

An Óige also publishes a regional guide to the hostels in Cork and Kerry which describes the mountains of both regions and includes numerous route descriptions for walks and bicycle trips from the hostels. This booklet is entitled:

- *An Óige—Irish Youth Hostel Association: Cork and Kerry.*

Both handbooks can be obtained for a nominal charge from An Óige.

Another useful resource for the hosteler is the 1:600,000 *Ireland Map: Youth Hostel Edition* which shows the locations of youth hostels throughout Ireland. The map, which is also an excellent aid to motorists, is available for a nominal charge from Bord Fáilte.

Mountaineering Club Huts

Members of foreign mountaineering and walking clubs may stay in the huts operated by the constituent clubs of the F.M.C.I. Arrangements to stay in the huts, however, must be made well in advance with the secretary of the club that runs the hut. Keys also must be obtained since all of the huts are kept locked. To obtain the key, you must have proof of your club membership.

The four club huts are located in:

Kerry: Hut-type accommodation is available at the Climber's Inn (see *Address Directory*).

Wicklow: Three huts:

1. Irish Mountaineering Club hut. Map reference: 115975. Located on the left, about half a mile up Wicklow Gap Road from Glendalough. Sleeps 30. Nearest shop is in Laragh.

2. Dublin University Climbing Club hut. Located near Glendalough, about half a mile up the track on the south side of Glendasan from the Royal Hotel. Sleeps 20. Nearest shop is in Laragh.

3. The Farmhouse at Luggala. For bookings, telephone Eileen Clarke (see *Address Directory)* at least three days in advance. Sleeps 4.

Camping

With the permission of the landowner it is possible to camp almost anywhere in Ireland. In some areas you may see *no camping* signs, and these should be respected. Camping is also discouraged in the state forests (except for Killarney and Lough Key which have established sites), and the state foresters will ask you to move on if you camp.

There are numerous commercial campgrounds—known as caravan and camping parks—along Ireland's roadways. A list of these, with a list of the firms that rent tent and camping equipment, is available upon request from Bord Fáilte (see *Address Directory*). Ask for the pamphlet, *Ireland Tourism: Caravan & Camping Parks.*

Water

Tap water is safe throughout Ireland, and you should depend on it for most of your water needs. The peat soil covering most of Ireland's hills gives water a brackish taste. Many streams also may contain seepage either from piggeries or from a farm's silage. Most farmers will give you water from their wells if you ask. Pubs are also a good source of water, although you may get a quizzical look if you walk into one and simply ask for water.

Equipment Notes

No specialized equipment is required for walking in Ireland, although you should always be sure to carry spare woolen clothing, a windproof jacket, good raingear and a map and compass. For boggy areas you may also want to bring a pair of rubber boots in addition to your regular hiking boots.

Organized Walks

Several marathon walks and walking tours are organized by a variety of associations in Ireland. Among these are:

See *Address Directory:*

An Óige: Organizes numerous weekend activities throughout the year. Details are published in the Dublin *Evening Herald* each Wednesday. Midweek hill walks are organized during the summer, along with courses in rock climbing, orienteering and caving. The courses are designed primarily to interest participants in an activity rather than to teach technique. A list of upcoming activities and their dates can be obtained by writing the An Óige office in Dublin.

Association for Adventure Sports (AFAS): Offers a comprehensive series of courses in all aspects of mountaineering. Also organizes numerous adventure holidays, both in Ireland and abroad. The one- and two-week holidays are of two types: 1) fairly leisurely outdoor holidays offering a certain amount of free time and activities which are not too strenuous, and 2) more demanding specialist holidays for the outdoor enthusiast. Available activities include walking, rock climbing, canoeing, orienteering, caving and field studies. Walking tours are held in Wicklow and Kerry, with accommodation in youth hostels and guesthouses. The adventure holidays are open to people 15 years of age or older. Full details are available from the Tiglin Adventure Centre.

Castlebar's International Four Days' Walks: These walks are patterned after the 63-year-old KNBLO Four-Day Walk in Nijmegen, The Netherlands. They are held each year at the end of June in Castlebar, County Mayo. On each of the four days there is a long walk varying from 24 to 27 miles (38 to 43 kilometers), a short walk varying from 12 to 17 miles (19 to 27 kilometers) and a mini-walk of about 8 miles (13 kilometers), which follow lightly traveled roads and country lanes. In addition, there is a cross-country walk or *ramble* across moorland and over heather-clad hills each day. Participants choose the length and type of walk they wish and are given plenty of time—10 hours maximum—to complete the walks. Because the walks are non-competitive, you are free to choose your own pace, rest when you wish and pause at any point to enjoy the rolling, lake-studded countryside. All the routes are signposted, and guides are available. A rescue service is provided in case of a mishap or inability to complete the selected walk. There are also food stops and refreshment points along the way. Each participant who completes one or more walks receives a Certificate of Fitness. Walkers who complete the four days' walks also receive a bronze medal. After participating in the walks for five years, a person receives a silver medal and, after 10 years, a solid gold medal. Footwear is important. For the short and long walks on the country roads and lanes, you should wear comfortable, well-fitting walking shoes, running shoes or soft boots—not hiking boots. On the cross-country rambles, however, good boots are essential since most of the terrain is trackless and boggy. Full details on the walks are available on request from Castlebar's International Four Days' Walks.

Dublin International Two Days' Walks: These walks are similar to those held in Castlebar. They are organized by the Dublin Walking Club in the northern part of County Dublin and are held each year on the last weekend in June. Participants have the choice of a short walk of 15.5 miles (25 kilometers) each day, for which a silver medal is awarded, and a long walk of 25 miles (40 kilometers) each day, for which a gold medal is awarded. Participants must complete the walks in order to receive the medals. A commemorative certificate of fitness is awarded to all participants. Special awards are also given to the largest foreign team, the largest home (Irish) team and to all teams with 11 or more members.

The routes for the non-competitive walks pass through pleasant, rolling countryside and follow the seashore with its picturesque headlands. The center for the walks is based in a large school, which is only a 20-minute drive from the car-ferry terminals and the international airport. Reasonably priced accommodation and meals are provided at the school for foreign participants. Other accommodation includes first class hotels, guesthouses and private houses. Refreshments are provided at various rest points each day. Free entertainment is also provided each evening of the walks, including traditional Irish music and dancing. Full details are available on request from: Dublin International Two Days' Walks.

Galtees Seven Peaks Walk: Of Ireland's marathon walks, this is one of the easiest, with gradual climbing (4,500 feet), few navigational problems and a relatively short distance (17 miles, or you can choose a shorter walk of 12 miles). Starts near Anglesborough at the west end of the Galtee Mountains in County Tipperary. Finishes at Cahir at the east end of the range. Can be left early with no great difficulty, although the walk out could be long. Organized in June by the Tipperary Adventure Sports Club. Details can also be obtained from the F.M.C.I.

Lugnaquillia Walk: Organized in June by the Irish Ramblers Club in the Wicklow Mountains. The 33-mile walk starts at Stone Cross, Ballinascorney and finishes at the Glen of Imaal. It has 7,500 feet of climbing, crosses several bogs and takes from 9 to 14 hours to complete. Climbs are relatively gentle. Care is needed in navigation, although there are no major difficulties. The walk can easily be left before the finish (it crosses two paved roads). Full details are available from the Irish Ramblers Club.

Maam Turks Walk: This is Ireland's toughest walk, if not the longest. It also is one of the most enjoyable. The 14-mile walk stretches from Maam Cross, at the base of Leckavrea, to Leenane. It has 8,000 feet of climbing. There are no paths to follow, the map has serious errors (for instance, a complete coombe is ignored), and navigation in the mist is extremely difficult. In 1975 only 8 walkers out of 50 who started finished the whole walk, and in 1976 only 4 out of 60 finished. (On the other hand, nearly 100 participants finished in both 1977 and 1978.) The walk is organized in May by the University College Galway Mountaineering Club. Details are also available from the F.M.C.I.

Mountain Marathon (Northern Ireland): This walk is divided into three classes: 1) a severe test of fell-running and navigational ability over a distance of 20 miles, 2) an equally severe test, but over a shorter distance (15 miles), and 3) a slightly less severe test over a distance of 10 miles. The first two classes are competitive events. The walk is held in June in the Mourne Mountains of Northern Ireland. It is organized by the Northern Ireland Orienteering Association

Mourne Wall Walk (Northern Ireland): A 22-mile walk with 10,000 feet of climbing. Starts and finishes at Rourkes Park. Crosses roads a few times and can be left before the finish. Navigational problems are nil; most of the walk follows the Boundary Wall of the Belfast Water Supply Catchment area. Generally held on the first Sunday in June by the Youth Hostel Association of Northern Ireland.

Reeks Walk: From Kate Kearney's Cottage at the Gap of Dunloe to Lough Acoose, part of the way along a knife-edge arête with vast drops on either side. This is the shortest of Ireland's walks (11 miles), but passes through some of the most splendid mountains of any. It requires some scrambling, is difficult to leave before the finish, and has 6,000 feet of climbing, some of which is up long, steep slopes, such as the final climb up Carrantouhill, Ireland's highest peak. Organized in June by the Laune and Killarney Mountaineering Club. Details are also available from the F.M.C.I.

Other Walks: Comeragh Bog Trot, County Waterford, April, about 15 miles, 4,000-foot ascent; Blackstairs Walk, County Wexford, May, 16 miles, 5,000-foot ascent; Knockmealdowns Walk, Waterford/Cork, Glover Marathon, County Donegal, September, about 15 miles, 6,000-foot ascent. Details are available from the F.M.C.I.

With the exception of the Mountain Marathon, none of the walks are strictly competitive. Nonetheless, each walk has its record time (2½ hours for the Seven Peaks Walk, for instance) and there is keen unofficial competition on the walks among the good hill walkers.

Several of Ireland's mountaineering clubs, such as the Irish Ramblers Club, organize walking and climbing tours for their members. Details on these are reported in the club newsletters. In addition, walking holidays are organized by the C.H.A. Walking Club and Holiday Fellowship. Details on these holidays are available upon request from the two associations.

Mountaineering Courses

The Association for Adventure Sports (AFAS) runs numerous mountaineering and outdoor activity courses throughout the year. The courses cover rock climbing, hill walking, winter mountaineering, mountain rescue, first aid, orienteering, caving, canoeing, hang gliding, snorkeling, skiing, surfing and board sailing.

For those already active in these activities there are courses in leadership and advanced skills, while novices can attend one of the many introductory courses. There are also special courses for groups.

Most of the mountaineering courses are held at the AFAS Tiglin Adventure Centre in the Wicklow Mountains. In addition, several courses are held at Caragh Lake and Glencar in County Kerry, on Achill Island (noted as a hang-gliding center), and in Connemara, the Galtees, Sligo and Clare. Accommodation during the courses is usually in small, youth-hostel-type dormitories.

Among the advanced courses offered by the AFAS are:

Orienteering map-making: Covers all aspects of map-making, including geodesy (determining the exact locations and elevations of specific points and the relationships and sizes of topographical features), ground surveying and cartography—the production of maps.

Mountain rescue: A comprehensive course covering all aspects of mountain rescue from search operations and communications to helicopter rescue and improvised equipment. Designed for club members, mountain leaders, defense personnel and Outdoor Pursuit Centre staff members.

Mountain safety: These courses, which are spread over two weekends, deal with clothing and equipment, map reading, navigation, walking skills, safe movement on rough ground, and accident procedure. The courses are intended for teachers and youth leaders who are thinking of taking young people walking in the hills. They offer an elementary level of training.

Mountain Leadership Training Courses: These courses provide training in the technical skills required by people who wish to lead groups of beginners and young people in the mountains. The courses are part of a training and assessment program operated by the Irish Mountain Leadership Training Board (Bord Oiliunt Sleibhe). All courses are approved by the board. A Mountain Leadership Certificate is issued to those who successfully complete the training courses.

Founded in 1969, the AFAS is a non-profit association administered almost entirely by voluntary workers. It receives support from the National Sports Council and Bord Fáilte. All courses are run by a fully qualified staff of professional instructors.

Further information on the AFAS and its courses can be obtained by writing:

Tiglin Adventure Centre (see *Address Directory*).

Special Train & Bus Fares

The Irish Transport System, C.I.E., offers several reduced fares on its rail and bus services to the major cities and towns throughout the Republic of Ireland. These include special Youth/Student "Rambler" tickets, and tickets which provide unlimited standard-class travel for a period of 8, 15 or 30 days. Some of the tickets must be purchased prior to arrival in Ireland.

Full details on these special fares, as well as on transportation to and from Ireland, and boat services to the Irish Islands may be obtained from Bord Fáilte (see below).

Useful Addresses
& Telephone Numbers

General Tourist Information

In Ireland:

Bord Fáilte (The Irish Tourist Board). See *Address Directory*. Staff speaks English, French and German (and, of course, Irish). Extremely helpful. Publications are numerous and include lodging lists, 25 holiday-information booklets covering all areas of the country (available in three languages), an information-packed and concisely written book entitled *The Ireland Guide,* a bimonthly magazine with enticing articles and color photographs entitled *Ireland of the Welcomes,* plus a stack of free one-page Information Sheets, each of which highlights a different aspect of Ireland—Seaside Resorts (Information Sheet No. 1), Climate (No. 2), Libraries, Art Galleries, Museums (No. 5), Tracing Your Ancestors (No. 8), Canoeing (No. 21), Orienteering (No. 24), and so on. A full list of publications is available on request. Bord Fáilte can also provide a list with the addresses and telephone numbers of the local tourist information offices and room-reservation services throughout Ireland.

Abroad:

Branch offices of the Irish Tourist Board are located in NORTHERN IRELAND: Belfast; GREAT BRITAIN: Birmingham, Bristol, Edinburgh, Glasgow, London and Manchester; EUROPE: Amsterdam, Brussels, Düsseldorf, Frankfurt, Hamburg, Munich and Paris; AUSTRALIA: Sydney; NEW ZEALAND: Auckland; ARGENTINA: Buenos Aires; CANADA: Toronto; and the U.S.A.: Chicago, Los Angeles, New York and San Francisco.

London: Irish Tourist Board, 150 New Bond Street, London W1Y 0AQ. Tel. (01) 493 3201.

New York: Irish Tourist Board, 590 Fifth Avenue, New York, New York 10036. Tel. (212) 246-7400.

Sport Shops

There are several sport shops in Ireland where you can buy equipment for hill walking, rock climbing and other mountain activities. Two good shops in Dublin are:

See *Address Directory:*

Scout Shop. Located in Dublin, off Dame Street.

Great Outdoors. Located in Dublin, behind Woolies on Grafton Street. The staff includes experienced mountaineers, canoeists and scuba divers who are happy to advise visitors.

Search & Rescue

In case of an emergency: Immediately contact the nearest police station or telephone the police emergency number: Tel. 999.

Although the police may themselves be unable to mount a full rescue operation they will, if necessary, arrange for experienced mountain rescue teams to undertake the rescue or search.

The mountain rescue teams and mountain rescue posts in Ireland are listed in the *An Óige Handbook* and on Bord Fáilte's *Information Sheet No. 11: Hill Walking and Rock Climbing* (both of which are described in the section on *Where to Get Walking Information*). Both lists give the grid reference numbers of the rescue posts and the current telephone numbers of the rescue teams. You should carry one of these lists with you in the hills—just in case.

Ireland's Long-Distance Footpaths

While Ireland has few marked paths, and virtually no long-distance footpaths at present, plans are underway to change this. In 1976 the government formed a Long-Distance Walks Committee to begin laying out long-distance footpaths in Ireland. Little was done until the spring of 1978, when committee members, representing such groups as F.M.C.I., An Taisce, Bord Fáilte, AFAS, Forestry and Wildlife, An Óige, the Department of the Environment and the Irish Sports Council, were selected.

The committee's first project is to open up a long-distance path known as the Wicklow Way, a 306-kilometer (190-mile) route that was plotted out and first espoused by J.B. Malone of An Taisce in one of his weekly articles in the Dublin *Evening Herald* in 1966.

The route, as proposed by Malone, would virtually encircle the Wicklow Mountains, beginning from Three Rock Mountain. The first leg would pass through Glencullen and Glencree, go around the side of Maulin to the top of Powerscourt Waterfall (121 meters; highest waterfall in Ireland and Great Britain), climb over Djouce to the Sally Gap Road near Luggala, head cross-country to Lough Dan, follow back roads to Glandalough, and then go over Mullacor to Glenmalure. From there, the path would head back up the west side of the range to Three Rock Mountain.

Much of the route can now be followed on existing forest tracks, with overnight stops in youth hostels and guesthouses. None of the tracks are marked, and there are still stretches where walkers must strike off cross-country or go across private property, where no rights-of-way agreements exist. But this could change in the near future and the Wicklow Way may soon become Ireland's first long-distance footpath.

Other long-distance footpaths are also on the drawing board. In Donegal, the County Council is planning a route to link up with the Ulster Way in Northern Ireland (see the chapter on Northern Ireland). The towpaths along the Barrow Navigation and the Grand and Royal canals are being looked at as possibilities, and proposals have been put forth to use the green roads in Kerry as the basis for paths.

There is some debate on whether Ireland needs long-distance footpaths. Some walkers see them as an intrusion by officialdom into a territory best left to individual walkers. Others fear they may attract swarms of people, with the attendant degradation of areas that are currently wild and solitary.

But long-distance footpaths also have some strong support. In the Winter, 1978 *F.M.C.I. Newsletter*, Joss Lynam says: "My own opinion is that LDP's [long-distance paths] could open up new areas for walkers, and offer a series of new challenges. If properly routed, they will not encroach on the wilderness areas. I would hate to see a 'Pennine Way' following the backbone of Wicklow, but the Ulster Way, the coastal paths in Britain, like the Pembrokeshire Coast path, and the downland paths such as the Ridgeway seem a great idea to me."

Information on the current status of the Wicklow Way, and the other proposed long-distance footpaths in Ireland, can be obtained from the F.M.C.I. or:

National Sports Council (see *Address Directory*).

Where to Walk in Ireland

Ireland has more than 1,000 mountains that rise to an altitude in excess of 305 meters (1,000 feet), each with a different character and attraction for the hill walker. From a climber's standpoint, the finest mountains are in the south and west—the cones of quartzite in Connemara, the rugged slates of the Reeks, and the Silurian and sandstone formations of the Galtees, for instance. The walker, on the other hand, can find lovely hill country practically everywhere in Ireland. Even in the heart of Dublin, you can see hills rising from the suburbs, and an inexpensive bus ride will take you into wonderful hill walking country in less than an hour.

Some of Ireland's principal hill walking areas are listed below, along with the sheet numbers of the maps and titles of guidebooks that cover each region, the addresses of local tourist offices, and the names of towns which provide a good base for hikes into the surrounding countryside. Where possible, a few suggested walks have also been given—just to get you started. Nonetheless, this is only a brief introduction to the Irish hills. For a fuller description, Claud W. Wall's *Mountaineering in Ireland* (described in the section on *Guidebooks*) is recommended.

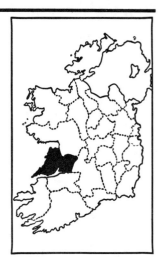

Clare

Clare is a hilly rather than a mountainous county, although it has 26 summits which exceed 1,000 feet. In the northwest is a wild region known as the Burren district, where limestone peaks overlook Galway Bay. On a clear day, these peaks provide views to the rugged mountains of Connemara and Kerry. The region's strange, lunar-like landscape features many turloughs (lakes which disappear overnight), streams which disappear into potholes and nearly 700 stone forts and dolmens left over from prehistoric times. Along the coast between Hags Head and O'Brien's Tower, the Burren ends abruptly at the perpendicular Cliffs of Moher, which plunge into the Atlantic from a height of more than 180 meters (600 feet). The district also has numerous caves, including Pollnagollum at Slieve Elva, the longest cave system in Ireland. One possible walk is from Ballyvaughan on Galway Bay across the summits of Cappanwalla, Gleninagh and Carnsefin to Black Head—about three to four hours each way.

In the south the steely gray ridge of Slieve Bernagh rises from the western shores of Lough Derg, culminating in the two highest peaks in Clare—Cragnamurragh (527 meters; 1,729 feet) and Glennagallaigh (532 meters; 1,746 feet). At the base of the mountains is the old-world town of Killaloe on the River Shannon, a good starting place for a stiff day's walk among the principal summits of the 10-mile ridge of the Slieves.

Elsewhere in the county, you can walk in the sandstone uplands of Slieve Callan, and in the Cratloe Hills and Slieve Aughty, which tower above the River Shannon. For diversion, there are also 190 castles, 150 ancient churches and more than 2,000 stone and earthen forts you can visit.

Tourist Information

Mid-Western Region Tourist Information (see *Address Directory*).
Other local tourist offices open all year are located in Ennis and at
Shannon Airport.

Bord Fáilte's Holiday Information Booklet, *Co. Clare*, is packed with
useful information for the visitor. It is available in English, French and
German for a nominal charge from Bord Fáilte (see *Address Directory*).

Maps

- Ordnance Survey half-inch series (1:126,720), sheets 14, 15, 17
  and 18 (recommended).
- Ordnance Survey one-inch Black Outline (1:63,360), sheets 114,
  122, 123, 124, 125, 131, 132, 133, 134, 141 and 142.

Guidebooks

- *Irish Walk Guides/2: West* by Tony Whilde, Gill & Macmillan,
  Dublin.
- *The Burren Hills*, a 50-page guide published by An Óige.

Walking Bases

The town of Ballyvaughan provides a good base for exploring the Burren
district and the Cliffs of Moher, as does the Doorus House youth hostel at
Kinvara, County Galway. Slieve Callan can be reached relatively easily
from the town of Ennis, Killaloe provides access to Slieve Bernagh, and the
Mountshannon youth hostel at Mountshannon is close to the Slieve Aughty
Mountains.

The Comeraghs

The Comeraghs offer some of the finest walking in County Waterford. The mountains form an elevated plateau, bounded by steep slopes and numerous grassy hollows containing tarns. Long, winding ridges connecting the principal summits provide sweeping views of the surrounding countryside. From the town of Clonmel, you can climb up to the northern spur of Knockmohra (665 meters; 2,181 feet) in about two hours, where you can follow the cliff edge to Knockanaffrin (755 meters; 2,478 feet), then descend into a Gap where there is a bridle path leading eastwards to Carrick-on-Suir and westwards back to Clonmel. Another circular walk can be undertaken through the mountains to the south of the Gap—Knocknalingady, Fauscoum, Knockaunnapeebra, Coumalocha and Coumfea—all of which rise to altitudes in excess of 727 meters (2,384 feet).

Tourist Information

> **South Eastern Region Tourist Information Office** (see *Address Directory*).
>
> Holiday Information Booklet: *Co. Waterford*, available from Bord Fáilte.

Maps

- Ordnance Survey half-inch series (1:126,720), sheets 22 and 23 (recommended).
- Ordnance Survey one-inch Black Outline (1:63,360), sheets 156, 166, 167, 177 and 178.

Guidebooks

- *Irish Walk Guides/5: South East* by Frank Martindale, Gill & Macmillan, Dublin, 1979.
- *The Irish Peaks*, Joss Lynam, general editor, Constable & Company, London. Due to be published in 1980.
- *A Visitors' Guide to the Comeragh Mountains* by Patrick Warner, Blackstaff Press, Belfast, 1978. Describes several walking routes. Also covers traditions, local crafts, camping and fishing. Recommended.

Walking Bases

The towns of Clonmel and Carrick-on-Suir are good bases for exploring the Comeraghs, while the Lismore youth hostel, located at Glengarra (4 miles north of Lismore), is a good center for exploring the Knockmealdown Mountains and the Blackwater Valley to the west of the Comeraghs.

The Connemara Mountains

Connemara is a spectacular region of brooding mountains, desolate boglands and numerous lakes in the west of County Galway. Long a popular touring area, it has been the subject of many paintings and poems, and many of its Irish-Gaelic speaking residents flatly assert there is no prettier place in Eire. They may be right. The sparsely populated region is an enclave of ancient Irish tradition and folklore where stone walls enclose green, rock-strewn fields and wild ponies race beneath a backdrop of impressive peaks—the Twelve Bens, the Maamturks, the Sheefry Hills,

Mweelrea, the Partry Mountains, the Joyce Country Mountains and Croagh Patrick, Ireland's holy mountain, site of an annual pilgrimage on the last Sunday of July when up to 80,000 people ascend the Pilgrim's Path to pray on the summit.

The rocky horseshoe of the Twelve Bens dominates the landscape, rising in steep, cliff-bound ridges from valleys only a few meters above sea level. The mountain group is neither extensive nor high, but climbing its rocky slopes requires considerable stamina and the deep-cut saddles between its summits make for long descents and re-ascents between the peaks. As a result, a generous allowance of time should be made, even for climbs that look short on the map.

The Maamturk Mountains are a wild and barren range of peaks which stretch between Lough Corrib and Killary, and overlook Lough Inagh. Seven of its summits exceed 610 meters (2,000 feet). The traverse of the range from Maam Cross to Leenane, which is made in May of each year by Ireland's top hill walkers, is the toughest marathon walk in the country. A less strenuous walk is along the zigzagging ridges between Shannakeela, Skannive and Leckavrea, which can be done in about six hours from Maam Cross.

Other hikes can be taken in the Benchoona group, north of the Twelve Bens; up Mweelrea, which rises from the northern shores of Killary Harbour and can be climbed from Delphi; in the Sheefry Hills, directly north of Delphi; in the Partry Mountains, to the west of Lough Mask; and in the Joyce Country Mountains.

Tourist Information

Western Region Tourist Information Office (see *Address Directory*).

Holiday Information Booklet: *Co. Galway*, available from Bord Fáilte.

Maps

- Ordnance Survey half-inch series (1:126,720), sheets 10 and 11 (recommended).
- Ordnance Survey one-inch Black Outline (1:63,360), sheets 83, 84, 85, 93, 94 and 95.

Guidebooks

- *The Twelve Bens,* edited by Joss Lynam, F.M.C.I., Dublin, 1971.
- *Irish Walk Guides/2: West* by Tony Whilde, Gill & Macmillan, Dublin, 1978.
- *The Irish Peaks,* Joss Lynam, general editor, Constable & Company, London, 1980.

Walking Bases

The Twelve Bens youth hostel at the foot of Ben Lettery is an ideal base for exploring the Twelve Bens. The town of Clifden is also a good base. A bus runs along the southern edge of the mountain range from Clifden to Maam Cross through Recess; another runs between the two towns via Kylemore and Leenane. Both buses leave you within half a mile of the Bens. Bus schedules and routes vary on the southern route each day of the week however, so be sure to study the timetables carefully. For those who want to be close to the Twelve Bens, enjoy luxury (and can afford it), you might consider staying at Ballynahinch Castle. Simpler accommodation is available at Recess.

From the Killary Harbour hostel at Rosroe, it is sometimes possible to arrange with local boatmen to ferry you across the harbor to climb Mweelrea from its best approach. For the Maamturk and Partry mountains, the village of Leenane is a good base as is the bunkhouse at Maam. The Sheefry Hills can also be easily reached from Leenane.

Suggested Walks

Derryclare-Bencorr Horseshoe. A high cross-country circuit in the Twelve Bens beginning and ending in Derryclare Wood, north of the village of Recess. The route climbs westward to the summit of 677-meter (2,220-foot) Derryclare, then along the ridge to Bencorr (712 meters; 2,336 feet) and Bencorr Beg (582 meters; 1,908 feet). From there the route descends toward Lough Inagh before turning south back to Derryclare Wood. Fine views along the summit ridge, especially from Bencorr Beg. **Length:** 9.7 kilometers (6 miles). **Walking Time:** 3½ to 4 hours. **Difficulty:** Moderately difficult to difficult (3,000-foot ascent with some scrambling). **Path Markings:** No path, no markings.
Maps:
• Ordnance Survey half-inch series (1:126,720), sheet 10 (recommended).
  Or:
• Ordnance Survey one-inch Black Outline (1:63,360), sheet 94.

Glencoaghan Horseshoe. High cross-country circuit in the Twelve Bens, beginning and ending at Benlettery Youth Hostel. Follows the horseshoe-shaped ridge connecting Derryclare, Bencorr, Bencollaghduff, Benbreen, Bengower and Benlettery. Excellent views. May be walked in either direction. **Length:** 16 kilometers (10 miles). **Walking Time:** 6 to 7 hours. **Difficulty:** Moderately difficult to difficult (rough ground; steep climbs and descents). **Path Markings:** No path, no markings.
Maps:
• Ordnance Survey half-inch series (1:126,720), sheet 10 (recommended).
  Or:
• Ordnance Survey one-inch Black Outline (1:63,360), sheets 93 and 94.

Maam Turks Walk. From near Maam Cross to Leenane. A high, rugged traverse of the entire Maam Turks ridge, including ascents of eight peaks. Steep cliffs, rugged terrain and marvelous views. **Length:** 22.5 kilometers (14 miles). **Walking Time:** 10 hours. **Difficulty:** Difficult to very difficult, with numerous steep ascents and descents over barren scree. Total elevation gain: 8,000 feet. **Path Markings:** No path, no markings.
Maps:
• Ordnance Survey half-inch series (1:126,720), sheet 10 (recommended).
 Or:
• Ordnance Survey one-inch Black Outline (1:63,360), sheet 94.

Muckanaght and Benbaun. A high, trackless circuit to 730-meter Benbaun, the highest of the Twelve Bens and the hub of the range from which its several ridges radiate. Route begins and ends at Glencorbet farm. **Length:** 8 kilometers (5 miles). **Walking Time:** 3 to 3½ hours. **Difficult:** Moderately difficult; steep ascents with unstable footing in places. **Path Markings:** No path, no markings.
Maps:
• Ordnance Survey half-inch series (1:126,720), sheet 10 (recommended).
 Or:
• Ordnance Survey one-inch Black Outline (1:63,360), sheets 93 and 94.

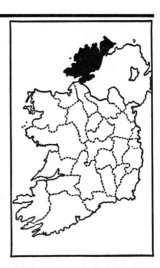

Donegal

Donegal offers some of the finest hill walking and rock climbing of any county in Ireland. Other counties can boast of loftier peaks, but none have such an extensive array of hills as Donegal. More than 130 peaks exceed 305 meters (1,000 feet) elevation, and several top 610 meters (2,000 feet).

Errigal, the highest summit in the county, is a symmetrical quartzite cone 752 meters (2,466 feet) high.

What's more, many of Donegal's "hills," despite their modest elevations, resemble true mountains: summit crags and steep rock faces plunge scores of meters either to glacier-carved valleys or directly into the sea. The Donegal coast for most of its length consists of a succession of sheer cliffs, rocky headlands and narrow coastal loughs (fjords) winding inland through the mountains.

Donegal's mountains offer numerous excellent walking tours, most of which are rather difficult, although very rewarding. Because paths are virtually nonexistent, a map and compass are essential. Ample time should also be allowed for completing all routes.

The Banagh Mountains of southern Donegal occupy most of the peninsula immediately north of Donegal Bay. They include 21 peaks, the highest of which is 601-meter (1,972-foot) Slieve League, whose southern face is a sheer rock wall dropping from the summit to the Atlantic. The beauty of this awesome precipice is further enhanced by the varied colors of its exposed quartzites, schists, slates and conglomerates. A track from the village of Carrick leads to the 300-meter cliffs of Bunglass, from which you can continue on to the summit of Slieve League, crossing the narrow ridge known as "One Man's Pass" enroute.

East of the Banagh Mountains are the Croaghgorm, or Blue Stack Mountains, a spectacular range rising abruptly behind the northern shore of Lough Eske. The range is about 11 kilometers (7 miles) long. From Lough Eske, you can follow the tumbling Corab River to Lough Belshade, which lies in a high basin beneath 600-meter peaks. From there, you can ascend 676-meter (2,219-foot) Croaghgorm, or Blue Stack Mountain, via the impressive bluff on the west side of the lake. Having reached the summit, it is possible to continue to Lavagh More and Silver Hill, from which you can descend through a wild, lake-speckled moorland to the village of Glenties. Another route runs from Barnesmore Gap, 11 kilometers from Donegal town, to Glenties.

The highest and, in the view of many, finest mountains in Donegal are found in the northwestern part of the county and include the hills surrounding Errigal and the Derryveagh Mountains immediately to the south. From the summit of Errigal, which can be climbed in a few hours, you can see virtually all of Ulster as well as a vast stretch of ocean to the north and west. Errigal is a showy quartzite cone, from which it is possible to walk northward to the craggy spurs of Aghla More and Aghla Beg and from there to 670-meter (2,197-foot) Muckish ("Pig's Back"), from which a descent is possible to the village of Dunfanaghy.

South of Errigal rise the precipitous granite peaks of the Derryveagh Mountains, highest of which is the glacially polished granite dome of 683-meter (2,240-foot) Slieve Snaght. Nearby is the Poisoned Glen, a flat-floored glacial valley, largely barren and flanked by sheer granite cliffs almost 300 meters high. These walls, along with those above Lough Barra, offer some of the most challenging climbing in Ireland, with routes ranging in difficulty from severe upward. A spectacular tour of the Derryveagh Mountains begins at the head of Poisoned Glen, follows a winding stream upward to Ballaghgeeha Gap, and from there crosses a valley to a road leading northeastward to Glenveagh. This rugged gorge contains a lake bounded by sheer cliffs on the west shore. You can walk down the valley to a road leading to the village of Gweedore, 16 kilometers distant. Another route follows the main summit ridge of the Derryveagh Mountains from 499-meter (1,636-foot) Crocknasharragh to 654-meter (2,147-foot) Dooish, passing above the head of Poisoned Glen.

Donegal's North Coast, from Horn Head east to Inishowen Head, offers spectacular walks both along the coast and among the inland hills. Horn Head is a massive promontory whose perpendicular cliffs plunge directly to the surf. A 19-kilometer (12-mile) walk along the crest of the cliffs, rising more than 180 meters (600 feet) high in places, offers spectacular views of the Atlantic and the craggy Tory Island to the northwest.

The Fanad Peninsula, a few miles east of Horn Head, also offers splendid walking, although of a different sort. Here the main attraction is rolling moorland studded with small loughs. The coastal cliffs are lower than those at Horn Head, but the natural rock formation of the Seven Arches—a series of tunnels extending some 90 meters (300 feet) in length—is a worthwhile attraction along the coast north of Portsalon.

The Fanad Peninsula is bounded on the east by Lough Swilly, a magnificent fjord extending several kilometers inland. The cliffs of Dunaff Head—the lough's eastern promontory—rise more than 180 meters (600 feet) from the water. On a clear day the view from the top is spectacular, taking in the islands off Scotland toward the east and the grand sweep of Donegal headlands to the west. South of Dunaff Head you can follow the crest of the Urris Mountains, whose seaward faces plunge directly to Lough Swilly.

These mountains line the western coast of the Inishowen Peninsula, which is bordered on the east by Lough Foyle. The entire peninsula is mountainous, with the highest peaks rising in the west-central section. A mile beyond Ballmagan, along the road leading to the Crana River valley, you can climb a hillside to the summit of Crocknamaddy, and from there proceed northeastward to Slieve Main and 615-meter (2,019-foot) Slieve Snaght ("Snow Mountain"), the highest peak in Inishowen. From the summit you can see the Donegal Highlands to the west, Antrim to the east and the coast of Scotland across the sea to the north. From Slieve Snaght, the route continues northeast to Tullymore and a descent to the road near Carndonagh.

Malin Head, the northernmost point in Ireland, commences a fine stretch of seacliffs extending southeastward to Culdaff. Along this coast, the cliffs commonly exceed 120 meters (400 feet) in height. From Glengad Head to Stookarudden—a 16-kilometer section—you can walk along the crest of broken cliffs rising up to 250 meters above the ocean.

Tourist Information

North Western Region Tourist Information Office (see *Address Directory*).

Another local tourist office open all year is located at Letterkenny.

Holiday Information Booklets: *North Donegal* and *South Donegal*, available from Bord Fáilte.

Maps

- Ordnance Survey half-inch series (1:126,720), sheets 1 and 3 (recommended).
- Ordnance Survey one-inch Black Outline (1:63,360), sheets 1, 2, 3, 4, 5, 6, 9, 10, 11, 12, 15, 16, 17, 22, 23, 24, 25, 31 and 32.

Guidebooks

- *Climbing in the British Isles: Ireland* by H.C. Hart, Longmans, Green and Co., London, 1895. Reprinted by Joss Lynam, Dublin.
- *The Irish Peaks,* Joss Lynam, general editor, Constable and Company, London, 1980.
- *Irish Walk Guides/3: North West* by Patrick Simms and Gerry Foley, Gill & Macmillan, Dublin, 1979.
- *Mountaineering in Ireland* by Claude Wall (revised), F.M.C.I., Dublin, 1976.

Walking Bases

The youth hostel at Carrick is an excellent center for walks in the Banagh Mountains. The Blue Stack Mountains are best approached from Donegal town, a few kilometers to the south, or from the village of Glenties on the west. The finest centers for exploring the Derryveagh Mountains and North West Highlands are the village of Gweedore and the youth hostel near Errigal. The Tra na Rossan youth hostel offers access to Horn Head and the Fanad Peninsula. The Bunnaton youth hostel is situated on the east side of the peninsula on Lough Swilly. The town of Letterkenny offers easy access to the North Coast as well as to Errigal and the Derryveagh Mountains. The Inishowen Peninsula is the least settled part of Donegal and is most often explored from the city of Londonderry, just across the border in Northern Ireland.

Suggested Walks

Glengad Head to Stookarudden. Strenuous clifftop walk along the Inishowen coast northwest to Culdaff; 200- to 250-meter cliffs. **Length:**

About 16 kilometers (10 miles). **Walking Time:** 6 to 8 hours. **Difficulty:** Moderately difficult. **Path Markings:** No path, no markings.
Maps:
• Ordnance Survey half-inch series (1:126,720), sheets 1 and 2 (recommended). Or:
• Ordnance Survey one-inch Black Outline (1:63,360), sheets 1, 2 and 6.
Gweedore to Dunfanaghy. The grand tour of the North West Highlands, including an ascent of Errigal and rough rambling along the ridge leading to Muckish, from which it is an easy hill walk to the village of Dunfanaghy, near Horn Head. **Length:** 24 to 32 kilometers (15 to 20 miles). **Walking Time:** 12 to 14 hours. **Difficulty:** Moderately difficult to difficult. **Path Markings:** No path, no markings.
Maps:
• Ordnance Survey half-inch series (1:126,720), sheets.1 and 3 (recommended). Or:
• Ordnance survey one-inch Black Outline (1:63,360), sheets 4, 9 and 10.

Horn Head. Clifftop walk around Horn Head, beginning and ending at Dunfanaghy. Spectacular cliffs and great ocean views. **Length:** 16 to 19 kilometers (10 to 12 miles). **Walking Time:** 6 to 8, hours. **Difficulty:** Moderately difficult. **Path Markings:** No path, no markings.
Maps:
• Ordnance Survey half-inch series (1:126,720), sheet 1 (recommended). Or:
• Ordnance Survey one-inch Black Outline (1:63,360), sheet 4.

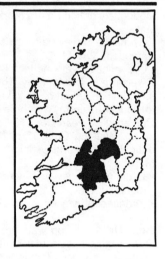

Galtee Mountains, Northern Tipperary & Slieve Bloom

A few kilometers south of the town of Tipperary, the great northern escarpment of the Galtee Mountains rises abruptly from the Glen of Aherlow to a grassy summit ridge crowned with rocky peaks of ancient red sandstone. The monarch of the range is 920-meter (3,018-foot) Galtymore, the highest inland peak in Ireland. Six other summits exceed 730 meters (2,400 feet). In contrast to the abruptness of the range's northern face, its southern flank slopes gently from the ridgecrest to the road connecting the towns of Mitchelstown and Cahir. The range extends in an east-west direction between these two towns, a distance of about 24 kilometers (15 miles). The highest peaks are arrayed along the western half of the crest.

Numerous lakes are tucked among hollows carved from the green, terraced cliffs of the northern escarpment. The cliffs flanking Lough Muskry tower some 365 meters (1,200 feet) above the water to the summit of 803-meter (2,636-foot) Greenane. The north face of Galtymore drops about 300 meters (1,000 feet) to the shore of Lough Curra. The summit of Galtymore—which is crowned with a cross commemorating the 1500th anniversary of St. Patrick's arrival in Ireland—offers perhaps the most extensive view in the country.

About 6.5 kilometers (4 miles) east of Michelstown, a track climbs the gentle southern slope of the Galtees to 786-meter (2,579-foot) Temple Hill, from where it is possible to walk the entire length of the range to Cahir. You can cut the trip short either by following a track from the shoulder of Galtybeg southeast to the Mountain Lodge youth hostel, or by descending from Greenane to Lough Muskry and from there following a track northward to Rossdrehid Wood and the youth hostel at Ballydavid Wood, in the Glen of Aherlow. It is also possible to cross the range from one youth hostel to the other.

West of Michelstown, the Galtees are succeeded by Slievereagh and the Ballyhoura Hills, which are lower and less rugged, but offer a fine grassy walk along the ridge connecting the main summits. You can also walk along the ridge of Slievenamuck, from which the Galtee Mountains can be seen to the south, across the Glen of Aherlow.

North of Tipperary town lies a great expanse of high moorlands that contains some 45 summits more than 300 meters in height. These largely uninhabited hills are crossed by few roads, and convenient walking bases are few. The walker exploring this district therefore should be prepared to camp out. The best ridge walk is along the Silvermines, with three peaks over 460 meters (1,500 feet). You can also climb 695-meter Keeper Hill (2,279-foot), the highest summit in the district, or 462-meter (1,517-foot) Tountinna, which offers a splendid view west over Lough Derg to the Slieve Bernagh Mountains of Clare.

In northeastern Tipperary, the Devil's Bit offers a good 8- to 10-kilometer (5- to 6-mile) ridge walk from the town of Templemore. And further northeast, along the border of counties of Offaly and Laois, the Slieve Bloom Mountains extend for a distance of some 32 kilometers (20 miles). The gentle summit ridge of grass and peat offers easy rambling.

Tourist Information

South Eastern Region Tourist Information Office (see *Address Directory*).

Holiday Information Booklets: *Limerick and North Tipperary* and *Laois and Offaly,* available from Bord Fáilte (see *Address Directory*).

Maps

- Ordnance Survey half-inch series (1:126,720), sheets 18 and 22 (recommended).
- Ordnance Survey one-inch Black Outline (1:63,360), sheets 154, 155, 165 and 166.

Guidebooks

- *Climbing in the British Isles: Ireland* by H.C. Hart, Longmans, Green and Co., London, 1895. Reprinted by Joss Lynam, Dublin.
- *The Irish Peaks,* Joss Lynam, general editor, Constable & Company, London, 1980.
- *Irish Walk Guides/5: South East* by Frank Martingale, Gill & Macmillan, Dublin, 1979.
- *Mountaineering in Ireland* by Claude Wall (revised), F.M.C.I., Dublin, 1976.

Walking Bases

The best walking base on the north side of the Galtees is the youth hostel at Ballydavid Wood, in the Glen of Aherlow, although the town of Tipperary, a few kilometers north, may also be used. A track leads south from the youth hostel to Lough Muskry, where a route avoiding the steep cliffs leads to the summit of Greenane. The youth hostel at Mountain Lodge offers the best walking base on the south side of the mountains, although the villages of Michelstown and Cahir may also be used. A track leads northwest from Mountain Lodge to near the summit of Galtybeg. Roads lead into the hills of northern Tipperary from the towns of Tipperary, Limerick and Nenagh, and from the village of Templemore. The town of Portlaoise is the best walking base for the Slieve Bloom Mountains.

Suggested Walks

Ballydavid Wood to Mountain Lodge. Across the Galtees via Lough Muskry, Greenane and Galtybeg, with possible sidetrips to Galtymore and other peaks. Beautiful lakes, precipitous cliffs and splendid views from the crest. **Length:** 10.5 kilometers (6.5 miles). **Walking Time:** 5 hours. **Difficulty:** Moderately difficult. **Path Markings:** None. No path from Lough Muskry to Galtybeg.
Maps:
• Ordnance Survey half-inch series (1:126,720), sheets 18 and 22 (recommended). Or:
• Ordnance Survey one-inch Black Outline (1:63,360), sheets 154, 155 and 156.

The Seven Peaks Walk. From Cahir to Anglesborough. Along the crest of the Galtees, including ascents of the seven highest peaks. An annual Seven Peaks Walk is hosted by the Tipperary Adventure Club in late June. **Length:** 27 kilometers (17 miles). **Walking Time:** 9 hours. **Difficulty:** Moderately difficult; 1,400 meters (4,600 feet) of ascents. **Path Markings:** None; no path from Galtybeg to Temple Hill.
Maps:
• Ordnance Survey half-inch series (1:126,720), sheets 18 and 22 (recommended). Or:
• Ordnance Survey one-inch Black Outline (1:63,360), sheets 154, 155, 165 and 166.

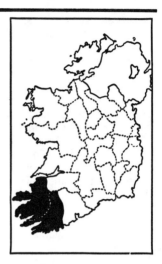

Kerry & West Cork

Southwestern Ireland culminates in five rocky, mountainous peninsulas that together form a great claw extending into the Atlantic. Here, in Kerry and West Cork, rising abruptly from the sea, are the highest, most rugged mountains in Ireland. Well over 300 peaks more than 300 meters high are distributed among more than a dozen ranges. Sixty-five peaks exceed 600 meters, and nine, including Ireland's four highest summits, tower above 915 meters (3,000 feet).

The region boasts perhaps the finest mountain scenery in Ireland, most of it accessible only on foot. Numerous tracks and cross-country routes ascend the ranges to mountain lakes cupped in spectacular cliff-bound cirques, or *corries;* follow jagged ridges to lofty summits with sweeping views of the rugged coast; and meander through high moorlands strewn with lakes and surrounded by peaks.

Enroute, you may pass one of the few hill farms remaining in the district or—more likely—the remains of the many that bad weather and poor soils long ago caused to be abandoned. Old stone walls, cairns, ruined shepherds' huts and the remains of entire settlements stand as mute testimony to the unforgiving nature of these mountains—a warning that the hill walker would do well to keep in mind. In many places you encounter the ruins of monastic settlements dating back to the 6th century, including beehive cells, oratories and cross-inscribed stones and pillars.

The mountains of Kerry and West Cork consist mostly of old red sandstone similar to that of the Galtees. During the Ice Age, much of the region was overrun by glaciers, which chiseled steep cliffs and scoured numerous corries that are now filled with tarns. The narrow bays separating the five major peninsulas of Kerry and West Cork are actually fjords, glacial valleys later submerged by a rising sea. Inland, similar valleys are bounded by steep slopes and often contain one or more lakes. The Iveragh Peninsula is the largest and most mountainous in the district. Here, extending west from the town of Killarney, are the magnificent Macgillycuddy Reeks, a great, rugged horseshoe of peaks culminating in 1,041-meter (3,314-foot) Carrauntoohil, Ireland's highest mountain. Nearby are 1,010-meter (3,314-foot) Beenkeragh and 975-meter (3,200-foot) Caher, the second and third highest summits in the country. In many places the peaks drop away in sheer precipices to corrie basins spangled with tarns 300 to 500 meters below. Portions of the main ridge are crowned with serrated peaks connected by narrow walkways falling away on both sides in awesome rock walls. Other stretches, though steep, offer less precarious walking.

To reach the summit of Carrauntoohil, you can follow a track leading up the Gaddagh River valley to Loughs Gouragh and Callee, where a steep gully (the "Devil's Ladder") leads to a grassy saddle just below the peak. From Carrauntoohil you have a choice of two difficult ridge routes (over Caher or Beenkeragh) leading back to Lough Acoose, near Glencar.

The main ridge of the Reeks extends eastward from the saddle at the head of Devil's Ladder. It connects five 915-meter peaks, as well as several lower summits, before dropping away to the Gap of Dunloe. The ridge is bounded in the north by high cliffs and, in its succession of rocky crags and sheer precipices, offers the most rugged mountain scenery in the Reeks, perhaps in all of Ireland. The walk along the Ridge of the Reeks is the finest ridge walk in the country, but should be attempted only by experienced, well-equipped hill walkers. Storms and mists can swiftly envelop these mountains, making a descent to safety either perilous or impossible. An annual Reeks Walk is held by the Kerry Mountain Rescue Association on the first Sunday in June.

Southwest of the Reeks, a somewhat lower, but scarcely less impressive, chain extends some 32 kilometers (20 miles) to the sea. The entire range is spangled with lakes, above which rise great cliffs and numerous peaks over 600 meters high. The impressive ring of cliffs and summits flanking Lough Reagh, near Glencar, offer numerous opportunities for roaming among high peaks and glacial lakes. One of the most spectacular routes is from Broaghnabinnia, the northernmost peak of the range, to Ballaghbeama Gap, then to Mullaghanattin ("mountain of the gorse") and finally to the peaks above Lough Reagh. The entire route is strenuous, and the descent to Lough Reagh is difficult and should be undertaken with great care.

To the north lies yet another mountain range—the Coomacarrea group—with steep, mostly grassy peaks, several of which exceed 600 meters. The range also includes a series of fine north-facing, tarn-filled coums. The ridge connecting the modest Seefin, Coolroe and Beenraugh peaks offers easy walking. Farther west rises the isolated mass of 690-meter (2,265-foot) Knocknadobar, from the top of which is a sweeping view that includes Dingle Bay to the north.

The Gap of Dunloe separates the Macgillycuddy Reeks to the west from

Purple Mountain, which can be seen across Lough Leane from Killarney. Three of its summits exceed 600 meters. Southeast of Lough Leane stretches the high moorland of the Mangerton group, with three peaks over 600 meters. East of the Mangertons rise the twin summits of the Paps, which offer one of the finest views of Killarney. A day's walk begins on the west shore of Lough Leane with an ascent of Tomies Mountain and Purple Mountain and from there south to Turc Mountain and Mangerton. You can then either strike northward across the moorlands back to Killarney or head west to include the Paps in your circuit. Additional walks are possible in the Derrynasaggart and Boggeragh mountains, southeast of Mangerton and the Paps.

The Derrynasaggart Mountains are succeeded in the southwest by an imposing chain of peaks extending down the Bæra Peninsula from the picturesque gorge of Gougane Barra to the town of Glengariff. The main summit ridge offers a difficult day's walk. You can also walk across the range from the youth hostel at Ballingeary to the ones at Bonane or Loo Bridge. Other possible walks include a circuit through the Shehy Mountains to the south of the Ballingeary youth hostel.

West of Glengariff, the picturesque Caha Mountains form the backbone of the Bæra Peninsula, a slim finger of land between the Kenmare River on the north and Bantry Bay on the south. A few peaks top 600 meters, but the summit ridge tends to be flat and boggy, making for a difficult walk, but one rewarded by views of deep valleys and mountain lakes. From the youth hostel at Glanmore Lake, you can walk the Lauragh Horseshoe, a circuit that includes Toogh, Coomacloghane, Eskatariff and Lackabane mountains.

The Slieve Miskish Mountains continue westward from the Cahas, extending nearly to the tip of the Bæra Peninsula. A good cross-country route links the main peaks.

The Dingle Peninsula is the northernmost of the peninsulas of Kerry and West Cork. It is bounded on the south by Dingle Bay, across which can be seen the mountains of Iveragh. Toward the tip of the Dingle Peninsula, the Brandon Mountains form a picturesque chain running north-south for a distance of some 16 kilometers. These mountains have boulder-strewn ridges, broken cliffs, wild moorlands and several chains of lakes. Brandon, 953 meters (3,127 feet), is the highest peak in Ireland outside the Macgillycuddy Reeks. Commanding a beautiful view of the Atlantic and the surrounding mountains, Brandon was named for Brendan the Navigator, patron saint of Kerry, whom the Irish claim was the first European to discover the New World—and they may be right. The ruins of his stone oratory can be found near the summit. The ridge walk from Connor Pass northward to Brandon is spectacular. Another fine walk begins at the village of Cloghane, passes Lough Cruttia, Lough Nalackan and a chain of glacial lakes, and reaches the summit ridge by means of a rough scramble. From there you can head northward over Masatiompan peak to Brandon Head, where cliffs over 300 meters high plunge into the Atlantic.

East of Connor Pass the Brandons are succeeded by a more extensive, if less impressive, mountain range offering numerous summit ascents but few ridge walks. One of the best ridge walks is from Ballyduff to Castlegregory, taking in a number of peaks near or over 600 meters elevation.

The Slieve Mish Mountains form the backbone of the narrow neck of land connecting the Dingle Peninsula to the mainland. They include several peaks over 600 meters elevation, including Baurtregaum, on whose northern face three enormous glens have been carved out from summit to base. A fine ridge walk extends from Annascaul to Camp and from there to the summit of Baurtregaum.

East of the Slieve Mish Mountains and the town of Tralee to the north are several minor ranges extending across the Kerry mainland into neighboring Limerick. These ranges include the Stack Mountains, Glanaruddery Hills, Mullaghareir Mountains and Nagles Mountains, none of which exceed 460 meters (1,500 feet) elevation. All offer pleasant walking, however.

Tourist Information

Cork/Kerry Region Tourist Information Office (see *Address Directory*).

Other tourist information offices open all year are found in Killarney, Tralee and Skibbereen.

Holiday Information Booklets: *South Kerry, North Kerry,* and *West Cork,* available from Bord Fáilte.

Maps

- Ordnance Survey half-inch series (1:126,720), sheets 20, 21 and 24.
- Ordnance Survey one-inch Coloured District Map (1:63,360), *Killarney* (recommended).
- Ordnance Survey one-inch Black Outline (1:63,360), sheets 160, 161, 162, 171, 172, 173, 174, 175, 182, 183, 184, 185, 186, 190, 191, 192, 193, 197, 198, 199, 200, 203, 204 and 205.

Guidebooks

- *Climbing in the British Isles: Ireland* by H.C. Hart, Longmans, Green and Co., London, 1895. Reprinted by Joss Lynam, Dublin.
- *Cork and Kerry: A Hosteller's Guide,* An Óige, Dublin, 1969.
- *The Irish Peaks,* Joss Lynam, general editor, Constable & Company, London, 1980.
- *Irish Walk Guides: South West* by Sean O'Suilleabhain, Gill & Macmillan, Dublin, 1978.

- *Journeys into Muskerry: Wanderings and Excursions in the Country West of Cork City and the Kerry Borderland of Southern Ireland* by J.C. Coleman, Dundalgan Press (W. Tempest) Ltd., Dundalk.
- *Mountaineering in Ireland* by Claude W. Wall (revised), F.M.C.I., Dublin, 1976.
- *The Mountains of Killarney* by J.C. Coleman, Dundalgan Press, Dundalk, 1948.

Walking Bases

A network of 10 youth hostels provides access to all the mountains of Kerry and West Cork, save those of the Dingle Peninsula.

The Ballingeary youth hostel is a good walking base for the Derrynasaggart Mountains, the peaks west of Gougane Barra and the Sheny Mountains.

A route leads from the Black Valley youth hostel to the summit of Carrauntoohil and the entire Ridge of the Reeks. You can also gain access to the Reeks from the hostel via an easy track to the Gap of Dunloe. This hostel is also a good walking base for the Purple Mountains.

The Bonane youth hostel is convenient to the Caha Mountains, the Mangertons and the high ridge between Glengariff and Gougane Barra.

The finest route to the summit of Carrauntoohil and the entire Macgillycuddy Reeks strikes southward from the Corran Tuathail youth hostel on the north side of the range. The hostel also provides excellent access to the mountains north and west of the village of Glencar.

The Glanmore Lake youth hostel is located on the north slope of the Caha Mountains and offers the best base for exploring both this range and the Slieve Mikish Mountains to the west.

The Killarney youth hostel is the best base for exploring the Purple Mountains and is also convenient to the Paps, the Mangertons and the Derrynasaggart Mountains.

The Loo Bridge youth hostel is situated in a valley flanked by the Mangertons on the west, the Paps on the east and the Derrynasaggart Mountains on the south.

Other youth hostels in the region are located at Alihies, Ballinskelligs, Cape Clear—on Clear Island southwest of Skibbereen—and Valentia.

The Dingle Peninsula has no youth hostels. The most convenient centers are the towns of Dingle for the Brandon Mountains and Tralee for the Slieve Mish Mountains. Regular bus service connects the two towns. Both offer easy access to the mountains in the center of the peninsula.

Killarney, of course, can serve as a center for the entire Kerry/West Cork region, particularly the Iveragh Peninsula. The bunkhouse accommodation at the Climber's Inn in Glencar is convenient to all the major mountain areas on the peninsula.

On the Bæra Peninsula, the village of Glengariff is a good walking base for the Caha Mountains and the peaks running east to Gougane Barra. During the summer, buses run regularly between Glengariff and Killarney.

The best center for the Boggerah Mountains is the village of Millstreet, which also offers access to Caherbarnagh Mountain and the Paps to the west.

Suggested Walks

Ballingeary Youth Hostel to Loo Bridge Youth Hostel. Across the mountains north of Gougane Barra to Morley's Bridge, following a track between Lackabaun and Coomataggart Mountains; then north along a road leading to Loo Bridge. **Length:** 27 kilometers (17 miles). **Walking Time:** 8½ to 10 hours. **Difficulty:** Moderately difficult. **Path Markings:** None.
Maps:
• Ordnance Survey half-inch series (1:126,720), sheets 21 and 24.
• Ordnance Survey one-inch Coloured District Map (1:63,360), *Killarney* (recommended). Or:
• Ordnance Survey one-inch Black Outline (1:63,360), sheets 184 and 192.

The Reeks Walk. Along the wild, precipitous Ridge of the Reeks from the Gap of Dunloe to Lough Acoose. Spectacular mountain scenery. **Length:** 18 kilometers (11 miles). **Walking Time:** 6 to 8 hours. **Difficulty:** Difficult to very difficult, with steep scrambles and some precarious ridge crossings. **Path Markings:** None; trackless most of the way.
Maps:
• Ordnance Survey half-inch series (1:126,720), sheets 20 and 21 (recommended). Or:
• Ordnance Survey one-inch Black Outline (1:63,360), sheets 183 and 184.

The Nephins & North Mayo Highlands

The Nephin Beg, or Corslieve Range, is an isolated mountain group occupying a remote, almost roadless district in northwestern County Mayo. Walking bases are few and widely scattered in this, the wildest region in Ireland. As a result, the Nephins do not lend themselves to casual excursions. But they are ideal for the hill walker prepared to travel long distances over rough terrain and to spend a night or two camping on the high moorlands or bedding down in a hill cabin.

Nephin Mountain is an isolated, symmetrical quartzite cone situated just west of large Lough Conn. The 807-meter (2,646-foot) summit overlooks a vast sweep of terrain because no peaks of comparable height stand nearby to block the view. To the north, across Donegal Bay, you can see the mighty cliff of Slieve League and the great cone of Errigal. The Sperrin Mountains of Tyrone and Derry are visible in the northeast. Nearer at hand is the rocky crest of Slieve Gumph in County Sligo. Lough Conn spreads out at the eastern base of the mountain, and the wild moorlands leading to Nephinbeg and Slieve Car extend toward the west. To the south rises Croagh Patrick, Ireland's holy mountain.

The Nephinbeg Range, crowned by 629-meter (2,065-foot) Nephinbeg, rises to the west, joined to Nephin by high, rolling moorlands. Beyond Nephinbeg, the range splits, extending north to Bangor and south to Mulrany and Newport. The Nephinbeg Range offers rugged scenery, grand views and some of the wildest, loneliest walking in Ireland. From the village of Mulrany, you can walk north to Slieve Car and beyond. Halfway there, you have the choice of heading east toward Nephin.

The moorlands of the North Mayo Highlands continue north from the Nephinbeg Range to the coast. The highlands themselves have few summits exceeding 300 meters elevation, but they are very wild. At the coast, they culminate in sheer precipices of 300 meters or more. An excellent cliff walk from Belmullet to Killala takes about three days.

West of Mulrany, at the southern end of the Nephinbeg Range, an extremely short, narrow neck of land connects the mainland to the Corraun, where three hills look out to Achill Island and the Atlantic. The island is accessible by a bridge that crosses the narrow strait separating it from the peninsula. The two highest peaks on the island—Slievemore (672 meters; 2,204 feet) and Croaghaun (668 meters; 2,192 feet)—are both easy climbs offering fine views. Croaghaun is particularly noteworthy for its great cliffs, which plunge in stages to the Atlantic.

Tourist Information

Western Region Tourist Information Office (see *Address Directory*).

A second tourist information office open all year is located at Westport.

Holiday Information Booklet: *Co. Mayo*, available from Bord Fáilte.

Maps

- Ordnance Survey half-inch series (1:126,720), sheet 6 (recommended).
- Ordnance Survey one-inch Black Outline (1:63,360), sheets 39, 40, 41, 51, 52, 53, 62, 63 and 64.

Guidebooks

- *Climbing in the British Isles: Ireland* by H.C. Hart, Longmans, Green and Co., London, 1895. Reprinted by Joss Lynam, Dublin.
- *The Irish Peaks,* Joss Lynam, general editor, Constable & Company, London, 1980.
- *Irish Walk Guides/2: West* by Tony Whilde, Gill & Macmillan, Dublin, 1978.
- *Mountaineering in Ireland* by Claude W. Wall (revised), F.M.C.I., Dublin, 1976.

Walking Bases

There is no convenient center for taking day walks into the Nephinbeg Range. The closest villages are Mulrany, Newport and Bangor. Nephin is accessible by way of a road south from the village of Crossmolina. The Currane youth hostel is a good center for walks on Achill Island. The Pollatomish youth hostel is near the North May Highlands and coast.

Sligo & Leitrim

The hills of Sligo and Leitrim are unlike those found anywhere else in Ireland. Composed mostly of limestone, they typically have flat tops bounded by steep blocky cliffs that fall away to skirts of talus and grass-covered scree. Many walkers will find the firm, dry footing on the grassy plateaus a welcome change from the boggy undulations of most Irish hills. Although the steep cliffs make for rugged scenery, the hills of Sligo and Leitrim are not high. One hundred summits exceed an elevation of 300 meters, of which only three top 600 meters.

The Dartry Mountains north of Sligo are the most striking hills in the two counties, forming a horseshoe-shaped tableland about 10 kilometers around. The western end of the horseshoe culminates in the great prow-shaped mass of Ben Bulben (527 meters; 1,730 feet), which is bounded on three sides by limestone cliffs scores of meters high. The grave of W. B. Yeats, the greatest of Irish poets, lies in a churchyard in the village of Drumcliff "Under bare Ben Bulben's head." Some scrambling is required to ascend the ridge near Ben Bulben, but the walk around the perimeter to Carrownamaddoo, at its northern end, is easy. Due west of the summit, a gap in the cliffs leads down to the Bundoran-Sligo highway.

Just east of Ben Bulben is the Gleniff Valley, hemmed in by limestone cliffs. On the east side of the valley are the two highest summits in Sligo and Leitrim: Cloghcorrah (612 meters; 2,007 feet), and Truskmore (644 meters; 2,113 feet). The summits are undistinguished, but on their eastern flanks are high, steep cliffs enclosing the amphitheater of Glenade.

South of Glencar, with its lovely lake and two waterfalls, are the Castlegal Mountains. The ridge linking the principal summits is studded with rock outcrops and offers fine walking. This range is also known as *Slieve gan baiste,* the "mountains without rain," which in Ireland would be a novelty indeed.

To the west and south of Sligo town, you can wander among the low hills of Slieve Daeane or those near Collooney, both of which have picturesque outcrops, not of limestone, but granite. Of greater interest, however, is Slieve Gumph, or the Ox Mountains, which run southwest for some 32 kilometers from the village of Skreen to the border of County Mayo. From Skreen a good ridge walk leads over granite peaks to Lough Easky.

The headwaters of the Shannon River, Ireland's longest, rise in a green meadow—known as the "Shannon Pot"—at the foot of 594-meter (1,949-foot) Tiltinbane, in eastern County Leitrim. The ridge leading southeast to Knockatoona (579 meters; 1,744 feet) offers fine walking. A second, somewhat lower ridge parallels the course of the river on the southwest, culminating in 545-meter (1,787-foot) Slievenakilla.

Lough Allen, the first of the large lakes that punctuate the Shannon's course down the center of Ireland, lies among dark ranges where limestone is less prominent than elsewhere in the district. The best walking is found in the Slieveanierin Mountains on the east side of the lake, which can be followed from the town of Drumshambo, at the foot of Lough Allen, northward to Ballingleragh at its head. The Arigna Mountains, on the west side of the lake, are noted for their coal deposits and are of less interest to hill walkers than to miners.

Tourist Information

North Western Region Tourist Information Office (see *Address Directory*).

Holiday Information Booklets: *Co. Sligo* and *Co. Leitrim*, available from Bord Fáilte.

Maps

- Ordnance Survey half-inch series (1:126,720), sheet 7 (recommended).
- Ordnance Survey one-inch Black Outline (1:63,360), sheets 42, 43, 44, 53, 54, 55, 56, 65, 66 and 67.

Guidebooks

- *The Irish Peaks,* Joss Lynam, general editor, Constable & London, 1980.
- *Irish Walk Guides/3: North West* by Patrick Simms and Gerry Foley, Gill & Macmillan, Dublin, 1979.
- *Mountaineering in Ireland* by Claude W. Wall (revised), F.M.C.I., Dublin, 1976.

Walking Bases

Sligo is a good walking base for the Daltry Mountains, Gleniff Horseshoe and other nearby ranges. It is less convenient to the Slieve Gumph Range and the mountains of eastern Leitrim. Walks in the Slieve Gumph Range are possible from Skreen, at its northern end, and from Lough Talt, which lies on its west side not far east of the town of Ballina in County Mayo. Drumshambo is a possible base for exploring the mountains around Lough Allen and the Shannon Pot.

The Wicklow Mountains

The foothills of the Wicklow Mountains are visible on the southern outskirts of Dublin. They spread southward through County Wicklow, presenting the hill walker with a vast area of wild moorlands across which countless walks are possible. Some 150 hills top 300 meters, of which one-third exceed 600 meters. Ten peaks are higher than 760 meters (2,500 feet), and one—Lugnaquilla Mountain—is 926 meters (3,039 feet), making it the highest Irish peak outside Kerry. The Wicklows have the highest average elevation of any hill district in Ireland.

The main backbone of the range, from Sally Gap south to Lugnaquilla, consists of rounded granite domes, most of which are densely blanketed with tussocky moorlands and peat. Patches of drier grassland are scattered throughout the boggy upland, and forests cover many of the lower slopes and glens. East of the main crest, the granite tops are flanked by summits of schist and quartzite.

Glacier-carved glens penetrate deeply into the hills. At their heads and along their flanks there are often steep cliffs chiseled by ice from the mountainsides. Tarns often lie at the feet of the cliffs, but overall these mountains contain fewer lakelets than found in the west and north of Ireland.

Numerous streams rush down the glens on either side of the range. The River Liffey, which flows through the center of Dublin to the Irish Sea, rises on the west flank of the Tonduff hills south of the city, flows southwest through Poulaphouca Reservoir, then northwest into the plain of Kildare, before swinging back eastward to the city and the sea. On the opposite side of the Tonduff Ridge, the Dargle River tumbles eastward toward Deer Park, dropping 120 meters (392 feet) along the way to form the Powerscourt Waterfall, the highest in Ireland.

Although the Wicklows contain numerous cliffs and rocky summits they are, overall, a gently contoured range. Even so, the dense mantle of wet, hummocky moorland and heather so characteristic of these hills makes walking very difficult in some areas. In others, grassy tracks and forest paths ease the hill walker's way.

The most difficult walking is encountered along the main crest of the range from Sally Gap south to Lugnaquilla. Much of the region is trackless moorland and peat, and the walker must negotiate not only steep ascents, but precarious tussocks and wet bogs, both of which may impede progress. Few roads cross this region, however, so it provides the loneliest, wildest walking in the Wicklows, with splendid views from a succession of high peaks. This grand tour of the range, however—from Sally Gap southward to Mullaghcleevaum (850 meters; 2,788 feet), Tonelagee (819 meters; 2686 feet) and Lugnaquilla—should be attempted only by well-equipped, experienced hill walkers.

Numerous shorter routes are found throughout the Wicklows, including many that connect the Wicklows' nine youth hostels. Even the wild heartland of the range is accessible from numerous points around its perimeter. The Military Road, Sally Gap Road, Wicklow Gap Road and Glenmalure Road all provide good starting points for one-day rambles into the wilds.

Several good routes begin near the outskirts of Dublin. One touches Three Rock Mountain, Two Rock Mountain, Kilmashogue Mountain and Tibradden Mountain—all below 600 meters elevation. The burial mound of the Irish King Niall (killed doing battle with the Danes in 917) is found on the summit of Tibradden. A more difficult route follows the Dublin-Wicklow boundary from 650-meter (2,131-foot) Seechon to Corrig (620 meters; 2,035 feet), Seefingan (721 meters; 2,364 feet) and Kippure (754 meters; 2,475 feet), the highest peak in the Dublin Hills. From here, it is possible to follow the range eastward to Tonduff (642 meters; 2,107 feet), Maulin (570 meters; 1,871 feet) and Djouce (727 meters; 2,385 feet).

South of the Wicklows is the narrow, rocky ridge of the Blackstair Mountains, which extends along the Carlow-Wexford boundary into Kilkenny. The range consists of peat-covered cones more boldly shaped than those of the Wicklows. The highest peak is Mt. Leinster (796 meters; 2,610 feet). The ridge is 32 kilometers long and drops abruptly to the plains on either side. It is possible either to walk its entire length or to descend to the lowlands at several points along the way.

Tourist Information

City of Dublin Region Tourist Information Office (see *Address Directory*).
Eastern Region Tourist Information Office (see *Address Directory*).
Holiday Information Booklets: *Co. Kildare* and *Co. Wicklow*, available from Bord Fáilte.

Maps

- Ordnance Survey 1:500,000, one sheet: Wicklow. Recently published. Shows the Wiclow Way.
- Ordnance Survey one-inch Coloured District Maps (1:63,360), two sheets: *Dublin* and *Wicklow* (also recommended).
- Ordnance Survey half-inch series (1:126,720), sheet 16.
- Ordnance Survey one-inch Black Outline (1:63,360), sheets 120, 121, 129, 130, 147, 148, 157 and 158.

Guidebooks

- *Dublin and Wicklow Mountains: Access Routes for the Hill Walker,* edited and published by members of the Irish Ramblers Club, 1976.
- *The Irish Peaks,* Joss Lynam, general editor, Constable & Company, London, 1980.
- *Irish Walk Guides/4: East* by David Herman, Jean Boydell, Michael Casey and Eithne Kennedy of the Irish Ramblers Club, Gill & Macmillan, Dublin, 1979.
- *Mountaineering in Ireland* by C.W. Wall, F.M.C.I., Dublin, 1976.

Walking Bases

The hills south of Dublin can be easily explored from the city itself. Numerous roads lead into the hills, and regularly scheduled buses serve many approaches. The Military Road heads south from Dublin and runs the length of the Wicklows, offering convenient access to most of the major walking areas. Roads also lead into the hills from the town of Naas on the west and from the towns of Bray, Wicklow and Arklow on the east.

The best walking bases for the Wicklows, however, are the nine youth hostels scattered the length and breadth of the range. No part of these hills is more than a day's walk from one of the hostels. As a result, you can take extended walks in the Wicklows, using the hostels for overnight accommodation. There are also two mountaineering club huts at Glendalough.

The Blackstairs Mountains are more remote, but convenient access is available from the village of Bunclody on the north and the town of New Ross on the south.

available from the village of Bunclody on the north and the town of New Ross on the south.

Suggested Walks

Aghavannagh Youth Hostel to Tiglin Youth Hostel. A grand tour of the Wicklows, including an ascent of Lugnaquilla, the fifth highest peak in Ireland. Through forest and moorland; along mountain streams and past lakes flanked by cliffs; over summits with splendid, wild views in all directions. The trip can be taken in two or three days with overnight stays at the Ballinclea, Glendalough or Glenmalure youth hostels. From the Aghavannagh youth hostel, the route follows a forest track to near the summit of Lugnaquilla, then descends westward to a road leading to the Ballinclea youth hostel. From there, the Table Track—a cairned route in places—climbs through forest and moorland before dropping into Glenmalure. A short way past the youth hostel, the route climbs to a shoulder of Lugduff Mountain and strikes northward cross-country to the Glendalough youth hostel. From there the route heads east on a rural track, attaining a couple of summits before descending through forest to roads leading to the Tiglin youth hostel. The route may be followed in either direction. **Walking Time:** 19 hours: 2 to 3 days. **Difficulty:** Moderately difficult, with some difficult sections. **Path Markings:** Cairns along the Table Track; elsewhere no markings; some cross-country sections.
Maps:
• Ordnance Survey half-inch series (1:126,720), sheet 16.
• Ordnance Survey one-inch Coloured District Map (1:63,360), *Wicklow* (recommended). Or:
• Ordnance Survey one-inch Black Outline (1:63,360), sheets 121, 129 and 130.

Dublin-Wicklow Boundary Walk. From the 49A bus terminus at Bohernabreena to the Glencree youth hostel. Along an open, often boggy ridge to Kippure, highest of the Dublin Hills, and down a gap in the cliffs on its east side to upper and lower Lough Bray. From there, it's an easy walk north to the Glencree youth hostel. The walk may also be continued to the Knockree youth hostel, 6.5 kilometers (4 miles) east. **Walking Time:** 7 hours to Glencree. **Difficulty:** Difficult; the boggy section between Seefingan and Kippure is extremely difficult. **Path Markings:** Boundary stones along the ridge; otherwise none.
Maps:
• Ordnance Survey half-inch series (1:126,720), sheet 16.
• Ordnance Survey one-inch Coloured District Map (1:63,360), *Dublin* (recommended). Or:
• Ordnance Survey one-inch Black Outline (1:63,360), sheets 111, 112, 120 and 121.

Address Directory

A

- *An Óige,* Myles Caulfield, 39 Mountjoy Square, Dublin 1. Tel. (01) 74 57 34.
- *An Taisce,* The National Trust for Ireland, 41 Percy Place, Dublin 4. Tel. (01) 68 19 44.
- *Association for Adventure Sports,* Tiglin Adventury Center, Ashford, County Wicklow. Tel. (0404) 4169.

B

- *Bord Fáilte* (The Irish Tourist Board), Baggot Street Bridge, Dublin 2. Tel. (01) 76 58 71. For postal enquiries, you should write to P.O. Box 273, Dublin 8.

C

- *C.H.A. Walking Club,* (Hon. Sec.) 2 Ardenza Park, Blackrock, County Dublin.
- *Castlebar's International Four Days' Walks,* Courthouse, Castlebar, County Mayo. Tel. (094) 21 0 33.
- *Clarke, Eileen.* Tel. (01) 74 83 13.
- *Climber's Inn,* Glencar, County Kerry. Contact the proprietor, Jack Walsh. Tel. Glencar 104.
- *Comeragh Mountaineering Club,* Garry Farrell, 17 Cluain a Laoi, Cork Road, Waterford.
- *Cork/Kerry Region Tourist Information Office,* Tourist House, Grand Parade, Cork. Tel. (021) 23 2 51.
- *Cork Mountaineering Club,* Paul Brennan, Flat 1, Bellair Gardens, Douglas Road, Cork.

D

- *Dalriada Mountaineering Club,* Harry O'Brien, 43 Cherryfield Avenue, Walkinstown, Dublin 12.
- *Danum Mountaineering Club,* Carol Bardon, 18 Henley Park, Churchtown, Dublin 14.
- *Dublin International Two Days' Walks,* 61 Ardcollum Avenue, Artane, Dublin 5. Tel. (01) 31 28 97.

- *Dublin Region Tourist Information Office,* 51 Dawson Street, Dublin 2. Tel. (01) 74 77 33.
- *Dublin University Mountaineering Club,* 23. 31 Trinity College, Dublin 2.

E

- *Eastern Command Mountaineering Club,* Ann Lane, 41 Raglan Road, Dublin 4.
- *Eastern Region Tourist Information Office,* 1 Clarinda Park North, Dun Laoghaire, County Dublin. Tel. (01) 80 85 71.
- *Eileen Clarke,* see *Clarke, Eileen.*
- *Emerald Star Line Ltd.,* St. James Gate, Dublin 8. Tel. (01) 75 67 01.
- *Emergency:* Tel. 999.
- *Ennis Tourist Information Office.* Tel. (065) 21 3 66.

F

- *The Farmhouse,* Luggala. For bookings, telephone Eileen Clarke (01) 74 83 13.
- *Federation of Mountaineering Clubs of Ireland (F.M.C.I.),* Patricia Murray, secretary, 3 Gort na Mona Drive, Foxrock, County Dublin. *General Enquiries:* Fino la Donoghue, 20 Leopardstown Gardens, Blackrock, County Dublin.
- *Forest and Wildlife Service,* 22 Upper Merrion Street, Dublin 2. Tel. (01) 78 92 11.

G

- *Geological Survey,* Photo Section, Bishop Street, Dublin 2. Tel. (01) 760 855. A full set of aerial photographs is on file at the survey office.
- *Gill & Macmillan,* Goldenbridge, Inchicore, Dublin 8.
- *Glenfoffany Climbing Club,* Liz Wallace, 4 Craiglee Way, Newtownards, County Down.
- *Government Publications Sales Office,* G.P.O. Arcade, Henry Street, Dublin 1. Tel. (01) 74 25 41.
- *Great Outdoors,* Chatham Street, Dublin 2. Tel. (01) 77 33 57.

H

- *Holiday Fellowship,* 92 Lower Baggot Street, Dublin 2.

I

- *Irish Mountaineering Club, Belfast Section*, Robin Merrick, 82 Marlborough Park North, Belfast BT9 6HL.
- *Irish Mountaineering Club, Dublin Section*, Patricia Murray, 3 Gort na Mona Drive, Foxrock, County Dublin.
- *Irish Orienteering Association*, 34 Dun Emer Drive, Dundrum, Dublin 14.
- *Irish Ramblers Club*, Finola O'Donoghue, 20 Leopardstown Gardens, Blackrock, County Dublin.
- *Irish Tourist Board, London*, 150 New Bond Street, London W1Y 0AQ, England. Tel. (01) 493 3201.
- *Irish Tourist Board, New York*, 590 Fifth Avenue, New York, New York 10036, U.S.A. Tel. (212) 246-7400.

K

- *Killarney Tourist Information Office*. Tel. (064) 31 6 33.

L

- *Laune Mountaineering Club*, Brid O'Donoghue, "Cum A Ciste", Park Road, Killarney, County Kerry.
- *Letterkenny Tourist Information Office*. Tel. Letterkenny 348.

M

- *Mid-Western Region Tourist Information*, 62 O'Connell Street, Limerick. Tel. (061) 47 5 22.

N

- *National Library of Ireland*, Librarian, Kildare Street, Dublin 2.
- *National Sports Council*, 11th Floor, Hawkins House, Dublin 2. Tel. (01) 714 311.
- *New University of Ulster Mountaineering Club*, New University of Ulster, Coleraine, County Londonderry.
- *North Western Region Tourist Information Office*, Stephen Street, Sligo. Tel. (071) 24 36.
- *Northern Ireland Orienteering Association*, 20 Graystown Avenue, Belfast BT9 6UL.
- *Northwest Mountaineering Club*, Maurice Simms, Murlough House, Lifford, County Donegal.

O

- *Ordnance Survey Office*, Phoenix Park, Dublin. Tel. (01) 38 31 71.

P

- *Peaks Climbing Club*, Willie Neil, 27 Cherrymount, Clonmel, County Tipperary.

Q

- *Queens University Mountaineering Club*, Students Union, Queens University, University Road, Belfast BT7 1PE.

S

- *Scout Shop*, 14 Fownes Street, Dublin. Tel. (01) 78 79 55. Located off Dame Street.
- *Shannon Airport Tourist Information Office*. Tel. (061) 61 6 64.
- *Skibbereen Tourist Information Office*. Tel. Skibbereen 189.
- *Slieve Bloom Association*, 9 John's Mall, Birr, County Laois.
- *Slieveadore Club*, Gordon Murray, 74 Rodden's Crescent, Belfast BT5 7JP.
- *Sligo Mountaineering Club*, Alex Carey, 2 Flynns Terrace, College Road, Sligo.
- *South Eastern Region Tourist Information Office*, 41 The Quay, Waterford. Tel. (051) 75 8 23.

T

- *Tiglin Adventure Centre*, Ashford, County Wicklow. Tel. (0404) 4169.
- *Tipperary Adventure Sports Club*, 4 Dawson Villas, Tipperary Twon. Tel. (062) 51 470.
- *Tralee Mountaineering Club*, Sean Kelly, Dromore, Caherslee, Tralee, County Kerry.
- *Tralee Tourist Information Office*. Tel. (066) 21 2 88.

U

- *Ulster Polytechnic Mountaineering Club*, c/o Students Union, Ulster Polytechnic, Jordanstown, Country Antrim.
- *University College Dublin Mountaineering Club*, Arts Block, Belfield, Dublin 14.

• *University College Galway Mountaineering Club,* Raphael Frendo, Porters Office, Concourse, University College, Galway.

W

• *Wayfarers Association,* Catherine Flemming, "Athassal," Burnaby Road, Greystones, County Wicklow.
• *Weather Forecast.* Dublin, Tel. (01) 74 33 20 or Cork Airport, Tel. (021) 2 67 86.
• *Western Region Tourist Information Office,* Aras Fáilte, Galway. Tel. (091) 63 0 81.
• *Westport Tourist Information Office.* Tel. Westport 269.

Y

• *Youth Hostel Association of Northern Ireland,* 93 Dublin Road, Belfast BT2 8HO. Tel. (0232) 24 7 33.

A Quick Reference

In a hurry? Turn to the pages listed below. They will give you the most important information on walking in Ireland.

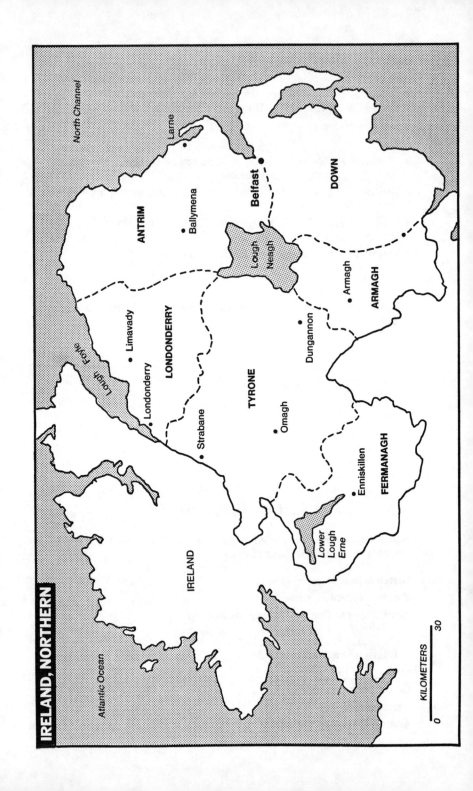

IRELAND, NORTHERN

Ireland, Northern

NORTHERN IRELAND—or Ulster—has long had an unfortunate prominence in news reports—adverse publicity that has already dissuaded many potential visitors from entering the country. Indeed, stories of agitation in Ulster made it seem hardly worthwhile—let alone safe—to enter the country to gather information for this chapter.

But to have stayed away would have been a sad mistake.

Despite reminders in Belfast of the past decade's incidents of violence—barricades, military patrols, armed security guards and the like—life goes on normally. And any jitters that a first-time visitor might experience are quickly stilled by the outgoing friendliness and hospitality of the people. Belfast is neither a war zone, nor is its atmosphere one of a city under siege. If anything, urban renewal projects have recently created more havoc than the unpleasant confrontations that have occasionally dominated the headlines.

Life is even more relaxed in the countryside, and if possible the hospitality is even better. You are constantly reassured both by locals and your own observation and experience that there is little to fear in Northern Ireland; instead, only a country and a people to be enjoyed. After a day or two, the reassurances sink in. As in the Republic of Ireland, the people are extraordinarily friendly and seemingly ever ready to chat with strangers or assist walkers on their way.

The Ulster countryside is open, green and largely rolling, like that of the Republic to the south. Pleasant farms and villages nestle among lush pastures divided by hedgerows and clumps of woodland. Rivers pour from the hills ringing the Central Lowlands, where Lough Neagh—the largest lake in Great Britain and Ireland—forms a vast, shallow inland sea fringed in some places with marshes. Lakes spangle much of Northern Ireland, occupying glacial hollows left over from the Ice Age.

The Ulster hills range from rolling downs to rugged massifs such as the Mournes Mountains, where 14 peaks reach heights in excess of 610 meters (2,000 feet). Slieve Donard, at 850 meters, is the highest point in Northern Ireland. Hill walkers have a variety of high, seldom visited, largely trackless moorlands to choose from—in addition to the Mournes, the Sperrin Mountains, the Cuilcagh Mountains and the wild Antrim Plateau.

You can also walk along much of the Ulster Coast, which is most often rugged, but also has long sandy beaches and peaceful estuaries. The Antrim Coast, with its spectacular cliffs, headlands, sea stacks and bays, is rightfully considered one of the most beautiful in Europe.

And everywhere in Northern Ireland you encounter history in the form of Stone Age monuments, cairns, castles and monasteries and rather outlandish architectural ventures known locally as "follies."

Altogether, Northern Ireland has less than 500 kilometers of marked footpaths—not a lot as European countries go, but far more than the Irish Republic. Most are fairly short walks—usually under 16 kilometers (10 miles)—but many of the paths can be linked to form longer routes. And for the hill walker who prefers to leave the path for the adventure of rambling over the open moorlands, the walking possibilities are numerous.

You can walk almost anywhere in Northern Ireland. Most farmers will grant permission to cross their lands. Many will even suggest the best routes. But they do not welcome uninvited guests walking or camping without their permission, especially in cultivated areas or where livestock is penned.

So when walking in the Ulster countryside, observe the Country Code, a series of 10 reminders written to help visitors enjoy their rural jaunts with a minimum of disturbance to the land and its people:

1. Guard against careless use of fire. Plantations, woodlands and heaths are highly flammable.
2. Fasten all gates—except those you find open.
3. Keep dogs on leashes, especially on private farmlands or along country roads.
4. When crossing farmlands, stick to established paths to avoid trampling crops.
5. Avoid damaging fences, hedges and walls.
6. Leave no litter.
7. Do not pollute lakes, streams or other waters.
8. Do not pick plants, disturb wildlife or deface trees and rocks.
9. Walk carefully on country roads; stick to the right, facing oncoming traffic.
10. Respect the life of the countryside.

The actions of one careless or thoughtless person can spoil things for every one who follows. A farmer who has seen his hay trampled or livestock let loose by one walker may well think twice about letting the next cross his land. By observing the Country Code—a simple blend of courtesy and common sense—you can help to preserve the beauty of the Ulster countryside and the cordial hospitality of its residents.

Flora & Fauna

Although woodlands now cover only 4 percent of Northern Ireland, the Forest Service is engaged in a vigorous reforestation program that envisions 120,000 hectares of woodland by the year 2000. More than 49,000 hectares have already been planted, and 7 forest parks and more than 130 state forests are now open to visitors.

Most of the state forests lie above 200 meters elevation on boggy soils unsuited for agriculture. Sitka spruce, a native of North America's Pacific Northwest, accounts for 62 percent of the planted trees. Noble fir, Douglas fir and lodgepole pine, also natives of western North America, make up another 12 percent. Altogether, 97 percent of the state forests consist of conifers, all introduced.

Native hardwoods—such as ash, birches and oaks—are also planted in the state forests to create diversity and provide wildlife habitat. Privately owned forests, which cover 12,000 hectares, contain a higher proportion of hardwoods. A few remnant stands are also protected in county parks and nature reserves.

Approximately 1.1 million hectares (2.7 million acres)—82 percent of Northern Ireland's total land area—are devoted to agriculture, 90 percent of which is livestock production. Forage grasses are the chief crops, and large fields and pastures accented by hedgerows and small stands of trees are characteristic of Northern Ireland's landscape.

Uncultivated lands, which include undrained lowland tracts and virtually all upland regions other than those planted in forest, are covered by a variety of wetland communities—bogs, fens, marshes, callows, and turloughs. Of these, blanket bog—a community of moisture-loving and acid-tolerant mosses, sedges, grasses and dwarf shrubs—is most widespread and forms a dense, soggy turf on upland slopes.

Plants are protected only in nature reserves and state forest lands. Elsewhere, plant picking is legal, but discouraged. Cutting turf for fuel is still a widespread practice and is even permitted in some state forests.

Northern Ireland's extensive loughs, marshes and seacliffs support a wide variety of nesting sites for waterfowl, wading birds and seabirds. Lough Neagh, the large shallow lake in the center of Northern Ireland, Strangford Lough and the cliffs of the Antrim coast are especially rich in bird life. Altogether, more than 130 species of birds occur in Northern Ireland. Several are protected by law.

Native mammals include Irish hare, red fox, marten, stoat, badger, common otter and red deer. Introduced mammals such as the American gray squirrel, mink, fallow deer and Sitka deer have fared well in various parts of Northern Ireland. In addition, feral goats inhabit many of the upland regions, such as the Antrim Plateau and Mourne Mountains. The gray seal is the only protected mammal.

As in the rest of Ireland, snakes and mosquitos are absent, although clouds of midges can be annoying during the summer. A variety of leaflets and booklets on the flora and fauna of Ulster are available from the Forestry Service and the Northern Ireland Tourist Board. A complete list of these publications can be obtained on request from both organizations. (For their addresses, see the *Address Directory* at the back of this chapter.)

Climate

Northern Ireland's maritime climate is characterized by cool summers and mild winters. Average daily temperatures range from about 4.5°C. (40°F.) in January to 14.5°C. (58°F.) in July and August. On hot, clear summer days the temperature may exceed 27°C. (81°F.), but such days are uncommon. The average minimum temperature in winter is about 1.5°C. (35°F.), but frosts may occur anytime between October and April.

Ireland sits astride the main Atlantic storm track and is the first landfall for storms pushing eastward into Northern Europe. As a result, rainfall is plentiful. Precipitation in the Mournes Mountains, in the southeastern corner of the country, averages more than 1,800 mm (74 inches) per year. Totals are also high in the Western Uplands and the Antrim Plateau. Lying in the rainshadow of the Western Uplands, the Central Lowlands around Lough Neagh average only 850 mm (33 inches) a year. The Ards Coast, in the extreme east of the country, is the driest place in Northern Ireland, receiving as little as 800 mm (31 inches) of precipitation a year. Throughout Ulster, however, precipitation totals for individual years—or months—can vary widely from the averages.

Spring is the driest season of the year, but even then monthly totals typically exceed 51 mm (2 inches), even in the drier sections of the country. December and January are the wettest months, and rainfall during the summer is usually above the monthly average. Dry spells, however, sometimes occur in September and October. Snowfall is sparse and occasional in Northern Ireland, although the higher peaks may be lightly dusted with white during cold winter storms and, on rare occasions, in summer.

Like the climate of Ireland as a whole, that of Northern Ireland is extremely changeable, especially in the hill country. Storms can boil up rapidly, and summer fogs and stratus clouds can suddenly shroud hikers rambling through the uplands, making route finding extremely difficult.

Weather Forecasts

The weather forecasts given in newspapers and on radio and television broadcasts are usually too general to be of much use to walkers. Instead, you should telephone the Meteorological Office directly:

Meteorological Office: Belfast, Tel. (0232) 28 4 57. Provides forecasts for areas within a 24-kilometer radius of Belfast.

Belfast Airport: Crumlin, Tel. (02384) 52 3 39. Provides forecasts for the entire country.

Be sure to tell the person to whom you speak the exact area where you are going to walk; variations in weather can occur even over short distances. You should also specify the dates you intend to be in an area and the weather features that are of interest to you, such as wind speed and direction, temperature and anticipated rainfall. In addition, be sure to ask for the anticipated cloud level. Clouds often hang below 1,000 meters (3,200 feet) and thus can envelop the higher mountain tops in swirling mist.

Where to Get Walking Information

Information on walking, mountaineering and orienteering can be obtained from:

The Sports Council for Northern Ireland (for its address and telephone number, see the *Address Directory* at the back of this chapter).

The Sports Council is a statutory body established in 1974 to promote sports and physical recreation in Northern Ireland. It works closely with government departments, district councils and sports organizations of all kinds and represents Northern Ireland on international sports bodies, such as the International Olympic Committee.

The Sports Council can put you in touch with organizations devoted to walking, mountaineering, orienteering and skiing. It can also suggest places to walk in Northern Ireland and tell you where to obtain guidebooks and maps. Its Tollymore Mountain Centre on the northern edge of the Mourne Mountains offers courses in mountaineering and other outdoor activities (for information, see the section on *Mountaineering Courses* later in this chapter). The Sports Council also coordinates the work of several organizations involved in the development of the Ulster Way, Northern Ireland's only long-distance footpath. The council publishes leaflets describing several different sections of the path (listed in the section on *Guidebooks)* and has a comprehensive guidebook in the works.

YHANI

The Youth Hostel Association of Northern Ireland (YHANI) is also a valuable source of information on walking. The *YHANI Handbook* describes walks near each of Northern Ireland's 13 youth hostels, lists the

Ordnance Survey maps that cover the area around each hostel, and contains information on proper clothing and equipment, safe-walking tips and first aid. In addition, YHANI sponsors the annual Mourne Wall Walk, a 35-kilometer trek along the watershed-boundary wall through the Mourne Mountains. This walk is held the first Sunday in June and is open to all comers for a nominal entry fee. YHANI's Peak-a-Month Club organizes hill walks from different hostels about once a month. And the Fell Walking Group organizes weekend walks through hill country, forests, lakelands and coastal areas.

To obtain the *YHANI Handbook*, information on the Mourne Wall Walk, and schedules of walks organized by the Peak-a-Month Club and Fell Walking Group, contact:

YHANI Information Centre (see *Address Directory*).

Most youth hostel wardens can give you a wealth of information on the areas in the immediate vicinity of the hostels and, if you have the appropriate Ordnance Survey maps, they will often mark out suggested walks on them.

State Forests & Forest Parks

Northern Ireland's state forests and forest parks offer numerous walking opportunities. Forest trails, which are waymarked and range in length up to 13 kilometers (8 miles), have been established in many forest areas. Together, these forest areas contain more than 1,100 kilometers (700 miles) of traffic-free roads and paths. Several of the forests also have campgrounds, caravanning sites, picnic areas, wildlife enclosures, interpretive centres and arboretums. Other forest areas are less developed and still do not have established footpaths, but you can roam nearly anywhere you wish within them. Walks can easily be planned in these forests by referring to the appropriate Ordnance Survey sheets. Bus service is available to most forest parks and many state forests. Information on the forest areas, plus a series of free leaflets to the forest areas and walks within them, is available from:

Forest Service (see *Address Directory*).

These leaflets include:

- *Fermanagh Lakeland Route* (Navar and Big Dog Trails). Published by The Sports Council for Northern Ireland. Describes a 40-kilometer (25-mile) section of the Ulster Way stretching between Lough Erne and Lough Macnean through the Lough Navar, Big Dog and Ballintempo forests. Includes a sketch map.
- *The Moyle Way.* Also published by the Sports Council for Northern

Ireland. Describes a 29-kilometer (18-mile) path from Ballycastle on the North Antrim Coast to Glenariff. Includes a sketch map.

• *Somerset Forest Trim Trail.* Describes a 2-kilometer keep-fit trail with 14 exercise stations.

• *Hillsborough Forest Wayfaring Trail.* A 1:5,000 color map showing three orienteering courses. The map shows contour lines and all man-made and natural features important to route finding. Control points are numbered and indicated by red circles. Other information on the course is printed on the back of the map.

• Six guides to short nature trails: *Gosford Forest Park Nature Trail; Baronscourt Forest Nature Trail; The Grace Drennan Woodland Trail, Pomeroy Forest; The Augustine Henry Trail, Portglenone Forest; Tollymore Forest Park Tree Trail 1;* and *Tollymore Forest Park Tree Trail 2.*

Many of the Forest Service leaflets and trail guides are available from the individual forest parks and state forests, as well as from the Northern Ireland Tourist Board. Each of the forest parks is also described in a series of booklets which can be purchased for a small charge from:

Her Majesty's Stationery Office (see *Address Directory*).

These booklets include *Outdoors in Ulster's Forests,* which gives details of all forest recreational facilities in Northern Ireland; five booklets with descriptions of various walks in the forest parks—*American Trail, Gortin Glen Forest Park; Drum Manor Forest Park; Florence Court Forest Park; Gosford Forest Park;* and *Glenariff Forest Park*—plus a brochure entitled *Gortin Glen Forest Park* with a color map showing the routes of five marked paths in the park.

The Forest Service publishes more than 40 other leaflets to Ulster's forest areas, most of which are free on request. A complete list of these publications, entitled *Northern Ireland Forest Service Publication List,* can be obtained from both the Forest Service and the Northern Ireland Tourist Board.

County Parks & Nature Reserves

Northern Ireland contains 7 country parks and more than 35 national nature reserves, most open to walkers. The reserves are managed for the protection and maintenance of vegetation, wildlife and other natural features of interest. The system of reserves contains representative samples of most of the natural habitats found in Northern Ireland—woodland, scrub, grassland and heath, bogland, coastal areas and freshwater habitats. It is forbidden to disturb plants, animals or other natural features in the reserves.

The county parks also encompass a variety of habitats and include such visitor facilities as campsites, picnic areas, interpretive centres, caravanning areas and footpaths.

You can obtain information on the nature refuges and county parks from:

Department of Environment (see *Address Directory*).

Among the free publications available from the department is:

• *Guide to the National Nature Reserves, Forest Nature Reserves, Areas of Scientific Interest and Bird Sanctuaries in Northern Ireland* (in English). Lists each of the areas, describes their main features and gives their locations. Does not describe walks.

The Department of Environment also operates the Lagan Valley Regional Park south of Belfast. Several free guides to various features of the park are available from the department.

National Trust Lands

The National Trust is a privately endowed, charitable organization devoted to purchasing and maintaining properties of natural, scenic and historical interest. Its holdings include castles, large estates, woodlands, gardens, wildlife refuges and the famous Giant's Causeway, a magnificent formation of columnar basalt located on the Antrim coast. National Trust properties are open to the public, and several have nature walks in the vicinity. In addition, the National Trust maintains two footpaths: 1) the North Antrim Cliff Path, a 17-kilometer (11-mile) path along the Antrim Coast, passing the Giant's Causeway enroute (described under "Suggested Walks" in the regional description of *County Antrim)* and 2) the Mourne Coastal Path, a one-mile walk along Northern Ireland's rocky southeast coast.

Each year the National Trust publishes a small booklet describing properties open to the public. The booklet—entitled *Properties Open in 1980*—lists each property by county, describes its main features of interest and indicates those properties with walking opportunities. This booklet, as well as other information on National Trust properties, can be obtained from:

The National Trust, Regional Information Officer (see *Address Directory).*

There is a small charge for the booklet.

Walking & Mountaineering Clubs

The Federation of Mountaineering Clubs of Ireland (F.M.C.I.) has seven member clubs in Northern Ireland:

See *Address Directory:*

Feorgortha Mountaineering Club.
Glenfoffany Climbing Club.
Irish Mountaineering Club (Belfast Section).
New University of Ulster Mountaineering Club.
Queen's University Mountaineering Club.
Slieveadore Club.
Ulster College Mountaineering Club.

The F.M.C.I. also has about 20 member clubs in the Republic of Ireland (see the section on *Irish Mountaineering Clubs* in the chapter on Ireland). Most of the clubs take a keen interest in foreign walkers who are visiting Northern Ireland and often go out of their way to provide assistance. In addition, foreign walkers may join one of the member clubs in either Northern Ireland or the Republic of Ireland. Membership allows you to stay in the mountain huts maintained by member clubs in the Mourne Mountains, as well as in the Republic of Ireland. As a member you will also receive the club newsletters, which provide information on places to walk and climb and which keep you up to date on new guidebooks, upcoming activities and the development of trails and huts in Ireland.

Enquiries about the F.M.C.I. in Northern Ireland should be addressed to:

Patricia Murray (see *Address Directory*).

Other Walking Associations

See *Address Directory:*

Keep Fit Association of Northern Ireland.
Northern Ireland Orienteering Association.
Ulster Federation of Rambling Clubs. Can provide information on all of Northern Ireland's many walking clubs and their activities.

Maps

The Ordnance Survey of Northern Ireland publishes three series of topographical maps suitable for walkers:

One-Inch Map: Third Series (1:63,360). The nine sheets in this series cover all of Northern Ireland. Topographical relief is indicated by both contour lines and shading in seven colors. In addition to footpaths, the maps show all public roads and most private roads, as well as cities, towns, villages, railways, National Trust properties, youth hostels, antiquities and other features of interest. The Irish Grid is shown at one-kilometer intervals. Sheets are periodically updated. The maps in this series are also available in a black-and-white outline edition without contours. When ordering, be sure you ask for the *colour edition.*

1:50,000 Map. In 1978 the Ordnance Survey of Northern Ireland began publishing a completely new 1:50,000 map series covering the entire country. The 18 sheets in the series will supercede the one-inch maps. The sheets covering Belfast, the North Down area, County Antrim and parts of Counties Londonderry and Armagh are now available. Another three sheets per year are expected to be published until the series is completed in 1983. These are the most detailed maps of Northern Ireland suitable for walkers. In addition to the information shown on the one-inch maps, the 1:50,000 maps will show open and undisputed sections of the Ulster Way, Northern Ireland's only long-distance footpath. To facilitate walking over mountain and moorland areas, the series also shows prominent fences and stone walls in these areas.

Half-Inch Map: Second Series (1:126,720). The four sheets in this series cover all of Northern Ireland. Roads, water, contours, afforestation areas, relief and other features are distinguished by color. The Irish Grid is shown at 10-kilometer intervals. The maps in this series are also available in a black-and-white outline edition without contours. When ordering, be sure to ask for the *colour edition.* These maps show less detail than the one-inch maps, but are still suitable for walking on marked paths. Walkers following unmarked routes, however, should obtain the one-inch maps or, for the areas they are available, the 1:50,000 maps.

In addition to these maps, the Ordnance Survey of Northern Ireland publishes a single 1:25,000 sheet covering the Mourne Mountains, entitled *Mourne County* and a 1:250,000 sheet entitled *Holiday Map, Northern Ireland,* covering all of Northern Ireland and parts of the Irish Republic which shows antiquities, National Trust properties, Country Parks and the route of Ulster Way.

All these maps, plus a free map catalog and index sheets, are available by mail or in person from:

Ordnance Survey of Northern Island, Chief Survey Officer (see *Address Directory).*

The maps are also available at principal bookshops in Belfast—including the **Government Bookshop** (see *Address Directory)* in Belfast and other towns. Outside Belfast, however, the availability of specific maps is uncertain, so you should obtain the sheets you need before leaving the city.

Guidebooks

Relatively few guidebooks exist to the footpaths and hill country of Northern Ireland. A handful of leaflets, sketch maps and booklets cover walks in the state forests and forest parks as well as along completed sections of the Ulster Way. Where marked trails do not exist, you must rely on the Ordnance Survey maps to find your way.

The guidebook situation is likely to improve, however, in the years to come. The Sports Council for Northern Ireland has published a general guide to the entire Ulster Way. Also, a volume in the series of six hill-walking guides published by Gill & Macmillan of Dublin covers all of Northern Ireland:

- *Irish Walk Guide/4: North East* by Richard Rogers. Available from principal bookstores in Belfast, or from the publisher, Gill & Macmillan (see *Address Directory).*

For the time being, however, the most comprehensive guide to walks in Northern Ireland is a map rather than a book:

- *Popular Walks: A map folder with table of routes in forests, county parks, rural lanes and by the shore* (in English) published by the Northern Ireland Tourist Board. Includes a 1:253,440 outline map of Northern Ireland showing walking routes in red. Each route bears a red number keyed to a list on the reverse side of the sheet. The list gives the name of each walk and its approximate length. The names of forest parks, state forests and other areas of interest to walkers are also shown in red on the map. Youth hostels are indicated by red triangles. In addition to the list of walks, the back of the map contains a list of youth hostels, with their addresses (and in some cases telephone numbers); a list of publications of interest to walkers, with their prices and where to obtain them; a section on walking etiquette; and a brief summary of the walking opportunities in Northern Ireland. Although the map does not include individual route descriptions and is not sufficiently detailed for trail use, it is invaluable as a planning aid. After deciding which walks you want to take, you can refer to the indexes of the Ordnance Survey maps to find out which topographical sheets you will need. Altogether, the map shows more than 80 walking routes. Nonetheless, it does not exhaust the walking possibilities in Northern Ireland, particularly those on unmarked routes in the hill country. Available for a small charge from the Northern Ireland Tourist Board or the Sports Council for Northern Ireland. (Recommended)

The only comprehensive regional walking guide for Northern Ireland is:

* *Hill Walks in the Mournes* (in English) by J.S. Doran, Mourne Observer Press, Newcastle. Describes in great detail 18 walks in the Mourne Mountains. Six sketch maps show the routes of the walks. These maps, however, are not accurate enough for use on the trail and should be supplemented with the appropriate Ordnance Survey one-inch or 1:25,000 maps. Useful information is also provided on fitness, equipment, safety and particularly hazardous sections of the walks. Available by mail from the F.M.C.I. (see *Address Directory)* and from principal bookstores in Belfast. (Recommended)

Details on walks in the vicinity of Northern Ireland's youth hostels are given in the *YHANI Handbook,* described in the section on *Trailside Lodgings.* It can be obtained from the Youth Hostel Association of Northern Ireland.

The Forest Service leaflets listed in the section on *Where to Get Walking Information* are also useful for planning walks in Northern Ireland.

The Ulster Way

Free leaflets describing open sections of the Ulster Way are published by The Sports Council for Northern Ireland. When used in conjunction with the appropriate Ordnance Survey one-inch or 1:50,000 maps, the leaflets provide you with all the information necessary to walk the routes. The following leaflets (all in English) are currently available:

* *North Antrim Coast.* Describes a 64-kilometer (40 miles) coastal walk from Fair Head to the River Bann, passing the Giant's Causeway.
* *North Coastal Down Path.* Describes an 18-kilometer (11-mile) path running along the shore northeast of Belfast from Holywood to Groomsport.
* *Fermanagh Lakeland Route.* Describes a 40-kilometer (25-mile) route from Lower Lough Erne to Belcoo. Includes a sketch map.

- *The Moyle Way.* Describes a 29-kilometer (18-mile) route from Ballycastle to Glenariff. Includes a sketch map.
- *The Lagan Valley.* Describes several short walks in the Lagan Valley, a richly wooded area outside Belfast.
- *The Mourne Trail (Section 1).* Describes a 16-kilometer (10-mile) walk along back roads between the old town of Newry and the village of Rostrevor in County Down.
- *Belfast and Cave Hill.* Describes a walk through woods to the top of Cave Hill (358 meters; 1,280 feet), overlooking the City of Belfast.

The leaflets may be obtained separately or in conjunction with a booklet entitled:

- *The Ulster Way* (in English) by The Sports Council for Northern Ireland. Describes the major regions of Northern Ireland through which the completed Ulster Way will pass. Includes a map showing the projected route, alternative routes and a proposed network of secondary routes and links. Available free of cost from The Sports Council for Northern Ireland.

Climbing Guides

The Federation of Mountaineering Clubs of Ireland publishes three rock-climbing guides (both in English) covering portions of Northern Ireland. These are:

- *Mournes* by John Forsythe, 1980.
- *Antrim Coast* by Calvin Tottans and Clare Sheridan, 1981.
- *F.M.C.I. New Climbs Bulletin,* issued annually.

A general guide published by the F.M.C.I. also contains information on walking in Northern Ireland:

- *Mountaineering in Ireland* (in English) by Claud W. Wall, revised by Joss Lyman. For a description, see the section on *Guidebooks* in the chapter on Ireland.

These guides may be purchased by mail from:

Federation of Mountaineering Clubs of Ireland (F.M.C.I.). See *Address Directory.*

Trailside Lodgings

A variety of lodgings are available to walkers in Northern Ireland—family hotels, guesthouses, country homes and youth hostels. There are also four mountaineering club huts in the Mourne Mountains. In other mountain areas, lodgings are readily available in nearby towns and villages. Nevertheless, if you plan to walk in the Mourne Mountains, Sperrin Mountains or Antrim Plateau, you should consult a map and accommodation list beforehand to ensure that lodgings can be easily reached from your planned route. Sizeable detours may sometimes be necessary to reach lodgings in adjacent valleys. Advance reservations are also advisable, especially in July and August.

You can obtain the following accommodation list from the Northern Ireland Tourist Board (see *Address Directory*):

- *Northern Ireland: All the Places to Stay* (in English, French and German). Gives full details on Ireland's hotels, guesthouses, and farm and country house accommodation. Includes prices (not guaranteed). Indicates daily, weekend and weekly rates. The towns and villages with accommodation are listed alphabetically.

- *Farm and Country Holidays* (in English, French and German). Gives details on these attractive and inexpensive lodgings where you get to stay with the people of the province.

Youth Hostels

The Youth Hostel Association of Northern Ireland (YHANI) operates 13 hostels, most located in good walking areas. For example, four hostels are located near the Mourne Mountains, four along the Antrim Coast and one near the Sperrin Mountains. The hostels provide excellent bases for walking in the surrounding countryside. Several are also located within a day's walk apart.

Some of the hostels have been specially designed and built as hostels. Others are converted castles or fine old homes. All have separate dormitories for men and women. Beds and blankets are provided, and sheet sleeping bags, which are required, can be rented. None of the hostels provide meals, though all have fully equipped kitchens in which you can prepare your own. You must, however, bring your own cutlery and food.

Most of the hostels close for a month or two in the winter. During July and August the hostels are heavily used, and reservations made at least a month in advance are advisable. Advance reservations may also be necessary if you wish to stay in a hostel during weekends in May and June, or in September and October. Booking should be made in person at the YHANI Information Centre in Belfast. The information centre can also tell you which hostels permit camping on their grounds.

Full details on the hostels are included in the YHANI Handbook, including their addresses, opening dates, number of beds and the location of such facilities as the nearest shops, post office, churches and public transportation. The locations of the hostels are shown on sketch maps, and photographs of some are included. The handbook also contains a good deal of information for hikers, including the one-inch Ordnance Survey maps covering the regions in which the hostels are located, distances to the nearest hostels, points of interest and suggested walks in the vicinity. The handbook can be purchased from the YHANI Information Centre in Belfast (see Address Directory).

Mountain Huts

Members of foreign mountaineering and walking clubs may stay in four Mourne Mountain huts operated by constituent clubs of the F.M.C.I. Arrangements to stay in the huts, however, must be made well in advance with the secretary of the club that runs the hut. Keys must also be obtained since all of the huts are kept locked. To obtain the key, you must have proof of your club membership.

The Mourne Mountain huts are operated by the following clubs (see Address Directory):

1. The Bloat House, a hut located at Dunnywater, near Annalong. Operated by the Irish Mountaineering Club, Belfast Section.

2. The Queen's University Mountaineering Club hut. Located up a lane on the north side of the road leading from the Silent Valley to Dunnywater; about ½ mile from the entrance to the Silent Valley reservoir. Operated by the Queen's University Mountaineering Club.

3. The Slieveadore Club hut. Located at 38 Old Road, Kilkeel Road, Newcastle, County Down. Operated by the Slieveadore Club.

Camping

With the permission of the landowner it is possible to camp almost anywhere in Northern Ireland. Farmers are usually friendly and will allow you to pitch a tent on an uncultivated section of their land, but they do not like someone entering or camping on their property without permission. In some areas you may see no camping or no trespassing signs, and these should be respected. Camping is also discouraged in state forests and forest parks except where authorized caravan and camping sites exist. At present, however, so few campers use the state forests that most state foresters will grant you permission to camp in certain locations.

There are numerous commercial caravan and camping sites along roads, in state forests and forest parks and in other public recreation areas. A list of these, entitled *Caravaning and Camping Sites 1981,* is available upon request from the Northern Ireland Tourist Board (see *Address Directory*).

Water

Tap water is safe throughout Northern Ireland, and you should depend on it for most of your water needs. The peat soil covering most hill country gives water a brackish taste. Many streams also may contain seepage contaminated by livestock. Most farmers, however, will give you water if you ask.

Equipment Notes

No specialized equipment is required for walking in Northern Ireland, although you should be sure to always carry spare woolen clothing, a windproof jacket, good raingear and a map and compass. For boggy areas you may also want to bring a pair of rubber boots in addition to your regular hiking boots.

Organized Walks

Marathon walks and walking tours are organized by a variety of associations in Northern Ireland. Among these are:

See *Address Directory:*

YHANI: Sponsors the annual Mourne Wall Walk, generally on the first Sunday in June. The walk is 35 kilometers (22 miles) long and involves 3,000 meters (10,000 feet) of climbing. It follows the boundary wall enclosing the two large reservoirs of the Silent Valley watershed, which supplies water for Belfast. The walk begins and ends at Rourkes Park, at Dunnywater, near Annalong. Navigation is not difficult, but there are several strenuous sections. You can, however, leave the walk before the finish.

YHANI's Peak-a-Month Club organizes one walking trip per month from various youth hostels, and the Fell Walking Group organizes weekend walks throughout Northern Ireland. Information on the Mourne Wall

Walk, the Peak-a-Month Club and the Fell Walking Group is available from the YHANI Information Centre in Belfast.

Northern Ireland Orienteering Association: Sponsors two walks, an 80-kilometer (50-mile) two-day walk in the Mourne Mountains with overnight camps held in September, and a one-day Mountain Marathon held in June. The Mountain Marathon is divided into three classes: 1) a severe test of fell-running and navigational ability over a distance of 32 kilometers (20 miles), 2) an equally severe test, but over a shorter distance (24 kilometers), and 3) a slightly less severe test over a distance of 16 kilometers (10 miles). The first two classes are competitive events. For information, contact the Northern Ireland Orienteering Association.

The Sports Council for Northern Ireland: Offers a full program of mountaineering activities through its Mountain Centre in the Mourne Mountains. Details are available from The Sports Council for Northern Ireland.

Local walking clubs also offer a variety of walks for their members. For information on the club walks, contact The Sports Council for Northern Ireland or the Ulster Federation of Rambling Clubs.

Mountaineering Courses

Numerous mountaineering and outdoor-activity courses are offered throughout the year at the Northern Ireland Mountain Centre in the Mourne Mountains. The courses cover basic and advanced climbing, mountain rescue, mountain leader training and walking. In addition, the centre conducts mountaineering trips to Scotland in the winter and to the Alps and Pyrenees in July and August. It also provides special courses for school and youth groups. For information, contact The Sports Council for Northern Ireland (see *Address Directory*).

The Northern Ireland Mountain Training Board offers courses on such topics as mountaineering, first aid, weather, mountain hazards and mountain navigation. The courses are geared primarily for people who intend to lead walking groups in the hill country. The courses, however, are open to anyone. For information, contact:

Northern Ireland Mountain Training Board (see *Address Directory*).

A schedule of courses and its newsletter, *Peak Viewing* (published bi-annually in winter and summer), are available upon request.

Special Train & Bus Fares

A special discount bus ticket good for seven days of unlimited travel throughout Northern Ireland is available from:

Ulsterbus (see *Address Directory*).

The ticket may also be purchased at any Ulsterbus depot.
Northern Ireland Railways offers a Rail Runabout ticket good for seven days of unlimited travel at reduced rates. Information on this ticket, as well as on special excursion fares, can be obtained from any railway station or from:

Northern Ireland Railways (see *Address Directory*).

Useful Addresses
& Telephone Numbers

General Tourist Information

In Northern Ireland:

Northern Ireland Tourist Board (see *Address Directory*). Staff speaks English. A few staff members also speak French and German. Extremely helpful. Among its many publications, the following are particularly useful to walkers:

- *Discover Northern Ireland* (in English) by Ernest Sandford. An exhaustive guide to all of Northern Ireland. Contains numerous line drawings and photographs as well as seven maps showing main roads, towns and points of interest. Indicates a number of possible walking areas, although specific routes are not described. Useful for deciding which parts of Northern Ireland especially interest you. (Recommended)

- *Northern Ireland: A Map for Tourists.* A 1:250,000 map showing all of Northern Ireland and adjacent parts of the Republic of Ireland. An excellent map for general touring or for planning walks in Northern Ireland, but not suitable for trail use. Shows the locations of scenic routes, antiquities, telephone call boxes, airports and airfields, bird sanctuaries, National Trust properties, state forests and forest parks, railway lines and stations, caravan and camping sites, youth hostels, viewpoints and other features of interest. Topographical relief is indicated in seven colors. Information on the back side of the map gives suggested auto tours; lists National Trust properties, caravan camps, forests, county parks; and gives the addresses of tourist information offices, motoring organizations, public transportation services and hospitals with 24-hour casualty departments. (Recommended)

The Northern Ireland Tourist Board also publishes a series of leaflets to the various regions in Ulster. These describe main points of interest, provide information on accommodation and sometimes mention areas where walking opportunities exist. The leaflets include color photographs and a sketch map of each region.

The Tourist Board can also provide an address list of local tourist information offices.

Abroad:

Branch offices of the Northern Ireland Tourist Board are located in ENGLAND: London and Sutton Coldfield (near Birmingham); SCOTLAND: Glasgow; and the REPUBLIC OF IRELAND: Dublin.

London: Northern Ireland Tourist Board, 11 Berkeley Street, London WIX 6BU. Tel. (01) 493 0601.

Elsewhere, information on Northern Ireland can be obtained from the branch offices of the British Tourist Authority located in EUROPE: Amsterdam, Brussels, Copenhagen, Frankfurt, Madrid, Oslo, Paris, Rome, Stockholm and Zurich; AUSTRALIA: Sydney; NEW ZEALAND: Wellington; SOUTH AFRICA: Johannesburg; JAPAN: Tokyo; CANADA: Toronto, and in the U.S.A.: Los Angeles, Chicago, Dallas and New York.

New York: British Tourist Authority, 680 Fifth Avenue, New York, New York 10019. Tel. (212) 581-4700.

Sport Shops

There are only a few shops specializing in hiking and mountaineering equipment in Northern Ireland. Of these, some of the best are:

See *Address Directory:*

YHANI Shop. Located in Belfast. The staff is very helpful and will direct you to an appropriate store if they don't have what you need.

The Scout Shop. Located in Belfast.

Jackson Sports Equipment. Located in Belfast.

The Hill Trekker. Located in Newcastle, County Down.

Base Camp. Located in Newtownards, County Down.

Search & Rescue

In case of emergency: Immediately contact the nearest police station or telephone the police emergency number: Tel. 999.

Search and rescue operations are conducted either by the police or in some areas—notably the Mourne Mountains—by volunteer groups. There is no charge for the service. Donations to the mountain rescue volunteers for equipment purchases, however, are welcomed.

Northern Ireland's
Long-Distance Footpath

The 805-kilometer (500-mile) Ulster Way is Northern Ireland's only long-distance footpath. It completely circumnavigates the country, forming a large undulating loop through the most scenic regions of mountains, forests, lakes and coast. Although the path was first conceived in its present form in 1946, active work was not begun until 1974, when The Sports Council for Northern Ireland was asked by the Ulster Society for the Preservation of the Countryside to supervise the project and coordinate the activities of other participating agencies and private organizations.

Nearly all of the path can now be walked. Nevertheless, rights-of-way have yet to be obtained for long stretches, and you should obtain the permission of local landowners before attempting to walk these portions of the route. Officially open sections of the Ulster Way are marked by signposts bearing yellow arrows and are maintained either by District Councils or by organizations—such as the Forest Service or National Trust—over whose lands the route crosses.

Although the Ulster Way has been divided into several convenient sections in the following route descriptions, you can pick up the route wherever you choose and walk in either direction for as far as you like. Before setting out, however, be sure to check with The Sports Council for Northern Ireland whether the section or sections you wish to walk have been marked, and where permission must be obtained to cross private lands.

The Ulster Way

Length: Over 805 kilometers (500 miles). To purchase supplies and find overnight accommodation you must often leave the route. This significantly increases the distance walked. **Walking Time:** 35 to 45 days.
Difficulty: See the difficulty gradings for the individual sections below.
Path Markings: Yellow arrows; most sections unmarked.
Lodgings: Youth hostels at Belfast, Minerstown, Newcastle, Slievenaman, Kinnahalla, Gortin, Stradreagh, White Park Bay, Ballycastle, Moneyvart and Ballygally; four mountaineering club huts in the Mourne Mountains (for their locations, see the section on *Trailside Lodgings*); innumerable family hotels and guesthouses. Many farm and country homes also accept lodgers (see the *Farm and Country Holidays* accommodation booklet, listed in the section on *Trailside Lodgings*).

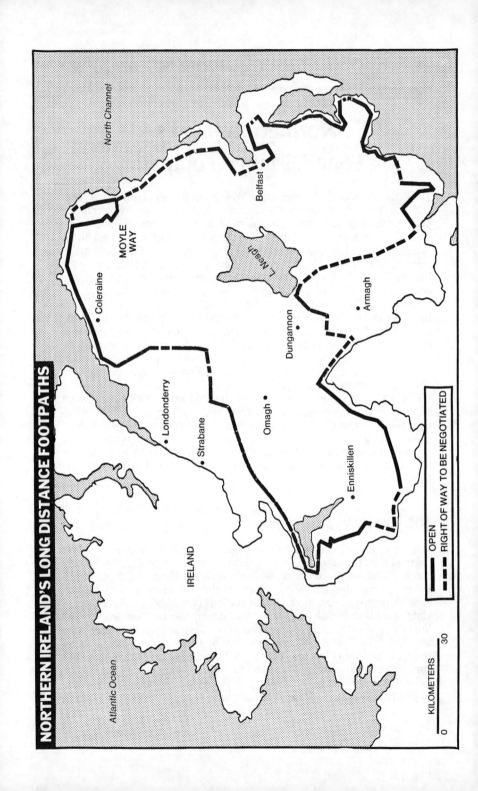

NORTHERN IRELAND'S LONG DISTANCE FOOTPATHS

Atlantic Ocean

North Channel

IRELAND

Coleraine

MOYLE WAY

Londonderry

Strabane

Belfast

L. Neagh

Dungannon

Armagh

Omagh

Enniskillen

KILOMETERS

0   30

OPEN
RIGHT OF WAY TO BE NEGOTIATED

Maps:
- Ordnance Survey of Northern Ireland One-Inch Map: Third Series (1:63, 360), sheets 1, 2, 3, 4, 5, 6, 7, 8 and 9.

Guidebook:
- *The Ulster Way,* available from The Sports Council for Northern Ireland (see *Address Directory*).

From Newtownabbey to Ballycastle. Over the high moor ands of the Antrim Plateau; along portions of the rugged Antrim Coast, with its white cliffs; and across the Glens of Antrim, with their tumbling streams and spruce forests. An alternate route (the Moyle Way, described in the regional description on *County Antrim)* is possible fr< n Glenariff to Ballycastle. **Length:** About 100 kilometers (62 miles). **Walking Time:** 4 days. **Difficulty:** Easy to moderately difficult; some steep climbs; rough going over untracked, boggy moorlands. **Path Markings:** None except along the Moyle Way.

Maps:
- Ordnance Survey of Northern Ireland One-Inch Map: Third Series (1:63, 360), sheets 3 and 6, and 1:50,000, sheets 5, 9, and 15.

From Ballycastle to Castlerock. Along the spectacular North Antrim coast, with its rugged cliffs and headlands, beautiful bays, the Giant's Causeway and seabird colonies. Near Ballintoy, the Carrickarade rope bridge, swinging 90 feet above the sea, links the mainland to a small island. **Length:** About 64 kilometers (40 miles). This distance will be reduced considerably once the ferry over River Bann is in operation. **Walking Time:** 2 to 3 days. **Difficulty:** Easy. **Path Markings:** None.

Maps:
- Ordnance Survey of Northern Ireland One-Inch Map: Third Series (1:63,360), sheet 1, and 1:50,000, sheets 4 and 5.

From Castlerock to Gortin Glen Forest. A ridge walk through forests and high, boggy moorland; fine views over the Foyle River to the hills of Donegal; route crosses the eastern end of the Sperrin Mountains. The section from Castlerock to Moydamlaght (60 kilometers) is known as the "Sperrin Way." **Length:** About 97 kilometers (60 miles). **Walking Time:** 4 to 6 days. **Difficulty:** Moderately difficult. **Path Markings:** Waymarked from Castlerock to Dungiven and through Gortin Glen Forest.

Maps:
- Ordnance Survey of Northern Ireland One-Inch Map: Third Series (1:63,360), sheets 1, 2, 4 and 5. Partly covered by 1:50,000, sheet 4.

From Gortin Glen Forest to Belcoo. Along narrow country roads to the river Strule and the Ulster American Folk Park, site of the cottage from which Thomas Mellon emigrated to establish his banking empire in the United States. The park also contains replicas of a Presbyterian meeting house, school, shop and other buildings like those Mellon knew in Ulster,

as well as log farmhouses and buildings similar to those built by the early Ulster settlers in the New World. From the Folk Park the route winds over hills and across broad moorlands to Lough Erne. The last 42 kilometers (26 miles) to Belcoo take you through forests, alongside small lakes bedecked with water lilies and over hills rising to almost 305 meters (1,000 feet). **Length:** 122 kilometers (76 miles). **Walking Time:** 4 to 5 days. **Difficulty:** Easy to moderately difficult. **Path Markings:** Yellow arrows on wooden posts from the Donegal border (near Pettigoe) to Belcoo; otherwise unmarked.
Maps:
• Ordnance Survey of Northern Ireland One-Inch Map: Third Series (1:63,360), sheets 4 and 7.

From Belcoo to Maghery. Over high, wet moorlands along the border with the Republic of Ireland; across the lake-strewn valley of Upper Lough Erne; along the forested ridge southwest of Slieve Beagh and around the north side of the peak to Favour Royal Forest. From there, the route follows a long, winding course along the River Blackwater through the Central Lowlands to the southern shore of Lough Neagh. **Length:** About 172 kilometers (107 miles). **Walking Time:** 7 to 10 days. **Difficulty:** Easy to moderately difficult. **Path Markings:** None.
Maps:
• Ordnance Survey of Northern Ireland One-Inch Map: Third Series (1:63,360), sheets 5, 7 and 8.

From Maghery to Rostrevor. Along small roads close to the River Bann to Portadown, south along the Newry Canal to Newry, then across low hills to the forest at Rostrevor on the southwestern end of the Mourne Mountains. **Length:** About 64 kilometers (40 miles). **Walking Time:** 3 to 4 days. **Difficulty:** Easy. **Path Markings:** From Newry to Rostrevor waymarked.
Maps:
• Ordnance Survey of Northern Ireland One-Inch Map: Third Series (1:63,360), sheets 5, 8 and 9.

From Rostrevor to Downpatrick. Through Rostrevor Forest and over Slievemoughanmore and Pigeon Rock mountains before dropping down to the Spelga road. Then through Tollymore Forest Park to Newcastle. From Newcastle the route mostly sticks close to the shore, sometimes running along clifftops, sometimes along sandy beaches to Strangford Lough, where St. Patrick landed in 432 A.D. to start his Christian mission at Saul. It was his second visit to Northern Ireland. As a youth, he was a slave in County Antrim, where he herded sheep on Llemish Mountain. **Length:** About 113 kilometers (70 miles). **Walking Time:** 5 to 6 days. **Difficulty:** Easy to moderately difficult; some steep ascents and descents, as well as wet moorlands. **Path Markings:** From Rostrevor to Newcastle waymarked.

¯ Maps:̄
• Ordnance Survey of Northern Ireland One-Inch Map: Third Series (1:63, 360), sheets 6 and 9, and 1:25,000 map covers the area from Rostrevor to Newcastle.

From Downpatrick to Newtownabbey. Along the western shore of Strangford Lough, with its thousands of wintering birds to Holywood, on the south shore of Belfast Lough, then by way of the North Down Coastal Path, passing the Ulster Folk and Transport Museum; then southeast through Lagan Valley Regional Park, following the old Lagan Towpath. From Drumbeg, the route winds north skirting the suburbs of Belfast, climbs the ridge west of the city, then heads north along the ridge (good views) before dropping down to Newtownabbey. **Length:** About 108 kilometers (67 miles). **Walking Time:** 4 days. **Difficulty:** Easy to moderately difficult. **Path Markings:** None.
Maps:
• Ordnance Survey of Northern Ireland One-Inch Map: Third Series (1:63,360), sheets 6 and 9. North County Down and South County Antrim covered by 1:50,000 map, sheet 15.

Where to Walk in Northern Ireland

Northern Ireland's state forests and forest parks have numerous marked footpaths, most of them under eight kilometers in length. Walkers looking for longer routes can follow sections of the Ulster Way or wander through the Mourne Mountains, Sperrin Mountains or Antrim Plateau. Hill walkers should be prepared, however, for rugged country, faint or nonexistent tracks, wet moorlands and foul weather. Skill in using map and compass are essential in trackless hill country. And hill walkers should always carry proper clothing and raingear (see *The Equipment Rack* in *On Foot Through Europe: A Trail Guide to Europe's Long-Distance Footpaths*).

Excellent walking possibilities exist in all six of Northern Ireland's counties. The suggested walks listed below under each county all follow established paths, though not all are marked. For additional walks, consult the map brochure *Popular Walks* (see the section on *Guidebooks)*, which also indicates areas where more challenging routes are possible.

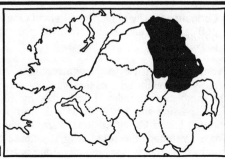

County Antrim

Antrim is the northeasternmost county in Northern Ireland. Its spectacular coastal cliffs and headlands, wooded glens and untrampled hill country offer some of the finest walking in Northern Ireland.

The coast is bounded mostly by cliffs, including the famous Giant's Causeway, a magnificent formation of columnar basalt resembling a stairway into the sea. Consisting of some 37,000 columns, the Giant's Causeway is a remnant of a 60 million-year-old lava flow. Here and there along the coast, the cliffs culminate in massive headlands such as Fair Head, from the top of which you can see Rathlin Island. Murlough Bay, to the east, is considered one of the most beautiful in the country.

At the mouths of the glens the coastal cliffs give way to sandy beaches and estuaries, where villages such as Cushendun and Carnlough nestle near the shore. The glens themselves are steep-sided glacial valleys formed during the Ice Age. At the upper end of Glenariff, the Queen of the Glens, the valley narrows to a deep, wooded gorge with a series of waterfalls. Glenariff Forest Park, which encompasses the gorge, offers a number of fine walks.

The Antrim Plateau rises steeply from the coast and slopes gently westward to the broad valley of the River Main. The hills west of Belfast—in the extreme southeast corner of the county—are its southernmost outposts. From there, it extends northward for a distance of about 70 kilometers (43 miles) to Fair Head, which plunges steeply into the sea.

The plateau is a basaltic tableland, part of the same lava flow that created the Giant's Causeway. Few roads cross this upland, and the Garron Plateau—that part of the Antrim Plateau between Glencloy and Glenariff—is the largest roadless area in Northern Ireland. The highest point on the plateau is Trostan (550 meters), which rises north of Glenariff. Most of the Antrim Plateau is an undulating moorland dotted with numerous small lakes.

Tourist Information

See *Address Directory:*

Information Office, Ballycastle.
Information Office, Cushendall.

Other local tourist offices open all year are located in Larne, Larne Harbour, Bushmills, Portballintrae and Portrush.

The Northern Ireland Tourist Board's leaflets, *The Glens of Antrim, The Causeway Coast, Rathlin Island, Belfast* and *Lough Neagh,* contain much useful information, as does *Discover Northern Ireland* by Ernest Sandford (see description under the section on *Useful Addresses & Telephone Numbers).*

Maps

- Ordnance Survey of Northern Ireland One-Inch Map: Third Series (1:63,360), sheets 1 and 3. 1:50,000 maps, sheets 4, 5 and 9. 1:250,000 Holiday map: "Ireland North."

Guidebooks

- *Irish Walk Guides/4: North East* by Richard Rogers. Gill & Macmillan, Dublin.
- *The Moyle Way, Belfast and Cave Hill* and *North Antrim Coast.* Three leaflets describing walks. Published by The Sports Council for Northern Ireland, Belfast.
- *The Causeway Coast.* A leaflet to the North Antrim Coast Path published by The National Trust.

Suggested Walks

The Moyle Way. From Ballycastle to Glenariff. Over high moorlands of the Antrim Plateau, including the summits of Knocklayd, Slieveanorra and Trostan. Streams, waterfalls, lakelets and forests. An alternate section of the Ulster Way. **Length:** 32 kilometers (20 miles). **Walking Time:** 2 days. **Difficulty:** Easy to moderately difficult. **Path Markings:** Yellow arrows on wooden posts at frequent intervals.
Maps:
- Ordnance Survey of Northern Ireland One-Inch Map: Third Series (1:63, 360), sheets 1 and 3.
- Ordnance Survey of Northern Ireland 1:50,000, sheets 5 and 9. Cover of the path. The path is labeled on the map and shown with red dashed lines.

North Antrim Coast Path. From Ballintoy to Portballintrae. Along a spectacular stretch of coast that includes steep cliffs, rocky headlands, sea caves and the Giant's Causeway. Part of the Ulster Way. **Length:** 17 kilometers (11 miles). **Walking Time:** 1 day. **Difficulty:** Easy. **Path Markings:** Unmarked except for occasional National Trust acorn signs. (When following the coastline, no waymarks are necessary.)
Maps:
• Ordnance Survey of Northern Ireland One-Inch Map: Third Series (1:63, 360), sheet 1.
• Ordnance Survey 1:50,000, sheet 5.

From Cushendun to Ballycastle. There are two choices of routes from the National Trust village of Cushendun to Greenanmore—along the Ulster Way by way of a green track which takes you toward Hungry House and over Carnanmore, or along the beautiful, winding scenic coast road. From Greenanmore to Murlough Bay the route follows a ridge overlooking the sea, then takes you along the cliff edge and past the spectacular Fair Head to Ballycastle. A very beautiful walk. **Length:** 24 kilometers (15 miles). **Walking Time:** 1 to 2 days. **Difficulty:** Easy to moderately difficult. **Path Markings:** None.
Maps:
• Ordnance Survey of Northern Ireland One-Inch Map: Third Series (1:63, 360), sheet 1.

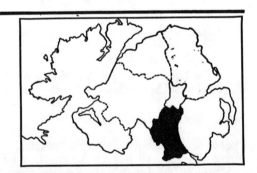

County Armagh

County Armagh stretches south from Lough Neagh to the border with the Republic of Ireland. The northern part of the county consists of fertile lowlands, known as the "garden of Ireland," and is one of the few places in the country able to support extensive commercial orchards. Southward, a range of low, rolling hills stretch to the international border.

The county is bordered on the west by the River Blackwater, one of Northern Ireland's best angling streams, and on the east by the River Bann. Extended walks are possible along the banks of both rivers.

In the southeast corner of Armagh is the impressive old volcano Slieve Gullion, which rises abruptly from the surrounding valley to a height of 575 meters. A ring of rugged volcanic hills surrounds the peak, constituting what geologists call a "volcanic ring dike." There are two ancient monuments on the peak, a passage grave dating from about 2500 B.C. and a cist cairn dating from between 1700 and 2000 B.C. Near the mountain Glendoey Gap, the legendary chief Cuchullain defended Ulster from the army of Connaught. Slieve Gullion offers excellent walking, and on a clear day, there is a wonderful view from the summit.

Tourist Information

See *Address Directory:*

Council Office and Astronomy Center, Armagh.

The Northern Ireland Tourist Board's leaflets, *Armagh, Lough Neagh, The Mourne Mountains* and *Slieve Gullion and Newry,* contain much useful information. Also refer to *Discover Northern Ireland* by Ernest Sandford (see the section on *Useful Addresses & Telephone Numbers).*

Maps

- Ordnance Survey of Northern Ireland One-Inch Map: Third Series (1:63, 360), sheets 5 and 8.
- Ordnance Survey 1:50,000, sheet 19. Covers most of the country.

Guidebook

- *Irish Walk Guides/4: North East* by Richard Rogers. Gill & Macmillan, Dublin.

Suggested Walks

Newry Canal Towpath (part of the Ulster Way). See the section on *Northern Ireland's Long-Distance Footpath.*

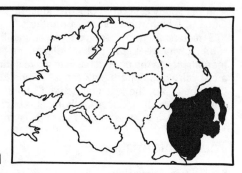

County Down

The Mourne Mountains, Northern Ireland's finest hill walking region, rise abruptly from the coastal plain in southernmost County Down. This ancient range contains five types of granite intruded into beds of folded slate. Fourteen peaks rise above 610 meters, encompassing Northern Ireland's highest and most rugged mountain area. The interior of the range is often simply referred to as "the Wilderness." Slieve Donard (850 meters) is the highest point in Northern Ireland.

North of the Mourne Mountains, the remainder of County Down is a region of broad lowlands broken by lush, gently rolling downs. The only summit of any note in this region is Slieve Croob (532 meters), the northernmost outpost of an upland ridge extending north from the Mournes.

The long, convoluted Down coast offers excellent walking for much of its length. Along some stretches, cliffs and headlands plunge steeply to the water. In others, gentle plains culminate in long, sandy strands—some of the finest beaches in Northern Ireland.

The North Down coast is deeply indented by the 24-kilometer (15 mile) long Strangford Lough—meaning the "violent fjord"—so named by the Vikings for the treacherous currents in its narrow inlet. On the east side of the lough stretches the narrow Ards peninsula, the driest spot in Northern Ireland, where coastal paths take you to sandy beaches.

Strangford Lough is the largest sanctuary for wintering birds in the British Isles. About 12,000 brant geese—almost half the world's total population—winter at the lough, as do upwards of 20,000 dunlin and 100,000 knot. Numerous other species of shorebirds and waterfowl also spend the winter at Strangford Lough. The Ulster Way follows the lough's western shore, and shorter paths provide access to different sections of the eastern shore.

Tourist Information

See *Address Directory:*

Information Office, Bangor.
Information Office, Warrenpoint.

Other local tourist offices open all year are located in Banbridge, Newcastle, and Kilkeel.

The Northern Ireland Tourist Board's leaflets, *North Down and the Ards, The Heart of Down and the Brontë Homeland, The Mourne Mountains, Slieve Gullion and Newry* and *Lough Neagh,* contain much useful information. Also refer to *Discover Northern Ireland* by Ernest Sandford (see *Useful Addresses & Telephone Numbers).*

Guidebooks

- *Hill Walks in the Mournes* by J.S. Doran, Mourne Observer Press, Newcastle (described in the section on *Guidebooks* earlier in this chapter).
- *Irish Walk Guides/4: North East* by Richard Rogers, Gill & Macmillan, Dublin.

Maps

- Ordnance Survey of Northern Ireland One-Inch Map: Third Series (1:63,360), sheets 5, 6 and 9.
- Ordnance Survey 1:50,000, sheet 15, covers the northern part of the country and 1:25,000 covers the Mourne Mountains.

Suggested Walks

The Brandy Pad. From Slieveneman Youth Hostel, across the Mourne Mountains, to Bloody Bridge on the Mournes Coast. Rugged mountain scenery featuring streams, some cliffs, Slieve Donard and other peaks. Trails branch off the Brandy Pad to all parts of the mountains. **Length:** 14 kilometers (8.7 miles). **Walking Time:** 4 to 6 hours, depending on side trips and rest stops. **Difficulty:** Moderately difficult (rough surface; some fairly steep sections). **Path Markings:** White splashes painted on rocks.
Map:
- Ordnance Survey of Northern Ireland One-Inch Map: Third Series (1:63,360), sheet 9, and 1:25,000 map "Mourne Country."
Guidebook:
- *Hill Walks in the Mournes* by J.S. Doran, Mourne Observer Press, Newcastle.

Mourne Boundary Wall Circuit. A loop trip through the very heart of the Mourne Mountains. Follows the stone boundary wall surrounding the Silent Valley watershed. Climbs nine of the Mourne Peaks over 610 meters (2,000 feet). **Length:** 35 kilometers (22 miles). **Walking Time:** 1 to 2 days. To find overnight accommodation you must leave the route. **Difficulty:** Moderately difficult to difficult (involves 3,000 meters—10,000 feet—of climbing). **Path Markings:** The boundary wall itself.

Special Note: Although walkers are permitted to venture for short distances on the watershed side of the boundary wall, those who approach too closely to the Silent Valley Reservoir will be asked to leave.

Map:
• Ordnance Survey of Northern Ireland One-Inch Map: Third Series (1:63,360), sheet 9 and 1:25,000 map "Mourne Country."

Guidebook:
• *Hill Walks in the Mournes* by J.S. Doran.

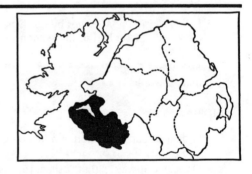

County Fermanagh

Fermanagh, Northern Ireland's westernmost county, is a land of lakes, both large and small, strewn in a broad valley surrounded by hills. Large, island-studded Lower Lough Erne fills the northern end of the Erne Basin. Upper Lough Erne to the south is a maze of islands, inlets and subsidiary lakelets connected to the main body by narrow channels. A completed section of the Ulster Way crosses this labyrinthine wetland via the Lady Craigavon Bridge.

The hill country west of the lakes offers splendid walking through forests and over high moorlands. The Fermanagh Lakeland Way, a completed section of the Ulster Way, crosses the northern part of this upland from Lough Navar Forest to Belcoo. South of Belcoo rise the wild Cuilcagh Mountains, which extend west into the Republic of Ireland. The highest summit in this range—Cuilcagh (667 meters)—lies across the border, but walkers will encounter no difficulties with customs if they choose to cross the boundary. It should be stressed, however, that the Cuilcagh Mountains are largely trackless moorlands in which proper equipment and skill with map and compass are essential.

East of Upper Lough Erne, another range of hills runs along the border, extending north into County Tyrone, where Slieve Beagh rises to a height of 370 meters. These hills contain large forests as well as open moorlands, and a completed section of the Ulster Way winds through them from end to end.

Tourist Information

See *Address Directory:*

Information Office, Enniskillen.

The Northern Ireland Tourist Board's leaflet, *The Fermanagh Lakeland,* contains much useful information. Also refer to *Discover Northern Ireland* by Ernest Sandford.

Maps

- Ordnance Survey of Northern Ireland One-Inch Map: Third Series (1:63,360), sheets 4 and 7.

Guidebook

- *Irish Walk Guides/4: North East* by Richard Rogers, Gill & Macmillan, Dublin.

The Northern Ireland Tourist Board's *Fermanagh Leisure Guide* contains a list of short walks in the Fermanagh Lakeland, as well as useful information on local fishing spots. Available from the Northern Ireland Tourist Board.

Suggested Walks

Fermanagh Lakeland Route (part of the Ulster Way). Also:

Cuilcagh Mountains to Slieve Beagh (part of the Ulster Way). See the section on *Northern Ireland's Long-Distance Footpath.*

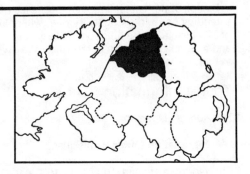

County Londonderry

From the basalt cliffs of Benevenagh, which rise abruptly from the Foyle lowlands of northwestern Northern Ireland, a narrow upland swings south and then west, culminating in the Sperrin Mountains, of which Sawel Mountain (680 meters) is the highest. This upland forms a natural barrier cleaving County Londonderry in two. To the east lie the Central Lowlands bordering Lough Neagh; to the west, the rolling hills and stream-laced valleys of the Foyle lowlands.

The rounded summits of the Sperrin Mountains are covered mostly by blanket bog, although large state forests are found in the eastern Sperrins and on the upland extending northward to Benevenagh. These mountains offer excellent walking, particularly for those who prefer to venture off established routes. The slopes of 527-meter Slieve Gallion, east of the Sperrins, also offers good walking, with excellent views from the summit.

The Londonderry Coast is for the most part gentler than that of Antrim to the east. Northern Ireland's longest stretch of sandy beach extends from Castlerock to Mulligan Point at the narrow mouth of Lough Foyle. Along the southeastern shore of the lough, farmlands have been reclaimed from the sea by a system of dikes. A few miles up the River Foyle, which empties into Lough Foyle, sits Londonderry, Northern Ireland's second largest city. To the east rise the beautiful hills of Donegal in the Republic of Ireland.

Tourist Information

See *Address Directory:*

Information Portakabin, Londonderry.

Other local tourist offices open all year are located in Portstewart and in Castlerock.

The Northern Ireland Tourist Board's leaflets, *Londonderry-Foyle Valley, The Sperrin Mountains* and *Lough Neagh,* contain much useful information. *Discover Northern Ireland* by Ernest Sandford is also useful.

Maps

- Ordnance Survey of Northern Ireland One-Inch Map: Third Series (1:63,360), sheets 1, 2, 3 and 5.
- Ordnance Survey 1:50,000, sheet 4, covers much of the northern part of the country.

Guidebook

- *Irish Walk Guides/4: North East* by Richard Rogers. Gill & Macmillan, Dublin.

Suggested Walks

From Dunluce Castle to Magilligan Point. Along the north Derry coast, first crossing clifftops, then following Northern Ireland's longest sand beach—Magilligan's Strand—with its sand dunes and abundant seashells. Dunluce Castle is a romantic old ruin situated on a sea crag reachable only by bridge; well worth a visit. At the mouth of the River Bann, between Portstewart and Castlerock, it is necessary to detour southward along the river to the town of Coleraine, then northward up the opposite bank back to the coast. **Length:** 40 kilometers (25 miles). **Walking Time:** 2 days. **Difficulty:** Easy. **Path Markings:** From Castlerock to Binevenagh only.
Map:
- Ordnance Survey of Northern Ireland One-Inch Map: Third Series (1:63,360), sheet 1.
- Ordnance Survey 1:50,000, sheet 4.

Sawel Mountain Circuit. From Learmont Castle Youth Hostel to Sawel Mountain, the highest in the Sperrins, via Meeny Hill, Learmount Mountain and Dart Mountain; return via Dreen and Park Village. High, open bog and moorlands with sweeping views in all directions. **Length:** 19 to 24 kilometers (12 to 15 miles), depending upon the route taken. **Walking Time:** 1 day. **Difficulty:** Moderately difficult. This ridge of the Sperrins can be quite taxing because of its numerous deep channels and gullies. **Path Markings:** None.
Map:
- Ordnance Survey of Northern Ireland One-Inch Map: Third Series (1:63,360), sheet 2.

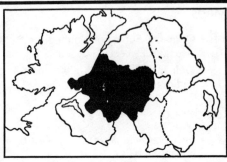

County Tyrone

The town of Omagh in central Tyrone is situated in a broad, roughly circular valley almost entirely surrounded by hills. Rivers draining the hills join near Omagh to form the River Strule, the county's largest, which flows through a gap in the hills to the north, entering the River Foyle near Strabane. On either side of the gap are large forests—Baronscourt Forest on the west and Gortin Glen Forest Park on the slopes of 539-meter Mullaghcarn on the east. Both offer good walking and are crossed by the Ulster Way.

Wilder hill country suitable for cross-country rambling lies along Tyrone's southwestern border with the Republic of Ireland and County Fermanagh, especially in the region of Killeter Forest and 370-meter Slieve Beagh. Both areas have numerous forest tracks and unmarked paths. Slieve Beagh lies on a signposted 89-kilometer (55-mile) stretch of the Ulster Way linking the Fermanagh Lakeland with the Favour Royal Forest on the Blackwater River.

Excellent hill walking is also available in the Sperrin Mountains, which run east-west along Tyrone's border with County Londonderry. The Southern Sperrins, which are separated from the main mountain massif by the valley of the Glenelly River, offer difficult, but rewarding walks through high, untracked moorlands.

Tourist Information

See *Address Directory:*

District Council Offices, Strabane.

Other local tourist offices open all year are located in Omagh and Cookstown.

For more information on Tyrone, refer to *Discover Northern Ireland* by Ernest Sandford.

Maps

- Ordnance Survey of Northern Ireland One-Inch Map: Third Series (1:63,360), sheets 2, 4, 5, 7 and 8.

Guidebook

- *Irish Walk Guides/4: North East* by Richard Rogers, Gill & Macmillan, Dublin.

Suggested Walks

The Ulster Way, from Slieve Beagh to Maghery, on Lough Neagh (described in the section on *Northern Ireland's Long-Distance Footpath*).

Address Directory

B

- *Ballycastle Tourist Information Office,* 61 Castle Street. Tel. (026 57) 62 0 24.
- *Banbridge Tourist Information Office.* Tel. Banbridge 22164.
- *Bangor Tourist Information Office,* The Esplanade. Tel. Bangor 2092.
- *Belfast C.H.A. Rambling Club* (affiliated with the Country-wide Holidays Association in Manchester, England), 6 Cross Avenue, Belfast 6.
- *British Tourist Authority,* 680 Fifth Avenue, New York, New York 10019, U.S.A. Tel. (212) 581-4700.
- *Bushmills Tourist Information Office.* Tel. (026 57) 31 3 43.

C

- *Castlerock Tourist Information Office.* Tel. Castlerock 258.
- *Cookstown Tourist Information Office.* Tel. 62205.
- *Council Office and Astronomy Center,* Armagh. Tel. (0861) 52 36 89.
- *Cushendall Tourist Information Office,* Mill Street. Tel. (026 672) 415.

D

- *Department of Environment,* Conservation Branch, Castle Grounds, Stormont, Belfast BT4 3SS. Tel. (0232) 76 78 16.

E

- *Emergency:* Tel. 999.
- *Enniskillen Tourist Information Office,* Townhall Street. Tel. Enniskillen 3110.

F

- *F.M.C.I.,* see *Federation of Mountaineering Clubs of Ireland.*
- *Federation of Mountaineering Clubs of Ireland,* Patricia Murray, 3 Gort na Mona Drive, Foxrock, Dublin.
- *Federation of Mountaineering Clubs of Ireland,* 183 Clonkeen Crescent, Pottery Road, Dun Laoire, County Dublin.
- *Forest Service,* Public Relations and Education Branch, Room 26, Dundonald House, Belfast BT4 3SB. Tel. (0232) 65 01 11.

G

- *Gill & Macmillan,* 15 Eden Quay, Dublin 1.
- *Glenfoffany Climbing Club,* Joe Cannon, 4 Rathdrum Park, Newtonabbey, County Antrim.
- *Government Bookshop,* 80 Chichester Street, Belfast BT1 4JY. Tel. (0232) 34 4 88.

H

- *Her Majesty's Stationery Office,* 80 Chichester Street, Belfast BT1 4JY. Tel. (0232) 34 4 88.
- *Hill Trekker,* Central Promenade, Newcastle, County Down.

I

- *Information Portakabin,* Foyle Street, Londonderry. Tel. (0504) 61 5 04.
- *Irish Mountaineering Club,* (Belfast Section), Robert Merrick, 82 Marlborough Park North, Belfast 9.

J

- *Jackson Sports Equipment,* 70 High Street, Belfast BT1 2DS.

K

- *Keep Fit Association of Northern Ireland,* 17 Fairview Park, Dunmurry, Belfast BT16 9HL. Tel. (0232) 61 09 33 (home) or 66 11 11 (business).
- *Kilkeel Tourist Information Office.* Tel. Kilkeel 62278.

L

- *Larne Harbour Tourist Information Office.* Tel. (0574) 2270.
- *Larne Tourist Information Office.* Tel. (0574) 2313.

M

- *Mourne Observer Press,* Newcastle, County Down, Northern Ireland.
- *Murray, Patricia,* 3 Gort na Mona Drive, Foxrock, Dublin.

N

- *National Trust Regional Information Officer,* Rowallane, Saintfield, Ballynahinch, County Down, BT24 7LH. Tel. Saintfield (0238) 51 07 21.
- *New University of Ulster Mountaineering Club,* New University of Ulster, Coleraine, County Londonderry.
- *Newcastle Tourist Information Office.* Tel. Newcastle 22222.
- *Northern Ireland Mountain Training Board,* 49 Malone Road, Belfast BT9 6RZ. Tel. (0232) 66 31 54.
- *Northern Ireland Orienteering Association,* 23 Ferndale Crescent, Newtonabbey BT36 8AN.
- *Northern Ireland Railways,* Central Station, Belfast. Tel. (0232) 30 3 10 or 30 6 71.
- *Northern Ireland Tourist Board,* Belfast, River House, 48 High Street, Belfast. Tel. 46 6 09.
- *Northern Ireland Tourist Board,* London, 11 Berkeley Street, London W1X 6BU. Tel. (01) 493 0601.

O

- *Omagh Tourist Information Office.* Tel. 45 321.
- *Ordnance Survey of Northern Ireland,* Chief Survey Officer, 83 Ladas Drive, Belfast BT6 9F. Tel. (0232) 58 2 25.

P

- *Patricia Murray*, see Murray, Patricia.
- *Portballintrae Tourist Information Office*. Tel. (026 57) 672.
- *Portrush Tourist Information Office*. Tel. (0265) 3333.
- *Portstewart Tourist Information Office*. Tel. Portstewart 2286.

Q

- *Queen's University Mountaineering Club*, c/o Students Union, Queen's University, University Road, Belfast 9.

S

- *S. A. Climbing Club*, William J. Blacker, 108 Legahory Court, Brownlow, Craigavon, County Armagh.
- *Scout Shop*, 14 College Square East, Belfast BT1 6DD. Tel. (0232) 20 5 80.
- *Slieveadore Club*, Maggie Clark, 47 Deramore Drive, Belfast BT9 5JS.
- *Sports Council for Northern Ireland*, 49 Malone Road, Belfast BT9 6RZ. Tel. (0232) 66 31 54.
- *Strabane District Council Offices*, Derry Road, Strabane. Tel. 88 32 04.

U

- *Ulsterbus*, Milewater Road, Belfast BT13. Tel. (0232) 74 52 01.
- *Ulster College Mountaineering Club*, Lorraine Crothers, c/o Students Union, Ulster Polytechnic, Jordanstown, Country Antrim.
- *Ulster Federation of Rambling Clubs*, 5 Rowan Road, Ballymoney, Antrim.

W

- *Warrenpoint Tourist Information Office*, Boating Pool. No telephone.
- *Weather Forecast, Belfast*. Tel. (0232) 28 4 57.
- *Weather Forecast, Northern Ireland*. Tel. (02384) 52 3 39.

Y

- *YHANI Information Centre and Shop*, 56 Bradbury Place, Belfast BT7. Tel. (0232) 24 7 33.

A Quick Reference

In a hurry? Turn to the pages listed below. They will give you the most important information on walking in Northern Ireland.

Search & Rescue, page 212.

Weather Forecasts, page 196.

Associations to Contact for Information:
On Walking, page 197.
On the Principal Footpaths in Northern Ireland, page 213.
Tourist Information, page 210.

Maps, page 202.

Guidebooks, page 203.

Equipment, page 208.

Address Directory, page 229.

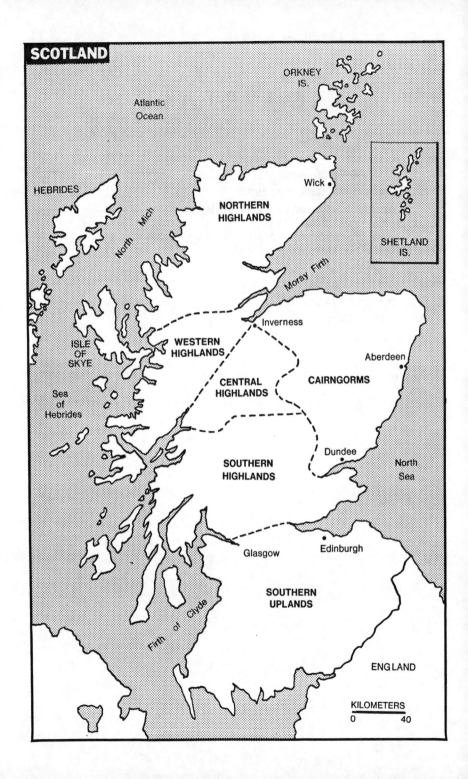

Scotland

SCOTLAND OFFERS SOME OF THE MOST REMOTE—and challenging—walk-ing in the British Isles. Half the size of England, with only one-tenth the population, most of Scotland's land is wild and unpopulated. Bare mountain and moor, scattered with hundreds of tiny lochs, stretch out beneath white massed clouds in the north, a vivid carpet of purple heather from early August through mid-September. To the west, great sea lochs bite into the land, and massive rock intrusions and numerous pine forests dominate the scenery. Peaks many millions of years older than the Alps, their glens slowly and deliberately gouged by glaciers, rise from sea loch to summit, every chiselmark of nature visible on their rocky, grass-covered flanks. Here and there, small crofts dot the landscape, marking the spots where people have tried, often in vain, to wrest a living from the barren earth.

To the south, where most of Scotland's 5 million people live, is gentler terrain. Fertile valleys are bounded by green, rolling hills whose broad, grassy slopes rise to ridges and high moorland amid rounded hilltops. Signposted walks, many designed with families in mind, follow forest trails created by the Forestry Commission, and wind along nature trails, more than 200 of which are described in the Scottish Tourist Board's booklet, *Walks and Trails in Scotland* (see the section on *Where to Get Walking Information* later in this chapter). Other marked paths take you up the Pentland Hills for the view across Edinburgh and the Firth of Forth to the hills of Fife, and, near Moffat, alongside the steep Tail Burn, which tumbles down from Loch Skeen in a series of falls and cascades culminating in the Grey Mare's Tail, a beautiful waterfall in an im-pressively narrow gorge.

Off the coast there are more than 700 islands, the best-known of which are the Hebrides in the western seas. One of the most spectacular of these is the Isle of Skye, highlighted by the Black Cuillin Hills, the steepest and rockiest mountains in Britain, and among the most potentially dangerous. Unless you are an experienced ridge-walker or rock climber, there is not much you can do in the Cuillins, except get as close as you can to admire them. Elsewhere on the island there are wide open spaces and broad hillsides dark from peat, dotted with little white crofts. Farther south lie the islands of Islay and Jura, famed for their distinctive whiskies, and Arran, once the hunting ground of kings, where palm trees and two unique varieties of the service tree flourish in its warm climate. Remains of civilizations long past are to be found at Callanish on the western Isle of Lewis where there are dramatic standing stones, second only to Stonehenge in size and importance, and nearby, the Dun Carloway broch, one of the best preserved Iron Age fortified towers in Britain.

More than 5,000 other standing stones, brochs, ruined towers and other reminders of the distant past are scattered across the Scottish landscape. There are also numerous castles, like Glamis, famous for its ghost and connections with Shakespeare's Macbeth, and Blair, whose white turrets stand stark against the heather. In much of the Highlands, however, one more often sees ruins of another kind. Scattered across the moors and in deserted glens are hundreds of ruined stone cottages, bleak memorials to the Highland Clearances, that black period in Scottish history when whole families were evicted from their ancestral homes to open up grazing areas for sheep.

Today the Highlands remain mostly wild and unspoiled, a vast, sparsely inhabited region covering nearly half of Scotland's 78,774 square kilometers (30,414 square miles), which supports only sheep farming, forestry, sports shooting, deer-stalking and fishing.

Much of the Highlands is privately owned and has few official footpaths. But there is technically no law of trespass in Scotland and, providing private and commercial interests are scrupulously respected, the walker enjoys tremendous freedom. There are numerous old military roads, cart tracks and drove roads dating back to the 16th and 17th centuries which can be followed, as well as a network of rights of way. Many private paths and tracks can also be used, providing you first ask permission and don't interfere with sporting interests and the lambing or clipping season.

Walking in Scotland, however, requires a high degree of care and discretion. The freedom to roam almost at will across the countryside is based largely upon the goodwill of landowners. It is not a legal right; it is a *privilege*.

Many of the wilder parts of Scotland belong to large estates where shooting, fishing and deer-stalking are the major underpinnings of the local economies. The sporting interests are also an important factor in Scotland's tourist industry and, hence, the economy of the country. Throughout much of the year, walkers are usually welcome to use the private access roads and tracks on the estates which, in many cases, lead into country poorly served by paths. But during the shooting and deer-stalking season—from the beginning of August until the middle of October—these access routes may be closed. It is essential to respect these closures. A walker can stampede a deer herd simply by being upwind of it. And while that walker may never know he or she caused any harm, future walkers will: they may be denied access across the estate. By asking locally where shooting and stalking is taking place, and which routes will be good to follow, you can avoid those areas where your presence will be a nuisance. In most instances, there will be alternate routes where you won't get in the way.

Grouse shooting is another major economic factor. Again, you should enquire locally during August and September where shooting is taking place—not only to avoid scattering grouse to the winds, but for your own safety.

You must also be careful to not interfere with sheep. Sheep are easily frightened, and once startled, they may run a kilometer. During most of the year the only risk here is that a startled sheep may fall in a gully and injure itself. But it becomes even more critical during lambing and clipping seasons. A shepherd may spend two or three days gathering his sheep, yet one careless walker can scatter the entire flock just by walking through the wrong place at the wrong time.

Consequently, it is important to always ask *where* you can go and *when* you are going to be a nuisance. A farmer who previously has had a bad experience with walkers may give you a cool—even hostile—reception and an emphatic "no" when you ask to cross his property, but most people will welcome you. By asking, you may also learn where some of Scotland's elusive *bothies*—abandoned buildings which can be used for shelter—are located. Because there is a feeling in Scotland against publicizing the locations of bothies (primarily to prevent them from becoming overcrowded) this is one of the few ways of learning where they are. The same feeling extends to rights of way. The contention of most Scots is that, through the consistent use of some routes, legal rights of way do exist, but once a path is marked and officially designated by law as a right of way, it may be contested by the landowner and lost as a right of way or, at the least, walkers will be restricted to the designated rights of way and lose their freedom to roam at will across the countryside. The result is that many rights of way remain unmarked and little publicized, and the only way to find out about them is to ask.

Information on the location of bothies and local walking routes, the dates and places where shooting and deer-stalking are taking place, and the times when lambing and clipping are coming due can be obtained from local post offices and police stations; from the proprietors of pubs, hotels and youth hostels; from local game wardens and the estate manager's—or *factor's*—offices; and from the landowners and their neighbors.

It is also wise to ask local advice on the condition of the walking routes you intend to follow. By Alpine standards the Scottish mountains are not high; only seven peaks exceed 1,220 meters (4,000 feet) and the highest of these, Ben Nevis, only reaches to 1,343 meters (4,406 feet). Nevertheless, all Scottish mountains—whether dramatic and rocky like those on Skye, or gentle and rolling like some of the Border Hills—are potentially dangerous and subject to rapid weather changes. Many mountains present exacting route-finding difficulties, and a certain amount of scrambling—elementary rock climbing without a rope—is necessary on some paths. Fatigue and hypothermia are constant hazards. Ankles are easily twisted in holes in the heather, and once immobile, a walker can get dangerously cold very easily. In a mist, a simple walk up a hillside can quickly turn into a serious undertaking requiring a high degree of skill and experience. As a result, the line between walking and mountaineering is often difficult to draw.

Sudden blanket mists, heavy winds and rain must be expected, especially in the western parts of Scotland. And in winter, the conditions can truly become arctic with temperatures well below minus 18° C. (0° F.) and winds so strong it is impossible to walk against them. Even in summer, there are blizzards, and snow is likely to lie in some of the corries until June.

Because of the uncertain weather and the likelihood of thick mists, survival frequently depends upon the accuracy of your route finding. In the Cairngorm range of eastern Scotland, for instance, many of the hills rise up to 1,200 meters and are bounded by cliffs, huge gullies and deep glens. Many of the peaks are poorly defined, which makes it exceedingly difficult to take bearings in bad weather. From some of the ridges, there are gently sloping grassy rakes which, in a mist, may appear to offer safe routes for a descent. But these can be deceptive. Some lead to relatively easy gullies which, in turn, plunge without warning over sheer rock walls. Others lead onto steeply sloping rock slabs which are often wet and slippery, and can send you on a fatal skid into the valley below. Often, even a small error in a compass reading can lead you into one of these areas. The combination of rain and high winds, even in warm temperatures, is also a threat, for the cooling effect of such conditions rapidly leads to hypothermia—the major cause of mountain deaths in the region.

Before walking in Scotland, it is absolutely essential that you have the proper clothing and equipment, be expert with map and compass, never walk alone, tell someone responsible where you are going and when you will be back, take proper account of weather forecasts and be ready to turn back the moment the weather begins to deteriorate.

Otherwise, don't go. Or stick to the walks described in the Scottish Tourist Board's *Walks and Trails in Scotland.*

Footpath Laws in Scotland

The laws relating to Scotland's rights of way differ considerably from those in England and Wales. Unlike the rest of Britain, local authorities are not obliged to record public paths on Definitive Maps. The Ordnance Survey maps covering Scotland also do not distinguish between those paths which are private and those which are public rights of way. Nonetheless, Scotland has an abundance of rights of way, many of which have their roots deep in the past. Because access to open land is seldom refused, and trespassing—in the sense of simple passage over another person's land—is not an offense, walkers generally enjoy a greater freedom than they do in areas of England and Wales. But this is based more upon tradition—and respect for others' interests—than upon law.

Even though you are not restricted solely to the recorded rights of way in

Scotland, it is worthwhile to understand the laws relating to them. The attitude of Scottish landowners to walkers generally is not an unfriendly one. Nevertheless, disputes do arise as to whether a particular route is or is not a public right of way. The more considerate a walker is toward the rights and interests of landowners, and the more careful walkers are to cause the least possible inconvenience to others, the more likely is the number of cases of contested rights of way to decrease. By seeking out and walking Scotland's rights of way, you also help preserve them as rights of way.

Many of Scotland's rights of way are old cross-country routes, once traversed on foot or horseback, which are today mere tracks through the heather, not always even visible. Many of these routes were drove roads, along which cattle and sheep were—and in some cases, still are—driven to market. *Kirk* and *coffin* roads are also common, the first being a route to church and the latter a route to the graveyard. Whatever their former use, nearly all the rights of way have two things in common: they had their origin in the public's need for a route from one place to another, and they have been in use for at least 20 years. (Prior to 1973, the prescriptive period for the creation of a public right of way was 40 years.) Local planning authorities have also recently been given statutory powers to establish public rights of way compulsorily.

Generally, the highlights of the law relating to rights of way in Scotland are as follows:

Acquisition. There are four criteria for acquiring a right of way under common law in Scotland. These are:

1. The route must have been used by the general public for a continuous period of not less than 20 years. It is not necessary that this be the *last* 20 years; it is sufficient if the route has been used any time *within* the last 20 years, and for a period of 20 years prior to that time. The amount of use necessary to establish a right of way also depends upon local circumstances; in thinly populated areas a lesser degree of use is required than in more populous districts.

2. The use must be a matter of right and not attributable to mere tolerance on the part of the landowner.

3. The route must connect two public places, or places to which the public habitually and legitimately resort, such as the tops of mountains.

4. The right of way must follow a more or less defined route. It is not necessary that there be a visible track, nor that the route be marked in any way. Minor deviations are also of no importance. It must be shown, however, that the public has always followed approximately the same route and the path is capable of being used along its entire length.

A right of way may also be acquired by statute. In this case a local planning authority may enter into an agreement with a landowner to create a public path or, failing this, a path may be created by order. For a creation order to take effect, it must be confirmed by the Secretary of State for Scotland after objections have been invited.

Enforcement. The Countryside (Scotland) Act, 1967, imposes a duty upon local planning authorities to: "assert, protect, and keep open and free from obstruction or encroachment any public right of way which is wholly or partly within their area, and they may for these purposes institute and defend legal proceedings and generally take steps as they may deem expedient." Any member of the public may also bring an action to vindicate a public right of way. It is not necessary for that person to reside locally. Anyone who walks in the district may raise an action, as may any society, organization or public group which has banded together for the purpose of protecting a right of way.

The legal procedure is by action of a *declarator* that a right of way exists. This action may be raised either in the Court of Session or in the Sheriff Court of the County. At the same time, evidence must be presented that the route has been used by the general public without interruption for a continuous period of 20 years. Evidence may be in the form of old maps, guidebooks, public records or statements of elderly persons with personal knowledge of the path. Hearsay evidence—what persons now dead have told witnesses concerning the path—is also accepted in the absence of other proof.

If the judgment is in favor of the existence of the right of way, the question cannot be reopened. But if the judgment is against the existence of the right of way, the matter can be reopened if more evidence comes to light.

Maintenance. The owners of land crossed by public rights of way are under no obligation to maintain or repair the routes. The public may repair or improve a right of way—cut back bushes, bridge streams, make marshy areas easier to walk over, or erect stiles, for instance—but only if no damage is caused to the owner's property. Local planning authorities also have the power to maintain paths, but they are under no obligation to do so, except in the case of public paths which have been created by agreement or creation orders, which they have a duty to maintain. If the Secretary of State for Scotland thinks they have failed in this duty, he has the power to order local planning authorities to carry out the necessary work.

Guideposting. Guideposts and direction posts may be erected by local planning authorities upon any right of way. Local authorities may also make a financial contribution to any person or society carrying out such work.

Obstructions. No obstruction that impedes a person's free passage may be placed on a right of way. Landowners may erect gates, providing they open and shut easily. A landowner may also erect a fence or wall across a right of way, but only if a gate or stile is installed to allow access. A landowner may not, at any time, lock or wire up a gate across a right of way. It is the responsibility of the users of the path, however, to ensure that all gates are properly shut after use.

A walker who encounters any obstruction may, without prior notice or protest, remove as much of the obstruction as is necessary to restore free passage along the right of way. Obstructions which cannot be dealt with in this manner should be brought to the attention of the local planning authority. The only condition in removing obstructions is that the action must be taken within a reasonably short period following erection of the obstruction.

Misleading notices. This is a less obvious form of obstruction. Examples are signs saying *Private, Private Road, Trespassers will be Prosecuted, No Dogs Allowed* and so on. A *Private* notice applies only to private ground, not the right of way. A *Private Road* notice on a right of way merely means it is a private road for vehicles but remains a right of way for pedestrians. A *Trespassers will be Prosecuted* sign may be true in certain unlikely cases, but to be prosecuted for trespassing in Scotland you must first cause damage (and trampling grass might be claimed as damage), but your mere presence on another person's land is not, strictly speaking, an offence. A walker is also entitled to be accompanied by his or her dog, providing it is kept under control and does no damage.

Plowing. Landowners and tenants have the right to plow a public right of way, unless this right has been excluded by a public path creation or diversion order. The landowner or tenant must inform the local planning authority within seven days after plowing and must reinstate the surface of the right of way as soon as possible. In the meantime, the public is entitled to tread down the ground and continue to use the right of way. In most cases, however, it makes more sense to walk around the edge of the field.

Bulls. The law on this issue is murky. Technically, a bull may be pastured in a field crossed by a public path if it is less than 10 months old, is not a recognized dairy breed, or is in a field in which cows or heifers are also at large. Nonetheless, the Scottish Rights of Way Society believes that under common law it is illegal to have any bull running free in a field crossed by a public right of way, although there has been no legal decision in Scotland on this point.

Diversion. A landowner cannot alter the route of a public right of way without due legal process, although there is usually no difficulty if walkers using the route accept minor changes as reasonable.

A landowner who wishes to alter the route of a public path—say from one side of his property to the other—must apply to the local planning authority for a diversion order. The planning authority must then invite objections to the diversion and, once they have been heard, decide the issue in the light of the circumstances.

A local planning authority may also make a diversion order closing an existing right of way and substituting a new one, but only if the new path will not be substantially less convenient to the public. In addition, a local planning authority may divert a path to allow development to take place. These diversion orders must be confirmed by the Secretary of State for Scotland after any objections have been heard.

The Secretary of State for Scotland may also divert a path to allow development—again, after objections have been invited. When closing or diverting a path, local planning authorities and the Secretary of State have the power—but not the obligation—to create or improve other rights of way.

Extinguishment. A right of way is extinguished by common law if it has fallen into disuse for a period of 20 years. This disuse, however, must be with the acquiescence of the public. Also, a right of way is not considered lost until a full 20 years have elapsed without the exercise of the public right. (Consequently, many routes in Scotland which have not been walked for a long period could still be saved as rights of way if walkers would simply seek them out and use them.)

A public path may also be extinguished by statute. Local authorities and certain statutory bodies, such as the Electricity Board, may acquire ground disburdened of all public rights of way, or may have the rights of way declared closed after acquisition. In this case, notice of the intention to close a right of way must be given.

In addition, local planning authorities have the power to close a right of way on the grounds it is not needed for public use. To do this, they must submit a "public path extinguishment order" to the Secretary of State for Scotland for confirmation. The Secretary of State for Scotland may also issue an order extinguishing any right of way if the land crossed by the path has been acquired for planning purposes by the local authority. The Secretary of State, however, must be satisfied that an alternative right of way has been provided, will be provided or is not required.

Rights-of-way maps. Scotland, unlike England and Wales, has no procedure for the registration of rights of way. Instead, rights of way in Scotland are merely *recorded*. Although there are no Definitive Maps in Scotland, local authorities have, in some cases, prepared lists of the rights of way and maps showing their routes. These maps and lists are available for the public to review upon request. (Information on where you can see them can be obtained from the Scottish Rights of Way Society. For its address and telephone number, see the *Address Directory* at the end of this chapter.)

Under the Countryside (Scotland) Act, 1967, all local planning authorities have a duty to prepare and keep up to date maps showing details of all land which has been acquired for public access or which is subject to access agreements. All orders for access, creation, diversion and extinguishment of the paths must be recorded on these maps, together with notices of any restrictions affecting access. The Secretary of State for Scotland must also prepare maps of the Scottish Countryside showing rights of way, although burghs of 5,000 inhabitants or more are excluded from this provision. But this is a slow process, and the job is far from complete.

The Scottish Rights of Way Society has signposted many of the principal cross-country rights of way and is now recording these routes on maps which will be passed on to the local planning authorities. The Society, however, does not have a comprehensive record of rights of way throughout the country. It also has not published a detailed list of cross-country routes because, the Society says: "The publication of such a list inevitably gives rise to controversy, and the Directors of the Society feel that there are already available to the public accounts of the hill-paths which are open to walkers, whether or not their status as rights of way could be satisfactorily established in a court of law."

Perhaps the best record of these rights of way are the two books by D.G. Moir, *Scottish Hill Tracks: Southern Scotland* and *Scottish Hill Tracks: Northern Scotland* (see the section on *Guidebooks*), which describe more than 300 walks on old highways and drove roads through Scotland, most of which are rights of way under common law.

What the public can do. The existence of most of the major cross-country routes in Scotland is now well established. But there are hundreds of other routes of lesser importance which may be lost forever if action is not soon taken to preserve these routes as rights of way. Walkers can help, first of all, by walking these rights of way at reasonable intervals and, secondly, by reporting to a member of the local Council any threatened loss or obstruction of a right of way. The Scottish Rights of Way Society is also available to advise the public and local authorities on any questions concerning rights of way.

If you would like to obtain more information about Scotland's rights of way—or the laws relating to them—you should contact the Society. You may also join the Society. Its address and phone number will be found in the *Address Directory*. Details on its publications are included in the section on *Where to Get Walking Information*.

Scotland's Mountain Code

When walking in Scotland, you should observe the Scottish Mountain Leadership Training Board's mountain code, both for the sake of others and your safety. Here is the code:

Before You Go

1. Learn the use of map and compass.
2. Know the weather signs and local forecast.
3. Plan within your capabilities.
4. Know simple first aid and the symptoms of hypothermia.
5. Know the mountain distress signals.
6. Know the Country Code (see the introduction to the chapter on England).

When You Go

1. Never go alone.
2. Leave written word of your route and report your return.
3. Take windproofs, woollens and a survival bag.
4. Take map and compass, flashlight and adequate food.
5. Wear climbing boots.
6. Keep alert all day.
7. Be prepared to turn back if the weather becomes bad or if any member of your party is becoming slow or exhausted.

If There Is Snow on the Hills

1. Always have an ice axe for each person.
2. Carry a climbing rope and know the correct use of rope and ice axe.
3. Learn to recognize dangerous snow slopes.

Flora & Fauna

The extensive forests of Scots pine that once covered much of Scotland below 380 meters (1,250 feet) were gradually destroyed through the expansion of cultivation, the need to drive out wolves and the use of timber for smelting, charcoal and shipbuilding. Remnants of the primeval forest remain in the Highlands, the best examples being the Black Wood of Rannoch in Perthshire, Rothiemurchus Forest in Speyside and the Glen Affric area. On river banks and in marshy areas woods of alder, willow, birch and ash are found, along with a rich meadow and river bank flora of herbs in which meadowsweet and whorled caraway are characteristic. Woods of oak, ash, birch, hazel, elm, rowan and holly grow on better drained ground, and in October their brilliant russets and golds stand out against the snow-covered mountains.

On higher ground heather moorland is dominant on the poorer soils, coloring whole hillsides purple during August and September, while the well-drained, fertile soils of the glens often support bright green turfy grasslands. Mixed through the heather moorland is sedge, rush, bog asphodel, cotton grass and purple moor grass. On blanket bog, where the peat is a meter or more deep, the abundant cotton grass gives a grayish-brown color to the hills. Large areas are also covered with wild hyacinths, primroses, anemones and violets, as well as the small scrubby blaeberry.

Much of the moorland is artificial, maintained as open heath by burning, grazing and tree-pulling. This produces economic benefit in grouse and deer for the estates and in sheep and cattle for the hill farmer. If burning and stock grazing were stopped, forests and scrub would spread over much of the ground again, and in some areas you can see this process at work.

Above the moorland are a large number of Arctic-Alpine plants. In the Cairngorms the special snow-patch vegetation is richer in its extent and number of species than anywhere else in Britain. It also has a remarkable variety, depending upon the length of snow cover. Ridges of wind-swept granite, where the snow usually blows off, are sparsely dotted with the three-pointed rush which grows commonly in the high Arctic. Where the snow lies longer on slightly less-exposed ground, the circumpolar dwarf willow commonly creeps low over the ground. Over the schists, where soils are more fertile than over granite, plateaus tend to be covered with a complete coat of vegetation, mainly composed of Arctic sedge and woolly fringe moss.

You often see a big change in vegetation around 750 meters (2,500 feet), where you pass from the moorland zone dominated by long heather, to an obvious Arctic-Alpine zone with many screes, dwarfed blaeberry and crowberry, clubmosses and a few patches of cloudberry. Here, the grassland contains alpine meadow-rue, the alpine lady's mantle and the moss campion, whose green cushion-like masses are covered with bright pink blossom in early summer. Among the rarer species are the alpine lady fern, the holly fern, the bog bilberry and alpine saw-wort.

In the lowlands during spring and early summer, fresh, pale green breaks through the dun of field and woods; the trees suddenly have a shimmer of green, which soon bursts into fresh leaf. Spring isn't even officially started when the first masses of snowdrops are to be seen, then come the daffodils—on the grounds of estates, in woods and gardens. Soon, too, come the rhododendrons, particularly in the west; not isolated bushes, but kilometers of them, often growing wild—great bunches of reds and pinks and purples and whites greeting you as you walk across the hills, contrasting vividly with the masses of yellow gorse and broom which, in Scotland, ushers you into summer.

Well before the end of April, the spring migrants are flying in to add their chorus to the rich variety of bird life which stays in Scotland all year—birds like the snowy owl of Shetland, the crested tit in Speyside and the capercaille and ptarmigan of the forest and moors—a few of the 400-odd species to be seen and heard in Scotland.

Great colonies of gannets are to be seen on Bass Rock off North

Berwick, at Ailsa Craig off Givan, and on the bird island of St. Kilda. Cormorants and shags, kittiwakes and skuas are seen in many parts of the country. Geese visit Scotland in the winter and can be seen, 10,000 at a time, on the Solway Coast near Caerlaverock. Swans and all kinds of ducks are permanent residents, as are birds of prey such as the golden eagle, peregrine falcon, buzzard and kestrel.

Red deer range over the Highlands, and roe deer are found in the lower woodlands. A herd of reindeer, introduced from Sweden in 1954, can even be seen at a reserve in Speyside in the Cairngorms. The wildcat is still common in the north, while the pine marten, once almost extinct, is occasionally seen in the forests. There are also badgers, stoats, weasels, blue hares, red squirrels and foxes. And in the southwest, you can see the shaggy goats of Talnotry.

The only poisonous snake in Scotland is the adder, and it is extremely rare, although a bite should receive immediate medical attention. Mosquitoes are not much of a problem, except in the Western Highlands, but midges, clegs and horse flies can be annoying during the early evening in the Highlands in August and September. Although the midges have a bothersome habit of ignoring most repellents, you will be more comfortable in wet and marshy areas if you bring some along.

Climate

There is an old saying in Scotland about its weather: "If you can see the mountains, it's going to rain; and if you cannot, it's raining." This is not strictly true, but raingear is important for any walk in Scotland.

Rainfall averages are actually no greater in Scotland than elsewhere in the British Isles. Long-term measurements of precipitation show that each area in England and Wales can be matched by one in Scotland: London by the Edinburgh area, for instance, the English Lake District and Welsh Hills by the Scottish Highlands, the coastal area of Yorkshire by the Aberdeenshire coast, the Devon coast by the Ayrshire and Galloway coasts, and so on.

Many districts in north and east Scotland have an annual precipitation of less than 762 mm (30 inches). Nevertheless, the ruggedly scenic areas of western Scotland, which cover much of the country, are very wet because of their high hills. Large parts of the Highlands have an average precipitation exceeding 2,032 mm (80 inches) per year, while some areas receive as much as 3,675 mm (150 inches) of precipitation per year. Many of the coastal islands, such as Skye, also have a high annual precipitation. The low-lying coastal strips flanking the high ground, however, are often relatively dry and it is sometimes possible to escape heavy and prolonged showers by heading to a place on one of the nearby coastal strips.

Spring is generally the driest season, with the months of May and June being the best months for warm, dry weather in the Highlands and on the coastal islands. The days are also long and during June you can walk and climb till midnight. July and August are warmer but wetter, while September and early October often provide good weather in lower parts of the country.

Far more important than rainfall, however, is the speed and severity with which conditions can change. The weather varies almost from hour to hour. Sudden blanket mists and heavy winds can occur at any time. The damp conditions combined with high winds pose a constant hazard of hypothermia for the ill-equipped, even in otherwise moderate temperatures. But temperatures can also plunge suddenly, creating near-Arctic conditions on the exposed mountainsides and peaks.

In the Cairngorms, you are more likely to encounter blizzards than on any other British range. And they occasionally can be very severe, with heavy snowfalls, drifting and frost.

Even in settled weather, there is a radical swing in the range of daily temperatures in the Highland glens, particularly in east and northeast Scotland. During July midday temperatures may reach 27° C. (80° F.) or more, yet plunge to near freezing at night.

The weather also varies a great deal locally. During spring and early summer, very strong, Föhn-like winds may be blowing down the lee slopes of the moors and higher hills. Exceptionally, these winds reach hurricane force and may cause a blizzard of ground drift. Yet only two kilometers away and 100 meters lower in elevation it may be a virtually calm day.

Generally, winter is no more severe in the lowlands of Scotland than it is in England. But the mountaintops have an Arctic-type climate, as opposed to the Alpine climate of most European mountain areas. The average mean temperature in Edinburgh for January, for instance, is 3° C. (37.4° F.). In contrast, winter temperatures of *minus* 18° C. (0° F.) are common in glens in the Cairngorms, and temperatures of *minus* 29° C. *(minus* 20° F.) have been recorded. You frequently hear the snow squeak beneath your boots and feel your hands sticking slightly to metal, both of which occur below *minus* 5° C. During sunny, windless days in winter, the cold air stays in the valley bottoms, sometimes producing a frosty fog, while on the mountain tops it feels much warmer. More often, however, it becomes much colder as you climb. This is virtually always the case if any wind blows, even a light wind. And winds on Scottish mountains can be far from light. Weather instruments on Cairn Gorm have proved it to be one of the windiest places in the British Isles; the top gust ever recorded in Britain— 125 knots (232 kilometers, or 144 miles per hour)—occurred there on March 6, 1967.

In some winters, snow storms with severe drifting occur in the exposed northern counties, particularly in Caithness, Sutherland and northeast Aberdeenshire. More typically, however, ski areas in the Cairngorms, Glencoe, Glenshee and elsewhere in Scotland rely more on long-lasting snow beds, which accumulate in corries, than on general snow cover. As in the Alps, there can be considerable variations in snowfall and snow cover from month to month and from year to year, but generally the skiing season in Scotland lasts from early December to the end of April.

Weather Forecasts

Because of the uncertainty of weather conditions in Scotland, it is advisable to always obtain a weather forecast prior to beginning a walk in the hills. A favorable forecast, however, does not negate the need for proper clothing and equipment. Remember that local conditions can sometimes vary greatly from the forecasts, and that while other forecasted conditions may appear favorable, a sudden mist can make even an easy hill walk hazardous. The forecasts are valuable in helping you avoid major storm systems, which may catch you unaware in the hills. But they should be taken only as a general guide.

Recorded telephone forecasts for the whole of Scotland may be obtained by dialing:

> **Weather Forecasts:** Tel. (031) 246 8091 in Edinburgh or (041) 246 8091 in Glasgow.

More specific information on local conditions can be obtained from one of Scotland's Meteorological Offices. Their telephone numbers are:

> **Glasgow Weather Centre** (Glasgow, Borders, West of Scotland): Tel. (041) 248 3451.
>
> **Aberdeen Airport** (Northeast): Tel. Aberdeen 72 23 34.
>
> **Edinburgh Airport:** Tel. (031) 339 7777.
>
> **Glenmore Lodge:** Tel. (047) 986 256.
>
> **Kinloss, Morayshire** (Moray Firth Area): Tel. Forres 72161, ext. 673 or 674.
>
> **Leuchars** (Fife): Tel. Leuchars 224.
>
> **Pitreavie** (Fife): Tel. Inverkeithing 3566.
>
> **Prestwick Airport** (West and Southwest): Tel. Prestwick 78475.
>
> **Orkney** (Kirkwall Airport): Tel. Kirkwall 2421, ext. 34.
>
> **Shetland:** Tel. Lerwick 2239.

The Meteorological Offices generally give information based on the forecasts prepared by the Glasgow Weather Centre. In all cases, these reflect sea level conditions, and may vary from the wind speeds, temperatures and precipitation experienced at higher altitudes.

For a nominal charge, you may request a 24-hour forecast from the Meteorological Offices for the specific locality in which you intend to walk. If you do this, you should ask for the Officer-in-Charge and tell him the exact area in which you are going to walk; the purpose for which the forecast is required; the weather features that are of interest to you, such as wind speed and direction, temperature, anticipated rainfall, and—importantly—the anticipated cloud level; the time at which the information is desired; and the telephone number to which the information is to be sent. The Meteorological Office will then prepare a forecast for you and call back with the information.

If you are unsure which Meteorological Office to call, you should direct your enquiries to the Glasgow Weather Centre. The Weather Centre generally will provide a forecast for any Scottish area upon request. You may also drop into the Glasgow Weather Centre for personal enquiries:

Glasgow Weather Centre (see *Address Directory*).

Where to Get Walking Information

There are several organizations from which you can obtain walking information. Many of the organizations offer specialized information on a particular aspect of walking in Scotland. Depending upon the kind of walking you want to do and where you want to go, you may have to contact more than one of the following organizations. For general enquiries it is best to contact either the Mountaineering Council of Scotland or the Scottish Tourist Board.

All addresses and telephone numbers will be found in the *Address Directory*.

Mountaineering Council of Scotland, Honorary Secretary, William Myles. Written enquiries only. Can provide information on any aspect of mountaineering and hill walking in Scotland. Also can provide a list of Scotland's mountaineering club huts, as well as information on the clubs. Very good about answering letters, providing you follow certain guidelines; see *How to Obtain Information from Walking Clubs* in *On Foot Through Europe: A Trail Guide to Europe's Long-Distance Footpaths* and enclose a self-addressed envelope and sufficient return postage. The honorary secretary, however, is a volunteer who must answer letters in his spare time. Please respect this. All enquiries should be in English.

The Backpackers Club. Will provide help in selecting walking routes and working out itineraries, providing you enclose a self-addressed envelope and sufficient postage (or international postal reply coupons) with your request. You should briefly describe the kind of walking you want to do, the type of terrain you wish to cross (or the area you wish to visit) and supply details on your walking and backpacking experience. For additional information on the club, see the sections on *Where to Get Walking Information* and *Walking Clubs in England* in the chapter on England.

Forestry Commission, in Edinburgh. Can provide information on waymarked footpaths, interpretive trails, forest and mountain walks, pony trekking trails and wayfaring courses in Scotland's forest areas. Also can provide information on forest cabins and cottages, backpacking campsites and other recreational facilities in the forests. Footpaths in the forests range up to 24 kilometers (15 miles) in length, and vary in difficulty from easy to strenuous. There are also nearly 16,000 kilometers of forest roads that can be walked, many of which are closed to automobile traffic. The Forestry Commission publishes several information pamphlets, detailed guides to each of Scotland's four Forest Parks and a leaflet entitled *See Your Forests: Scotland* covering the forest areas in Scotland, which gives details on the footpaths and walking possibilities in the forest areas. All the Forestry Commission publications are listed in the *Forestry Commission Catalogue of Publications,* along with their prices and information on where each can be obtained. The publication list is free upon request. Information on walking in the forests can also be obtained from the Forestry Commission regional offices in Aberdeen, Inverness, Dumfries and Glasgow.

Scottish Rights of Way Society, Ltd. Can provide information on Scotland's recorded rights of way, where you can see maps showing the rights of way, and supply details on the law in Scotland relating to rights of way. The Society publishes several useful publications, including:

- *The Principal Rights of Way in the West Central Highlands; The Cairngorm Passes;* and *The Knoydart & Moyer Passes* (all in English). Three maps showing recorded rights of way. The maps are meant only as a guide to the rights of way in these areas and should be supplemented with the appropriate Ordnance Survey maps (which are listed on the back of the SRWS maps). The map to the Cairngorm Passes also shows the locations of guideposts and youth hostels along the routes and includes a brief description of three principal rights of way. All the rights of way in the area are not shown on this map. The maps are available for a nominal charge from the Society or, if you become a member, you will receive all the Society's publications free. Foreign members are welcome.

- *A Walker's Guide to The Law of Right of Way in Scotland* (in English). Gives full details on the origin and nature of rights of way, their creation and extinction, the procedures for establishing and defending them, their maintenance, and what the public can do to help preserve Scotland's rights of way. Available for a nominal charge, or free with a membership in the SRWS.

The Scottish Landowners' Federation. Can provide information on the areas and dates when access may be restricted across private estates, whom to contact in various areas for permission to cross property and how to maintain good relations with landowners. A very useful—and highly recommended—publication is:

- *The Scottish Landowners' Federation: Access for Mountain Climbers* (in English). Compiled and issued in cooperation with the Mountaineering Council of Scotland. Gives brief guidelines on access routes, access permission, camping, bothies, cars and livestock. Also includes a detailed list of private properties in several mountain areas, with information for each on restricted periods, preferred routes, the telephone numbers of contacts and remarks to help you to get along better with the individual property owners. Available for a nominal charge. Please enclose a large self-addressed envelope with your request.

Scottish Youth Hostels Association. In addition to maintaining 80 youth hostels, the SYHA publishes seven walkers' guides; organizes numerous "Breakaway Holidays" for walking, climbing, canoeing, sailing, gliding and pony trekking throughout Scotland; offers several individual package holiday arrangements, such as its "Highland Wayfarer Package," which can be combined with hikes or any other activity you want to pursue on your own in the areas visited; and operates a travel service for members heading to the European continent. Brief descriptions of the walking opportunities around each of its hostels are included in the *SYHA Handbook,* along with a list of the Ordnance Survey map sheets that cover the region surrounding the hostels. The SYHA walkers' guides are listed later in this chapter under *Guidebooks.* Details on the other SYHA publications and activities are available on request.

The Scottish Sports Council. Can provide information on Scotland's sports organizations, and on outdoor activities such as orienteering, angling, birdwatching, canoeing, caving, cycling, diving, gliding, horseback riding and sailing. The Sports Council also organizes courses in rock climbing, snow and ice climbing, winter mountaineering, skiing, ski mountaineering, mountain rescue, hill craft, canoeing and field studies at its National Outdoor Training Centre in Aviemore. Details are available on request.

The National Trust for Scotland. Maintains nearly 100 properties in trust, including several mountain areas, such as 5,747 hectares (14,200 acres) in Glencoe and Dalness, which encompasses some of the finest climbing and walking country in Scotland. Other trust holdings include castles, historic sites, islands, waterfalls, notable viewpoints and the homes of "Famous Scots." The National Trust publishes an annual booklet listing all its properties:

- *The National Trust for Scotland Year Book* (in English). Gives a brief description of all the Trust's holdings, including locations, dates open, admission fees and the locations of visitor centers. No information is given on walking, but the booklet is useful for helping you decide where to go.

The National Trust also publishes several leaflets and guides to nature trails on its holdings. Several of these are listed later in this chapter under *Guidebooks*.

Scottish Tourist Board. Provides general information on all types of holidays in Scotland. Publishes numerous pamphlets and booklets giving information on where to go, what to do, where to stay and various outdoor activities. Can provide information on walking and climbing holidays, mountaineering and hill walking courses, skiing and just about anything else you might like to do in Scotland. Staff speaks English and most other European languages. Useful publications include:

- *Scotland for Hillwalking* (in English). Gives a brief description of each of Scotland's seven regions, with details on suggested walks in each. Also lists walkers' and climbers' guidebooks, and gives information on equipment and weather conditions in the mountains. Provides an excellent overview on walking in Scotland. (Recommended)

- *Walks and Trails in Scotland* (in English). Describes more than 200 walks in city and county parks, in forests, along the coast and across wild moorland. Most of the walks can be completed within a few hours, do not require specialist equipment and are suitable for families with children. Many are signposted and are described in guidebooks available locally. The walk descriptions include the addresses and telephone numbers of local contacts for further information on each path, list the titles of guidebooks and briefly describe the terrain crossed. The locations of the walks are shown on a series of sketch maps at the beginning of the booklet. (Recommended for those who like short, gentle walks).

Highlands & Islands Development Board. Can provide information and advice on holidays in the Highlands and on Scotland's islands. The Development Board maintains a number of local tourist organizations throughout the area, which can provide specific details on their locales.

The Countryside Commission for Scotland. Oversees the planning of long-distance footpaths in Scotland and assists local authorities in negotiations with landowners to secure formal rights-of-way agreements. The Commission is currently working to establish three long-distance footpaths in Scotland—the West Highland Way from Glasgow to Fort William, the Southern Uplands Way from Portpatrick to Cockburnspath and the Speyside Way from Spey Bay to the Cairngorms. But it will be many years before these routes are complete. The Commission maintains a set of one-inch Ordnance Survey maps, prepared by the Scottish Rights of Way Society, showing all the recorded rights of way in Scotland. The maps, however, are not printed and are not available for general sale to the public. The Commission also oversees the establishment and improvement of country parks in Scotland, several of which contain walking routes. Information on the country parks is available from both the Countryside Commission and the Scottish Tourist Board.

Scotland's Walking & Climbing Clubs

Scotland has more than 80 mountaineering and climbing clubs, most of which are members of the Mountaineering Council of Scotland. A list of these clubs, along with details on each, can be obtained on request from the MCS (see *Address Directory*).

The MCS is the representative body for mountaineering in Scotland, and is concerned with activities ranging from summer hill walking to exacting climbing in Scotland and abroad, both in summer and winter conditions. The Council does not seek to popularize the sport or influence the number of mountaineers, which it believes should change spontaneously. It does, however, seek to maintain the highest quality of mountain experience for those who climb. Its principal functions are to: 1) provide a democratic forum for the formulation of mountaineering policy; 2) represent mountaineering and the interests of mountaineers to the Scottish Sports Council and other bodies within Scotland and, with the British Mountaineering Council, to represent British mountaineering abroad; 3) maintain the freedom of access to Scotland's mountains and crags and the freedom to participate in mountaineering without external restrictions; and 4) ensure that proper standards are set for educational and training programs.

The MCS works in cooperation with its member clubs to educate mountaineers and the general public in their responsibilities toward the mountain environment and those who earn a living in the mountains, and to maintain public understanding of the ethics and value of the sport of mountaineering. The MCS also has access, through its members, to a wide mountaineering expertise and can serve as a valuable source of technical knowledge and advice on mountaineering.

Full membership in the MCS is open to mountaineering clubs and organizations whose principal objectives are mountaineering, who have headquarters in Scotland and who are owned and controlled by their members. Associate membership is open to bodies and individuals who do not qualify for full membership. Individuals may apply for membership in the MCS by providing personal details and an outline of interests and experience. Normally, however, individuals join one of the MCS's member clubs. One of the best known of these clubs—and one of particular interest to walkers because of its guidebooks—is:

Scottish Mountaineering Club (see *Address Directory*). A club with about 300 members. Membership is private, based upon the recommendations of sponsors and experience. Publishes an excellent series of eight district guidebooks covering all of Scotland with comprehensive descriptions of the mountains and valleys; information on each region's history, weather, geology, flora and fauna, estates and land use, accommodation, transport and local clubs; and details on mountain safety, equipment, rock and ice climbs, skiing routes and walking routes. The club also publishes an annual journal with comprehensive information on mountaineering in Scotland and abroad. Further details on the club and membership are available on request.

Maps

Scotland, like England and Wales, is covered by the maps published by the Ordnance Survey in Southampton, England. The OS publishes five maps series suitable for walkers and climbers:

1:25,000—First Series. Covers most of the Southern Uplands, Southern Highlands, the Orkney Islands and the Grampian region of the Cairngorms.

1:25,000—Second Series. Covers the rest of Scotland; will eventually replace the 1:25,000 First Series maps.

Outdoor leisure Maps based on the Second Series 1:25,000, two sheets: *The High Tops of the Cairngorms* and *The Cuillin and Torridon Hills* (includes two separate maps printed back to back).

1:50,000 Maps. Fifty-eight sheets in this series cover all of Scotland.

Tourist Maps, one-inch (1:63,360), two sheets: *Loch Lomond and the Trossachs,* and *Ben Nevis and Glen Coe.*

For further details on these maps, see the section on *Maps* in the chapter on England.

A list of retailers, a catalog with a map index and a price list are available from:

Ordnance Survey (see *Address Directory*).

The Ordnance Survey does not sell maps, but they can be purchased nearly everywhere in Scotland—from local tourist boards; from sports shops such as Graham Tiso in Edinburgh and Nevisport in Fort William, Glasgow and Aviemore; and from many booksellers, including John Smith & Son Ltd. in Glasgow and the Menzies Booksellers in most towns. The main agent for the Ordnance Survey in Scotland is:

Thomas Nelson & Sons Ltd. (see *Address Directory*). Can provide an OS catalog, indexes and a price list. Sells maps both in person and by mail.

Because few local booksellers and stationers stock the complete set of OS maps, it is advisable to either order them by mail before you arrive in Scotland, or to buy them in Edinburgh at the beginning of your trip. One other series of maps worth mentioning are those produced by:

John Bartholomew & Son Ltd. (see *Address Directory*).

These maps cover all of Scotland and are stocked by most booksellers. An index and price list may be obtained from the publisher upon request.

Climbers' Maps

The Scottish Mountaineering Club publishes three special climbers maps:

- *Black Cuillin of Skye,* Code SM, three inches to one mile (1:21:120). An outline map in two colors.
- *Black Cuillin of Skye,* Code CM 1:15,000. A topographical map in four colors.
- *Ben Nevis,* four inches to one mile (1:15, 840). A topographical map in four colors. Includes north face routes and descriptions on the reverse side.

The maps are produced and distributed by:

West Col Productions (see *Address Directory*).

Guidebooks

Scotland is covered by several very good guidebooks. In addition, there are numerous forest trail leaflets and local footpath guides. Perhaps the best of these guides are the eight district guidebooks published by the Scottish Mountaineering Club:

- *Southern Uplands* (in English) by K.M. Andrew and A.A. Thrippleton, produced and distributed by West Col Productions, Reading, England. Covers the region from Forth-Clyde Canal to the English border. Includes 116 photographs and illustrations.
- *The Southern Highlands* (in English) by Dr. Donald Bennet, West Col Productions. Covers Arrochar, Ben Lommond, the Trossachs, Crianlarich and the Lawers groups. Includes 79 photographs and illustrations.
- *The Central Highlands* (in English) by Campbell R. Steven, West Col Productions. Covers Blackmount, Glencoe, Lochaber, Ben Nevis, Mamore Forest and Creag Meaghaidh. Illustrated with 32 photographs and maps.

- *The Western Highlands* (in English) by G.S. Johnstone, West Col Productions. Covers Morvern, Ardgour, Moidart, Knoydart, Kintail Cannich and Strathfarrar. Illustrated with 30 photographs and maps.
- *The Northern Highlands* (in English) by Tom Strang, West Col Productions. Covers Ross-shire, Sutherland and Caithness. Includes 50 photographs and drawings, and 15 maps.
- *The Cairngorms* (in English) by Adam Watson, West Col Productions. Covers the Cairngorms, the Mouth and Lochnagar. Includes 50 photographs and illustrations, and 15 maps.
- *The Isle of Skye* (in English) by Malcolm Slesser, West Col Productions. Covers the mountains and hills of Skye, including the Black Cuillins. Illustrated with 75 photographs and maps.
- *The Islands of Scotland* (in English) by Norman Tennent, West Col Productions. A guide to all the Scottish islands excluding Skye. Includes 50 photographs and illustrations.

The SCM District Guides provide comprehensive descriptions of the mountains and valleys in each region, along with details on touring, skiing, walking and climbing routes. The guides are extremely well done and have few equals, even in other countries. The route descriptions are quite detailed, but contain a lot of solid text and therefore may be difficult to read for those who are not fluent in English. Also, all the books are hardbound, which adds to the weight of your pack.

Two lightweight guidebooks, which virtually everyone associated with walking in Scotland recommends, are:

- *Scottish Hill Tracks/Old Highways & Drove Roads: Southern Scotland* and *Scottish Hill Tracks/Old Highways & Drove Roads: Northern Scotland* (in English). Both by D.G. Moir, John Bartholomew & Son Ltd., Edinburgh.

These two books together describe 326 walks ranging in length from 4 to 39 miles (6.5 to 63 kilometers) on hill tracks and cross-country routes throughout Scotland. Many of the routes follow Roman roads, medieval roads, drove roads, kirk and coffin roads, and military roads abandoned by modern traffic. The two booklets also describe eight long-distance routes (see the section on *Scotland's Long-Distance Walking Routes* later in this chapter), which mostly follow the old Scottish hill tracks, with a few unavoidable links along short stretches of paved roads. A series of sketch maps at the beginning of the books show the routes of the walks and are keyed to the numbered route descriptions. Each route description is short enough to be understood by those who are not completely fluent in English, and have the necessary details on the beginning and end points of each walk, its length and the sheet numbers of the required Ordnance Survey maps (both one-inch and 1:50,000) set off from the rest of the text. If you buy only two guidebooks to walking in Scotland, these are the ones to get.

The SMC District Guides and the *Scottish Hill Tracks* can be obtained by mail from their publishers or from Graham Tiso in Edinburgh and Nevisport in Fort Williams, Glasgow and Aviemore (see *Address Directory*).

While these guides are extremely good, they are by no means the only recommended guidebooks to walking and climbing in Scotland. Some other guidebooks you may also find useful are listed below.

General Guidebooks

All the following guidebooks are in English. For the addresses of their publishers, see the *Address Directory*.

- *Backpacking Through the Highlands* by Cameron McNeish. Available from K.S.A. Whickam, England. A series of personal accounts of long-distance backpacks by the author in the Highlands with details of wildlife, history and ecology.
- *The Drove Roads of Scotland* by A.R.B. Haldane, Edinburgh University Press, Edinburgh.
- *Hillwalking in Scotland* by Richard F. Gilbert, Thornhill Press Ltd., Gloucester, England.
- *Scotland for Hillwalking* by Donald J. Bennet, Scottish Tourist Board, Edinburgh. Described under the section on *Where to Get Walking Information*. (Recommended)
- *Scottish Highlands* by W.H. Murray, West Col Productions, Reading, England. Another one of the Scottish Mountaineering Club guidebooks, this one covering all of Scotland's principal mountain areas.
- *The Scottish Peaks* by W.A. Poucher, Constable & Company Ltd., London, England. One in an excellent series of books to Britain's mountain regions. (Recommended)
- *Walks and Trails in Scotland,* Scottish Tourist Board, Edinburgh. Described under the section on *Where to Get Walking Information*. (Recommended)
- *Guide to the West Highland Way* by Tom Hunter, 1979. A good guide to Scotland's first long-distance footpath. Illustrated with photographs and a map. Available in most book shops.

Regional Guidebooks

For the addresses of the following publishers and mail-order outlets, see the *Address Directory*.

Available from the Scottish Youth Hostels Association:

- *Arran.* Gives details on touring and walking routes on this balmy island off the southeast coast of Scotland.
- *Cairngorms.*
- *Northern Highlands.*
- *Garth and Glyn Lyon.* Covers a lovely glen between Loch Rannoch and Loch Tay in the Southern Highlands.
- *Glencoe and Glen Nevis.* Two noted areas in the Central Highlands.
- *Loch Lomond and Trossachs.*
- *Skye.*

Available from the Forestry Commission:

- *Argyll Forest Park,* published by Her Majesty's Stationery Office, London, England.
- *Galloway Forest Park,* also published by HMSO.
- *Glen More Forest Park: Cairngorms,* HMSO.
- *Queen Elizabeth Forest Park: Ben Lomond, Loch Ard and the Trossachs,* HMSO.

Each of Forestry Commission's Forest Park guides provide detailed descriptions of the history and antiquities; legends and traditions; geology; plant, animal and marine life; and walking routes in the Forest Parks. The guide to Glen More Forest Park also includes descriptions of climbs and skiing areas in the park. The guides are illustrated throughout with photographs and wood block prints, and include large-scale color maps on which walking routes have been indicated. They may be obtained from the Forestry Commission, HMSO or from the Visitor Centres at the Forest Parks.

Locally Produced Guidebooks

For the addresses of the following publishers and mail-order outlets, see the *Address Directory.*

Available from the Grampian Regional Council:

- *Braemar Guide.* Describes a week of walks in Braemar.
- *Haughton and Murray Park Nature Trails.* Describes nine-mile and one-mile trails.
- *Hillwalking in the Grampian Region.* A general guide with several suggested walks.
- *Walks around Alford; Walks around Ballater; Walks around Banchory; Walks around Fettercairn;* and *Walks around Stonehaven.* Five leaflets describing local walks.

Available from the Forestry Commission, Dumfries:

- *Craig Forest Trail; Fleet Forest Trails; Glentress Forest Trails; Kilsture Forest Walk; Larg Hill and Bruntis Trails; Loch Trool Forest Walk; Pressmennan Forest Trail; Solway Mabie Walks; Stroan Bridge Trails;* and *Talnotry Trail.* Ten nature trail leaflets and guidebooks describing forest walks in southern Scotland.

Available from the Forestry Commission, Glasgow:

- *Walks in Queen Elizabeth Forest Park* (describes 70 miles of waymarked routes from 3 to 15 miles); *Barcardine Forest Walks; Sallochy and Balmaha Forest Trails; Carradale Forest Walks; Inverliever Forest Walks; Knapdale Forest Walks; Strathyre Forest Centre Walks;* and *Tighnabruaich Forest Walks and Caladh Castle Forest Trail.* Eight leaflets and guidebooks describing forest walks in the Southern Highlands.

Available from the Forestry Commission, Inverness:

- *Craig Phadrig Forest Trail; Culloden Forest Trail; Farigaig Forest Trail; Glen More Forest Trail; Inchcailloch Forest Walk; Kyle of Sutherland Forest Walks; Lael Forest Garden Trail; Lochaber Forest Walks; Reelig Glen Forest Walk; Slattadale Forest Trail and Tollie Path;* and *Torrachilty Forest Trail.* Eleven leaflets and guidebooks describing forest walks in northern Scotland.

Available from the National Trust for Scotland:

- *Ben Lawers Nature Trail; Crathes Castle Woodlands Nature Trail; Eildon Walk; The Hermitage; The House of the Binns Trail;* and *Linn of Tummel Trails.* Six leaflets describing nature trails on Trust properties.

Available from Buteshire Natural History Society:

- *Bull Loch Trail; Ettrick Bay Trail; Kilchattan Trail; Kingarth Trail; Loch Fad and Loch Ascog Trail;* and *Rothesay Walk.* Six leaflets describing trails on the island of Bute, west of Glasgow.

Available from the East Ross & Black Isle Tourist Organization:

- *Walks in the Black Isle.* Describes 19 walks on the Black Isle peninsula north of Inverness.

Three other guidebooks worth mentioning are:

- *Pentland Walks* by D.G. Moir, John Bartholomew & Son Ltd.,

Edinburgh. Describes walks in the Pentland Hills in southern Scotland.

- *Seventy Walks in Arran* by R.D. Walton. Available from the author. Describes walks on the island of Arran.
- *A Guide to Walks in Pitlochry and District* by the Pitlochry District Tourist Association. Describes walks in the area surrounding Loch Tummel in the Southern Highlands.

Numerous other guidebooks and forest trail leaflets are available in local areas throughout Scotland. Each of the SMC District Guides includes bibliographies of books of interest to walkers and climbers for each region covered. The Scottish Tourist Board's *Walks and Trails in Scotland* also tells you where leaflets covering each trail can be obtained locally.

Climbing Guides

The Scottish Mountaineering Club publishes nearly 15 guides to the principal climbing areas in Scotland. All the guides are produced and distributed by West Col Productions and may be obtained either by mail from West Col (see *Address Directory*) or from the sport shps in Edinburgh and Glasgow.

The guides are currently being updated. Consequently, any list presented here will soon be obsolete. A current list of titles and prices, however, can be obtained upon request from West Col Productions. The guides cover the following areas:

- Arran
- Arrochar
- Ben Nevis
- Cairngorms (several volumes)
- Cuillin of Skye (two volumes)
- Glencoe and Ardgour
- Northern Highlands (two volumes)

If ordering by mail, you should specify as clearly as possible the area in which you intend to climb so you are sure to obtain the right guide.

Trailside Lodgings

Scotland has numerous hotels, guesthouses, youth hostels and cozy little bed-and-breakfast establishments where you can sit by the hearth for oatcakes and scones after a day's trek in the hills. Many of these are located far from population centers and make ideal bases for walkers. Some of the highland crofts also offer bed-and-breakfast accommodation. Because many of these do not advertise, the only way to find out about them is to enquire locally.

Many walkers also stay in *bothies*—simple, unlocked (and somewhat elusive) mountain shelters maintained by, among others, the Mountain Bothies Association. Typically, these are abandoned farm workers' huts which the Mountain Bothies Association has obtained written permission from the owner to use. The association makes any necessary renovations to the bothy, then makes periodic checks to ensure its roof does not leak and that careless walkers have not left behind garbage.

Altogether, there are about 400 bothies in Scotland. The Mountain Bothies Association keeps an eye on about 40 of these, and there are about another 40 good ones. The rest are derelicts.

Problem is, it is difficult to find out where the bothies are located. No published list of locations exists, and the Mountain Bothies Association is reluctant to tell outsiders for fear a favorite bothy might become overused and lost as a bothy or, at the least, get filled to capacity and leave some of its members out in the rain. Then, too, a landowner might get tired of having walkers tramp across his property, put a padlock on the bothy and refuse to let walkers use it. So even if you use a bothy on one walk, there is no guarantee it will be usable the next time.

If you write to the Mountain Bothies Association or the Mountaineering Council of Scotland and tell them where you intend to walk, they may tell you where a few of the bothies are. You can also enquire about bothies locally—at a local post office, for instance. There generally is no feeling in Scotland against people using the bothies, just against publicizing them. Before you use a bothy, however, always be *sure* to ask the owner's permission. The best way to get up the hackles of a farmer—and to even have him refuse to let other walkers use a bothy—is to tell him you heard you were free to stay there. Remember they are owned by someone else.

Another way to find out where bothies are located is to join one of the Mountain Bothies Association work parties. In fact, by doing this you might even be able to find out where all the bothies that are currently in use are located. And you will be helping a good cause.

The whole concept of bothies began in 1965 when a small group of enthusiasts set to work on renovating a derelict cottage at Tunskeen in the Galloway hills. This involved lugging cement and corrugated iron sheets over trackless moorland by improvised sledge. Sand was panned from a nearby stream. As a result, what was almost a complete ruin was transformed into a weatherproof shelter. Following the considerable interest shown in the finished job, the idea of forming the MBA was born.

The association's primary aim is still that of renovating bothies and other shelters—not building new ones, but trying to prevent those that remain from falling into disrepair. Scotland's numerous empty cottages, derelict farms, refuge huts and *howffs* (boulder shelters or caves) sometimes play a vital role in saving lives on the hills, but many of these are falling into ruin through lack of attention or vandalism.

The association does not own any of the bothies, nor does it provide any accommodation, membership cards, passes or keys. The only rights the MBA has to the bothies are those expressly given by the landowner for a particular building. In the case of approved renovation projects, these include the owner's permission to carry out certain repairs and improvements.

Members of the association receive a periodic journal and can obtain a badge with the MBA emblem for their anorak or rucksack. But since the principal aim of the MBA is to renovate remote shelters, the main benefits of membership are in helping others by joining a work party or helping to finance a renovation project.

Staying in the Bothies

To stay in one of the bothies, you must bring everything with you—sleeping bag, stove, fuel, cooking gear, food and ground pad. The bothies provide shelter, but sometimes little else, not even bunks or mattresses. You should also observe the MBA's Bothy Code:

1. Wherever and whenever possible seek the owner's permission to use a bothy, particularly if you plan to stay more than one night.
2. Keep parties small, say three to four people.
3. Keep fires small. Large fires damage the stonework and waste fuel.
4. Leave the bothy—and its surrounding premises—cleaner, tidier and in better condition than you found it.
5. Burn all rubbish and bury all glass and tins (flattened) well away from the bothy (or better yet, take them home with you). Leave no litter behind.
6. Lay in a supply of fuel and kindling for the next user (but be sure not to cut live wood).
7. Sign the visitors' book (name, address, club and date).
8. Add unused stores to the food cupboard. Date perishables and leave safe from vermin.
9. Do not burn, deface or damage any part of the structure.
10. Guard against any risk of fire and ensure that the fire is safely out before leaving.
11. Secure windows and doors on departure. (Swinging doors are a trap to animals who get in and cannot get out.)
12. Observe the strictest sanitary precautions and safeguard the water supply.
13. Drop a postcard to the MBA Record Secretary reporting date of visit and state of bothy, with suggestions for bettering it and precise details of repairs if necessary.

For further information on the bothies, the MBA, its work parties and membership, you should write:

Mountain Bothies Association (see *Address Directory*).

Mountaineering Club Huts

Scotland has about 18 mountaineering club huts. These are open to members of the Scottish Mountaineering Club and to members of the clubs which make up the Mountaineering Council of Scotland and the British Mountaineering Council—and then only if there is room. Most of the huts sleep from 10 to 20 people, have gas lighting and cooking, and coal stoves for heat. Some—but not all—have cooking utensils. A few also have electric light, running water, a supply of blankets and, in two cases, hot showers. Several of the huts have space nearby for tents. Camping, however, is not permitted directly beside any of the huts. Members who use the huts should bring their own food and cutlery, a sleeping bag and should check beforehand if cooking utensils are necessary. They must also book in advance—sometimes as much as 12 weeks in advance, even during the winter.

A list can be obtained from the Mountaineering Council of Scotland giving the name of each hut, the club it is run by, its location and Ordnance Survey grid reference number, and information on access, camping, the number of people it can sleep, its facilities, overnight charges, where keys can be obtained and the address and telephone number of the person to write for reservations and further information. The hut list is entitled:

- *The Mountaineering Council of Scotland: Scottish Clubs' Huts.* Issued annually. Includes full details on each hut. Available only to members of the BMC and Mountaineering Council of Scotland.

Forest Cabins & Cottages

The Forestry Commission maintains 55 cottages and forest cabins in Scotland's forest areas. The self-catering lodgings accommodate between five and seven people, are comfortably furnished and equipped with refrigerators, stoves, cooking utensils, showers or baths, and have hot running water. Some of the older cottages have a coal or log fireplace. Blankets are provided, but you are expected to bring your own sheets, towels and pillow cases. The cottages and cabins can be rented for a week or more. Reservations, made far in advance for the summer months, are required. Information on the cabins and cottages is given in a leaflet published by the Forestry Commission (see *Address Directory*):

- *Forestry Commission Cabins and Holiday Houses* (in English). Issued annually. Gives full details on the cabins and holiday houses in forest areas in Scotland, including photographs. Booking information and a booking form are also included. Free upon request.

Youth Hostels

Scotland has 80 youth hostels scattered the length and breadth of the country, including 3 hostels on the Isle of Skye, 2 on Arran, 3 on the Orkney Islands, 1 in the Shetland Islands and 1 each on the islands of Harris, Raasay and Mull. There is even a hostel at John o' Groats at the northernmost tip of the Scottish mainland. The hostels are located in castles and old mansions as well as in cottages and timber buildings. All have dormitories, washrooms, a common room and members' kitchen which is equipped with cooking utensils and dishes. To keep prices low, members are expected to help with domestic duties, such as sweeping and dusting. Inexpensive meals are available at some of the hostels. In most cases, however, you must bring food and cook your own meals. You must also bring your own cutlery, a dish towel and a sheet sleeping bag.

There is no age limit at the hostels and a few, such as those at Cannich, Durness, Kirkwall and Loch Ness, have self-contained family units. Many of the hostels remain open for most of the year, although several close for one day a week between October 1 to May 31 to give the warden a day off. Camping is not permitted near any of the hostels. Full information on each hostel, including the dates they are open, is included in:

- *SYHA Handbook* (in English). Issued annually. Gives full details on each hostel, including a sketch drawing, location map, information on points of interest, the title of guidebooks covering nearby walks and the sheet numbers of Ordnance Survey maps covering the surrounding countryside. Information is also included in the booklet on the SYHA walkers' guides, and its holiday arrangements for walking, climbing, canoeing and other activities. (Recommended)

The SYHA also sells a 1:760, 320 map showing the locations of the hostels and of National Trust for Scotland properties. The map is entitled:

- *Touring Map of Scotland.* Published jointly by the SYHA and National Trust for Scotland. A good map for general planning. (Recommended)

Both the handbook and touring map are available for a nominal charge from the Scottish Youth Hostels Association (see *Address Directory*).

Reservations

During the summer, it is advisable to book ahead for all your lodgings—whether it be a youth hostel, bed-and-breakfast establishment, forest cottage or hotel. Bookings for youth hostels and mountaineering club huts must be made directly to the warden of the hostel or hut in which you wish to stay, while bookings for forest cottages must be made through the Forestry Commission in Edinburgh or its regional offices.

For other lodgings, the Scottish Tourist Board runs an invaluable service called the *Book a Bed Ahead* scheme, which can save you a lot of time, money and frustration during the peak holiday period. There are about 150 Tourist Information Centres throughout Scotland. Those displaying a symbol of a "bed" outside will book that night's accommodation for you, even if the place you are heading is a considerable distance away. You pay a small fee, plus a nominal deposit for each person in your party which is deducted from your bill at the end of your stay. All the bookings are firm, so you know your accommodation will be waiting for you when you arrive. They also cover virtually every type of lodging in Scotland— from large hotels to humble crofts.

Lodging Lists

In addition to the SYHA handbook and the lists of mountaineering club huts and forest cottages, there are several booklets published by the Scottish Tourist Board which provide comprehensive lodging information. These include:

- *Scotland: Where to Stay/Hotels & Guest Houses* and *Scotland: Where to Stay/Bed & Breakfast* (in English with an introduction and key to symbols in French and German). These two annual publications list more than 4,000 hotels and guesthouses, and over 2,000 bed-and-breakfast establishments throughout Scotland with full details on each. Both books are available for a nominal charge.

- *Scotland: Self Catering Accommodation* (in English with an introduction and key to symbols in French and German). This booklet gives details on do-it-yourself accommodation—furnished cottages, holiday flats and caravans for hire—throughout Scotland. Available for a nominal charge.

The Scottish Tourist Board also publishes numerous information booklets on more specific facilities such as hotels which have special amenities for children, the elderly and disabled; hotels with shooting or deer-stalking; hotels and restaurants with special Scottish entertainment; and Scotland's farmhouse accommodation. All these publications may be obtained from the Scottish Tourist Board (see *Address Directory*).

Other Lodging Possibilities

Most of the district guidebooks published by the Scottish Mountaineering Club (see the section on *Guidebooks*) provide details on lodgings or at least tell you where this information can be obtained. In some cases, the guides also list the Ordnance Survey grid reference numbers for remote occupied houses and mountain huts, as well as for selected bothies and other uninhabited shelters. The remote occupied houses are listed so you can find them in the event of an emergency. If you politely ask at these houses, you can sometimes get some kind of accommodation, usually in a nearby barn or shed where you can cook and stretch out a sleeping bag. Occasionally, the guides list uninhabited bothies and refuges in the higher hills. The mention of the bothies in the guidebooks, however, does not imply that permission exists for walkers and climbers to use them. Permission should always be sought beforehand.

In addition to the shelters mentioned in the district guides, you will see numerous stables, shooters' lunch huts and other uninhabited buildings in the Highlands, many of which have no locks. These shelters are specifically not listed in the SMC district guides because they are not meant as shelters for walkers. Also, the quickest way to have them locked or demolished would be to publicize them. In the Cairngorms, for example, there have been instances of forcible break-ins of unoccupied houses and lodges by hill walkers, and in one case this led to the immediate demolition by the owner of a building that had once been an excellent bothy.

You may sometimes stay in unoccupied shelters in the Scottish countryside. But the courteous custom in Scotland—before you walk across someone else's property, stay in a bothy, enter an unoccupied shelter, or pitch a tent—is *always* to ask.

Camping

Camping, like the use of bothies, can be a touchy subject in Scotland. A lot depends upon where and when you intend to camp. In the Highlands, camping is fairly open and free. Nonetheless, there are areas where you cannot camp—in some woodland areas and nature reserves, for instance, as well as near youth hostels and some mountaineering club huts. During the deer-stalking and grouse-shooting seasons care must be exercised in your choice of sites so you don't set up camp in the wrong place and inadvertently scatter deer and grouse, or wake up in a tent ventilated with buckshot.

Camping on Forestry Commission land is also frowned upon, although most foresters will let you camp somewhere out of sight if you ask. If you don't ask, just hope you're not caught; you'll be asked to move on. The Forestry Commission is currently cooperating with the Backpackers Club in an attempt to strike a balance between a "no camping" policy and *responsible* wild camping. For this to work, however, depends largely upon each individual camper. And a single abuse tends to stick in the foresters' minds a lot more than a score of responsible campers.

Near habitations you should always ask permission to camp. It is seldom refused without reason. But if it is refused, *respect* it. You can be prosecuted for camping on someone's land without permission.

In remote areas there are few restrictions on camping. And there is an abundance of peaceful campsites high in the glens, by the sides of lochs and in mountain corries. You rarely have to ask permission to camp in these areas and can freely pick and choose your sites. Nonetheless, it is still advisable to always enquire locally prior to your walk where you can and cannot camp—just to be sure. What looks to you like a remote glen may very well be part of a large estate where deer stalking is taking place.

The SMC district guides usually note areas where restrictions exist on camping. These restrictions should be respected when they are mentioned. There will usually be other places where you can camp.

Organized Campsites

Scotland has more than 400 campsites scattered along glens, near towns and villages, and on the shores of mountain-ringed lochs. These often provide a viable alternative to wild camping in areas where it is difficult to get permission to camp. While standards vary widely, some of the campsites are delightful. Information on the locations of these campsites can be obtained from local Tourist Information Centres and local inhabitants. The Scottish Tourist Board also publishes a booklet giving full details on campsites in Scotland:

- *Camping and Caravan Sites in Scotland* (in English with an introduction and key to symbols in French and German). Issued annually. Includes a set of maps showing the locations of the campsites, which is keyed to their numbered descriptions in the text. Available for a nominal charge from the Scottish Tourist Board (see *Address Directory*).

Fires

It is illegal to light a fire without the landowner's permission in the Scottish countryside. If you intend to camp, you should carry a stove and fuel, and be sure to guard against flare-ups. Once a fire is started, it may get down into the peat and burn for years.

Water

In the Highlands, you can drink from natural water sources nearly everywhere, even from the lochs. Water will often be clear brown, the natural color after draining from peat ground. This water is good and very soft. The only places where caution is advisable is below farms where chemicals may have leached into the water supplies and in the more densely populated lowlands. But in these places you can usually fill up your water bottle from the tap by asking at someone's house.

Equipment Notes

Clothing is important no matter where you intend to walk in Scotland, even if it is only for a few hours on one of the Forestry Commission paths in southern Scotland. Because of Scotland's fickle weather, strong winds and damp conditions, you must always be on the guard against hypothermia. Windproof outer clothing and a long cagoule that will hold in body heat are essential. Pants should be long and combined with shirts that won't come untucked and cause a cold draft up your back. Even if it is warm in the bottom of a glen when you start out, you should wear clothing made of wool so it will still keep you warm if it becomes damp. You should also carry a wool sweater, wool cap, wool scarf and wool mittens. On the hills—even the rolling Border Hills—you cannot afford to take anything for granted. Conditions can change rapidly, and hypothermia can occur just as readily in mild temperatures as it can in freezing temperatures. Because of this, it is always better to carry too much clothing rather than too little. If you get hot, you can always take something off, but if you start to chill seriously there is not much you can do if you are already wearing all your clothing on your back.

Always ensure you can keep both your clothing and the contents of your pack dry. You should also carry a spare jersey and set of dry wool socks. Boots should be watertight and treated with a good waterproofing, especially along the seams on the soles. They should also have profiled or vibram soles; smooth rubber and cork soles are potentially very dangerous. A pair of gaiters, to plug up the gap between the bottom of your cagoule and the tops of your boots, is advisable to keep your socks (and feet) dry. In addition, you should carry plenty of high-energy food—chocolate, nuts, dates and mint cake. It will be a godsend if you are feeling weary, the mist is down and progress is slow and tiring.

Finally, you should always be sure to carry the appropriate Ordnance Survey maps and a compass—and ensure you know how to use them competently. Your life may depend upon them. If your orienteering skills are shaky, stick to the well-marked paths described in the Scottish Tourist Board's *Walks and Trails in Scotland* (see the section on *Where to Get Walking Information*). But even on well-marked paths, be sure to carry a map and compass. In a mist, path markings can never be too close together, and it is frighteningly easy to stray from the path if you miss one of the markings.

Those are the essentials for a day trip.

For overnight trips, you should always carry a tent and sleeping bag. The chance that the bothy in which you intend to stay is locked or derelict, or a river has swollen, preventing a crossing, is very real. Even if you plan to stay in a youth hostel or guesthouse in the next valley, take adequate precautions so you will be able to survive a night out in freezing conditions if you are unable to reach your objective. For camping, and for staying in bothies, mountaineering club huts and youth hostels, you will have to carry your own food. Here, you must rely upon shops to replenish your supplies; you can rarely buy food from farmers. As a result, you must often carry tins of food, which will necessitate a sturdy plastic bag to carry the empty tins back out with you. Dried foods are often available only in the principal tourist centers such as Fort William and Aviemore, and freeze-dried backpacking foods can be bought only at specialized equipment shops. You should always check on the locations of shops before you begin your hike so you are sure to have adequate food, with an allowance for at least a day's delay, until you reach the next shop. In some areas in the Highlands and on the islands, mobile shops stop at outlying communities on certain days. By enquiring locally you can find out where and when they stop.

During the months of July through September, it is advisable to carry a midge repellent cream. *Moon Tiger,* a slow burning stick (available from most sport shops), is useful for keeping your tent midge-free. You can also avoid midges by camping where there is a slight breeze.

Many of the bothies and mountaineering club huts have fireplaces where you can cook, but you cannot always depend upon finding a supply of firewood or coal. Instead, carry a stove and fuel. You will be able to get plentiful supplies of paraffin (kerosene), even from some farmers. Camping gaz is also readily available nearly everywhere. But gasoline is only available at petrol stations and garages. You must also carry cooking and eating utensils.

All this equipment, of course, is going to add up to a relatively heavy pack. But it is much better to have a heavy pack than to be caught in a blizzard without adequate food or clothing. In many mountain areas the mark of an experienced climber or mountaineer is how little he or she is able to carry, yet still be prepared for all possible conditions. In Scotland, the situation is different. The experienced mountaineer always carries adequate equipment, clothing and food, just in case he or she is caught in a fierce summer blizzard and must sit it out for two or three days.

In winter, you must be prepared for Arctic conditions which are more severe than any found on the European continent. If you plan a winter trip in Scotland, you should be experienced in winter travel and always be sure to carefully check weather forecasts prior to your trip. It is also advisable to check with the Mountaineering Council of Scotland, or one of its member clubs, for advice on your itinerary and the equipment you intend to carry. What may seem adequate to you may not be suitable for the conditions in Scotland.

Crowded Trails

Scotland has few trails or mountain tracks that can be considered crowded. During the summer, some of the waymarked Forestry Commission paths are often walked daily by numerous people in its forest areas. But elsewhere—in the "open country"—the Scots consider guideposts and paint marks objectionable. Consequently, few mountain tracks are marked. Often, there is a well-trodden path to follow, but you must also strike off cross-country on many occasions. In Scotland, you have the freedom to do this. And there are often numerous routes by which you can climb up to a ridge or a peak (although the prevalence of rough terrain, heather, bog and boulders make many of these routes arduous and time-consuming). The preferred routes that you should follow are described in the SMC district guides and D.G. Moir's *Scottish Hill Tracks*. But even these sometimes give you more than one alternative, and if you enquire locally and ask permission from landowners, you can often learn of other acceptable routes. The result is that you can sometimes walk all day without seeing another climber or walker, even in August.

While paths generally do not become crowded in Scotland, there are *areas* which do. Glencoe, the Cairngorms, Torridon and the Black Cuillin of Skye, for example, attract numerous walkers and climbers during July and August. And the climb up the tourist path to the top of Ben Nevis, Scotland's highest peak, is perhaps the most popular in the country.

With the exception of Ben Nevis, however, the crowds are rarely so big that they detract from your enjoyment of the countryside. The presence of other climbers and walkers also increases the likelihood of someone coming to your aid should you injure yourself.

By referring to the SMC district guidebooks and *Scottish Hill Tracks* you can easily find routes in remote areas. But you will have to depend largely upon doing your own detective work with the appropriate maps, guidebooks and local enquiries. Writing to one of the walking clubs to ask about remote routes will be just about as effective as writing to the Mountain Bothies Association for a list of bothies. The Scots are reluctant to divulge too much information about their favorite spots for fear they might become overcrowded (and in Scotland, overcrowded means more than two people on the same peak), or worse, that an abuse might cause all walkers and climbers to lose their freedom to roam across a particular stretch of countryside. This may seem selfish, but it is really a matter of protective self-interest, based upon bitter past experiences. As the former secretary of the Mountaineering Council of Scotland says: "We prefer people, particularly larger parties, to avoid the more remote areas where solitude is valuable and we prefer to keep disturbance to a minimum."

If you take the initiative to do the necessary research to find these areas, you will also be rewarded with the same solitude and lack of disturbance. But don't expect anyone to tell you about these places. If they did, the solitude would soon become a thing of the past.

Walking & Climbing Tours

The following organizations offer walking and climbing tours in Scotland (for their addresses and telephone numbers, see the *Address Directory*):

Country-Wide Holidays Association. Offers week-long walking holidays based at its guesthouses at Ardenconnel overlooking the village of Rhu in the Southern Highlands, with access to the Trossachs, Oban and Dunoon; at Kinfauns Castle near Perth, with access to the Grampians; and at Creag Mhor Onich on Loch Linnhe with access to Glencoe and Ben Nevis in the Central Highlands. Two-week walking tours are also organized to the Orkney Islands, Aviemore and other areas in Scotland. All walks and tours are led by experienced leaders. Full details are given in the CHA's brochures, *Summer Holidays at Home and Abroad* and *Winter Holidays.* In addition, day and weekend rambles are organized by its local groups in Dundee, Edinburgh and Glasgow. For further information on the CHA, see the sections on *Walking Clubs in England* and *Walking & Climbing Tours* in the chapter on England.

Hamish Brown Mountain Holidays. Organizes numerous mountain holidays for hill walking and climbing, both summer and winter in Scotland and abroad. Details are available upon request.

Highland Guides Information. Organizes week-long walking holidays and other activities based in Aviemore and the Spey Valley. Also provides information and local advice on hill walking in the Cairngorms. Has a selection of equipment for hire. Full details are available upon request.

Holiday Fellowship. Offers week-long holidays at centers on the Isle of Arran, near Edinburgh, at Loch Awe and Loch Leven in the Western Highlands, and at Strathpeffer in the Northern Highlands. Full details are given in its free brochures: *Holidays that are Different; Autumn, Winter, and Spring Holidays; Holidays for Young People and School Parties;* and *Great Britain, Great Holidays.* Day and weekend rambles are also organized by its local groups on the Isle of Arran and in Edinburgh and Glasgow. For further information on the HF, see the sections on *Walking Clubs in England* and *Walking & Climbing Tours* in the chapter on England.

Ramblers Holidays Ltd. Organizes several mountain walking holidays, ski touring holidays and special holidays for photography, birdwatching and other interests. Full details are given in its free brochure, *Ramblers Holidays.*

Scottish Youth Hostels Association. Organizes numerous "Breakaway Holidays" for walking, climbing, canoeing and other outdoor activities. Examples include its Cairngorm Hill Walking and Mountain Adventure Holidays based at the Loch Morlich youth hostel; the Trossachs and Loch Lomond Walking Tour, based at the Stirling youth hostel; the Lairig Ghru Walking Tour, based at the King George VI Memorial hostel in Aberdeen; and the Strathclyde Walking Tour, based at the Ardgarten youth hostel. Full details on these and other SYHA holiday arrangements are available upon request.

Tulloch Mountain School. Offers hill walking and rock climbing courses and holidays, particularly for youngsters. Full details are available upon request.

Tweed Valley Hotel Sports Centre. Organizes holidays for hill walking, roe deer observation, birdwatching and other activities. Full details are available upon request.

YHA Adventure Holidays. Organizes numerous holidays for walking, climbing, mountaineering and other activities throughout Britain. The week-long holidays in Scotland are organized in cooperation with the SYHA in Glencoe, Skye and Speyside. Details are given in its free brochure, *YHA Adventure Holidays.*

Additional information on other mountain holidays in Scotland can be obtained from the Scottish Tourist Board.

Mountain Guides

Mountain guides may be hired for rock climbs and winter tours from the Glenmore Lodge in Aviemore (Cairngorms and Eastern Grampians), the Loch Eil Centre at Achdalieu in Fort William (Western and Central Highlands) and from Benmore Centre near Dunoon in Argyll (Southern Highlands). Guides are also available in Glencoe (Central Highlands), Glenelg (Western Highlands and Skye) and Edinburgh.

On rock climbs, the guides will take a maximum of three people. Ropes are provided by the guide, as is any necessary hardware, but the client must bring the rest of his or her equipment, including the proper clothing, vibram sole boots and, where necessary, a climbing belt, helmet, ice axe and crampons.

Arrangements are made directly with the guide. Also, you must book in advance. Fees are reasonable, but the number of guides is limited, so the earlier you book the better. A list of mountain guides, with their addresses and a list of recommended minimum fees, can be obtained by sending a stamped, self-addressed envelope to:

Colin G. Firth, Secretary, Association of British Mountain Guides (see *Address Directory*).

Mountaineering Courses

Courses in basic and advanced rock climbing, hill walking, snow and ice climbing, skiing, winter mountaineering, ski mountaineering, mountain rescue and field studies are conducted by 16 organizations and outdoor pursuit centres in Scotland.

A list of these mountain centres, entitled *Mountaineering Courses in Britain and Abroad,* is available from the Mountaineering Council of Scotland or the British Mountaineering Council (see *Address Directory*).

The list gives the address of each centre, a brief description of the courses available, their duration and the age groups accepted. The list is designed to help you choose the right course, not to answer all your questions. For full details, you must write the individual centres.

Of these centres, four are particularly noteworthy (see *Address Directory*):

> **Glencoe School of Winter Climbing.** Offers courses in snow and ice climbing from January until April.
>
> **Glenmore Lodge.** The National Outdoor Training Centre run by the Scottish Sports Council. Offers summer courses in rock climbing, hill craft, mountain rescue, field studies, canoeing, sailing and Scottish Mountain Leadership training. Offers winter courses in snow and ice climbing, winter mountaineering, skiing, ski mountaineering and mountain rescue, as well as courses for ski instructors, ski party leadership and Scottish Mountain Leadership training. Courses should be booked early. Full details are available from the Scottish Sports Council.
>
> **Hamish McInnes Scottish Winter Climbing.** Offers one-week courses in mountaineering, walking, rock climbing and advanced ice climbing from January through March.
>
> **Loch Eil Outward Bound.** Offers one-week and longer courses in mountaineering, hill walking, rock climbing and mountain rescue. Open all year.

Climbing and mountaineering courses are also conducted by several organizations listed previously in the section on *Walking & Climbing Tours* —Hamish Brown Mountain Holidays, Highland Guides Information, the Scottish Youth Hostels Association (at its Glen Brittle youth hostel on Skye) and the Tulloch Mountain Centre.

Cross-Country Skiing & Ski Mountaineering

Scotland offers numerous opportunities for ski touring and ski mountaineering from early December until the end of April. Marked and prepared cross-country tracks are few, but given the right conditions, virtually every one of the 544 peaks in Scotland which rise above 915 meters (3,000 feet) can be ascended on skis. You don't have to be an expert skier to climb many of these peaks, although you should be experienced in both mountaineering and winter travel.

Those who are less experienced in winter travel can take advantage of the ski tracks located near Scotland's downhill ski areas in the Cairngorms, Glenshee and Glencoe. There are also facilities for equipment rental and ski instruction at the ski areas.

For the experienced winter mountaineer, the Cairngorms and Southern Highlands offer the best ski mountaineering in Britain, with smooth, evenly weathered mountains, powder-filled corries and white glens lined by snow-laden pines. From high ground, the ski mountaineer looks out across a panorama of frozen hills receding into the distance in undulating waves, and to great cliffs plastered with thick ice and the frosty white feathers of hoarfrost.

The SMC district guidebooks to the Cairngorms, the Southern Highlands, and the Central, Western and Northern Highlands include descriptions on the possibilities in each area for ski mountaineering and ski touring. In many cases it is possible to ski tour on the walking routes described in the guides. A few specific ski tours are also suggested, along with brief information on equipment. By far the best guide to ski mountaineering in Scotland, however, is:

• *Scottish Mountains on Ski, Vol. I: Climbs and Tours for Winter and Spring* (in English) by Malcolm Slesser, West Col Productions (see *Address Directory*), 1970. Gives information on understanding Scottish snow conditions, equipment—including specialized equipment for the ascent and descent—safety, technique and stopping a fall. Describes 57 ski tours. Each description includes a sketch map, notes the skiing ability required, briefly describes the character of the terrain, tells you which season is best for the tour, lists the lengths of ascents and descents, gives the approximate time to climb to the main summit and lists the sheet number of the Ordnance Survey map required for the tour. In addition, approaches, ascent and descent routes, traverses and possible variants and alternate routes are described for each tour. An indispensable book for the ski mountaineer. (Recommended)

Two other useful booklets are:

• *Ski-ing in Scotland* (in English) by the Scottish Ski Club. Provides details on downhill skiing as well as on areas for ski mountaineering in Scotland.

• *Winter Sports in Scotland* (in English), issued annually by the Scottish Tourist Board. Describes Scotland's principal ski areas; gives the telephone numbers for snow reports; lists the addresses and telephone numbers of ski schools, places where equipment can be hired and the organizations offering ski holidays; and gives the dates and locations for Scotland's ski championships. Also includes a detailed list of lodgings near the ski areas. Free on request. (Recommended)

Two centers which offer courses specifically in ski touring and ski mountaineering are Glenmore Lodge and the Highland Guides Information, both located in Aviemore (see *Address Directory*). Instruction in ski touring is also offered by:

> **Scottish Norwegian Ski School,** Speyside Sports; two locations, one in Aviemore and another in Grantown-on-Spey (see *Address Directory*).

Further information on cross-country skiing and ski mountaineering in Scotland may be obtained from either the Scottish Tourist Board or:

> **Scottish Ski Club** (see *Address Directory*).

Special Train & Bus Fares

Scotland is reasonably well served by public transportation. Its rail network covers most of the country, except the extreme northwest, and scheduled buses and postbuses link virtually every village and town. Some of the bus services are operated by private carriers with no published schedule, so it is always advisable to enquire locally where you can catch the buses and what their schedules are. To reach the offshore islands, you have a choice of steamers or, in the case of many of the larger islands, air service.

Many of the special train fares that apply to England (see the section on *Special Train & Bus Fares* in the chapter on England) also apply to Scotland. In addition, Scotland has several special discount fare tickets which can save you money. These include:

> **Travelpass.** This ticket gives you unlimited travel for a period of either 8 or 12 days on almost any rail, bus or ship service in the Highlands and islands of Scotland. The tickets can be purchased anytime between March 1 and October 31 from the Highlands and Islands Development Board (see *Address Directory*).
>
> **Freedom of Scotland.** These discount tickets provide unlimited first- or second-class travel on Scotland's trains for a period of either 7 or 14 days. Available from all major train stations.
>
> **Runabout Season Ticket.** This is especially suited for holidays based in a single center. The ticket enables you to make a series of day trips within defined areas throughout Scotland for a period of seven consecutive days for a set price. Available from all major train stations.
>
> **Three Return Trips.** Another good ticket for one-center holidays. Simply choose three destinations from any of a dozen starting points

and travel when you like during the week. The ticket is valid for any three roundtrip journeys between Monday and Friday of the same week. Available from all major train stations.

Further information on rail travel can be obtained from the ticket sellers in the stations. For schedules and information on Scotland's postbuses, you should direct your enquiries to:

Scottish Postal Board (see *Address Directory*).

Useful Addresses & Telephone Numbers

General Tourist Information

In Scotland:

Scottish Tourist Board (see *Address Directory*). Provides general information on all types of travel in Scotland, including hill walking and mountaineering. Publishes numerous booklets on lodgings, camping, angling, golf, hill walking, architecture, a gazetteer of 1001 things to see and motor touring. A complete list of publications is available upon request. A list of Tourist Information Centres throughout Scotland may also be obtained upon request. Staff speaks English and most other European languages. Very helpful.

In England:

Scottish Tourist Board, (see *Address Directory*).Provides much the same information as the office in Edinburgh.

Abroad:

Information on Scotland may be obtained from the branch offices of the British Tourist Authority in EUROPE: Amsterdam, Brussels, Copenhagen, Frankfurt, Madrid, Oslo, Paris, Rome, Stockholm and Zurich; AUSTRALIA: Sydney; NEW ZEALAND: Wellington; SOUTH AFRICA: Johannesburg; JAPAN: Tokyo; CANADA: Toronto; and in the U.S.A.: Los Angeles, Chicago and New York.

New York: British Tourist Authority, 680 Fifth Avenue, New York, New York 10019. Tel. (212) 581-4700.

Sport Shops

There are several sport shops in Scotland which specialize in equipment for hill walkers and climbers. In addition to equipment and clothing, the shops sell guidebooks, special-interest magazines, mountaineering club journals and, in some cases, Ordnance Survey maps. They are also a valuable source of information on walking and climbing. The principal shops are listed below. For their addresses and telephone numbers, see the *Address Directory.*

> **Graham Tiso.** Located in Edinburgh. An excellent shop. Also sells guidebooks by mail.
>
> **Nevisport Ltd.** Located in Glasgow, Aviemore and Fort William.
>
> **Highrange Sports.** Located in Glasgow.
>
> **Black's.** Located in Glasgow, Dundee and Edinburgh.

Search & Rescue

> **In an emergency:** Go to the nearest rescue post or telephone— whichever is quickest. At the telephone, dial **999**. Ask for the **police.**

Before you go walking in Scotland, you should obtain a copy of:

- *Mountain and Cave Rescue,* The Handbook of the Mountain Rescue Committee, Herald Press, Arbroath, Angus, England.

This lists the official rescue teams and posts throughout Britain, gives their locations, grid reference numbers and the names, addresses and telephone numbers of their supervisors. The booklet is the most complete, up-to-date listing of rescue posts available. Nonetheless, the location of a post is sometimes changed and should be verified locally. There is a nominal charge for the booklet. It can be obtained from all climbing equipment shops and most bookshops, or by mail from:

> **John Hiade,** chairman, Mountain Rescue Committee of Scotland (see *Address Directory*).

The Mountain Rescue Committee of Scotland is in charge of rescue operations throughout the country, although, as in the rest of Britain, the police are the main coordinators and the Chief Constables bear the responsibility in their own areas. Unless it is quicker to get to a manned Mountain Rescue Post, all calls for help must go to the police. They will then call out the rescue teams and public services needed.

There is no charge for search and rescue. When needed, helicopters are provided gratis, and rescuers are volunteers. You will see donation boxes in the sport shops for the mountain rescue squads, to which you are encouraged to contribute. All donations go toward the purchase of equipment, not to the individual members of the rescue squads.

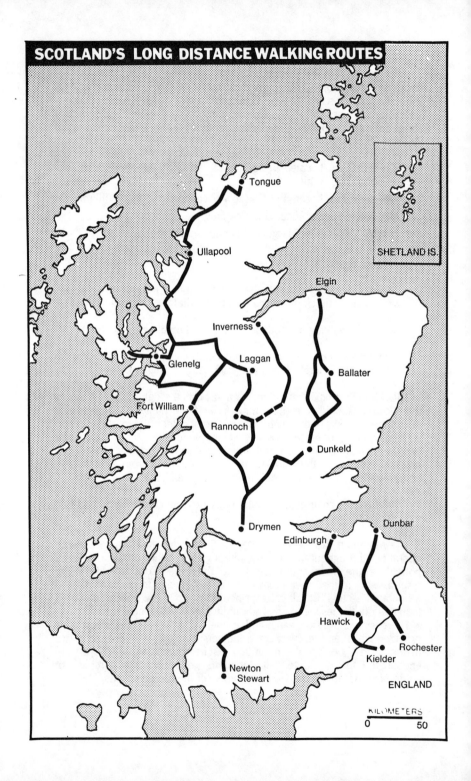

SCOTLAND'S LONG DISTANCE WALKING ROUTES

Tongue

Ullapool

Elgin

Inverness

Laggan

Ballater

Glenelg

Fort William

Rannoch

Dunkeld

Drymen

Dunbar

Edinburgh

Hawick

Rochester

Kielder

Newton Stewart

ENGLAND

SHETLAND IS.

KILOMETERS
0   50

Scotland's Long-Distance Walking Routes

Scotland has one official long-distance footpath: the 148-kilometer (92-mile) West Highland Way from Glasgow to Fort William. The Countryside Commission for Scotland is working to establish the 328-kilometer (204-mile) Southern Uplands Way from Portpatrick to Cockburnspath and the 97-kilometer (60-mile) Speyside Way from Spey Bay to the Cairngorms. Many people in Scotland's outdoor fraternity seriously question the need for these Ways and doubt whether it is advisable—or even desirable—to establish prominently marked, well-publicized ways across the open countryside. The objections to one route proposed through the Cairngorms were so overwhelming that it has since been dropped as a possible long-distance footpath. The Speyside Way and the Southern Uplands Way, however, have been accepted and progress is being made by the Countryside Commission in negotiations with landowners. Both paths are expected to be marked and established as official long-distance footpaths in 1983. In the meantime, they can presently be walked.

In fact, walkers can plan numerous long-distance walks by simply looking at a set of Ordnance Survey maps, or by linking together some of the routes described in D.G. Moir's *Scottish Hill Tracks* (see Guidebooks). Britain's most inveterate walker, John Merrill, walked around the entire coast of Britain in 1978, a distance of some 11,100 kilometers (6,900 miles). So there is no lack of possibilities.

Eight long-distance walks described in D.G. Moir's *Scottish Hill Tracks* are listed below. Most of the routes follow old drove roads, kirk and coffin tracks and Roman roads, although you must occasionally walk along stretches of paved road to link the tracks. None of the tracks are marked and, while altitudes are generally moderate, all the walks are potentially strenuous and very difficult to follow in bad weather. Many of the routes take you over rough and boggy ground with no path—particularly in the west and northwest of Scotland—and there are numerous streams to be forded which, after a rain, may be in spate and necessitate a long detour. These conditions require that you be a skilled mountain walker who is physically fit, well equipped and highly proficient in the use of a map and compass. Less experienced walkers should limit themselves to day and overnight walks along short segments of the routes in good weather. This is easily done, since all the routes described below are no more than a series of short routes linked together to form longer routes, which can easily be picked up and left at virtually any town or village enroute.

Northumberland to Edinburgh

Across rolling hills and farmland, through wooded valleys and over bare mountains in southern Scotland. Starts at the English town of Byrnes on the Pennine Way (see the section on *England's Long-Distance Footpaths* in the chapter on England). Stretches through Edgerston, Kielder, Newcastleton, Hawick, Yarrow, Peebles, West Linton, Carlops and Balerno to Edinburgh. Crosses the Cheviot, Moorfoot and Pentland Hills. Follows a lovely ridge over Kailzie Hill, Kirkhope Law and Birkscairn Hill between Peebles and St. Mary's Loch, as well as part of an old Roman road between Carlops and West Linton. Several old ruins enroute. **Length:** 213 kilometers (132 miles); can easily be shortened. **Walking Time:** 8 to 10 days. **Difficulty:** Easy to moderately difficult. **Path Markings:** None.

Trail Lodgings: Youth hostels in Byrnes and Edinburgh. For other lodgings, refer to the lodging lists described in the section on *Trail Lodgings* earlier in this chapter.

Maps:
- Ordnance Survey 1:50,000, sheets 65, 66, 72, 73, 79 and 80 (Recommended). Or:
- Bartholomew one-inch (1:63,360), sheets 41 and 45.

guidebook:
- *Scottish Hill Tracks: Southern Scotland* by D.G. Moir, John Bartholomew & Son, Ltd., Edinburgh. The route can be followed by reading the descriptions in the guide for hill tracks 8, 9, 11, 12, 31, 30, 22, 42, 54 and 50—in that order. Some of the hill tracks must be walked in reverse to the way they are described. The section of the route between Balerno and Edinburgh (about 8 kilometers) is not described in the guide.

Northumberland to Dunbar

From Rochester, across the border in England, to the coastal village of Dunbar. A splendid route over the Cheviots on a broad grassy track known as Dere Street, past the extensive Roman Camps at Chew Green, then over the Eildon Hills to Melrose and Lauder, and across the Lammermuir Hills to Dunbar. Much of the route follows the main Roman road into Scotland, in use by the Romans between A.D. 78 and 185, which ran from Durham to Forth. In the Middle Ages the road was known as Gamel's Path where it crossed the Cheviots. The walk can be started from the Pennine Way. **Length:** About 110 kilometers (68 miles); a fairly long stretch of paved road must be followed between Jedburgh and Melrose. **Walking Time:** 5 to 6 days. **Difficulty:** Easy to moderately difficult. **Path Markings:** None.

Trail Lodgings: Youth hostel at Ferniehirst Castle south of Jedburgh (about 8 kilometers off the route) and at Melrose. For other lodgings, refer to the lodging lists described under *Trail Lodgings* earlier in this chapter.

Maps:
* Ordnance Survey 1:50,000, sheets 67, 73, 74 and 80 (Recommended). Or:
* Bartholomew one-inch (1:63,360), sheets 41 and 46.

Guidebook:
* *Scottish Hill Tracks: Southern Scotland* by D.G. Moir, John Bartholomew & Son, Ltd., Edinburgh. The route can be followed by reading the descriptions in the guide for hill tracks 7, 39 and 33. If you start the walk from Dunbar, you can follow the hill tracks in the direction they are described—from north to south. The section of road between hill tracks 7 and 39 is not described in the guide, but is easily followed by map.

Edinburgh to Newton Stewart

Across pleasant rolling country in southern Scotland. Stretches from Edinburgh through Balerno, West Linton, Peebles, Broughton, Crawford, Wanlockhead, Sanquhar, Carsphairn and Glen Trool to Newton Stewart. Passes through Galloway Forest Park. Winds through woods, past streams and waterfalls, over barren hills and moors, and alongside small lochs. Primarily follows forest and drove roads, as well as a short segment of an old Roman road outside West Linton. **Length:** 250 kilometers (155 miles). **Walking Time:** 10 to 12 days. **Difficulty:** Moderately difficult. **Path Markings:** None.

Trail Lodgings: Youth hostels in Edinburgh, Wanlockhead and Newton Stewart. There is also a hostel at Kendoon, about 8 kilometers south of Carsphairn. For other lodgings, refer to the lodging lists described under *Trail Lodgings* earlier in this chapter.

Maps:
* Ordnance Survey 1:50,000, sheets 65, 66, 71, 72, 73, 77, 78 and 83 (Recommended). Or:
* Bartholomew one-inch (1:63,360), sheets 37, 40, 41 and 45.

Guidebook:
* *Scottish Hill Tracks: Southern Scotland* by D.G. Moir, Bartholomew & Son, Ltd., Edinburgh. The route can be followed by reading the descriptions in the guide for hill tracks 50, 54, 42, 19, 55, 56, 63, 62, 86, 80 and 73—in that order. The section of the route between Balerno and Edinburgh (about 8 kilometers) is not described. ⸝

Glasgow to Ballater and Elgin

Stretches across the Southern Highlands and Eastern Grampians. Primarily follows glens, skirting the highest peaks. Begins at Drymen, near Loch Lomond. Passes through Aberfoyle, Callander, Comrie, Amulree, Dunkeld, Kirkmichael, Clova, Ballater and Tomintoul to Elgin. Takes you past

Loch Ard, through Queen Elizabeth Forest Park, below the Trossachs, down Glen Artney to Strath Earn, through the village of Dunkeld with its 17th century cottages (National Trust for Scotland property), across Glen Shee and Glen Clova, around the 1,200-meter (4,000-foot) peaks in the central Cairngorm Massif to Speyside, then north to the coast. One long section of road must be followed between Amulree and Dunkeld. **Length:** 388 kilometers (241 miles). **Walking Time:** 18 to 20 days. **Difficulty:** Moderately difficult; some steep zigzags on the descent into Glen Clova. **Path Markings:** None.
Trail Lodgings: Youth hostels at Glen Doll (at the head of Glen Clova), Ballater and Tomintoul. For other lodgings, refer to the lodging lists described under *Trail Lodgings* earlier in this chapter.
Maps:
• Ordnance Survey 1:50,000, sheets 28, 36, 37, 43, 44, 51, 52, 53 and 57 (Recommended). Or:
• Bartholomew one-inch (1:63,360), sheets 44, 45, 48, 52 and 56.
Guidebooks:
• *Scottish Hill Tracks: Southern Scotland* by D.G. Moir, John Bartholomew & Son, Ltd., Edinburgh. The route through the Southern Highlands to Dunkeld can be followed by reading the descriptions in the guide for hill tracks 107, 111, 121, 123 and 125.
• *Scottish Hill Tracks: Northern Scotland* by D.G. Moir, John Bartholomew & Son, Ltd., Edinburgh. The remainder of the route through the Eastern Grampians is covered by the descriptions for hill tracks 1, 9, 11, 22, 34, 35 and 46.

Glasgow to Braemar and Inverness

Up glens and across mountains in the Southern Highlands, Cairngorms and Eastern Grampians. Includes a traverse of the central Cairngorm Massif over Lairig Ghru, a pass hemmed in on the east by the peaks of Cairn Gorm and Ben Macdui (at 1,309 meters, the second-highest peak in Britain), and to the west by Cairn Toul and Braeriach—one of the classic walks in Scotland. Begins at Drymen, near Loch Lomond. Takes you through the Trossachs, past Loch Tay and Loch Rannoch, along the shores of Loch Tummel, through the center of the Cairngorms from Blair Atholl to Aviemore, and along the Wade Road, built in 1729, to Inverness. A paved road must be followed for about 16 kilometers between Kinlochrannoch, at the end of Loch Rannoch, to Loch Tummel. **Length:** 259 kilometers (161 miles). **Walking Time:** 12 to 14 days. **Difficulty:** Moderately difficult; some difficult sections. **Path Markings:** None, except for some cairns on the higher reaches of Lairig Ghru.
Trail Lodgings: Youth hostels in the Trossachs, Killin, Inverey, Aviemore and Inverness. For other lodgings, refer to the lodging lists described under *Trail Lodgings* earlier in this chapter.

Maps:
- Ordance Survey 1:50,000, sheets 26, 27, 36, 42, 43, 51, 52 and 57 (Recommended). Also:
- Ordnance Survey Outdoor Leisure Map 1:25,000, one sheet, *The High Tops of the Cairngorms* (Recommended). Or:
- Bartholomew one-inch (1:63,360), sheets 44, 48, 51 and 55.

Guidebooks:
- *Scottish Hill Tracks: Southern Scotland* by D.G. Moir, John Bartholomew & Son, Ltd., Edinburgh. The route from Drymen to Blair Atholl is covered by the descriptions for hill tracks 108, 113, 115, 118, 139 and 136. The stretch of paved road which must be walked between Loch Rannoch and Loch Tummel is not described.
- *Scottish Hill Tracks: Northern Scotland* by D.G. Moir, John Bartholomew & Son, Ltd., Edinburgh. The remainder of the route, including the crossing of Lairig Ghru, is covered by the descriptions for hill tracks 25, 29 and 51.

Glasgow to Skye via Forth William

A wonderful walk along the west coast of Scotland. Follows several sections of the West Highland Way. Begins in Drymen, near Loch Lomond, and winds northward through Queen Elizabeth Forest Park, Inverlochlarig and Benmore glens, Crianlarich, the Moor of Rannoch, Glencoe, Kinlochleven, Fort William, Gairlochy, Strathan and Kinlochhourn to the Glenelg Ferry. An alternate route can also be taken along the eastern shore of Loch Lomond to Crianlarich. Dramatic countryside with high misty mountains, sparkling blue lochs and fertile wooded glens. **Length:** 324 kilometers (201 miles), or 353 kilometers (219 miles) with the alternate route along the eastern shore of Loch Lomond. **Walking Time:** 15 to 17 days. **Difficulty:** Moderately difficult. Some sections of the route are difficult to follow even in good weather; check weather forecasts before setting out. **Path Markings:** None.

Trail Lodgings: Youth hostels at the Trossachs, Crianlarich, Glencoe (slightly off the route) and Glen Nevis (near Fort William). For other lodgings, refer to lodging lists described under *Trail Lodgings* earlier in this chapter.

Maps:
- Ordnance Survey 1:50,000, sheets 33, 34, 40, 41, 50, 51, 56 and 57 (Recommended). Or:
- Bartholomew one-inch (1:63,360), sheets 44, 48 and 50.

Guidebooks:
- *Scottish Hill Tracks: Southern Scotland* by D.G. Moir, John Bartholomew & Son, Ltd., Edinburgh. The route from Drymen to Kinlochleven is covered by the descriptions for hill tracks 108, 113, 115, 117, 143 and 149 or, if you prefer to walk along the eastern shore of Loch Lomond, follow the route descriptions for hill tracks 108, 109, 110, 116, 117, 143 and 149.

- *Scottish Hill Tracks: Northern Scotland* by D.G. Moir, John Bartholomew & Son, Ltd., Edinburgh. The remainder of the route is covered by the descriptions for hill tracks 71, 81, 87, 88, 91 and 92.
- *The West Highland Way* by Dr. A. Aitken, available from the Scottish Tourist Board (see *Address Directory*).

Glasgow to Skye via Glen Affric

Another beautiful walk through the Central and Western Highlands beginning from Drymen. Takes you through Queen Elizabeth Forest Park and the Trossachs, then past Loch Tay, Loch Rannoch, Loch Ericht, Loch Ness and Loch Benevean in Glen Affric to the Glenelg Ferry. Lovely mountainous countryside. **Length:** 299 kilometers (186 miles). **Walking Time:** 13 to 15 days. **Difficulty:** Moderately difficult; some difficult sections. **Path Markings:** None.
Trail Lodgings: Youth hostels at the Trossachs, Killin, Glen Affric and Ratagan. For other lodgings, refer to the lodging lists described under *Trail Lodgings* earlier in this chapter.
Maps:
- Ordnance Survey 1:50,000, sheets 25, 26, 33, 34, 42, 51 and 57 (Recommended). Or:
- Bartholomew one-inch (1:63,360), sheets 44, 48, 50, 51 and 55.
Guidebooks:
- *Scottish Hill Tracks: Southern Scotland* by D.G. Moir, John Bartholomew & Son, Ltd., Edinburgh. The route from Drymen to Loch Rannoch is covered by the descriptions for hill tracks 108, 113, 115, 118 and 140.
- *Scottish Hill Tracks: Northern Scotland* by D.G. Moir, John Bartholomew & Son, Ltd., Edinburgh. The remainder of the route is covered by the descriptions for hill tracks 63, 48, 100, 104, 105 and 94.

Fort William to Tongue

Along the west coast of Scotland through the Western Highlands and Northern Highlands to the North Sea coast. Dramatic scenery of sea lochs, towering peaks and grassy glens dotted with small crofts. Stretches from Fort William through Fort Augustus, Tomich, Glen Affric, Strathcarron, Torridon, Kinlochewe, Dundonnel, Ullapool, Achiltibuie, Lochinver, Kylesku and Altnaharra to Tongue. Takes you past Loch Lochy, Loch Ness and the Falls of Glomach (National Trust for Scotland property), through the Torridon Hills and up the spectacularly beautiful Glen Affric. Long stretches of road must be followed between Achiltibuie and Lochinver (about 30 kilometers) and between Altnaharra and Tongue (also about 30 kilometers). **Length:** 472 kilometers (293 miles). **Walking Time:** 20 to 24 days. **Difficulty:** Moderately difficult; some difficult sections. **Path Markings:** None.

Trail Lodgings: Youth hostels at Loch Lochy, Glen Affric, Ratagan, Torridon, Ullapool, Achininver and Tongue. For other lodgings, refer to the lodging lists described under *Trail Lodgings* earlier in this chapter.

Maps:
• Ordnance Survey 1:50,000, sheets 10, 15, 16, 19, 20, 24, 25, 26, 33, 34 and 41 (Recommended). Also:
• Ordnance Survey Outdoor Leisure Map 1:25,000, one sheet, *The Cuillin and Torridon Hills* (Recommended). Or:
• Bartholomew one-inch (1:63,360), sheets 50, 51, 54, 55 and 58.

Guidebook:
• *Scottish Hill Tracks: Northern Scotland* by D.G. Moir, John Bartholomew & Son, Ltd., Edinburgh. The entire route,, except for the stretches of road between Achiltibuie and Lochinver and between Altnaharra and Tongue, is covered by the descriptions for hill tracks 82, 98, 100, 104, 105, 114, 115, 116, 135, 145, 151, 162, 166, 170 and 171.

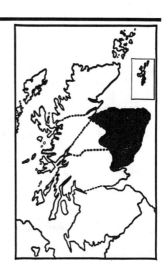

Cairngorms & Eastern Grampians

This big triangle of northeast Scotland is an area of contrasts. The long coastline east of Moray Firth has one of the sunniest climates in the country, plus a variety of coastal scenery ranging from the rocky headlands near Fraserburgh to the rolling sand dunes east of Nairn. Strung along the coast are small towns and villages, mostly fishing centers, often picturesque and always pleasant. The main center in this region is Elgin, an elegant town with the ruins of a once fine cathedral. On the east coast is the town of Aberdeen, noted for its granite buildings, its university, its fishmarket and now, North Sea oil.

Inland, there are rich, rolling farmlands and the stark, heatherclad hills of the Grampians and Cairngorms. Geologically, the Cairngorms are plateaus which have been eroded into mountains. From a distance, they appear rounded, rising between two of Scotland's finest rivers—the Spey and Dee—in deceptively gentle slopes which, on the opposite side, break suddenly into cliffs and magnificent corries. Four of the summits—Cairn Gorm, Ben Macdhui, Braeriach and Cairn Toul—rise above 1,200 meters (4,000 feet). Surrounding the summits is the largest area of high altitude mountain plateau in Scotland, characterized by an Arctic flora and climate, and severe storms which can arise suddenly at any time of year. Nowhere else in Britain can you feel so much that you are in Greenland or Arctic Canada. Streams from the Cairn Gorm and Ben Macdhui plunge over 240-meter cliffs into the great trench of Loch Avon, unsurpassed in Scotland for its grandeur and wild, remote setting. Between the two peaks is a vast, stony plateau, sparsely dotted with the three-pointed rush and other Arctic plants. The Cairngorms have significantly less precipitation than other mountain regions in Scotland, rarely exceeding 1,500 mm (59 inches) per year, but much of it comes in the form of snow. Extremes of temperature are also common, as are high winds which whip across the ridges and howl through Lairig Ghru, the rock-strewn pass separating the summits of Cairn Gorm and Ben Macdhui from those of Braeriach and Cairn Toul.

Angling along the base of the Cairngorms to the north is the Spey Valley, one of the most beautiful and varied in Scotland, with small lochs dammed by glacial debris, boreal pine forests, the Glen More Forest Park, small distilleries and the resort towns of Aviemore, Kingussie and Grantown-on-Spey. Strath Spey has the best set of forest lochs and forest bogs in Britain. One of the best examples of primeval forest remaining in Scotland is also to be found at Rothiemurchus Forest in Speyside.

To the south is the Dee Valley, with its steep wooded bluffs, natural pine and birch woods and multitude of small hills and side glens. Braemar, one of the highest and most attractive villages in the Highlands, nestles among the woods and small hills of the upper Dee, providing excellent access into the high Cairngorms, and the massive rolling hills of the Eastern Grampians to the south. Further down the valley is Ballanter, another good walking center, best known for its connections with Queen Victoria and Balmoral Castle; Banchory, with its two lovely National Trust for Scotland castles; and the bare brown moors and hills of the lower Dee, which are tinged a powder pink in August and September with a myriad of heather blooms.

Within the Grampians are several distinct massifs—the limestone outcrops of Beinn a' Ghlo above Glen Tilt to the west, rounded and green, well covered with moss and heath; the vast rolling plateaus and broad ridges of the Mounth above Glen Shee, Glen Callater and Glen Ey; the granite walls of Lochnagar—one of the loveliest hills in Scotland—whose magnificent northeastern corrie inspired Byron's verses in praise of "the steep frowning glories of dark Lochnagar"; and the Braes o' Angus, rising above the steep, broken slopes and brilliant green hillsides of Glen Clova.

The opportunities for hill walking in summer and ski mountaineering in winter abound. There are also numerous pitches to challenge climbers and no less than 23 forest areas with waymarked footpaths suitable for families. Those who venture into the hills, however, must be sure they are properly equipped and skilled with a map and compass.

Useful Addresses

See *Address Directory*:

> **Grampian Regional Council.** Provides general tourist information on the Grampian Region, including the Dee Valley and the North Sea coast. Also publishes eight leaflets and guidebooks to walks in the Grampians (see below).
>
> **Spey Valley Tourist Organisation.** Provides general tourist information on the Spey Valley, the Cairngorms and the little-frequented Manadhliath Mountains to the north of the Spey Valley.
>
> **Tayside Regional Council.** Provides general tourist information on the Tayside region, including the Grampian foothills, Glen Tilt, Glen Shee and Glen Clova.
>
> **Highland Guides Information.** Provides information and local advice on hill walking in the Cairngorms. Also organizes walking holidays; conducts climbing, mountaineering and ski touring courses; and rents mountaineering equipment. Does not provide tourist information.

Maps

The principal walking areas within the Cairngorms and Eastern Grampians are covered by the 1:50,000 Ordnance Survey maps, sheets 27, 28, 29, 35, 36, 37, 43, 44 and 53. These sheets cover the following areas:

> **Cairngorms:** sheet 36. Also covered by the 1:25,000 Ordnance Survey Outdoor Leisure Map, *The High Tops of the Cairngorms* (recommended), and the 1:63,360 Tourist Map, *Cairngorms*.
>
> **Eastern Grampians & Dee Valley:** sheets 43, 44 and 45.
>
> **Grampian Foothills & Sidlaw Hills:** sheet 53.
>
> **Spey Valley & Manadhliath Mountains:** sheets 28, 35 and 36.

One other useful map is *The Cairngorm Passes*, published by the Scottish Rights of Way Society, Ltd., which shows three principal rights of way in the Cairngorms and the locations of guideposts and youth hostels along the routes.

Guidebooks

- *The Cairngorms* by Adam Watson, Scottish Mountaineering Club district guidebook, West Col Productions, Reading, England. (Recommended)
- *Scottish Hill Tracks: Northern Scotland* by D.G. Moir, John Bartholomew & Son, Edinburgh. (Recommended)
- *Cairngorms,* Scottish Youth Hostels Association.
- *Glen More Forest Park: Cairngorms* by the Forestry Commission, HMSO, London. An extremely good guide with a 1:35,000 map covering Loch Morlich, the forest of Rothiemurchus and Glen More Forest Park at the base of the Cairngorms. Contains descriptions of hill walks, climbing and skiing in and around the park. Also has a chapter on Glenmore Lodge, the National Outdoor Training Centre on the eastern border of the park.
- *The Scottish Peaks* by W.A. Poucher, Constable & Company, London.
- *Walks and Trails in Scotland,* Scottish Tourist Board. Recommended for those who like short, gentle walks on waymarked paths.
- *Scotland for Hillwalking* by Donald J. Bennet, Scottish Tourist Board.
- *A Guide to Walks in Pitlochry and District* by the Pitlochry District Tourist Association. Describes several walks in the foothills of the Eastern Grampians.
- *Braemar Guide* by the Grampian Regional Council. Describes a week of walks around Braemar.
- *Hillwalking in the Grampian Region,* also by the Grampian Regional Council. Describes hill walks throughout the Grampian region.
- *Walks around Alford; Walks around Ballater; Walks around Banchory; Walks around Fettercairn; Walks around Stonehaven;* and *Haughton and Murray Park Nature Trails,* all by the Grampian Regional Council.

Numerous other guidebooks are also available. Many of these are listed in the SMC district guide and in the Scottish Tourist Board's *Walks and Trails in Scotland.* In addition, there are several Scottish Mountaineering Club climbers' guides to the Cairngorms, two of which cover the principal peaks in the Eastern Grampians.

Suggested Walks

Perhaps the most frequented—and classic—route through the Cairngorms is from Braemar to Aviemore through the Lairig Ghru. It is a long strenuous walk requiring 10 to 12 hours on a well-trodden path. But it is worth the effort. To walk the route, you should purchase D.G. Moir's *Scottish Hill Tracks: Northern Scotland,* turn to page 24 and follow hill track 29. The route can also be extended by beginning at Blair Atholl (hill track 25). For maps, you will need the 1:25,000 Ordnance Survey Outdoor Leisure Map, *The High Tops of the Cairngorms* and the 1:50,000 Ordnance Survey map, sheet 36.

Numerous other walks are also possible. For full details, it is best to consult the guidebooks listed above.

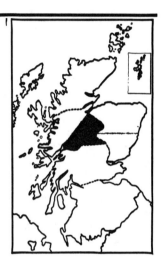

Central Highlands

For many visitors, the Central Highlands are the epitome of rugged Highland scenery. They also offer some of the most spectacular ridge walks and climbs in Scotland. The whole area is mountainous and includes Britain's highest peak, 1,343-meter (4,406-foot) Ben Nevis, as well as Glencoe, one of the principal mountaineering and skiing centers in Scotland. To the west is the fault of the Great Glen, running from Fort William to Inverness, which holds three lochs, including Loch Ness. The Central Highlands also encompass the upper Spey Valley, the bleak expanse of Rannoch Moor, the mountain-cradled lochs of Rannoch and Tummel, and several magnificently rugged mountain groups, including the Black Mount, Beinn a' Bheithir, the Mamores, the Aonachs and the Ben Alder group.

Glencoe is one of the finest glens in Scotland, its woods and pasture-lands enclosed by steep and rocky mountains, with the long ridge of the Aonach Eagach on the north, and the projecting spurs, huge buttresses and gullies of Bidean nam Bian on the south. On the north face of Aonach Dubh, the westernmost of the Bidean nam Bian peaks, is Ossian's Cave, a dark keyhole-like slit in the sheer face of the mountain. The foot tracks above Glencoe are steep and narrow, and can be extremely treacherous in a mist or wet weather. Nonetheless, numerous routes are possible, and there are two waymarked forest trails suitable for families in Glencoe Forest on the floor of the glen.

As with the rest of the Highlands, the true flavor of the Central Highlands is best captured on walks up their peaks and along their ridges. There is a good network of paths which lends itself to long-distance walks. But your time is often better spent taking day-long walks to the surrounding ridges and peaks from a single base. That way, you can concentrate your walking time on the best that the Central Highlands has to offer.

In fact, from just two bases you can reach six of the most spectacular walks in Scotland. From Ballachulish, for instance, you can easily reach the jagged, saw-edged ridge of Aonach Eagach above Glencoe. Bristling with rock towers and pinnacles, and offering magnificent views to the west, this is one of the narrowest and most exhilarating ridge walks in Scotland, surpassed only by the traverse of the main ridge on the Isle of Skye. You can also climb among the steep, closely clustered peaks, tree-hidden glens and high corries of Bidean nam Bian, considered by many to be Scotland's most beautiful mountain; explore the nearby Secret Valley; or clamber up numerous rewarding routes on the great rock-cathedral or Buachaille Etive Mòr. Another good base is Fort William, from which you can reach Ben Nevis and the broad, grassy shoulder of the Càrn Mòr Dearg Ridge.

These, of course, are merely a few of the highlights. The Central Highlands are—justifiably—among the most renowned mountain areas in Scotland, with a vast array of rewarding walking possibilities. Consequently, advance reading of the SMC district guidebook, *The Central Highlands,* is highly recommended.

Useful Addresses

See *Address Directory*:

Highlands & Islands Development Board. Provides general information on the entire Highlands region, including the northern part of the Central Highlands.

Fort William & Lochaber District Tourist Organisation. Provides tourist information on the region surrounding Fort William, including Ben Nevis and Glencoe.

Inverness, Loch Ness & Nairn Tourist Organisation. Provides information on the region surrounding Inverness and Loch Ness in the northern portion of the Central Highlands.

Strathclyde Regional Council. Provides general tourist information on the southern part of the Central Highlands, which includes Glen Coe and the Moor of Rannoch.

Tayside Regional Council. Provides general tourist information on the southeastern part of the Central Highlands, including Loch Rannoch, Loch Tummel and Loch Tay.

Maps

The Central Highlands are covered by the 1:50,000 Ordnance Survey maps, sheets 26, 34, 35, 41, 42, 49, 50 and 51. Among the areas covered by these sheets are:

Ben Nevis and Glencoe: sheet 41. Also covered by the 1:63,360 Ordnance Survey Tourist Map, *Ben Nevis and Glen Coe,* and the four-inch (1:15,840) Scottish Mountaineering Club climbers' map, *Ben Nevis.*

Ben Cruachan: sheets 49 and 50.

Guidebooks

- *The Central Highlands* by Campbell R. Steven, Scottish Mountaineering Club district guidebook, West Col Productions, Reading, England. (Recommended)
- *Scottish Hill Tracks: Northern Scotland* by D.G. Moir, John Bartholomew & Son, Ltd., Edinburgh. Covers the southern part of the Central Highlands, including routes around Glencoe, Loch Tay, Loch Rannoch and Ben Cruachan, and across the Rannoch Moors. (Recommended)
- *Glencoe and Glen Nevis,* Scottish Youth Hostels Association. Recommended for walks in these two areas.
- *Garth and Glen Lyon,* Scottish Youth Hostels Association.
- *The Scottish Peaks* by W.A. Poucher, Constable & Company, London.
- *Walks and Trails in Scotland,* Scottish Tourist Board. Describes walks on waymarked trails in 20 forest areas in the Central Highlands. Also tells you where locally produced guidebooks to the walks can be obtained.
- *Scotland for Hillwalking* by Donald J. Bennet, Scottish Tourist Board.

There are also several climbers' guides published by the Scottish Mountaineering Club covering Ben Nevis, and Glencoe and Ardgour.

Suggested Walks

In addition to the walks mentioned earlier—through the Secret Valley, up the Bidean nam Bian, Buachaille Etive Mòr and Ben Nevis mountains, and along the Aonach Eagach and Càrn Mòr Dearg ridges—one other ridge walk deserves particular mention: the traverse of the Ben Cruachan Ridge above Loch Awe, which involves 1,800 meters of ascents across seven peaks. All of these walks are described in the SMC district guidebook, *The Central Highlands*. There are also numerous wonderful walks described in D.G. Moir's *Scottish Hill Tracks*. One of these is:

From Laggan to Fort Augustus. Follows the Corrieyairack Road built by General Wade in 1731, and by which Prince Charles Edward marched south after raising the standard at Glenfinnan. Leads from the village of Laggan in the upper Spey Valley, past two small lochs, through Corrieyairack Forest, and over 764-meter Corrieyairack Pass (spectacular views on a clear day). The route then descends steeply into Glen Tarrf, which it follows to the main road leading to Fort Augustus. **Length:** 40 kilometers (25 miles). **Walking Time:** 1 long day or, if you camp, 2 days. **Difficulty:** Easy to moderately difficult. **Path Markings:** None.
Maps:
• Ordnance Survey 1:50,000, sheet 34.
Guidebook:
• *Scottish Hill Tracks, Northern Scotland* by D.G. Moir. See the description for hill track 58.

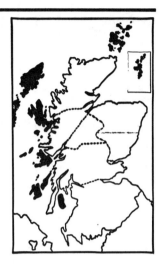

The Islands Of Scotland

Of Scotland's many islands only a few are mountainous, the most notable being Arran, Harris, Mull and Skye. Nonetheless, walks are possible on practically all of the inhabited islands, from the far-flung Shetlands to the Isle of Bute, which nestles close to the Cowal peninsula west of Glasgow. Each of the islands has its own particular charm—prehistoric remains, evidence of the Viking invasions, castles, age-old crofts and secluded, windswept promontories where you can look out over barren moors, rolling farmland and small fishing villages to the sea. Some of the islands, such as Colonsay, Gigha and Arran, are warmed by the Gulf Stream and have lush gardens in which subtropical plants flourish. Others, such as the islands of Barra, Vatersay, Uist and Benbecula in the Outer Hebrides, are remote, boulder-strewn and spangled with lochs. The most notable islands for walkers include:

Arran. This is a sheltered island set in the Firth of Clyde, the southernmost of Scotland's principal islands. Washed by the Gulf Stream its climate is soft and gentle, and its vegetation includes two varieties of the service tree and palms. Rocky mountains dominate the island to the north and east. To the south and west are lush pasturelands bordered by sandy beaches and towering cliffs. There are also several lochs—Tanna, Nuis, Urie and Iorsa—plus a lovely castle, owned by the National Trust for Scotland, near the town of Broderick. The island's highest peak, 874-meter (2,866-foot) Goatfell, is also a National Trust for Scotland holding. The island can be easily reached by regular steamer services between Ardrossan and Broderick, which is a good base for walks on the island. Two fine glens, Glen Rosa and Glen Sannox, provide access to the mountains. A nice walk, in fact, is up Glen Rosa and back down Glen

Sannox, crossing the pass between them known as the Saddle. There are six waymarked forest and hill walks in the region around Arran Forest which offer easy rambles past waterfalls, standing stones, the Giants' Graves and along the seashore. There are also opportunities in the north for serious climbs and challenging hill walks, especially along several splendid ridges. Bicycles may be rented on the island and can be extremely useful.

Harris. This island in the Outer Hebrides is a fantastic tableau of crag, cliff and white sand where the Gaelic language is still proudly maintained. Crofting—and the weaving of Harris Tweed—dominates the island's way of life. Scattered across the island are numerous archeological remains— ruined castles and chapels, brochs and standing stones—as well as isolated, thatched-roof houses. Most of the island is rugged and hilly, broken here and there by the gentle contours of rising moorland. The youth hostel at Stockinish provides a good base for exploring the island. Steamers ply between Uig, on the Isle of Skye, and Tarbert, which is situated on the narrow neck of land connecting Harris to the rolling Isle of Lewis to the north. The island also can be reached by air.

Mull. Situated in the Firth of Lorn and linked by steamer to Oban on the mainland, the island of Mull has many opportunities for fine walks. Much of the northern part of the island is comprised of rough moorland where sheepdog trials, sheepshearing competitions and Highland games are regularly held. Rising above the moors are dramatic mountains, domi- nated by 966-meter (3,169-foot) Ben More, which commands a magnifi- cent view of surrounding mountains, lochs and the island-littered sea. On the south coast, awesome cliffs soar to a climax at Malcolm's Point. Elsewhere, seals bask along the rocky coast as seabirds wheel high above. There are two impressive castles near Tobermory, the island's picturesque capital, and, according to legend, a Spanish galleon rests deep in its bay. Near the island to the west is Staffa, whose basalt mass rises abruptly from the waves in a wall of hexagonal columns which guard the mouth of Fingal's Cave, inspiration of Mendelssohn's Hebridean Overture. Among the many possible walks on Mull is the ascent of Ben More, beginning from the side of Loch na Keal and going directly up the northwest ridge of the mountain. There is also a waymarked cliff walk around the north- ernmost point of the island in Mull Forest, near Tobermory.

Skye. Sticking out from Scotland's west coast like a lobster's claw, Skye is the best-known and most mountainous of Scotland's islands. Among climbers and hill walkers it usually means one thing: the Black Cuillin, the steepest, rockiest and most treacherous mountains in Britain. The vertical black gabbro rock faces; a persistently narrow, ever-changing ridge that poses a constant challenge to the hill walker; and fickle weather which confounds all generalities, with anything possible from a three-month drought to a solid week of snow, would be enough to make the Cuillins notorious. But there is an additional twist. The mountain range is largely composed of magnetic rocks, which renders a compass nearly useless. In some places, a compass needle swings violently from side to side within a matter of a few steps. In fact, there are only three passes in the Cuillin which appear to have a normal compass reading—Bealach Coire Lochain, Bealach na Glaic Mhoire and Bealach Coire Lagan—but this offers little consolation, since in a mist you may not be sure on which pass you are standing. And in the Cuillin, one false step on its serrated ridge can be fatal. Even so, an experienced walker can traverse much of the Main Ridge, undoubtedly the most spectacular walk in Scotland.

There is, however, much more to Skye than the Cuillins—quiet coves, green valleys, glens and sheltered woodlands, a deeply indented coastline where seastacks and solid walls of rock rise out of the sea to a height of 300 meters, ruins and castles, small crofts standing in front of black silhouetted mountains with dramatic cliffs and waterfalls, and the hills of Sleat, Strathaird, Duirinish, Vaternish and Trotternish. Outside the Cuillin, the opportunities for walking are numerous, including several waymarked paths in Skye Forest.

But even on the gentler hills of Skye, you must be prepared for adverse weather. As Malcolm Slesser notes in the SMC district guidebook to Skye: "Here the weather fronts hold their sharp demarcations. The bright spell is bright. Squally means your tent needs all the holding down you can provide. To climb in a westerly gale is like being pumped full of ozone. When the summer anti-cyclone settles on the island, the heat even at three thousand feet may be oppressive."

He goes on to add that "Skye is no place for those who cannot take the rough with the smooth. Indeed after the first visit it is no place for those who do not accept its many virtues and ignore its defects. For sheer utter bleakness almost nowhere in the world can compare with Glen Drynoch in heavy rain. The capacity of Skye peatland to retain water after weeks of drought is worthy of special research. The island has few sandy beaches, and even her best are no competition to those of the mainland and other islands." Its plague of midges is also extremely annoying, especially during August. But the island's charms are many, and once you come under their spell you may find that you have to return again and again. Among the bases for walks on the island are the youth hostels at Uig and Broadford, as well as the Glen Brittle youth hostel at the foot of the Cuillins, which offers climbing courses in the summer. Easiest access to the island is by ferry from Glenelg.

This, of course, is but a sampling of Scotland's 700 islands. Further information on the other islands can be obtained from the tourist information offices listed below. The SMC district guidebook, *The Islands of Scotland*, also includes excellent descriptions of the islands that are of most interest to the walker and climber.

Useful Addresses

See *Address Directory*:

Highlands & Islands Development Board. Provides general tourist information on all the Scottish islands, along with information on access, lodgings and the addresses of local tourist information offices.

Dunoon, Cowal & Isle of Bute Tourist Organisation. Provides tourist information on the Isle of Bute.

Isle of Arran Tourist Information Centre. Provides tourist information on Arran.

Isle of Skye Tourist Organisation. Provides tourist information on Skye.

Oban, Mull & District Tourist Organisation. Provides tourist information on Mull.

Orkney Tourist Organisation. Provides tourist information on the Orkney Islands off the northern tip of Scotland.

Shetland Tourist Organisation. Provides tourist information on the Shetland Islands.

Western Isles Tourist Organisation. Provides information on the Isle of Harris, as well as on the other islands in the Outer Hebrides.

Maps

The islands of Scotland are covered by the following 1:50,000 Ordnance Survey maps:

Arran: sheet 69.

Bute: sheet 63.

Harris: sheets 14 and 18.

Mull: sheets 47, 48 and 49.

Orkney Islands: sheets 5, 6, and 7.

Skye: sheets 23, 32 and 33. Also covered by the 1:25,000 Ordnance Survey Outdoor Leisure Map, *The Cuillin and Torridon Hills;* the Scottish Mountaineering Club 1:15,000 climbers' map, *Black Cuillin of Skye Code CM;* and the Scottish Mountaineering Club three-inch climbers' map, *Black Cuillin of Skye Code SM.*

Shetland Islands: sheets 1, 2, 3 and 4.

Guidebooks

- *The Islands of Scotland* by Norman Tennent, Scottish Mountaineering Club district guidebook, West Col Productions, Reading, England. (Recommended)
- *The Island of Skye* by Malcolm Slesser, Scottish Mountaineering Club district guidebook, West Col Productions, Reading, England. (Recommended)
- *Scottish Hill Tracks: Northern Scotland* by D.G. Moir, John Bartholomew & Son, Ltd., Edinburgh. (Recommended)
- *The Scottish Peaks* by W.A. Poucher, Constable & Company, London.
- *Skye,* Scottish Youth Hostels Association.
- *Arran,* Scottish Youth Hostels Association. (Recommended)
- *Seventy Walks in Arran* by R.D. Walton, Dumfries. (Also recommended)
- *Bull Loch Trail; Ettrick Bay Trail; Kilchattan Trail; Kingarth Trail; Loch Fad and Loch Ascog Trail;* and *Rothesay Walk.* Six leaflets describing walks on the island of Bute. All available from the Buteshire Natural History Society, Isle of Bute.

There are also three climbers' guides published by the Scottish Mountaineering Club, two covering the Cuillin of Skye, and one covering Arran.

Suggested Walks

The walks enumerated in the Scottish Youth Hostel guidebooks and Bute Museum leaflets listed above are all worthy of attention. Few of the walks, however, can compete with the one described in *Scottish Hill Tracks: Northern Scotland* for Skye:

Around the Black Cuillin. A circular walk beginning from Sligachan. Circles around the Black Cuillin to the Glen Brittle youth hostel. Goes across glens and streams, past Loch Coruisk and over a shoulder of the Cuillins. The section between Glen Brittle to Loch Coruisk and Sligachan should be attempted only by *experienced walkers;* some river crossings may not be possible except in very dry weather. The route also strikes cross-country over a part of the Cuillins near the coast. The rest of the walk presents few complications. **Length:** 39 kilometers (24 miles). **Walking Time:** 3 days minimum. **Difficulty:** Easy to moderately difficult between Slighachan and Glen Brittle; difficult between Glen Brittle and Loch Coruisk; and moderately difficult between Loch Coruisk and Sligachan. **Path Markings:** None.

Maps:
- Ordnance Survey Outdoor Leisure Map 1:25,000, *The Cuillin and Torridon Hills.*

Guidebook:
- *Scottish Hill Tracks: Northern Scotland* by D.G. Moir. See the descriptions for hill tracks 127, 128 (possible detour from Loch Coruisk down the Strathaird Peninsula to Elgol) and 129.

Northern Highlands

The Northern Highlands are a blend of spectacular mountain scenery, deeply penetrating sea lochs, and wild, uninhabited hinterlands creased with verdant glens. Of 21 areas of outstanding beauty identified by the National Trust for Scotland, six are located in the Northern Highlands—the isolated, loch-bound peninsula of Applecross facing the mountains of Skye; the Ben Damph and Coulin Forests, sandwiched between Glen Torridon and Glen Carron west of Applecross; the sculpted sandstone of the Torridon Mountains, with their terraced bastions, sharp ridges and white quartzite pinnacles; the sparkling blue waters of Loch Maree, overlooked by an uninhabited maze of mountains rising to 980 meters (3,217 feet); the Fisherfield and Strathnasheallag Forests, which cloak the mountainsides to the north of Loch Maree; and the Inverpolly and Glen Canisp Forests east of Lochinver in the county of Sutherland, part of the Norseman's stomping grounds for over 400 years between 800 and 1263 A.D.

Scattered along the coast are old fishing villages and whitewashed crofts, which perch at the feet of complex mountain masses, crowned by numerous pinnacles. There are also numerous streams and the Eas-Coul

Aulin Falls in Sutherland, the highest in Britain, which leap over the cliff line of Leiter Dhubh in a vertical drop of 153 meters (502 feet), then cascade for yet another 45 meters (148 feet) at the foot of the cliffs. In addition, there are standing stones, brochs, chambered tombs and hut circles, above which golden eagles and peregrine falcons soar.

Despite the region's isolation, it is crossed by an intricate network of old drove roads, which provide excellent access to rolling moorland, lonely glens, brooding lochs and isolated peaks. Accommodation, however, is not as easy to come by and in the more remote areas you should plan on camping.

Useful Addresses

See *Address Directory*:

Highland & Islands Area Development Board. Provides general tourist information on the entire Northern Highlands region.

Caithness Tourist Organisation. Provides general tourist information on the county of Caithness, a region of gently rolling heatherland, lochs, pasture and high sea cliffs on the northeastern tip of Scotland.

Sutherland Tourist Organisation. Provides tourist information on the county of Sutherland, in the northern portion of the Northern Highlands.

Wester Ross Tourist Organisation. Provides tourist information on the county of Wester Ross, which takes in Applecross, the Torridon Mountains and Loch Maree.

Maps

The Northern Highlands are covered by the 1:50,000 Ordnance Survey maps, sheets 9, 10, 15, 16, 17, 19, 21, 24, 25, 26 and 29. These sheets cover the following areas:

Applecross Peninsula: sheet 24.

Assynt (including the Inverpolly & Glen Canisp Forests): sheet 15.

Ben Damph & Coulin Forests: sheet 25.

Loch Marre to Loch Broom: sheet 19.

Torridon Mountains: sheets 19 and 24. Also covered by the 1:25,000 Ordnance Survey Outdoor Leisure Map, *The Cuillin and Torridon Hills*. (Recommended)

Guidebooks

- *The Northern Highlands* by Tom Strang, Scottish Mountaineering Club district guidebook, West Col Productions, Reading, England. (Recommended)
- *Scottish Hill Tracks: Northern Scotland* by D.G. Moir, John Bartholomew & Son, Ltd., Edinburgh. (Highly recommended)
- *The Scottish Peaks* by W.A. Poucher, Constable & Company, London.
- *Northern Highlands*, Scottish Youth Hostels Association.
- *Walks and Trails in Scotland*, Scottish Tourist Board.
- *Hillwalking in Scotland* by Donald J. Bennet, Scottish Tourist Board.

Several leaflets describing walks on forest trails and nature paths in the Northern Highlands are available from the Forestry Commission in Inverness (see the section on *Guidebooks* earlier in this chapter). In addition, the Scottish Mountaineering Club publishes two climbers' guides to the Northern Highlands.

Suggested Walks

For good background reading, it is recommended that you purchase the SMC district guide *The Northern Highlands,* then get a copy of D.G. Moir's *Scottish Hill Tracks: Northern Scotland* for details on the best walks in the region. There is no single "best" walk, although you might try some of the following routes:

1. Hill track 133 from Applecross to Shieldaig across the Applecross Peninsula, 14.5 kilometers (9 miles).
2. Hill track 138 from Shieldaig to Torridon, 11 kilometers (7 miles).
3. Hill track 141 from Torridon to Gairloch along the shores of Loch Torridon and the Atlantic coast, 47 kilometers (29 miles).
4. Hill track 147 from Poolewe to Dundonnell through the remote, serrated mountains north of Loch Maree, 45 kilometers (28 miles).
5. Hill tracks 160 to 169. Virtually all of these are recommended, especially hill track 162 from Ullapool to Achtiltibuie, which includes a cliffside traverse of the precipitous slope of Ben More Coigach above Loch Broom, and hill track 163 from Lochinver to Elphin alongside Fionn Loch.

The maps covering these routes are: 1:50,000 Ordnance Survey, sheets 15, 19, 20 and 24; and the 1:25,000 Ordnance Survey Outdoor Leisure Map, *The Cuillin and Torridon Hills.*

Southern Highlands

Although the mountains in the Southern Highlands lack the lofty heights of the more northern peaks, they are easily one of Scotland's most popular walking areas. This is partly due to their close proximity to the major population centers of Glasgow and Edinburgh. But easy access is not their only virtue. Nearly 70 summits rise about 915 meters (3,000 feet), towering above tiny villages, lonely moorlands and turreted castles. There are also numerous lochs, such as Loch Lomond, one of the loveliest in Scotland, which spreads out beneath 973-meter (3,192-foot) Ben Lomond and is bordered to the east by the high hills and woods of Queen Elizabeth Forest Park. To the west is Argyll Forest Park, which stretches down the Cowal Peninsula across rugged mountains broken by sea lochs. Here you find the Arrochar Alps, clustered northwest of the village of Arrochar at the head of Loch Long, and the three rocky peaks of the Cobbler, one of the most impressive mountains in the Southern Highlands.

Beyond Loch Lomond to the east are the Trossachs, which rise to nearly 600 meters between Loch Katrin and Loch Achray near Callander; and the lovely hill-bound lochs of Rannoch, Tummel and Tay. Above Loch Tay is 1,214-meter (3,984-foot) Ben Lawers, rising at the center of a continuous ridge which is more than 11 kilometers long and connects seven distinct peaks over 915 meters in height.

The highest peaks in the Southern Highlands generally lie within Argyll and Pethshire. Elsewhere, there are ranges of low hills such as the Campsie Fells in Stirlingshire and the Lomond Hills in Fife, which offer opportunities for easy rambles through forests and moors. There are also more than 30 waymarked forest trails, plus numerous old drove roads.

Useful Addresses

See *Address Directory*:

Central Regional Council. Provides general tourist information on the Central region, which includes the Trossachs, Loch Earn, the Campsie Fells and part of Queen Elizabeth Forest Park.

Dunoon, Cowal & Isle of Bute Tourist Organisation. Provides tourist information on the Cowal Peninsula, which encompasses Argyll Forest Park and the Arrochar Alps.

Fife Tourist Authority. Provides tourist information on the Fife Peninsula to the east, lying across the Firth of Forth above Edinburgh. Takes in the Ochill Hills and numerous historical sites, including Kinross Castle, where Mary Queen of Scots was imprisoned in 1567.

Mid Argyll, Kintyre & Islay Tourist Organisation. Provides tourist information on the Kintyre and Argyll peninsulas, which jut out into the Atlantic between the islands of Jura and Islay, and the island of Arran.

Strathclyde Regional Council. Provides general tourist information on the Strathclyde region, which takes in the entire western portion of the Southern Highlands, including Cowal, Argyll, Kintyre and Loch Lomond.

Tayside Regional Council. Provides tourist information on Tayside, which takes in Loch Tay, Loch Rannoch, Loch Tummel and Ben Lawers, as well as the charming, historical village of Dunkeld and the town of Perth.

Maps

The Southern Highlands are covered by the 1:50,000 Ordnance Survey maps, sheets 49, 50, 51, 52, 55, 56, 57, 58, 59, 62, 63 and 68. These sheets cover the following areas:

Argyll & Kintyre: sheets 49, 50, 55, 62 and 68.

Cowal (including Argyll Forest Park & the Arrochar Alps): sheets 55, 56, 62 and 63.

Fife: sheets 58 and 59.

Loch Lomond & the Trossachs: sheet 57. Also covered by the 1:63,360 Ordnance Survey Tourist Map, *Loch Lomond and the Trossachs*.

Loch Rannoch, Loch Tummel & Loch Tay (including Ben Lawers): sheets 51 and 52.

Guidebooks

- *The Southern Highlands* by Donald J. Bennet, Scottish Mountaineering Club district guidebook, West Col Productions, Reading, England. (Recommended)
- *Scottish Hill Tracks: Southern Scotland* by D.G. Moir, John Bartholomew & Son, Ltd., Edinburgh. (Recommended)
- *The Scottish Peaks* by W.A. Poucher, Constable & Company, London.
- *Loch Lomond and Trossachs*, Scottish Youth Hostels Association. (Recommended)
- *Walks and Trails in Scotland,* Scottish Tourist Board. Recommended for those who want to explore waymarked forest trails.
- *Scotland for Hillwalking* by Donald J. Bennet, Scottish Tourist Board.
- *Argyll Forest Park* by the Forestry Commission, HMSO, London. An excellent guide with a 1:63,360 map and information on the park's history, legends, antiquities, walks and mountains.
- *Queen Elizabeth Forest Park: Ben Lomond, Loch Ard and the Trossachs* by the Forestry Commission, HMSO, London. Another excellent Forest Park guide.

Numerous locally produced leaflets and guidebooks to waymarked forest paths and nature trails are available from the Forestry Commission's regional office in Glasgow (see list of leaflets under "Locally Produced Guidebooks" in the section on *Guidebooks* earlier in this chapter). There is also a Scottish Mountaineering Club climbers' guide to the Arrochar Alps:

Suggested Walks

Two of the best walks in the Southern Highlands are on the long-distance walking routes beginning at Drymen on Loch Lomond, both of which wind through Queen Elizabeth Forest Park, one heading through Aberfoyle, Callander, Cromrie and Amulree to Dunkeld on hill tracks 107, 111, 121, 123 and 125; and the other taking you through Kinlochard, the Trossachs, Balquhidder and Killin, then along the western base of Ben Lawers to Loch Rannoch on hill tracks 108, 113, 115, 118 and 139. Both routes are described in D.G. Moir's *Scottish Hill Tracks: Southern Scotland.* The 1:50,000 Ordnance Survey maps required are sheets 51, 52 and 57.

Southern Uplands

This is the gentle side of Scotland, a land of broad valleys and rolling, grassy hills. The valleys are dotted with small towns, villages and farms. Above them rise the smooth grassy slopes of the Galloway, Pentland, Moorfoot, Lammermuir, Moffat and numerous other hills, which lead the walker upward through copses of woods, past cascading streams and waterfalls, and across high moorland to rocky ridges and rounded hill tops.

To the west, in the county of Galloway, is Galloway Forest Park, which encompasses seven forests, such as the rock-strewn hinterland of the Forest of Buchan in Glen Trool with its chain of lochs and network of paths and forest roads. Along the Galloway coast, there are indented bays, fringed with white sand and whitewashed fishing villages, overlooked by 843-meter (2,764-foot) Merrick, the highest knuckle of the Awful Hand Range and the highest hill in southern Scotland.

Near Moffat in the center of the Uplands, the Grey Mare's Tail tumbles down from Loch Skeen through a rocky, narrow gorge. To the east is a network of wooded valleys formed by the River Tweed and its tributaries. Here the hills are smooth in outline and grassy, looking out over farms, charming stone villages and numerous reminders of the past, including old Roman roads and camps, impressive castles and 12th century abbeys.

None of the hills in the Southern Uplands exceed 850 meters. Nonetheless, they contain summits almost as high as any in England, and in bad weather can be just as treacherous as the Highland peaks. They also offer a wide variety of walking experiences, from short signposted nature trails (of which there are more than 15 to choose from in Galloway alone) to tough moorland walks only for the experienced.

Useful Addresses

See *Address Directory*:

Borders Regional Council. Provides tourist information on the southeastern portion of the Southern Uplands.

Dumfries & Galloway Tourist Association. Provides tourist information on the southwestern portion of the Southern Uplands, including the rocky hills and forests of Galloway Forest Park.

Lothian Regional Council. Provides tourist information on the northeastern portion of the Southern Uplands, including the Pentland Hills, Lammermuir Hills and the coastal region along the Firth of Forth.

Strathclyde Regional Council. Provides tourist information on the northwestern portion of the Southern Uplands below Glasgow.

Maps

The Southern Uplands are covered by the 1:50,000 Ordnance Survey maps, sheets 63, 64, 65, 66, 67, 70, 71, 72, 73, 74, 75, 76, 77, 78, 79, 80, 81, 82, 83, 84, 85 and 86. Among the areas covered by these sheets are:

The Cheviot Hills: sheets 79, 80, 81, 86 and 87.

The Galloway Hills: sheets 76, 77, 82 and 83.

The Lammermuir Hills: sheets 66 and 67.

The Lead Hills & Lowther Hills: sheets 72 and 78.

The Moffat & Ettrick Hills (including Grey Mare's Tail): sheets 72, 73, 78 and 79.

The Moorfoot Hills: sheet 73.

The Pentland Hills: sheets 65 and 66.

Guidebooks

- *The Southern Uplands* by K.M. Andrew and A.A. Thrippleton, Scottish Mountaineering Club district guidebook, West Col Productions, Reading, England. (Recommended)
- *Scottish Hill Tracks: Southern Scotland* by D.G. Moir, John Bartholomew & Son, Ltd., Edinburgh. (Recommended)
- *Pentland Walks* by D.G. Moir, John Bartholomew & Son, Ltd., Edinburgh. (Recommended)
- *Galloway Forest Park* by the Forestry Commission, HMSO, London. An excellent guide with a 1:31,680 map and descriptions of nearly 20 walking routes.

- *Walks and Trails in Scotland,* Scottish Tourist Board. An indispensable guide to more than 50 signposted forest paths and nature trails.
- *Scotland for Hillwalking* by Donald J. Bennet, Scottish Tourist Board.

There are also numerous locally produced leaflets and guidebooks to forest walks and nature trails in the Southern Uplands. Ten of these can be obtained from the Forestry Commission's regional office in Dumfries (see list of leaflets under "Locally Produced Guidebooks" in the section on *Guidebooks* earlier in this chapter).

Suggested Walks

Three of the best walks in the Southern Highlands are along the long-distance walking routes from Northumberland to Edinburgh or Dunbar, and from Edinburgh to Newton Stewart (described in the section on *Scotland's Long-Distance Walker Routes*). Any of these walks can be broken down into smaller segments.

In D.G. Moir's *Scottish Hill Tracks: Southern Scotland,* there are a number of lovely walks through the Cheviot Hills (hill tracks 1 through 6). The walks in the 20's series in the hills southeast of Pebbles are also lovely, taking you through pleasant, rolling country above the banks of the Rivers Tweed, Yarrow and Ettrick.

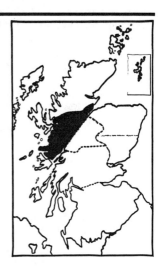

Western Highlands

The Western Highlands lie to the west of the Great Glen and comprise a remote, rugged countryside which is entirely mountainous. Few of the mountains have the character of, say, Ben Nevis or Bidean nam Bian and are therefore less frequented than other parts of the Highlands. But for those who seek peace and solitude, this is a distinct advantage.

There are only two main roads in the Western Highlands. The one from Fort William to Mallaig passes through grand mountain and loch scenery in country closely associated with Prince Charles and the ill-fated uprising of 1745. Much of the surrounding countryside is a tangle of lonely peaks and desolate glens, of which Ladhar Bheinn and Sgurr na Ciche, both rising above 1,000 meters (3,300 feet), are the most impressive summits. The two peaks are situated on the deeply indented western seaboard north of Mallaig near the heads of the fjord-like Loch Nevis and Loch Hourn. Yawning valleys lie beneath the steep sides and pointed summits of surrounding mountains, stirred only by the sounds of rushing streams and the wind.

In the center of the region are Glen Cannich and Glen Affric, divided by a mountainous massif which includes Carn Eige (1,182 meters; 3,877 feet) and Mam Soul (1,177 meters; 3,862 feet), the two highest mountains in the Western Highlands. Both glens are considered among the most beautiful in Scotland, and Glen Affric contains one of the largest stands of Scots pines remaining in the country. To the west of the two glens the Falls of Glomach plunge 113 meters (370 feet) in a cascade of spray through a rocky, forest-fringed gorge. Nearby are the Five Sisters of Kintail, culminating in 1,068-meter (3,505-foot) Sgurr Fhuran, northeast of Glen Shiel.

Finally, at the northeasternmost tip of the Western Highlands is the Black Isle, jutting out into Moray Firth above Inverness. The Black Isle is neither an island nor black. Instead it is a lush, green peninsula carpeted with wild flowers and ringed by sheltered bays with pink sand, and offers numerous opportunities for relaxed rambles.

Throughout much of the Western Highlands, you must be prepared to walk long distances and carry everything you need on your back. Outside of a few small crofts and a scattering of settlements along the roads to Mallaig and up Glen Shiel and Glen Affric, there are few opportunities for lodgings and few shops from which to buy provisions. You must also be prepared for wet weather. With the exception of the Black Isle, the Western Highlands has one of the highest rainfalls of any area in Scotland.

Useful Addresses

See *Address Directory*:

> **Highlands & Islands Development Board.** Provides general tourist information on the entire Western Highlands.

> **Fort William & Lochaber District Tourist Organisation.** Provides tourist information on the remote mountain area and seascape surrounding Mallaig.

> **Wester Ross Tourist Organisation.** Provides tourist information on the entire northern portion of the Western Highlands, including Loch Nevis, Loch Hourn, Glen Affric, Glen Cannich and the region surrounding the Falls of Glomach.

> **East Ross & Black Isle Tourist Organisation.** Provides tourist information on the region surrounding the Black Isle north of Inverness. Publishes a guidebook entitled *Walks in the Black Isle* which describes 19 walks on the peninsula.

Maps

The Western Highlands are covered by the 1:50,000 Ordnance Survey maps, sheets 25, 26, 33, 34, 40, 41, 47 and 49. Among the areas covered by these sheets are:

> **Black Isle:** sheets 21, 26 and 27.

> **Falls of Glomach & Five Sisters of Kintail:** sheet 33.

> **Glen Affric & Glen Cannich:** sheets 25, 26 and 34.

> **Loch Nevis & Loch Hourn:** sheets 33 and 40.

Guidebooks

> • *The Western Highlands* by G.S. Johnston, Scottish Mountaineering Club district guidebook, West Col Productions, Reading, England. (Recommended)

- *Scottish Hill Tracks: Northern Scotland* by D.G. Moir, John Bartholomew & Son, Ltd., Edinburgh. (Recommended)
- *The Scottish Peaks* by W.A. Poucher, Constable & Company, London.
- *Scotland for Hillwalking* by Donald J. Bennet, Scottish Tourist Board.
- *Walks in the Black Isle,* published by the East Ross and Black Isle Tourist Organisation (address above).

Suggested Walks

Numerous possible walks are described in D.G. Moir's *Scottish Hill Tracks: Northern Scotland.* You can explore virtually every glen and coastal promontory by following any of the hill tracks from hill track 72 upward to hill track 124. The long-distance route described in the section on *Scotland's Long-Distance Walking Routes,* for instance, begins in Fort William, takes you up the Great Glen to Loch Ness, across Glen Moriston to Glen Affric, along the base of the Five Sisters of Kintail to Loch Duich, past the Falls of Glomach and then northward through Glen Carron to the Torridon Hills. Virtually any segment of this route is well worth walking.

There are also numerous short, signposted walks on the Black Isle described in the guidebook *Walks in the Black Isle.* The classic walk in the region, however, is the traverse of the Five Sisters of Kintail, described in the SMC district guidebook, *The Western Highlands.*

Address Directory

B

- *Backpackers Club,* 20 St. Michaels Road, Tielhurst, Reading, Berkshire RG3 4RP, England.
- *Black's, Dundee,* 83-117 Princes Street, Dundee. Tel. (0382) 43766.
- *Black's Edinburgh,* 13-14 Elm Row, Edinburgh.
- *Black's, Glasgow,* 132 St. Vincent Street, Glasgow. Tel. (041) 221 4007.
- *Borders Regional Council,* Tourism and Industrial Development, Regional Offices, Newton, St. Boswells, Roxburghshire. Tel. (08352) 3301.
- *British Mountaineering Council,* Crawford House, Precinct Centre, Booth Street East, Manchester M13 9RZ, England. Tel. (061) 273 5835.

- *British Tourist Authority,* 680 Fifth Avenue, New York, New York 10019, U.S.A. Tel. (212) 581-4700.
- *Buteshire Natural History Society,* Bute Museum, Rothesay, Isle of Bute.

C

- *Caithness Tourist Organisation,* Whitechapel Road, Wick, Caithness. Tel. (0955) 2596.
- *Central Regional Council,* Tourist Department, Viewforth, Stirling, Stirlingshire. Tel. (0786) 3111.
- *Colin G. Firth,* see *Firth, Colin G.*
- *Constable & Company Ltd.,* 10 Orange Street, London WC2H 7EG, England.
- *Countryside Commission for Scotland,* Battleby House, Redgorton, Perth PH1 3EW. Tel. (0738) 27921.
- *Country-Wide Holidays Association,* Birch Heys, Cromwell Range, Manchester M14 6HU, England. Tel. (061) 224 2887.

D

- *Dumfries & Galloway Tourist Association,* Douglas House, Newton Stewart, Wigtownshire. Tel. (0671) 2549.
- *Dunoon, Cowal & Isle of Bute Tourist Organisation,* Pier Esplanade, Dunoon, Argyll. Tel. (0369) 3785.

E

- *East Ross & Black Isle Tourist Organization,* Information Centre, Muir of Ord, Ross and Cromarty. Tel. (046 382) 433.
- *Edenburgh University Press,* 22 George Square, Edinburgh EH8 9LF.
- *Emergency.* Dial 999. Ask for the police.

F

- *Fife Tourist Authority,* Fife House, North Street, Glenrothes, Fife. Tel. (0592) 754411.
- *Firth, Colin G.,* Secretary, Association of Mountain Guides, 64 Barco Avenue, Penrith, Cumbria England.
- *Forestry Commission, Aberdeen,* 6 Queen's Gate, Aberdeen AB9 2NQ.
- *Forestry Commission, Dumfries,* Greyston Park, 55/57 Moffat Road, Dumfries, DG1 1NP. Tel. (0387) 2425.

- *Forestry Commission, Edinburgh,* 231 Corstorphine Road, Edinburgh EH12 7AT. Tel. (031) 334 0303.
- *Forestry Commission, Glasgow,* Portcullis House, 21 India Street, Glasgow G2 4PL. Tel. (041) 248 3931.
- *Forestry Commission, Inverness,* 21 Church Street, Inverness IV1 1EL. Tel. (0463) 32811.
- *Fort William & Lochaber District Tourist Organisation,* Fort William, Inverness-shire. Tel. (0397) 2232.

G

- *Glencoe School of Winter Climbing,* Clachaig, Glencoe, Argyll.
- *Glenmore Lodge,* Aviemore, Inverness-shire. Tel. (047) 986 256. Enquiries: 1 St. Colme Street, Edinburgh EH3 6AA. Tel. (031) 225 8411.
- *Graham Tiso,* 13 Wellington Place, Edinburgh EH6. Tel. (031) 554 0804.
- *Grampian Regional Council,* Department of Leisure, Woodhill House, Ashgrove Road West, Aberdeen AB9 2LU. Tel. (0224) 23401.

H

- *Hamish Brown Mountain Holidays,* 21 Carlin Craig, Kinghorn KY3 9RX. Tel. (059 289) 422.
- *Hamish McInnes Scottish Winter Climbing,* Achnacon, Glencoe, Argyll. Tel. Ballachulish 258.
- *Her Majesty's Stationery Office,* Atlantic House, Holborn Viaduct, London EC1P 1BN, England. (Bookshop: 49 High Holborn, London, WC1V 6HB).
- *Highland Guides Information,* Inverdruie, Ariemore, Inverness-shire. Tel. (047 981) 729.
- *Highlands & Islands Development Board,* Bridge House, Bank Street, Inverness. Tel. (0463) 34171.
- *Highrange Sports,* 99 Great Western Road, Glasgow G4 9AH. Tel. (041) 332 5533.
- *Holiday Fellowship,* 142-144 Great North Way, London NW4 1EG, England. Tel. (01) 203 3381.
- *Hiade, John,* Chairman, Mountain Rescue Committee of Scotland, Loch Eil Centre, Achdalien, Corpach, Fort William, Inverness-shire.

I

- *Inverness, Loch Ness & Nairn Tourist Organisation,* 23 Church Street, Inverness. Tel. (0463) 34354.
- *Isle of Arran Tourist Information Centre,* Brodick, Isle of Arran. Tel. (2140) 2401.
- *Isle of Skye Tourist Organisation,* Meall House, Portree, Isle of Skye. Tel. (0478) 2137.

J

- *John Bartholomew & Son Ltd.,* 12 Duncan Street, Edinburgh EH9 1TA. Tel. (031) 667 9341.
- *John Hiade,* see *Hiade, John.*

K

- *K.S.A.,* 1 Warwick Avenue, Whickam, Newcastle-upon-Tyne, England.

L

- *Loch Eil Outward Bound,* Achdalieu, Fort William, Inverness-shire. Tel. Corpach 320.
- *Lothian Regional Council,* Department of Recreation and Leisure, 40 Torphichen Street, Edinburgh. Tel. (031) 229 9292.

M

- *MCS,* see *Mountaineering Council of Scotland.*
- *Mid Argyll, Kintyre & Islay Tourist Organisation,* Campbeltown, Argyll. Tel. (0586) 2056.
- *Mountain Bothies Association,* General Secretary, Richard Semmer, 9 Drysdale Lane, Mickleover, Derby DE3 5PR.
Mollison, 81 Dundas Street, Edinburgh EH3. Tel. (031) 556 3536.
- *Mountaineering Council of Scotland,* Honorary Secretary, William Myles, 59 Morningside Park, Edinburgh.

N

- *National Trust for Scotland,* 5 Charlotte Square, Edinburgh EH2 4DU. Tel. (031) 226 5922.
- *Nevisport Ltd.,* Aviemore, 43 Grampian Road, Aviemore. Tel. (0479) 819 0208.

- *Nevisport Ltd., Fort William,* 72 High Street, Fort William PH33 6EA. Tel. (0397) 3245.
- *Nevisport Ltd., Glasgow,* 261 Sauchlehall Street, Glasgow G23 EZ. Tel. (041) 332 4814.

O

- *Oban, Mull & District Tourist Organisation,* Boswell House, Argyll Square, Oban, Argyll. Tel. (9631) 3122 or 3551.
- *Ordnancy Survey,* Romsey Road, Maybush, Southampton SO9 4DH, England. Tel. Southampton 775555 ext. 706.
- *Orkney Tourist Organisation,* Junction Road, Kirkwall, Orkney. Tel. (0856) 2856.

P

- *Pitlochry District Tourist Association,* 28 Atholl Road, Pitlochry PH16 5DB.

R

- *Ramblers Holidays Ltd.,* 13 Longcroft House, Fretherne Road, Welwyn Garden City, Hertfordshire AL8 6PG, England. Tel. Welwyn Garden 31133.

S

- *SMC,* see *Scottish Mountaineering Club.*
- *Scottish Landowners' Federation,* 18 Abercromby Place, Edinburgh EH3 6TY. Tel. (031) 556 4466.
- *Scottish Mountaineering Club,* Honorary Secretary, W. Wallace, 22 Bonally Terrace, Edinburgh EH13.
- *Scottish Norwegian Ski School,* Speyside Sports, in Aviemore (Tel. Aviemore 656) and in Grantown-on-Spey (Tel. 2946).
- *Scottish Postal Board,* Operations Division, West Port House, 102 West Port, Edinburgh EH3 9HS. Tel. (031) 228 5241.
- *Scottish Rights of Way Society, Ltd.,* 28 Rutland Square, Edinburgh EH1 2BW. Tel. (031) 556 5245.
- *Scottish Ski Club,* Secretary, Zo Barnshot Road, Edinburgh. Tel. (031) 441 2494.
- *Scottish Sports Counc:',* 1 St. Colme Street, Edinburgh EH3 6AA. Tel. (031) 225 8411.

314 SCOTLAND

- *Scottish Tourist Board, Edinburgh,* 23 Ravelston Terrace, Edinburgh EH4 3EU. Tel. (031) 332 2433.
- *Scottish Tourist Board, London,* 137 Knightsbridge, London SW1X 7PN, England. Tel. (01) 930 8661 or 8662.
- *Scottish Youth Hostels Association,* 7 Glebe Crescent, Stirling FK8 2JA. Tel. (0786) 2821.
- *Shetland Tourist Organisation,* Alexandra Wharf, Lerwick, Shetland. Tel. (0595) 3434.
- *Spey Valley Tourist Organisation,* Aviemore Centre, Aviemore, Inverness-shire. Tel. (047 981) 363.
- *Strathclyde Regional Council,* Department of Leisure and Recreation, McIver House, Cadogan Street, Glasgow G2 7QB. Tel. (041) 204 1881.
- *Sutherland Tourist Organisation,* Masonic Building, Dornoch, Sutherland. Tel. (086 281) 400.

T

- *Tayside Regional Council,* Department of Leisure, Recreation and Tourism, Tayside House, 26-28 Crichton Street, Dundee DDI 3RD. Tel. (9382) 23281.
- *Thomas Nelson & Sons, Ltd.,* 51 York Place, Edinburgh EH16. Tel. (031) 557 3011.
- *Thornhill Press Ltd.,* 46 Westgate Street, Gloucester, England.
- *Tulloch Mountain School,* Railway Cottages, Fersit, Roy Bridge, Inverness-shire.
- *Tweed Valley Hotel Sports Centre,* Galashiels Road, Walkerburn, Peebles-shire. Tel. (089 687) 220.

W

- *Walton, R. D.,* 27 Castle Dougles Road, Dumfries DG1 1NP.
- *Weather Forecasts:* Tel. (031) 246 8091 in Edinburgh or (041) 246 8091 in Glasgow. Or call one of the local Meteorological Offices:
— *Glasgow Weather Centre* (Glasgow, Borders, West of Scotland): Tel. (041) 248 3451.
— *Aberdeen Airport* (Northeast): Tel. Aberdeen 72 23 34.
— *Edinburgh Airport:* Tel. (031) 339 7777.
— *Kinloss, Morayshire* (Moray Firth Area): Tel. Forres 72161, ext. 673 or 674.
— *Leuchars* (Fife): Tel. Leuchars 224.
— *Pitreavie* (Fife): Tel. Inverkeithing 3566.
— *Prestwick Airport* (West and Southwest): Tel. Prestwick 78475.
— *Orkney:* (Kirkwall Airport): Tel. Kirkwall 2421, ext. 34.
— *Shetland:* Tel. Lerwick 2239.

- *West Col Productions,* 1 Meadow Close, Goring-on-Thames, Reading, Berkshire RG8 0AP, England.
- *Wester Ross Tourist Organisation,* Sands Estate, Gairloch, Ross & Cromarty. Tel. (0445) 2139.
- *Western Isles Tourist Organisation,* South Beach Quay, Stornoway, Isle of Lewis. Tel. (0851) 3088.

Y

- *YHA Adventure Holidays,* Department HB, Trevelyan House, St. Albans, Hertfordshire AL1 2DY, England. Tel. St. Albans 55215.

A Quick Reference

In a hurry? Turn to the pages listed below. They will give you the most important information on walking in Scotland.

Search & Rescue, page 277.

Weather Forecasts, page 248.

Associations to Contact for Information:
On Walking & Climbing, page 249.
On Cross-Country Skiing & Ski Mountaineering, page 273.
General Tourist Information, page 276.

Maps, page 254.

Guidebooks, page 255.

Equipment, page 268.

Scotland's Mountain Code, page 243.

Address Directory, page 309.

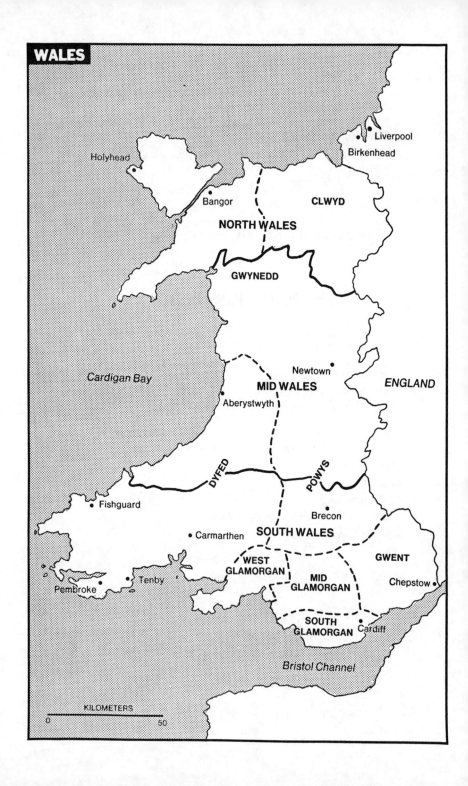

Wales

THE CONTRASTS between England and Wales are many. Across the border, the gentle rhythms of England's lowland landscape are replaced by the craggy, cloud-swept summits of the Welsh highlands. Mountain torrents plunge over high falls into dense forests and flow into natural lakes like Bala—Llyn Tegid to the Welshman—and reservoirs such as Vyrnwy, Nant-y-moch and Clywedog. Below the heights are deep valleys carved out by rivers with stony shallows and quiet pools. And to the north, west and south is the sea, edged by high, rocky cliffs, inlets and mountain-ringed estuaries.

Although both England and Wales share the same national government and are often considered together for administrative purposes (and by unknowing foreigners), Wales is, in many respects, a separate country. The Welsh people have their own distinctive culture and ancient language, the study of which is encouraged in the schools. Practically every bookseller stocks books in Welsh, along with English titles. And, in 1974, the names of most Welsh counties were changed from English to their native names. There are other differences as well—in the architecture of buildings, in the origins of the people and in their mannerisms of speech. The farther north and west you go, the more pronounced the differences become.

But there also are similarities. Every town has its ubiquitous bed-and-breakfast establishments and pubs—where conversations in both English and Welsh can be heard. The same government agencies and, for the most part, the same walking clubs cover England and Wales. The maps for both are published by the Ordnance Survey. Even the signposting and way-marking of footpaths is similar—and just as sporadic.

England's rights-of-way laws (see the chapter on England) also apply to Wales. But because Wales is, for the most part, wilder and less populous, you can walk nearly anywhere in its mountains and moorland above 300 meters (984 feet). Hence, with the aid of an Ordnance Survey map, you can often choose your own routes across the high country. There are also three national parks in which you can walk—Snowdonia, Pembrokeshire Coast and Brecon Beacons—and two long-distance footpaths: Offa's Dyke and the Pembrokeshire Coast Path. In addition, there are numerous local footpaths to explore, a few of which are ancient and little used tracks.

Wales is a small country. Including the Isle of Anglesey, it has an area of only 20,766 square kilometers (8,018 square miles)—less than 16 percent the size of England. Yet it includes Mount Snowdon, the highest peak south of the Scottish border, which rises to 1,085 meters (3,560 feet) in North Wales, and some of Britain's best rock climbing. It also has a varied scenery. You can walk through heath and moor, along beaches and high seacliffs, across lonely mountains and seaside dunes or up valleys with hedges and fields, historic ruins and clear, lusty streams that move past thickly wooded banks. And nowhere are you ever much more than 65 kilometers (40 miles) from the sea.

Flora & Fauna

Prior to the Industrial Revolution much of Wales was forested. In fact, one of Wales' native red squirrels easily could have traveled the 80 kilometers from the Brecon Beacons to the sea by simply hopping from one tree to another. No more. Most of Wales' sessile oaks were chopped down to be burned for charcoal—a sad irony since underneath the charcoal burners was one of the world's richest coal fields. Coal mining also changed the face of the Welsh landscape, and many of the scars—mining camps and coal slag heaps—still remain in parts of the south, while in the north, some areas show the scars of slate-quarrying. Forests are again being planted and, today, nearly 10 percent of Wales is forested—more than twice the percentage for the whole of England. The predominant tree is now Sitka spruce, followed by Lodgepole pine, Japanese larch and Western hemlock. Stands of sessile oaks still can be found but, for the most part, only in North Wales. There are also alders along the river banks and, on limestone soils, ash, birch and beech.

Outside of the coal-mining regions, much of the south is agricultural, devoted to dairying, growing potatoes and stock rearing. In the highlands, which comprise most of Wales, there are large stretches of open moorland and, at higher altitudes, a tundralike vegetation of lichens, mosses and bilberry. Here, the tilling of the soil is left to the lowland dwellers of the Severn and Wye valleys and, in the north, to a few broad valleys where the soils are rich enough to support crops of grain and corn. Millions of sheep roam the heather-clad hills and moorlands. Wales is a country where there are almost three sheep to every person. And most are on the hills of mid-Wales.

The wildlife is similar to that in England. There are gray seals on the coast and, inland, pine martens, red foxes, badgers, weasels and a few otters, as well as non-native red, roe and fallow deer. Wild goats, known locally as Welsh goats, are also seen in the northern sections of Snowdonia.

Birdlife includes thrushes, warblers, finches, swallows, cuckoos, owls, woodpeckers, swifts and sparrows, as well as the chough, a member of the crow family that is peculiar to Wales, and red kites, which exist nowhere else in Britain.

The only dangerous snake is the adder, or viper (recognizable by its "V" markings). The snakes are not numerous, but their bite is serious. Hence, you should watch for them and, if you are bitten, immediately seek medical assistance.

Climate

Wales' climate is influenced by its close proximity to the sea. Temperatures are generally moderate and winds common. The weather is also changeable, and mists can quickly move in and envelop mountaintops.

On an average, temperatures in the lower regions range from about 2.4°C. (36.3°F.) in January to 19.8°C. (67.6°F.) in August, although temperatures as low as *minus* 12.2°C. (10°F.) can occur in January, and the thermometer may reach 32°C. (89.6°F.) on exceptionally warm summer days. But these are lowland averages. In the mountains, temperatures drop by about 1.4°C. (3°F.) for every 300-meter rise in elevation. And the winds and sudden mists can make conditions at high elevations even more severe.

Rainfall on the coast ranges from an annual average of 676.4 mm (26.6 inches) at Rhyl in North Wales to 1,088 mm (42.8 inches) at Tenby on the South Pembrokeshire coast. In some areas, precipitation can be expected during as many as 201 days out of the year.

In the south, the weather gets progressively drier from January to June, then starts to swing back the other way. In mid-Wales, much of the land rises over 300 meters, culminating in mountains reaching more than 600 meters. And as elevation increases, so does rainfall. Winter in the mountains is cold and bitter. During this season the higher ranges are dusted with snow, although not enough to guarantee winter sports. The snow often persists until spring, when the pine needles again burst into an ocean of greens on the forested slopes. On the south and west coasts, however, spring comes early, and the average total hours of sunshine for the year is among the highest in Wales.

In North Wales, there is a wide variation in climate. The western coastal regions benefit from mild westerly winds during the winter, when the nearby mountain peaks are swept by biting-cold winds. Often, the areas east of the mountains, in the County of Clwyd, and on the low-lying coastal strips of Lleyn and the Isle of Anglesey, are basking in the sun when the hills are bathed in showers. Here, the driest months are usually April and May, while late July and August often are wetter than the other summer months.

Despite general trends, however, there is always the possibility of inclement weather in the mountains. When hiking in Wales, you should always be prepared for rain, mists, cold temperatures and strong winds.

Weather Forecasts

Recorded weather forecasts can be obtained by telephone for both North and South Wales. The numbers are:

Weather Forecasts, Cardiff Area: Tel. (0222) 8091.

Weather Forecasts, North Wales Coast: Tel. (0492) 8091.

These weather forecasts are for large areas, and variations in local topography may cause weather conditions to vary considerably from the forecasts—especially in the mountains.

For this reason, it is best to call the Meteorological Office directly. You can then request a 24-hour forecast for the specific locality in which you intend to walk.

If you do this, you should ask for the Officer-in-Charge and tell him:

1. The locality for which you wish a forecast;
2. The purpose for which the forecast is required;
3. The weather features of special interest to you—wind, rain, temperature, the possibility of hill fogs, etc.;
4. The time at which the information is desired; and
5. The telephone number to which the information is to be sent.

The Meteorological Office will then prepare a forecast for you and call back with the information. There is a nominal charge for this service, but you won't be able to get a more accurate forecast.

Even so, remember that weather conditions still can change, so pack your rucksack accordingly.

The telephone numbers of the Meteorological Offices in Wales are:

North Wales (Anglesey): Tel. (0407) 2288.

Mid-Wales (Aberporth): Tel. (0239) 810117.

South Wales: Swansea (summer only): Tel. (0792) 8011. Gloucester (all year): Tel. Churchdown (0452) 855566.

This service is only available during normal office hours, Monday through Friday.

Where to Get Walking Information

One of the best sources of information on walking in Wales is a booklet published annually by the Wales Tourist Board: *Wales Walking*.

The booklet gives details on more than 560 possible walks in Wales. Nearly 200 of these are on forest paths, nature trails and historic paths. These walks are either waymarked or described in guidebooks and, hence, are relatively easy to follow. For each, the booklet tells you: 1) the location of the path; 2) its starting place, length and walking time; 3) how you can get there on public transport; 4) what equipment is needed; 5) the walking ability that is required; 6) if there are any restrictions that apply to the path; and 7) the titles of publications that describe the walk's route, as well as their price and where they can be obtained. Details are also given on guided walks.

Another section briefly describes more than 300 unwaymarked routes that have been recommended by the members of the Ramblers' Association.

The walks are organized into chapters by Ordnance Survey sheet numbers. As a result, you can buy the booklet, an Ordnance Survey map and then base yourself in a convenient bed-and-breakfast establishment from which you can take day rambles. Once you have explored that area to your satisfaction, you can then turn the page to another chapter, buy another Ordnance Survey map and move onto another area.

In addition to the walking descriptions, the booklet tells you where you can obtain nature-trail leaflets and gives the addresses of holiday associations, youth hostel associations and organizations that offer courses in rock and ice climbing, hill walking, canoeing and mountain rescue. There is also a list of the addresses and telephone numbers of the tourist information offices in Wales and a generous supply of illustrations—sketch maps of the walks, drawings of the Welsh plant and animal life, and elevation charts of the areas in Wales above 300 meters where you can expect to roam at will.

The booklet can be obtained for a nominal charge from:

Wales Tourist Board (Bwrdd Croeso Cymru). For its address and telephone number, see the *Address Directory* at the back of this chapter.

Four other organizations can also provide information on various aspects of walking in Wales:

The Ramblers' Association (see *Address Directory*). Can provide general information on walking in Wales. The RA also has local Areas and Groups in Wales that can answer specific questions for you. Two of its publications are especially useful in helping you plan walks in Wales:

- *County Sheet—North Wales* and *County Sheet—South Wales.* This lists all the path guides to Wales known to the RA. Prices are given, as are the charges for postage within Britain and the addresses of publishers. The County Sheets also provide information on guided walks and excursions in Wales and list the names and addresses of RA Area secretaries. The County Sheets are available for a nominal charge.
- *Bed, Breakfast and Bus Guide.* This gives details for all of Britain on lodgings where ramblers are welcomed.
- The RA also sells *Wales Walking.*

For further information on the Ramblers' Association, see the section on *Walking Clubs in England* in the chapter on England.

Countryside Commission (see *Address Directory*). Can provide general information on the long-distance footpaths, national parks and Areas of Outstanding Natural Beauty in Wales.

Offa's Dyke Association (see *Address Directory*). This voluntary association exists to promote and protect the Offa's Dyke long-distance footpath. The association sells guidebooks and strip maps to the path, leaflets to the ancient monuments along Offa's Dyke, plus an accommodation list with public transport information. These publications, as well as other items available from the association, are listed in:

- *Offa's Dyke Association Publications.* Free, but please send a self-addressed envelope and one international postal reply coupon to cover postage.

Because the Offa's Dyke Association is a voluntary body that depends entirely upon the subscriptions of its members for existence, it is unable to maintain an information service for non-members. If you still have questions on the path once you have obtained the publications available from the association, either write to the Countryside Commission or send in a membership subscription to the Offa's Dyke Association with the questions you wish to have answered. Members receive newsletters, up-to-date "state of the path" information, and guidebooks and strip maps at reduced prices.

Backpackers' Club (see *Address Directory*). Can provide information on the routes in Wales where you can backpack and camp along the trails. Also will give help on compiling itineraries. Please enclose a self-addressed envelope and international postal reply coupon to cover postage.

Finally, many of the local tourist information offices and national park centers are good about providing information on walking in their areas. It is best, however, to visit the park centers in person. They do not believe in encouraging more people than necessary to come to the parks and, hence, are poor about providing information by mail. But once you are on the premises, the park staffs will willingly answer questions and can provide numerous free or inexpensive brochures.

Walking Clubs in Wales

As with the rest of Britain, there are numerous local rambling clubs and footpath societies in Wales. For the most part, however, the same national organizations cover both England and Wales. For information on these organizations, see the section on *Walking Clubs in England* in the chapter on England.

Maps

Walkers have the choice of four map series published by the Ordnance Survey:

1:25,000—First Series

1:25,000—Second Series

Outdoor Leisure Maps based on the First Series 1:25,000: Brecon Beacons (three sheets—East, Central and West), Snowdon, Conwy Valley, Bala, Harlech and Cader Idris-Dovey Forest.

1:50,000 Maps: For details on these maps, see the section on *Maps* in the chapter on England.

A list of retailers, a catalog with a map index and a price list are available from:

Ordnance Survey (see *Address Directory*).

The Ordnance Survey does not sell maps, but they can be purchased nearly everywhere in Wales—from local tourist boards, from the Offa's Dyke Association (for the Offa's Dyke Path only) and from many booksellers, including W.H. Smith & Son and Menzies. By mail, the maps can be purchased from:

Cook, Hammond & Kell, Ltd. (see *Address Directory*).

Guidebooks

In addition to *Wales Walking*, there are several guides that give details on walks throughout Wales. These include:

- *National Trust: Nature Walks,* available from the National Trust.
- *Nabod Cymru* (Knowing Wales) by Cledwyn Fychan, available from Y Lolfa. Written in Welsh.
- *Welsh Walks and Legends: North* and *Welsh Walks and Legends: South,* both by Showell Styles, John Jones Cardiff Ltd.
- *The Drovers' Roads of Wales* by Fay Godwin and Shirley Toulson, Wildwood House Ltd.

For the addresses of publishers, see the *Address Directory*.

Numerous guidebooks are also available to walks in the various regions of Wales, as well as to its long-distance footpaths and national parks. These are listed in the sections of this chapter that deal with each region. They are also included in the RA's *County Sheet—Wales* (see the section on *Where to Get Walking Information*).

In addition to the guidebooks to walks, numerous publications on the archeology, botany, geology and zoology of Wales are available from the National Museum of Wales. A publications list with their titles, prices and a short description of each is available on request from:

> **National Museum of Wales** (Amgueddfa Genedlaethol Cymru), Bookshop Manager (see *Address Directory*).

Trailside Lodgings

Lodgings can be found in youth hostels, bed-and-breakfast establishments, hotels and, occasionally, in farmhouses. For the most part, these lodgings are located in or near towns, which can be a long day's walk apart in some parts of the high country. Unless you intend to camp (see the next section), an accommodation guide is a must. It also is advisable to call ahead each morning to book a room for the night. Then, when you arrive, you will be assured of a place to stay. If you are unable to make it, however, be sure to let the person you booked with know. Three accommodation guides are available:

- *Bed, Breakfast and Bus Guide.* Published by the Ramblers' Association (see *Address Directory*). This lists reasonably priced lodgings that cater to walkers. Bus-schedule information also is included in the guide. The guide is free to members. Non-members may purchase it from the RA for a nominal charge.

- *YHA Handbook.* This lists the youth hostels in England and Wales where walkers of all ages are welcome. The Youth Hostels Association also publishes a map that shows the locations of its hostels. Both are available for a nominal charge from the Youth Hostels Association, England, as well as from the regional YHA offices for Wales:

YHA, North Wales and:
YHA, South Wales (see *Address Directory*).

- *Where to Stay in Wales.* Published by the Wales Tourist Board (see *Address Directory*). Lists hotels, motels, inns, guesthouses and farmhouse accommodation throughout Wales. Also gives information on furnished flats and mountain cottages that can be rented for a week or more, camping and caravanning sites, and organizations that offer accommodation in conjunction with tours and courses in rock and ice climbing, hill walking and canoeing. The booklet's introduction is translated into French and German, as is the key to symbols used to describe the facilities available from each accommodation.

Mountain Huts

Mountaineering and climbing clubs affiliated with the British Mountaineering Council maintain about 30 mountain huts, primarily in North Wales. The huts vary widely in size and amenities and are open only to members of the British Mountaineering Council and Mountaineering Club of Scotland. Members who use the huts should bring their own food and a sheet sleeping bag or, for those huts without blankets, a down sleeping bag. They also must book in advance—in one case, even as much as six months in advance. Details on the huts—and on membership in the BMC—are available from:

British Mountaineering Council (see *Address Directory*).

Camping

Because Wales is a small country and its open spaces are limited—and, in a few cases, such as in its national parks, heavily used—open camping is generally discouraged. Even so, with permission you can camp just about anywhere. All that is asked is that you use discretion—build no fires, safeguard all water supplies, dispose properly of all wastes, carry out all litter and leave your campsite so that no one can ever tell you were there.

In the high country it is sometimes difficult to determine who owns the land. But if you know approximately where you intend to camp for the night, a person in one of the towns you pass through often can tell you whom to ask for permission. On Forestry Commission land, permission to camp should be obtained from the forester.

A list of commercial campsites is included in *Where to Stay in Wales* (see above). The Camping Club of Great Britain and Ireland also publishes an extremely good camping list. In addition, members of the club benefit from reductions at many sites. The camping list and details on membership can be obtained from:

Camping Club of Great Britain and Ireland (see *Address Directory*).

Water

Water can be obtained from pubs, farmers and houses along your route. In the high country, some streams are perfectly safe. But many others pass through areas where sheep graze. The best rule is, if you drink from a stream, boil the water first.

Equipment Notes

When you hike in Wales you have to be prepared for changeable conditions—rain, winds, mists and sudden drops in temperature. Dry, warm clothing, rain and wind gear, a wool cap and mittens, and good boots are essential. A pair of stop-ems—short gaiters—is also advisable to help keep your feet dry.

Crowded Trails

The most heavily used paths in Wales are those that climb to the top of Snowdon. As a result, the paths have become rutted and have spread out until they resemble roads more than mountain tracks. If you don't mind crowds and must climb the mountain, at least stay on the paths (or take the train to the top). To avoid the congestion entirely, climb one of the other peaks in the park.

During the summer months, all the parks in Wales tend to be crowded. It is better to hike in the parks during May or early June. Not only will there be fewer people, but the weather is traditionally much clearer. During the summer, some of the best hiking is in the high country of mid-Wales. The countryside there is open and remote, and you often can walk for a day or two without seeing another person. When you do, it is more likely to be a shepherd than another hiker.

Walking & Climbing Tours

Numerous organizations offer walking and climbing tours in Wales. Some of the arrangements available include:

Week-long Walking & Climbing Tours

See *Address Directory*:

The Christian Mountain Center. Located in Snowdonia. Offers seven-day holidays and courses in mountaineering, walking, canoeing and mountain leadership. All equipment is supplied, with the exception of boots. Has accommodation for 30 people plus two leaders.

The Country-Wide Holidays Association. Offers walking and rock-climbing holidays with experienced leaders from its guesthouses at Barmouth, above Cardigan Bay and the Mawddach Estuary in Snowdonia; Llanfairfechan, on the southern slopes of Penmaenmawr mountain in Snowdonia; Lampeter, in the Teifi Valley beneath the hills of the Cambrian range in mid-Wales, and at Bangor, on the edge of Snowdonia National Park. Special holiday arrangements for young people are also available.

Holiday Fellowship Ltd. Offers walking and climbing tours with experienced leaders from holiday centers at Conwy, on the northern edge of Snowdonia; Llandudno, on the North Wales coast; Glasbury, in the Brecon Beacons; Tywyn, on the west coast of mid-Wales; Snowdon, at the base of Mount Snowdon; Maentwrog, also in Snowdonia; and at Llandogo, in the Wye Valley of mid-Wales. Special holiday arrangements for young people are also available.

Jesse James Bunkhouse. Located at the base of Mount Snowdon. Activities include rock climbing, hill walking, canoeing and pony trekking. Accommodation is in a bunkhouse, an annex, a flat and a house. Equipment is provided.

Penyrheol Adventure Centre. Address enquiries to: Minerva Outdoor Ventures. Located on the edge of the Brecon Beacons National Park in South Wales. Offers multi-activity holidays for hill walking, caving, rock climbing, orienteering, field studies and mountain craft. Specializes in holidays for young people between the ages of 9 and 18. Accommodation is in farmhouses and tents. All specialized equipment is provided.

Pentwyn Adventure Centre. Located on the northern edge of the Brecon Beacons in South Wales. Offers six-day multi-activity holidays for hill walking, caving, climbing, canoeing and sailing. Caters to people between the ages of 9 and 30. Accommodation is in tents.

YHA Adventure Holidays. The YHA organizes several walking tours in the Wye Valley and Snowdonia each summer. Details are given in its free brochure, *YHA Adventure Holidays.*

Weekend Excursions

Numerous weekend hikes are organized by the Ramblers' Association in various areas of Wales. General details on these walks are included in the RA's *County Sheet—Wales.*

Day-long Guided Walks

Penmaenmawr. Organized mountain walks into Snowdonia are arranged by the town's Publicity Association each July and August. Details on the walks are displayed on a notice board at Pant-yr-afon, Penmaenmawr.

Snowdon guided walks. Details on these walks up to the top of Mount Snowdon are available on request from Snowdonia National Park (see *Address Directory*).

Brecon Beacons National Park. A program of guided walks, devised by the park authority in conjunction with the Ramblers' Association, is available from the Brecon Beacons Park Information Centers (see *Address Directory*). The walks are available from the first week of June to the first week of October.

The National Museum of Wales also organizes guided walks in various parts of Wales. Details are available from:

National Museum of Wales, Information Officer (see *Address Directory*).

Forest Walks. From late June to the end of August, the Forestry Commission provides guided walks from the car parks at Garwnant (pronounced *Garroo-nant*) and Blaen-y-Glyn in the Brecon Beacons. Details can be obtained from the Forestry Commission, Talybont-on-Usk, and from its office in Brecon (see *Address Directory*).

Gwent. The Gwent County Council Countryside Warden Service operates an extensive program of guided walks in the Wye and Usk valleys from April to October. Most of the walks are on Saturdays and Sundays, and occasionally on weekdays during the summer. Details can be obtained from the Gwent County Council (see *Address Directory*). Ask for the *Guided Walks Programme*.

Pembrokeshire Coast National Park. The park authority arranges each year a program of summer guided walks in various sections of the park. Most of the walks begin at the car park in Broad Haven, near Haverfordwest. Details are publicized locally. They can also be obtained by writing the Pembrokeshire Coast National Park Information Service (see *Address Directory*).

Mountain Guides

Several mountain guides are based in North Wales. On rock climbs, they will take a maximum of three people. Ropes are provided by the guide, as is any necessary hardware, but the client must bring the rest of his equipment, including an anorak, vibram sole boots and, where necessary, a climbing belt, helmet, ice axe and crampons.

Arrangements are made directly with the guide. Also, you must book in advance. Fees are reasonable, but the number of guides is limited, so the earlier you book the better.

A list of mountain guides, with their addresses and a list of recommended minimum fees, can be obtained by sending a self-addressed envelope and international postal reply coupon to:

Association of British Mountain Guides (see *Address Directory*).

Information on climbing in North Wales can also be obtained from the personnel in the Joe Brown Mountaineering Shop in Llanberis (at the base of Snowdon). Or you can talk to Christopher Briggs, who runs the Penygwryd Hotel at the top of Llanberis Pass. Briggs is the local organizer for the mountain rescue squad. The hotel is also worth visiting. It is where the first Everest expedition based itself while training on Snowdon. In its pub, the ceiling is signed by the members of the expedition and the survivors still meet on special occasions for reunions.

Mountaineering Courses

Courses in basic and advanced rock climbing, mountaineering, hill walking, skiing and mountain rescue are offered by more than 20 organizations in Wales. Most of the courses are based in North Wales, but there also are six organizations that offer courses in mid- and South Wales.

A list of these organizations, entitled *Mountaineering Courses in Britain* and *Abroad,* is available from the British Mountaineering Council if you send a self-addressed envelope and international postal reply coupon.

The list gives the address of each organization, a brief description of the courses available, their duration and the age groups accepted. The list is designed to help you choose the right course, not to answer all your questions. For full details, you must write the organizations.

Two centers worth mentioning are:

The Christian Mountain Centre (see *Address Directory*). Located on the western edge of Snowdonia. Offers courses in mountain safety, map and compass navigation, rock climbing and, in winter, snow and ice climbing.

Plas-y-Brenin National Mountaineering Centre (see *Address Directory*). Located in Snowdonia National Park. A wide range of courses are offered—basic, advanced and instructors' courses in rock climbing; rock, snow and ice courses; a one-month mountaineering course; training in mountain leading and mountain rescue; family courses; mountain photography and mountain weather. A booklet describing the center and its courses is available from the center, as well as from the Sports Council.

Train & Bus Fares

A series of leaflets published by the Gwynedd County Council is of great help to the walker in Snowdonia National Park who is depending upon public transport to get around:

• *Bus to a Walk, or Walk to a Bus.* Four leaflets, covering: 1) *The Moelwyn,* 2) *Y Glyder,* 3) *Yr Arenig,* and 4) *Cader Idris.*

The pamphlets highlight bus services that are convenient for traveling to the starting points of various walks and indicate return bus services from where the walks finish. Brief details are also given on each walk. The pamphlets can be obtained from the National Park information offices and Wales Tourist Board information offices, as well as from:

Snowdonia National Park Information Service (see *Address Directory*).

The pamphlets are free, but if you request them by mail, please enclose a self-addressed envelope and sufficient international postal reply coupons to cover postage.

For details on special train and bus fares, see the section on *Special Train & Bus Fares* in the chapter on England.

Useful Addresses
& Telephone Numbers

General Tourist Information

In Wales:

Wales Tourist Board (Bwrdd Croeso Cymru). See *Address Directory*. Publishes a useful series of booklets on Wales with descriptions of each town and information on geology, climate, local traditions and architecture, legends and various activities. Each booklet also provides details on several short walks and gives information on forest and nature trails, spelunking and the activities available at various mountain centers. A nicely done series. There is a nominal charge for the booklets:

- *Mid Wales*
- *North Wales*
- *South Wales*

Other publications available from the office include *Wales Walking, Where to Stay in Wales, Wales—A Glimpse of the Past* (a tourists' guide to industrial trails, mines and mills), *Castles and Historic Places in Wales, Disabled Visitors' Guide, Crafts and Rural Industries, Museums and Art Galleries* and *Wales Tourist Map.*

Abroad

Enquiries about Wales are handled by the branch offices of the British Tourist Authority (for a list of the cities in which they are located, see the section on *Useful Addresses & Telephone Numbers* in the chapter on England).

Sport Shops

Among the shops in Wales that cater to backpackers, climbers and walkers are:

See *Address Directory*:
Ellis Brigham. Located in Capel Curig.
Joe Brown Mountaineering Shop. Located in Llanberis.
Comax (Leisure) Ltd. Located in Swansea.

Mountway Marine and Trek. Located in Abergavenney on the edge of the Brecon Beacons.

Outdoor Action. Located in Cathays.

YHA Services Ltd. Located in Cardiff.

Search & Rescue

In an emergency: Go to the nearest rescue post or telephone—whichever is quickest. **Tel. 999.** Ask for the police.

Before you go walking in Wales, you should obtain a copy of:

- *Mountain and Cave Rescue,* The Handbook of the Mountain Rescue Committee, Herald Press, Arbroath, Angus, England.

This lists the official rescue teams and posts throughout Britain, gives their locations, grid reference numbers and the names, addresses and telephone numbers of their supervisors. The booklet is the most complete, up-to-date listing of rescue posts available. Nonetheless, the location of a post is sometimes changed and should be verified locally. Cost of the booklet is 40p, plus postage (although it may have gone up and should be confirmed prior to ordering). It can be obtained from:

Mountain Rescue Committee (see *Address Directory*).

In Britain, the police forces are the main coordinators of the search and rescue effort. Unless it is quicker to get to a manned Mountain Rescue Post, all calls for help must go to the police. They will then call out the rescue teams and public services needed. There is no charge for this service. You will see donation boxes in many sport shops for the mountain rescue squads, to which you are encouraged to contribute. The donations, however, are for equipment. The squads are entirely voluntary.

Long-Distance Footpaths in Wales

There are two official long-distance footpaths in Wales—Offa's Dyke Path and the Pembrokeshire Coast Path. Both are waymarked with a symbol of an acorn and are maintained by local authorities with funds provided by the Countryside Commission.

Offa's Dyke Path

Traverses the length of Wales from Chepstow on the Severn Estuary to Prestatyn on the North Wales Coast. Closely follows 130 kilometers (81 miles) of the earthwork constructed between 750 and 800 A.D. by Offa, King of Mercia, to mark his boundary with Wales. Passes over the border hills and the eastern ridge of the Black Mountains, across the lonely, trenched moorland of Clun Forest and above the river valleys of the Dee and the thickly wooded Wye. Several medieval castles and market towns are along the route. The dyke itself is a simple earthwork consisting of a long mound of earth with a ditch, normally on the west side, from which the earth had been taken. **Length:** 270 kilometers (168 miles). **Walking Time:** 12 to 14 days.

Lodgings: Many available. An accommodation list, *Where to Stay: Offa's Dyke Path,* is available for a nominal charge from the Offa's Dyke Association (see *Address Directory*). The list also includes transport information.

Special Notes: Although parts of the path are generally easy to walk, there are some difficult sections. The two high sections over the Black Mountains and Clwydian Hills, for instance, can be treacherous in bad weather. Clothing should be suitable for muddy ways and rough hill walking. The route is fully signposted and waymarked, but over the occasional stretches of mountain and moorland the use of a compass is essential.

Maps:
- Ordnance Survey 1:50,000, sheets 116, 117, 127, 137, 148, 161 and 162.
- Ordnance Survey 1:25,000, sheets SJ-O6/16, SJ-07/17, SJ-08/18, SJ-15, SJ-20, SJ-21, SJ-22, SJ-23, SJ-24, SJ-25, SO-22, SO-23, SO-24, SO-25, SO-26, SO-27, SO-28, SO-29, SO-31, SO-32, SO-41, SO-50, SO-51 and SO-59.
- Outdoor Leisure Maps 1:25,000 (in lieu of sheets SO-22 and SO-23 and sheets SO-50, SO-51 and SO-59 above): *Brecon Beacons National Park* and *Wye Valley and Forest of Dean.* Alternatively, you can buy a set of strip maps in a scale of 1:63,360 and 1:25,000 from the Offa's Dyke Association.

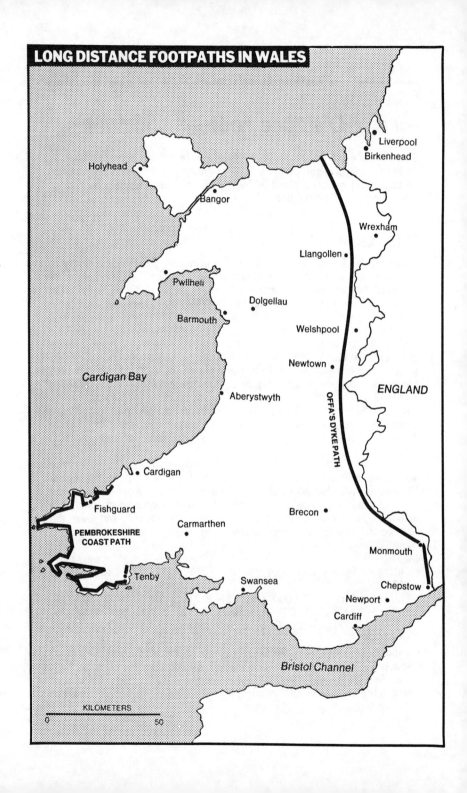

LONG DISTANCE FOOTPATHS IN WALES

Liverpool
Birkenhead
Holyhead
Bangor
Wrexham
Llangollen
Pwllheli
Dolgellau
Barmouth
Welshpool
Newtown
Cardigan Bay
OFFA'S DYKE PATH
ENGLAND
Aberystwyth
Cardigan
Fishguard
PEMBROKESHIRE
COAST PATH
Carmarthen
Brecon
Monmouth
Tenby
Swansea
Chepstow
Newport
Cardiff
Bristol Channel
KILOMETERS
0   50

Guidebooks:
Available from the Offa's Dyke Association:
• *A Guide to Offa's Dyke Path* by Christopher J. Wright, Constable & Company. (Recommended)
• *Through Welsh Border Country following Offa's Dyke Path* by Mark Richards, Thornhill Press.
• *The Offa's Dyke Path* by Arthur Roberts, The Ramblers' Association.
• *The ODA Book of Offa's Dyke Path* by Frank Noble, Offa's Dyke Association.
• *"Official" Guide Book to Offa's Dyke Path* by John B. Jones, Countryside Commission.

Pembrokeshire Coast Path

From Amroth to St. Dogmaels along the remote coastline of southwest Wales—an area of steep cliffs, secluded bays with sandy coves and rockbound islands that resound with the cries of seabirds. The seabirds are among the most numerous and diverse anywhere in Britain and include shearwaters, gannets, fulmars, guillemots, razorbills, puffins and kittiwakes. **Length:** 269 kilometers (167 miles). **Walking Time:** 12 to 14 days.
Lodgings: Plentiful. During summer, however, it is advisable to book ahead since lodgings often fill to capacity. There also are many campsites and nearby places where you can obtain water.
Special Notes: The path is extensively signposted and waymarked. The walking is generally easy, although there are some strenuous sections, particularly where there are climbs from coves to clifftops. The army occasionally uses a part of the Castlemartin Ranges, south of Pembroke, for artillery practice. When the army is firing, sections of the path in this area may be closed and red flags will be flown. Information on the dates and times of firing can be obtained from the park information offices (see *Address Directory*) and local post offices. With the exception of foulweather gear, no specialized equipment is required, although precautions should be taken against sunburn.
Maps:
• Ordnance Survey 1:50,000, sheets 145, 157 and 158.
• Ordnance Survey 1:25,000, sheets SM-70, SM-72, SM-80, SM-81, SM-82, SM-83, SM-90, SM-93, SN-01/10, SN-03, SN-04, SN-14, SS-09, SS-19 and SS-99.
Guidebooks:
• *The Pembrokeshire Coast Path* by John Barrett, HMSO. (Recommended)
• *Walking the Pembrokeshire Coast Path* by and available from Patrick Stark (see *Address Directory*).

In addition to the official long-distance footpaths, Wales has several "unofficial" long-distance walking routes devised by individuals and local walking organizations. One of the best-known of these is the Cambrian

Way, a high-level mountain path stretching the length of Wales from Conwy to Cardiff. Arguments for and against this path have rumbled on for more than 10 years and, although the idea is accepted in principle by the Countryside Commission, official designation of the route as a long-distance path is no nearer. Should it ever receive designation, it will be one of the most challenging and scenic long-distance paths in Britain, since it traverses the highest and wildest parts of Wales. But the last word on the Cambrian Way remains to be written. Opposition against the path is strong and well-organized.

Those who wish to try walking the Cambrian Way are very much on their own. No published guidebook exists to the path, most sections are unmarked and parts of the route pass through rugged countryside which presents a challenge to strong walkers even in good weather. In bad weather several sections of the path are exceedingly difficult and dangerous.

Currently, about 56 percent of the path either follows public rights-of-way or crosses land to which the public has a right of access. Another 41 percent of the route crosses rural commons or lies above 300 meters; to most of this land the public has traditionally enjoyed de facto access. Three percent of the path's proposed route, however, crosses areas to which no rights-of-way or access agreements exist. Farmers in these areas are generally friendly, providing you respect their boundary walls and fences, do not have a dog with you and ask permission before crossing their property. Nonetheless, the farmers' unions in Wales have vociferously opposed the Cambrian Way and have used their strong lobby to block it. Consequently, it is imperative that you respect property rights and be prepared for an occasional refusal of access along the route.

Cambrian Way

A coast-to-coast walk along the skyline of Wales, from Cardiff to Conwy. Follows the Taff Valley out of Cardiff, passing the castle of Castell Coch and looping through the Black Mountains along the Bal Mawr and the Pen Allt Mawr ridges. The route then dips south to the Brecon Beacons, passing above Llangattock, over Torpantau Pass and climbing the ridge leading to 886-meter (2,906-foot) Pen y Fan. From the Brecon Beacons, the route across the moors of Forest Fawr, near Fan Gihirych, is not common land and no rights of access exist; however, it is possible to detour to the south through a region of whitefoam rivers, caves and wooded valleys around Ystradfellte, then walk on a moorland path to Glyntawe and the Carmarthen Vans. From Llandovery, the route heads north into the Towy Valley, passing through the forest wilderness of Elenith, the Strata Florida Abbey ruins and the gorge at Devil's Bridge, then across the wild moors surrounding Plynlimon, source of the rivers Severn and Wye. Next comes rolling hill country north of the village of Dylife and the almost alpine scenery of Dinas Mawddwy in Snowdonia

National Park. Opinions differ on the best route for the path—and, for that matter, whether there should even be a waymarked path—in Snowdonia. One possibility is a tough, demanding mountain-top walk over Maesglasau and Mynydd Cieswyn to the craggy Cader Idris, then north along the sawtooth ridge of the Rhinogs, followed by the crests of the Moelwyns, Cnicht, Snowdon, the Glyders and Carnedds—a spectacular route to be sure, but one which involves some scrambling and can be extremely treacherous in foul weather, especially for anyone carrying a heavy pack. Another possibility is over Arenig Fawr pass, across the moor of Migneint, then via Nant Gwynant, Pen y Gwrd and Ogwen to the foothills on the east side of Carneddau, a much less strenuous route preferred by the Snowdonia National Park Authority. By looking at the Ordnance Survey maps listed below you can also work out other possible routes. **Length:** approximately 420 kilometers (260 miles). **Walking Time:** 20 to 24 days. **Path Markings:** Some of the existing paths which the route follows are waymarked; much of the route, however, crosses untracked terrain. Skill in mountain navigation is essential.

Lodgings: Available in most towns and villages near the route. On some sections, however, you must be prepared to camp.

Warning: The proposed route follows one of the trickiest mountain ridges to be found in North Wales—from Bwlch Tyddiad to Moel Ysgyfarnogod in the Rhinogs—which is susceptible to rapid weather changes and is extremely difficult to navigate even in a light mist. Other sections of the route can also be hazardous. Consequently, the route should be attempted only by strong mountain walkers who are well-equipped, prepared for rough (and sometimes very taxing) hill walking in foul weather, and are able to navigate across untracked terrain with a map and compass in adverse conditions. If you do not have this experience, walk one of the other paths in Wales.

Maps:
- Ordnance Survey 1:50,000, sheets 115, 116, 124, 135, 136, 147, 160, 161 and 171. Also:
- Ordnance Survey Outdoor Leisure Maps 1:25,000, *Brecon Beacons: East; Brecon Beacons: Central; Brecon Beacons: West; Snowdon;* and *Conwy Valley.*

Guidebook:
- *Cambrian Way Interim Report* by A.J. Drake (see *Address Directory*).

Two other possible long-distance walks are the Bay to Bay Walk, which stretches 206 kilometers (128 miles) from Liverpool to Barmouth over the Clwyd Range, Llantisilio Mountain, Berwyns, Arans and Cader Idris; and the 82-kilometer (51-mile) Lleyn Coast Walk from Pwllheli to Nanhoron around the Lleyn peninsula in North Wales. The 1:50,000 Ordnance Survey maps covering the Bay to Bay Walk are sheets 108, 116, 117, 124 and 125. Those covering the Lleyn Peninsula Walk are sheets 115 and 123. Both routes are described in *Backpacking in Wales* by Showell Styles, John Jones Cardiff Ltd.

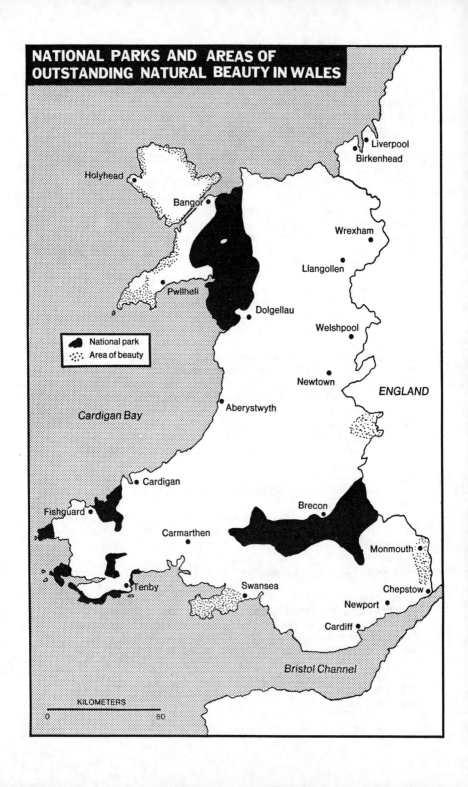

NATIONAL PARKS AND AREAS OF OUTSTANDING NATURAL BEAUTY IN WALES

Liverpool

Birkenhead

Holyhead

Bangor

Wrexham

Llangollen

Pwllheli

Dolgellau

Welshpool

National park
Area of beauty

Newtown

ENGLAND

Cardigan Bay

Aberystwyth

Cardigan

Brecon

Fishguard

Carmarthen

Monmouth

Tenby

Swansea

Chepstow

Newport

Cardiff

Bristol Channel

KILOMETERS

0   50

National Parks in Wales

There are three national parks in Wales. If you intend to walk in one of these parks, you should read the information about public rights-of-way, ownership and the locations of rescue posts at the beginning of the section on *England's National Parks* in the chapter on England. The comments also apply to the parks in Wales.

The Parks

Brecon Beacons

The Brecon Beacons—or, in Welsh, *Parc Cenedlaethol Bannau Brycheiniog*—lies in South Wales. At its heart is a range of red sandstone mountains, deeply cut by the broad, fertile valley of the Usk, that rises to a height of 886 meters (2,907 feet). The park also includes the Black Mountains in the east and a peak known as Black Mountain in the west, beyond the Fforest Fawr (once a royal hunting ground). To the south are rolling hills of carboniferous limestone and millstone grit, with many waterfalls and the most extensive cave system in Britain. Along the flat-topped mountains, it is possible to walk for hours without descending below 600 meters. There are also 52 kilometers (32 miles) of towpaths along the Brecon Canal for less strenuous walks. In addition, there are three nature reserves and numerous archeological sites.

Area: 1,344 square kilometers (519 square miles).

Towns with Park Information Centers (open from Easter until October): See *Address Directory.*

Written Enquiries: Brecon Beacons National Park (see *Address Directory*). Please enclose a *large* self-addressed envelope and at least two international postal reply coupons.

Special Notes: Walks in the park range from easy to difficult. On the heights, weather changes can be sudden and should be taken into account.

Lodgings: All types of accommodation are available. There are also several recognized campsites. Camping elsewhere—including unfenced moorland—requires the owner's permission. Details on lodgings and campsites are included in *Where to Stay in Wales* (see the section on *Trail Lodgings* earlier in this chapter). Information also can be obtained from park information centers in Abergavenny and in Brecon, both of which are open from Easter until the end of September.

Maps:
• Ordnance Survey 1:50,000, sheets 159, 160 and 161.
• Outdoor Leisure Maps 1:25,000, three sheets: 1) *Brecon Beacons: East,* 2) *Brecon Beacons: Central,* and 3) *Brecon Beacons: West.*

Guidebooks:
Available from the Brecon Beacons National Park Office:
• *Some short walks around Brecon,* Information Sheet No. 24. Describes eight walks.
• *Walking in the Beacons,* Information Sheet No. 25. Describes 10 walks.
• *Thirty Walks in the Abergavenny Area.*
• *Ystradfellte Area,* a sketch map with footpaths indicated.
• *Nature Trail: St. Mary's Vale, Abergavenny,* 3.2 kilometers (2 miles) in length.

Other Guidebooks:
• *Brecon Beacons National Park,* Margaret Davies, editor, HMSO. A general guide to the park. Does not include path descriptions.
• *Exploring the Waterfall Country* and *Walks in the Brecon Beacons,* both by Chris Barber, Pridgeon Publishing Ltd.
• *Walks and Rides in the Brecon Beacons* by H.D. Westacott, Footpath Publications.
• *The Welsh Peaks* by W.A. Poucher, Constable & Company.

Pembrokeshire Coast

This is the smallest of Britain's parks. Along the coast there are rock cliffs, bays and sandy coves. In the north is Mynydd Preseli—the Presely Hills—a small tract of moorland with numerous prehistoric remains. The park also includes numerous medieval castles, the reaches of the Milford Haven waterway and the ancient walled town of Tenby.

Area: 583 square kilometers (225 square miles).

Towns with Park Information Centers (open from Easter to October): See *Address Directory.*

Written Enquiries: Pembrokeshire Coast National Park Information Service (see *Address Directory*).

Special Notes: See the *Special Notes* for the Pembrokeshire Coast Path in the section on *Long-Distance Footpaths in Wales.*

Lodgings: Accommodation lists can be obtained from the park information centers at Fishguard, Kilgetty and St. David's. The other centers do not have accommodation services. Advance booking is necessary during summer.

Maps:
• Ordnance Survey 1:50,000, sheets 145, 157 and 158.
• Ordnance Survey 1:25,000, sheets SM-62, SM-70, SM-72, SM-80, SM-81, SM-82, SM-83, SM-90, SM-91, SM-92, SM-93, SN-00/10, SN-01/11, SN-02, SN-03, SN-04, SN-12, SN-13, SN-14, SR-89, SR-99, SS-09 and SS-19.

Guidebooks:
Available from the Pembrokeshire Coast National Park Information Service:
• *Presely Hills,* a free leaflet with a rights-of-way map.
• *Plain Man's Guide to the Path round the Dale Peninsula* by J.H. Barrett.
• *Nature Trails:* 1) *Dinas Island,* 2) *Marloes Sands,* 3) *Penally,* 4) *Slebech Forest,* 5) *Lydstep Headland,* and 6) *Skomer Island.*
Other Guidebooks:
• *Pembrokeshire Coast National Park,* Dillwyn Miles editor, HMSO. A general guide to the park. Does not include path descriptions.
• *Rambles around Tenby,* available from the South Pembrokeshire District Council.
• Also, see the guidebooks listed for the Pembrokeshire Coast Path in the section on *Long-Distance Footpaths in Wales.*

Snowdonia

Snowdonia encompasses some of the wildest country in Britain—and some of its highest peaks. Snowdon itself is the highest peak south of the Scottish Highlands and is surrounded by passes, gorges and numerous lakes. Above the Lleyn Peninsula are the peaks of Yr Eifl, and above Llyn Tegid—Bala Lake—remote moorlands stretch up to the tops of the Arans and Arenig. There are also many wooded valleys and several nature reserves, including the Cwm Idwal National Nature Reserve, which encompasses 398 hectares (984 acres) of ice-age flowers, some very rare. Less beautiful are the park's slate quarries—some of which are open and provide good rock-climbing practice, others of which have been turned into reservoirs. Paths are numerous, from the ancient causeways of the Romans to the tracks made by hill farmers, quarrymen and lead miners. Some lead up steep hillsides to high peaks, others to still, seldom seen lakes in remote valleys.
Area: 2,189 square kilometers (845 square miles).
Towns with Park Information Centers (open from Easter to October): See *Address Directory.*
Written Enquiries: Snowdonia National Park Information Services (see *Address Directory*).
Special Notes: The weather is changeable and can be extremely severe—even arcticlike—at high altitudes. Sudden drops in temperature and mists should be anticipated. A woolen hat and mittens, warm clothing and wind and raingear are essential, as is a compass, watch, whistle, flashlight, emergency rations and some coins for emergency phone calls.
Lodgings: Many lodgings are available. There are also several recognized campsites. Camping elsewhere—including unfenced moorland—requires the owner's permission. Accommodation lists may be obtained from the park information centers at Blaenau Ffestiniog, Conwy and Llanberis. The other information centers do not maintain accommodation services.

Maps:
- Ordnance Survey 1:50,000, sheets 115, 116, 123, 124, 125 and 135.
- Outdoor Leisure Maps 1:25,000, five sheets: *Snowdon, Conwy Valley, Bala, Harlech* and *Cader Idris.*
- Ordnance Survey 1:25,000, sheets SH-44, SH-45, SH-50, SH-51, SH-52, SH-53, SH-54, SH-55, SH-60, SH-62, SH-63, SH-64, SH-65, SH-66, SH-67, SH-70, SH-71, SH-72, SH-73, SH-74, SH-75, SH-76, SH-77, SH-80, SH-81, SH-82, SH-83, SH-84, SH-85, SH-86, SH-91, SH-93, SH-94, SJ-03, SN-59, SN-69 and SN-79.

Guidebooks:
Available from Snowdonia National Park Information Services:
- *Snowdon Sherpa Tourist Service.* Describes path routes on Snowdon and gives timetable information of special buses circling the mountain. Free.
- *Footpaths from Pen y Pass: The Miners' Track, the Pyg Track.*
- *Bus to a Walk, Walk to a Bus* (for a description, see the section on *Train & Bus Fares* earlier in this chapter).
- *Precipice Walk* (Dolgellau).

Available from the Forestry Commission in Aberystwyth:
- *Beddgelert Forest Trail* (leaflet).
- *Gwydyr Forest Trail* (leaflet).
- *Walks in Gwydyr Forest* (booklet).

Other Guidebooks:
- *Snowdonia National Park* by G. Rhys Edwards, HMSO. A general guide to the park. Does not include path descriptions.
- *Snowdonia Forest Park Guide,* edited by Herbert L. Edlin of the Forestry Commission, HMSO. Includes two chapters on walks in the park.
- *The Snowdon Log: Rambles and Scrambles in the Snowdon District* by C. Williams and H. Light and *The Idwal Log: Rambles and Scrambles in the Ogwen District* by Roland Helliwell, both published by Merseyside Youth Hostels Ltd.
- *Betws-y-Coed and the Conway Valley* by I.W. Jones, John Jones Cardiff Ltd.
- *Welsh Northern Footpaths* by S.M. Perry, James Pike Ltd.
- *The Welsh Peaks* by W.A. Poucher, Constable & Company.
- *Walking Snowdonia* and *Exploring Gwynedd from Porthmadog,* both by Showell Styles, John Jones Cardiff Ltd.
- *Snowdon Range* by Showell Styles, West Col Productions.
- *Hillwalking in Snowdonia* and *The Ascent of Snowdon,* both by E.G. Rowland, Cicerone Press.
- *Twenty Walks in North Wales* by "Rambler" of the *Liverpool Echo;* Philip, Son & Nephew.
- *Walk in the Beautiful Conwy Valley* by Ralph Maddern, Focus Publications.
- *Llangollen Town and Country Walks* by and available from Alan Williams.
- *Read about Walks in Snowdonia,* Photo Precision Ltd.
- Several walks in Snowdonia—and the publications describing each—are also listed in *Wales Walking* (see *Where to Get Walking Information*).

Areas of Outstanding Natural Beauty

In addition to the national parks, there are three designated Areas of Outstanding Natural Beauty in Wales. These are described in the sections that follow on mid-Wales, North Wales and South Wales.

Forests and Forest Parks

A free leaflet that shows the locations of the forests in Wales to which the public has access is available from:

Forestry Commission in Cardiff (see *Address Directory*).

The leaflet, *See Your Forests: Wales,* gives a brief description of forest walks and trails, along with the grid reference numbers of their starting points and places where leaflets describing them may be obtained.

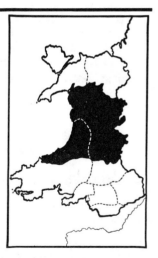

Mid-Wales

Between the northern border of the Brecon Beacons and Snowdonia, in the counties of Dyfed and Powys, is a wide expanse of unspoiled countryside, a region of rounded hills and undulating moorland, devoted almost entirely to the rearing of sheep. On the far side is the Cardigan Coast, with its sandy coves, smooth beaches and gorse-covered cliff tops. Inland, mid-Wales is largely a landscape of the scattered hut, the remote holding, the out-of-the-way hamlet and the country town. Without major industry, the region relies upon inherited skills in the handmaking of crafts from local materials. Foremost is woolen weaving, which is perpetuated in small riverbank mills. North of the Mawddach Estuary there is gold, little mined now, but the Royal Family's wedding rings are still made from it. Here, too, are the mountains of Meirionnydd, dominated by 892-meter (2,927-foot) high Cader Idris, in the southern part of Snowdonia, a popular area of walking, which is bounded by two fjordlike fissures.

Throughout mid-Wales there are numerous nature and forest trails, and to the east is the route of Offa's Dyke Path (see page 000). But the experienced walker is not limited solely to the marked routes, for much of mid-Wales lies above 300 meters where one can roam at will, guided only by a compass and a 1:50,000 Ordnance Survey Map.

Often, on the open moorland and mountain tracks, you will suddenly hear a piercing whistle, the sound of a shepherd working his flock, as his dog rounds up, drives and pens the wayward sheep. Each year, throughout mid-Wales, shepherds come together to compete in local and regional sheepdog trials. When you see such an event advertised on little barn door posters, go along. You will be welcome.

Useful Addresses

Tourist Information: The booklet *Mid Wales* (see the section on *Useful Addresses & Telephone Numbers*) lists all the tourist information offices in mid-Wales, gives brief descriptions of each town and describes several nature trails and forest paths. There is a nominal charge for the booklet, but it is the best source of general tourist information on the area. It can be obtained from the Wales Tourist Board (see *Address Directory*).

Walking: Contact The Ramblers' Association (see *Address Directory*).

Maps

- Ordnance Survey, 1:50,000, sheets 124, 125, 126, 135, 136, 137, 145, 146, 147 and 148.

Guidebooks

For the addresses of the following publishers and mail-order outlets, see the *Address Directory*.

- *Rambling round the Upper Wye: Part 1, Builth Wells Area* and *Part 2, Rhayader Area*, both by Carl D. Ehrenzeller, St. Christopher's.
- *From Offa's Dyke to the Sea through Picturesque Mid-Wales* and *Rambles round Radnorshire*, both by Carl D. Ehrenzeller.
- *Elenith* by Timothy Porter, YHA Cardiff. Describes several walking routes in mid-Wales.
- *Radnorshire (Bleddfa) Nature Trail No. 1* (leaflet), available from the Book Shop in the town of Llandrinod Wells. Describes a 13-kilometer (8-mile) long path in the Radnor Forest.

- *Hafren Forest Walks* (leaflet), available from the Forestry Commission in Aberystwyth.
- Several other walks—and the publications describing each—also are listed in *Wales Walking* (see *Where to Get Walking Information*).

Suggested Walks

On waymarked routes, the possibilities include Offa's Dyke Path, the Vale of Rheidol Railway Nature Trail (19 kilometers from Aberystwyth to Devil's Bridge), the Precipice Walk near Dolgellau (a guide by the same name is available from Snowdonia National Park Information Services and the Hafren Forest Walks and Radnorshire Nature Trail No. 1; (the leaflets describing each are listed above). Better yet, buy *Wales Walking,* along with the appropriate Ordnance Survey maps, and make your own decision.

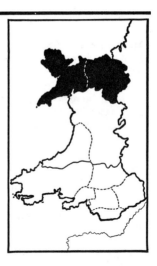

North Wales

North Wales is a land of mountains and lakes, of hill farms and tumbling rivers bounded by the sea and its beaches. Apart from a pocket of heavy industry on the banks of the Dee, and light industries here and there near the larger towns, the economy of North Wales relies almost wholly on tourism and various forms of agriculture. Most of the land is over 180 meters (600 feet) in height, with much over 350 meters. Inland, slate has long dominated the lives and landscape. There are old quarry faces at Blaenau Ffestiniog, Llanberis, Trefor and Bethesda, where a four-year-long strike in the late 19th century was instrumental in giving workers in Britain the right to speak with their employers through a union. Wooden framed buildings with white plastered infills are found in the Welsh Marches, the old counties straddling the once turbulent boundary with England. But in the mountains, most buildings are of local stone. The old custom of building a house on common land and lighting a fire on its hearth—all to be accomplished in one night between dusk and dawn—has also left its mark in the form of many hill cottages of Snowdonia built of large boulders. *Tai Unnos*—one-night houses—they are called.

Along the coast—above the low-lying Vale of Clywd, around the Isle of Anglesey and off the Lleyn Peninsula—boats gather lobsters, crabs and shrimp. And at Conwy there are mussels and in the Menai Strait, oyster beds.

Snowdonia National Park covers most of the county of Gwynedd. This is where most walkers go. Yet the county of Clwyd, to the east, also has numerous nature and forest paths, and large tracts of open moorland above 300 meters where you can roam at will. And, away from the industry and caravan sites along the coast in the north, there are few crowds—only sheep and an occasional country town.

Useful Addresses

Tourist Information: The best source of general tourist information is the booklet published by the Wales Tourist Board: *North Wales*. The booklet lists all the local tourist information offices in North Wales, gives a brief description of the mountain centers in Snowdonia as well as of the other towns in the region, and includes details of several nature and forest paths. It is available for a nominal charge from the Wales Tourist Board. Information on lodgings and the footpaths in Snowdonia can also be obtained from the Snowdonia National Park Information Centers (see *Address Directory*).

Walking: Contact The Ramblers' Association (see *Address Directory*).

Guided Walks: See the information on the Penmaenmawr and Snowdon guided walks in the section on *Walking & Climbing Tours*.

Climbing: See the sections on *Mountain Guides* and *Mountaineering Courses*.

Maps

- North Wales is covered by eight 1:50,000 Ordnance Survey maps, sheets 114, 115, 116, 117, 123, 124 and 125. In most places, these are sufficient for following mountain tracks and wandering across the high, open moorland. For walking in Snowdonia, however, the five 1:25,000 Outdoor Leisure Maps, *Snowdon, Conwy Valley, Bala, Harlech* and *Cader Idris*, are recommended.

Guidebooks

Most of the guidebooks for North Wales concentrate on Snowdonia National Park. These are listed in the description of the park in the section on *National Parks in Wales*. For walking outside the park, there are five guidebooks of use:

- *Twenty Walks in North Wales* by '' Rambler'' of the *Liverpool Echo;* Philip, Son & Nephew.
- *Llangollen Town and Country Walks* by and available from Alan Williams.
- *Welsh Northern Footpaths* by S.M. Perry, James Pike Ltd.
- *Exploring Gwynedd from Porthmadog* by Showell Styles, John Jones Cardiff Ltd.
- *Wales Walking* by the Wales Tourist Board.

Areas of Outstanding Natural Beauty

Anglesey

A small island off the north coast of Wales with rocky headlands, crescent-shaped bays and, inland, a low plateau with a few isolated hills and shallow valleys. On the Menai Strait beaches, the Romans put Druidic priests and their flower maidens to the sword in the first century A.D., an action that broke the mystique of ritual and sacrifice that flourished in the island's ancient oak groves. The Area of Outstanding Natural Beauty covers 218 square kilometers (84 square miles), mostly along the island's coast.

Maps:
- Ordnance Survey 1:50,000, sheet 114.
- Ordnance Survey 1:25,000, sheets SH-27, SH-28, SH-29, SH-36, SH-37, SH-38, SH-39, SH-46, SH-47, SH-49, SH-57, SH-58, SH-67 and SH-68.

On the island, the 1:25,000 maps are recommended for walking.

Guidebooks:
- *Isle of Anglesey,* published by R.E. Jones, Llandudno. Available from the Isle of Anglesey Tourist Association.

Further Information: Contact the Isle of Anglesey Tourist Association.

Lleyn

A remote peninsula thrusting westward into the Irish Sea, Lleyn is a region of small farms, irregularly enclosed fields, white cottages and rocky headlands indented by small coves. One of the oldest lands in Wales, it is the stronghold of the Welsh language and way of life. Prehistoric remains are numerous. There are narrow lanes that run through gorse, bracken and rough pasture and, on its northern coast, craggy peaks that rise up to 550 meters (1,800 feet). Covers 155 square kilometers (80 square miles).

Maps:
• Ordnance Survey 1:50,000, sheet 123 (see note below).
• Ordnance Survey 1:25,000, sheets SH-12, SH-13, SH-22, SH-23, SH-32, SH-33, SH-34, SH-43, SH-44 and SH-45.
Guidebooks:
• *Exploring Gwynedd from Porthmadog* by Showell Styles, John Jones Cardiff Ltd.

Suggested Walks

Best to refer to *Wales Walking* and the guidebooks listed above. There is no one route that can be recommended over others. There are many walks, each with its own rewards. The choice has to be yours.

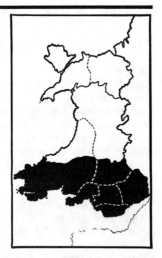

South Wales

South Wales is a region of contrasts. The grassy mountains and wild moorland of the Brecon Beacons lie north of the valley towns of Tonypandy, Merthyr and Rhymney, site of the Welsh coal fields, early railroads and industry. Farther south are the fields of the Vale of Glamorgan, and the Bristol Channel. To the east are the rolling hills of Gwent and the wooded Wye Valley; to the west, the sandy coves and smooth beaches of Dyfed and Gower. Medieval castles and sites of prehistoric interest—the Cathedral of St. David's and the Preseli Mountains, source of the bluestones at faraway Stonehenge—lie inland from the coves and cliffs of the Pembrokeshire Coast. And in the southern part of the Brecon Beacons is an extensive limestone region honeycombed with caves and caverns—described on *Information Sheet No. 3,* available from the Brecon Beacons National Park, which lists the locations of all the caves and gives the addresses of the caving clubs that explore them.

The region has its coal slag heaps, mining camps and industrial cities, but just eight kilometers inland from the city of Swansea, along the Tawe River, is a steep green valley. Although the walking is not as open and free as in mid- and North Wales, there are many unspoiled areas with forest paths, and remote moors above 300 meters where you can roam at will. In fact, South Wales has nearly as many waymarked paths as all the rest of Wales put together, plus one Area of Outstanding Natural Beauty and two national parks.

Useful Addresses

Tourist Information: Contact the Wales Tourist Board (see *Address Directory*). The booklet *South Wales* is also recommended for its list of local tourist information centers and information on the towns, activities and footpaths in the area.

Walking: Contact The Ramblers' Association (see *Address Directory*).

Guided Walks: See the information on guided walks in Gwent, the Brecon Beacons and the Pembrokeshire Coast in the section on *Walking & Climbing Tours*.

Maps

- South Wales is covered by 10 1:50,000 Ordnance Survey maps, sheets 145, 146, 157, 158, 159, 160, 161, 162, 170 and 171. In addition, there are four 1:25,000 Outdoor Leisure Maps: *Brecon Beacons:* 1) *East,* 2) *West,* and 3) *Central,* and *Wye Valley and Forest of Dean.* Much of the region south of the Brecon Beacons and a section of the Pembrokeshire Coast is also covered by the Second Series 1:25,000 Ordnance Survey maps, which show rights-of-way in addition to field boundaries (for information as to where an index of the 1:25,000 sheets can be obtained, see the section on *Maps* earlier in this chapter).

Guidebooks

Brecon Beacons

- See the description of the Brecon Beacons in the section on *National Parks in Wales.*

Dyfed and Pembrokeshire National Park

- See *National Parks in Wales.*

Glamorgan

- *Walks in the Taff Valley* (between Cardiff and Merthyr) by David Rees, Starling Press.
- *Thirty Walks in Gower* by and available from Roger Jones.
- *Ten Walks in Gower* by Stephen Rees, Gower Society.
- *Porthcawl Walks 1, 2 and 3* by Porthcawl Civic Trust Society.
- Cardiff City Parks Department Walks: 1) *Bute Park Nature Trail*, 2) *Canton to Llandaff*, 3) *Cefn-Qnn Walk*, 4) *Glamorgan Canal Nature Reserve*, 5) *Nant Fawr Walk*, 6) *Rhymney Walk*, 7) *Taff Valley Walk* and 8) *Wenallt Nature Trail*. All available from Cardiff City Parks Department.
- *Four Nature Trails in Glamorgan* and *Three Walks in the Coalfield*, both by Glamorgan County Naturalist Trust.
- Forest Trail leaflets: 1) *Rudry (Caerphilly)*, 2) *Graig Nantgwidden (Gelli)*, 3) *Garwnant and Llwyn-onn Reservoir Forest Walks (Merthyr Tydfil)*, 4) *Talybont Forest Walks* (four leaflets), 5) *Taf Fechan Long Distance Walk (Pontsticill)*, and 6) *Tair Onnen Forest Walk (Welsh St. Donat's)*. All available from the Forestry Commission, Churchill House, Churchill Way, Cardiff.
- *Wales Walking* by the Wales Tourist Board.

Gwent

Available from the Gwent County Council:

- *Walks in Gwent: No. 1 Upper Cwmbran, Little Porton, Llanbedr* and *No. 2 Llanhennock, Llanfrechfa, St. Julians Park*.
- *Gray Hill Countryside Trail, Wentwood Reservoir*.
- *Walking in Wentwood Forest*.
- *Lower Wye Valley Walk*. (Recommended. For details of the route see "Suggeted Walks" under the *Heart of England* in the chapter on England.)

Other Guidebooks

- *Tracking through Mercia, Vol. 2* by Donna Baker, Express Logic Ltd. Describes 24 walks, six of them in the Black Mountains.
- *A Walk in the Tintern Forest* (leaflet), available from the Forestry Commission.
- *Wyndcliff Nature Trail* (leaflet), available from the Nature Conservancy Council. (A recommended walk in the Wye Valley.)

Areas of Outstanding Natural Beauty

Gower
A peninsula west of Swansea with high cliffs, prehistoric caves, sandy coves and, inland, pleasant farmlands, a Stone Age burial chamber at Parc le Breos and four medieval castles. This was the first area in Britain to be designated an Area of Outstanding Natural Beauty. Covers 189 square kilometers (73 square miles).
Maps:
• Ordnance Survey 1:50,000, sheet 159.
• Ordnance Survey 1:25,000, sheets SS-48, SS-49, SS-58, SS-59, SS-68 and SS-69.
Guidebooks:
• *Thirty Walks in Gower* by and available from Roger Jones.
• *Ten Walks in Gower* by Stephen Rees, Gower Society.
• *A Guide to Gower,* published by the Gower Society. Available from Gower tourist information centers.
• *Gower Farm Trail* by Roscoe Howells. Available from the West Glamorgan Planning Department.

Suggested Walks

The possibilities are numerous—the Pembrokeshire Coast Path and Offa's Dyke Path (see *Long-Distance Footpaths in Wales*); the Wye Valley Walk (see the *Heart of England* in the chapter on England); the Brecon Beacons (see *National Parks in Wales*); and, of course, the many marked and unmarked routes detailed in *Wales Walking,* such as the Gwent Walks and Dale Peninsula Path. Two other walks worth mention are:

Taff Valley Long Distance Walk. Up the Taff River from Cardiff to Merthyr at the entrance to the Brecon Beacons. **Length:** 80 kilometers (50 miles). **Walking Time:** 3 to 4 days.
Maps:
• Ordnance Survey 1:50,000, sheets 160, 170 and 171.
Guidebook:
• *Walks in the Taff Valley* by David Rees, The Starling Press.

Coed Morgannwg (Morgannwg Wood Way). From Craig-y-llyn to Margam Forest Park through rolling parklands. **Length:** 37 kilometers (23 miles). **Walking Time:** 2 days.
Map:
• Ordnance Survey 1:50,000, sheet 170.
Guidebook:
• Forestry Commission leaflet, *Coed Morgannwg (Morgannwg Wood Way)* is in preparation.
Further Information: Contact Forestry Commission, Cardiff or the Wales Tourist Board.

Address Directory

A

- *Aberdyfi Park Information Center,* Located at The Wharf, Tel. Aberdyfi 367.
- *Abergavenny Park Information Center,* Lower Monk Street, Abergavenny, Gwent NP7, Tel. Abergavenny 3254.
- *Alan Williams, see Williams, Alan.*
- *Amgueddfa Genedlaethol Cymru, see National Museum of Wales.*
- *Association of British Mountain Guides,* Colin G. Firth, Secretary, Newstead, Eleven Trees, Keswick, Cumbria CA12 4LW.

B

- *Backpackers' Club,* Eric R. Gurney, Honorary National Organising Secretary, 20 St. Michaels Road, Tilehurst, Reading, Berkshire RG3 4RP England, Tel. (home) Reading (0734) 28754 or (business) Checkendon (0491) 680541 ext. 250.
- *Bala Park Information Center,* Located in the Old British School on High Street. Tel. Bala 367.
- *Blaenau Ffestiniog Park Information Center,* Located in the Caerblaidd Offices, Queen's Bridge, High Street. Tel. Blaenau Ffestiniog 360.
- *Brecon Beacons Mountain Centre,* Glamorgan Street, Brecon, Powys LD3 7DP. Tel. Brecon 3378.
- *Brecon Beacons National Park Information Center,* 6 Glamorgan Street, Brecon, Powys LD3 7DW. Tel. Brecon 2763.
- *Brecon Beacons National Park Information Centres* (open from Easter until October):
  —*Abergavenny,* Gwent NP7 5NA. Located on Lower Monk Street. Tel. Abergavenny 3254.
  —*Brecon,* Powys LD3 7DW. Located at 6 Glamorgan Street. Tel. Brecon 2763.
  —*Llandovery,* Dyfed SA20 0AR. Located at 8 Broad Street. Tel. Llandovery 20693.
  —*Brecon Beacons Mountain Centre.* Located near Libanus, Powys LD3 8ER. Tel. Brecon 3366.
- *Brecon Tourist Information Center,* Market Car Park, Brecon. Tel. (0874) 2485.
- *British Mountaineering Council,* Crawford House, Precinct Centre, Booth Street East, Manchester M13 9RZ, England.

- *Broad Haven Information Center,* Located in the Pembrokeshire Countryside Unit at the Car Park. Tel. Broad Haven 412.
- *Bwrdd Croeso Cymru,* see *Wales Tourist Board.*

C

- *Camping Club of Great Britain and Ireland,* 11 Lower Grosvenor Place, London SW1W 0EY, England. Tel. (01) 828 9232.
- *Cardiff City Parks Department,* City Hall, Cardiff.
- *Carl D. Ehrenzeller,* see *Ehrenzeller, Carl D.*
- *Christian Mountain Center,* Gorffwysfa, Tremadog, Porthmadog, Gwynedd. Tel. Porthmadog 2616. Enquiries to: The Warden.
- *Cicerone Press,* 16 Briarfield Road, Worsley, Manchester M28 4GQ, England.
- *Comax (Leisure) Ltd.,* 10 Nelson Street, Swansea. Tel. Swansea 41788.
- *Constable & Company,* 10 Orange Street, London WC2H 7EG, England.
- *Conwy Park Information Center,* Located in the Old Gas Showrooms, Castle Street. Tel. Conwy 2248.
- *Cook, Hammond & Kell Ltd.,* London Map Centre, 22-24 Caxton Street, London SW1 H0QU, England. Tel. (01) 222 2466.
- *Countryside Commission,* Public Relations Department, John Dower House, Crescent Place, Cheltenham, Gloucestershire GL50 3RA, England. Tel. Cheltenham (0242) 21381.
- *Country-Wide Holidays Association,* Birch Heys, Cromwell Range, Manchester M14 6HU, England. Tel. (061) 224 2887.

D

- *Dolgellau Park Information Center,* Located at Bridge End. Tel. Dolgellau 422888.
- *Drake, A. J.,* 2 Beechhodge, The Park, Cheltenham, Glouchestershire GL50 2 RX, England.

E

- *Ehrenzeller, Carl D.,* St. Christopher's, Ithon Road, Llandrinod Wells, Powys.
- *Ellis Brigham,* Capel Curig, Gwynedd. Tel. Capel Curig 232.
- *Emergency.* Tel. 999.
- *Express Logic Ltd.,* Foley Estate, Herford HR1 2SJ, England.

F

- *Fishguard Information Center,* Located in the Town Hall. Tel. Fishguard (0348) 873484.
- *Focus Publications,* 9 Priors Road, Windsor, Berkshire SL4 4PD, England.
- *Footpath Publications,* Adstock Cottage, Adstock, Buckingham, England.
- *Forestry Commission, Aberystwyth,* Victoria House, Victoria Terrace, Aberystwyth.
- *Forestry Commission, Brecon.* Tel. Brecon 2557.
- *Forestry Commission, Cardiff,* Churchill House, Churchill Way, Cardiff CF1 4TD.
- *Forestry Commission, Talybont-on-Usk,* Powys.

G

- *Glamorgan County Naturalist Trust,* c/o Nature Conservancy Council, 44 The Parade, Roath, Cardiff.
- *Gower Society,* Royal Institution, Victoria Street, Swansea.
- *Gwent County Council,* Planning Department, County Hall, Cwmbran, Gwent NP4 2XH.

H

- *HMSO,* Atlantic House, Holborn Viaduct, London EC1 1BN, England.
- *Holiday Fellowship Ltd.,* 142-144 Great North Way, London NW4 1EG, England. Tel. (01) 203 3381.

I

- *Isle of Anglesey Tourist Association,* Information Office, Coed Cyrnol, Menai Bridge, Isle of Anglesey. Tel. (0248) 712626.

J

- *James Pike Ltd.,* St. Ives, Cornwall, England.
- *Jesse James Bunkhouse,* Buarth-y-Clytiau, Penisarwaun, Llanberis, Gwynedd. Tel. Llanberis 521. Enquiries to: J. James.
- *Joe Brown Mountaineering Shop,* Llanberis, Gwynedd. Tel. Llanberis 327.
- *Jones, Roger,* Green Close, Llannorlais, West Glamorgan SA4 3TL.

K

- *Kilgetty Park Information Center,* Located in the Kingsmoor Common. Tel. Saundersfoot (0834) 813672.

L

- *Llanberis Park Information Center,* Located at the entrance to Padarn Country Park at the lakeside. Tel. Llanberis (028682) 765.
- *Llandovery Park Information Center,* 8 Broad Street, Llandovery, Dyfed SA20 0AR. Tel. Llandovery 20693.

M

- *Merseyside Youth Hostels Ltd.,* 40 Hamilton Square, Birkenhead, England.
- *Meteorological Office, Mid-Wales* (Aberporth): Tel. (0239) 810117.
- *Meteorological Office, North Wales* (Anglesey): Tel. (0407) 2288.
- *Meteorological Office, South Wales:* Swansea (summer only): Tel. (0792) 8011. Gloucester (all year): Tel. Churchdown (0452) 855566.
- *Minerva Outdoor Ventures,* Crown House, 19 London Road, High Wycombe, Buckinghamshire, England. Tel. High Wycombe 445383.
- *Mountain Rescue Committee,* The Secretary, 9 Milldale Avenue, Temple Meads, Buxton, Derbyshire SK17 9BE, England.
- *Mountway Marine and Trek,* Brecon Road (A40), Abergavenny, Gwent. Tel. 4193.

N

- *National Museum of Wales* (Amgueddfa Genedlaethol Cymru), Cathays Park, Cardiff CF2 3NP. Tel. (0222) 397951.
- *National Trust (Country Walks),* 42 Queen Anne's Gate, London SW1H 9AS, England.
- *Nature Conservancy Council,* Penrhos Road, Bangor, Gwynedd.

O

- *Offa's Dyke Association,* Old Primary School, West Street, Knighton, Powys LD7 1EW. Tel. Knighton 753.
- *Ordnance Survey,* Romsey Road, Maybush, Southhampton S09 4DH, England. Tel. Southampton 775555 ext. 706.
- *Outdoor Action,* 12 Wyeverne Road, Cathays, Cardiff. Tel. (0222) 28892.

P

- *Patrick Stark,* see *Stark, Patrick.*
- *Pembrokeshire Coast National Park Information Service,* County Offices, Haverfordwest, Dyfed. Tel. 3131.
- *Pembrokeshire Coast National Park Information Centres* (open from Easter until October):
  —*Broad Haven.* Located in the Pembrokeshire Countryside Unit at the Car Park. Tel. Broad Haven (043783) 412.
  —*Fishguard.* Located in the Town Hall. Tel. Fishguard 3484.
  —*Kilgetty.* Located in the Kingsmoor Common. Tel. Saundersfoot 81 36 72. Open all year.
  —*Pembroke.* Located in Drill Hall on Main Street. Tel. Pembroke 2143.
  —*St. David's.* Located in the City Hall. Tel. St. David's (043788) 392.
  —*Tenby.* Located in Guildhall, The Norton. Tel. Tenby 3510.
- *Pentwyn Adventure Centre,* Llangadog, Dyfed. Tel. Gwynfe 669.
- *Penyrheol Adventure Centre,* Ystradgynlais, Nr. Swansea, West Glamorgan.
- *Philip, Son & Nephew,* 7 Whitechapel, Liverpool L69 1AN, England.
- *Photo Precision, Ltd.,* Caxton Road, St. Ives, Huntingdon, Cambridgeshire, England.
- *Play-y-Brenin National Mountaineering Centre,* Capel Curig, Betws-y-Coed, Gwynedd. Tel. Capel Curig 214 or 280. Enquiries to: The Warden.
- *Porthcawl Civic Trust Society,* 17 West Drive, Porthcawl, Mid Glamorgan.
- *Pridgeon Publishing Ltd.,* Marks Farmhouse, Llangrove, Ross on Wye, Hertfordshire, England.

R

- *Ramblers' Association,* 1/5 Wandsworth Road, London SW8 2L5, England. Tel. (01) 582 6878.
- *Roger Jones,* see *Jones, Roger.*

S

- *St. David's Park Information Center,* Located in the City Hall. Tel. St. David's (043788) 392.
- *Snowdonia National Park Information Service,* Yr Hen Ysgol, Maentwrog, Blaenau Ffestiniog, Gwynedd. Tel. 360.
- *Snowdonia National Park Information Centres* (open from Easter to October):
  —*Aberdyfi.* Located at The Wharf. Tel. Aberdyfi (065472) 321.
  —*Bala.* Located in the Old British School on High Street. Tel. Bala (0678)520367.
  —*Blaenau Ffestiniog.* Located in the Caerblaidd Offices, Queen's Bridge, High Street. Tel. Blaenau Ffestiniog (076681) 360.
  —*Conwy.* Located in the Old Gas Showrooms, Castle Street. Tel. Conwy 2248.
  —*Dolgellau.* Located at Bridge End. Tel. Dolgellau (0341) 422888.
  —*Llanberis.* Located at the entrance to Padarn Country Park at the lakeside. Tel. Llanberis 765.
- *South Pembrokeshire District Council,* Llanion Park, Pembroke Dock, Dyfed.
- *Sports Council,* Department B, 70 Brompton Road, London SW3 1EX, England.
- *Stark, Patrick,* The Bush Inn, Robeston Wathen, Narberth, Dyfed.
- *Starling Press,* Tredegar Street, Risca, Newport, Gwent NP1.

T

- *Tenby Park Information Center,* Located in Guildhall, The Norton. Tel. Tenby (0834) 3510.

W

- *Wales Tourist Board* (Bwrdd Croesco Cymru), 3 Castle Street, Cardiff CF1 2RD. Tel. (0222) 27281.
- *Weather Forecasts,* Cardiff Area: Tel. (0222) 8091.
- *Weather Forecasts,* North Wales Coast: Tel. (0492) 8091.
- *West Col Productions,* 1 Meadow Close, Goring on Thames, Reading, Berkshire RG8 9AA, England.
- *West Glamorgan Planning Department,* 12 Orchard Street, Swansea, West Glamorgan.
- *Wildwood House Ltd.,* 1 Prince of Wales Passage, 117 Hampstead Road, London NW1 3EE, England.
- *Williams, Alan,* Bryntysilio Lodge, Llangollen, Clwyd.

Y

- *Y Lolfa,* Talybont, Ceredigion, Dyfed.
- *YHA,* see *Youth Hostels Association.*
- *YHA Adventure Holidays,* Department HB, Trevelyan House, St. Albans, Hertfordshire. Tel. St. Albans 55215.
- *YHA Services Ltd.,* 131 Woodville Road, Cardiff CF5 4DZ. Tel. (0222) 31370.
- *Youth Hostels Association, England,* Trevelyan House, 8 St. Stephen's Hill, St. Albans, Hertfordshire AL1 2DY, England.
- *Youth Hostels Association, North Wales,* 40 Hamilton Square, Birkenhead L41 5BA. Tel. (051) 647 7348 or 647 7258.
- *Youth Hostels Association, South Wales,* 131 Woodville Road, Cardiff CF5 4DZ. Tel. (0222) 31370.

A Quick Reference

In a hurry? Turn to the pages listed below. They will give you the most important information on walking in Wales.

Search & Rescue, page 332.

Weather Forecasts, page 320.

Associations to Contact for Information:
    On Walking, page 321.
    On Climbing, page 327.
    Tourist Offices, page 331.

Maps, page 323.

Guidebooks, page 324.

Equipment, page 326.

Address Directory, page 352.

Also, see the special notes on equipment—and the listings of maps and guidebooks—for:

Long-Distance Footpaths, page 333.

National Parks, page 339.